Alfonso Gálvez

Commentaries on the Song of Songs

First Volume

Translated from the Spanish by
Michael Adams

Second Edition
New Jersey
U.S.A. – 2022

Commentaries on the Song of Songs, First Volume by Alfonso Gálvez. Copyright © 2022 by Shoreless Lake Press. American edition published with permission. All rights reserved. No part of this book may be reproduced, stored in retrieval system, or transmitted, in any form or by any means, electronic, mechanical, photocopying, recording or otherwise, without written permission of the Society of Jesus Christ the Priest, P.O. Box 157, Stewartsville, New Jersey 08886.

CATALOGING DATA

Author: Gálvez, Alfonso, 1932–
Title: Commentaries on the Song of Songs, First Volume

First Printing   New Jersey, 1995
Second Printing   New Jersey, 2022

Library of Congress Control Number: 2022902178

ISBN: 978-1-953170-20-0 (hardcover)
        978-1-953170-21-7 (e-book)

Published by
Shoreless Lake Press
P.O. Box 157
Stewartsville, New Jersey 08886

"Causa diligendi Deum, Deus est;
modus, sine modo diligere."

Saint Bernard, "De diligendo Deo", I,1.

NOTE TO THE ENGLISH VERSION

The publisher and the author of this book feel themselves quite satisfied with the careful and excellent work accomplished by the translator. The task was not easy: biblical quotations are numerous, poems are of various kinds and abundant, often written in a highly literary, even archaic, Spanish. The translation of a literary book, such as this one is, keeping the elegance of the style and faithfully preserving the author's thought is an endeavor which has proved itself to be difficult.

It is well known that it is impossible to achieve an adequate translation of poetry: the beauty and the meaning contained in the words can be duly appreciated only in the original language in which they were written. This is the reason why it has been decided to maintain both the original Spanish of the poems and their English translation, so that those who have some acquaintance with the Spanish language may savor their poetic beauty and the doctrinal content they intend to convey.

The author has considered convenient to add some few and brief clarifications to the English language version. Such additions are almost always related to the doctrinal content of this book, and are intended to facilitate a better understanding of it to the English speaking reader. Since these additions belong to the author himself, they do not alter in the least the original Spanish.

THE EDITORS

INTRODUCTION

As anyone can appreciate, the task of writing about the themes dealt with in this book is not just a difficult one. Here, more than anywhere else, honesty demands that one's life conform to what one writes —or at least to some degree, which is perhaps all one might hope for. Moreover, love is something one cannot understand unless one experiences it, and this applies particularly when the love in question is something as complex and mysterious as divine–human love, the mutual love of God and the human person. So, since it would be too daring to claim to possess this honesty and this experience, one must admit that, in all logic, this is a book that should never have been written.

However, as everyone knows, people often behave based on motives which reason does not understand. And in spite of everything it can sometimes be valid to act in that way, because many good and even necessary things might otherwise remain undone. As far as this book is concerned, the only justification one can put forward for it, the only thing that can be said in its favour, timidly, by way of justification, is that it does seek to fill a certain void and meet a certain need, even if it does so clumsily and partially. The void and need referred to spring from a state of deprivation felt by a number of people who need to hear about such things as intimacy with God, prayer, and above all, true love, and Him who is Love in essence and the source of all love.

With every day that passes many Christians feel more and more uneasy, and more hungry for God. Their uneasiness is caused partly by the attitude of the Church: it spends so much time speaking about the things of this world that it seems to have forgotten the next. The hunger these Christians feel (it is perhaps a consequence of their uneasiness) is a hunger for the heavenly places: they miss them, because they are tired of treading earthly paths.

However, it is not true to say (as people sometimes suggest) that these Christians think that the Church should never speak about the things of the world. The problem is rather one of reference and degree. A problem of reference, in the sense that what they yearn for is that the Church, when it speaks of earthly things, should relate them to heavenly things; unfortunately, that does not always seem to happen. And a problem of degree, in the sense that they would feel much happier if the Church spoke more about the things of God, even at the expense of speaking less about the things of the world. In this connexion, they are mindful of the words of St Paul: *If for this life only we have hoped in Christ, we are of all men most to be pitied.*[1]

Many Catholics think like that. And those who do not probably include people who do not do much thinking anyway, or who have decided not to think at all. There are even some who say, obviously exaggerating, that it scarcely makes sense to talk of Catholicism nowadays, because there is no longer any sound rule of teaching,

---

[1] 1 Cor 15:19.

Introduction

either in the field of dogma or in that of morals. However, despite the upheavals that have occurred in our time, as against what anyone may say, the truth is that a Magisterium does exist which cannot err, because it is supported by the Holy Spirit.

There is, then, no room for error. But, regrettably, due to human weakness, wrong practical behaviours do take place often enough. One does find, among some Pastors, silence, tolerance, opportunism, and even certain attitudes which lead them to speak only about those subjects which the world wants to hear, and also in the style it wants to hear. Besides, as everybody knows, there is good reason to doubt the competence of ecclesiastics on certain topics on which they too eagerly and too often speak, albeit their knowledge of the matter is rather scanty.

For example, it is difficult to understand the zeal with which certain Pastors promote the case for democracy in particular countries. For some years, in South America, when the Pinochet and Castro dictatorships (in Chile and Cuba respectively) overlapped in time, one could observe an extremely discriminatory conduct on the part of certain Shepherds towards each r,gime. With respect to Cuba, we heard, "We must accept the *status quo*"; whereas, as regards Chile, the same people were loud in denunciation: "This is a situation which affronts the rights of man; it must be changed whatever it takes"; some, with regard to Chile, even went as far as to justify recourse to assassination. One gets the impression that, for some, r,gimes are *good* or *bad* depending on whether they are on the way up or down. In the mind of a number of Pastors, it seems as if goodness or evil depends on the whims of Power or on which way the wind blows; they hardly take into account the irreducibility of Christian morality. This type of opportunism suggests a prediction: if one day the Cuban dictator falls, the presumed model liberator, whom progressive Catholics have been extolling for so many years, will immediately be seen as abominable.[2]

Moreover, though it is scarcely ever mentioned, it is plain for all to see that the dividing line between Catholic and Protestant theology has become very blurred —and it is also true that what is currently being taught in Catholic faculties of theology is very far away from what one would find in the old "Denzinger Enchiridion."

Catholic bookshops are chock–a–block with books which, even thirty years ago, would have been officially rejected as heretical. And the Bibles on sale in those shops are "modern" translations of the Holy Book which no longer looks very holy: *people's* Bibles, *accessible* Bibles, and in general a whole range of *up–dated* Bibles, are the norm —with slang, Marxoid jargon, and vulgar language predominant; so much so that to claim that this is the word of God is nothing less than blasphemous. This kind of corruption has even crept into versions approved for liturgical use, which can at best be described as coarse and bland.

Preaching has become politicized, vapid and empty. It comes as no surprise; no more could be expected when clergy are trained, in large part, under the auspices of Kantian and Hegelian philosophy and practical Feuerbachian and Marxist derivatives. On top of this, things which one thought sacrosanct are being called into question. There is, for example, the whole debate about "priestly identity," which questions the role of the clergy and consecrated persons in

---

[2]It is painful to see that many ecclesiastics —as usual, years behind the times compared with the world at large— do not yet realize that Marxism is an obsolete and dead doctrine. In this connexion, it is difficult to explain the great following won by the liberation theologies, with their incredible claim to be renewing Christianity, working from so–called *progressivist* positions which are in fact nothing but a concoction of Utopian and antinatural doctrines and indeed the most serious attempt yet at regression to dark ages that belong firmly in mankind's past.

general: the Hierarchy's reaction has often been much too mild, with the effect that priests and religious have deserted *en masse*, and seminaries and novitiates are virtually empty; even now there are no signs of an increase in vocations, despite the statistics that are bandied about, as full of good will and fantasy as they are empty of truth.

One of the sectors most affected by the crisis is that of youth, although strangely enough all this has happened at a time when more work is seemingly being done with young people. In recent years, as everyone knows, many *experts* have become involved in this field, all eager to engage in every possible method of pastoral and even (some say) other kinds of experiments. There has been no end of meetings, encounters, pilgrimages and even *youth councils*, backed up by a whole orchestra of specialized and ever more technical literature.

In its desire to adapt to the modern world, and the world of youth, this sort of pastoral action has lost sight of the core of the problem. By trying to find what they think will be acceptable to the youth of today, people who adopt this type of pastoral approach have down–played the supernatural, if not suppressed it completely. Many are the Pastors (Bishops, priests, theologians, pastoral experts...) who think that the supernatural world cannot be reached by young people. They spend time adapting themselves to the fashions and customs of the youth and talking about what they think young people are interested in. Underlining this attitude is a lack of faith in both the supernatural world and the youngsters —an attitude that places important questions out of focus, turning them upside down; it is precisely the supernatural and the heroic paths that lead to it which would truly seduce young people; only the old in spirit are unable to understand it. The problem is always approached in the same way: the Christ who has been preached heretofore is inaccessible to young people, so one needs, instead, to offer them a *more human* Christ. There is no objection to that —except that in practice this kind of Christ is usually a *less divine* Christ.³ What this means is that instead of setting out from Christ to reach the young person, one sets out from the young person to reach Christ. But that kind of Christ is too like to the young person; the only qualities he possesses are those *human* (in the sense of *not so divine*) qualities which can be grasped and accepted by modern youth and modern man. The after–effects of immanentist philosophy have brought things to the point that no longer does one try to bring young people (and people in general) to start out from Christ, the Alpha and Omega, but rather from themselves, on the grounds that that is what human dignity demands. Thus we

---

³Here once again is the old error —the idea that in order to make Christ more human He must be made less divine. However, starting from the basis that Christ is *true* God and *true* man (or, if one prefers to put it another way, *perfect* God and *perfect* man), every attempt to deeply explore his humanity can only help to manifest his divinity more clearly. Once again, those theologians and pastoral experts have let themselves be seduced by old, nineteenth–century theories which make out that man has been alienated by the Godhead. However, if they really managed to make Christ *more human*, they would in fact also show Him to be *more divine*. In the perfect assumption of human nature by the Person of the Word by means of the hypostatic union, the divinity of Christ is revealed and *channelled* only through that human nature (Jn 14:9; 1:18; 1 Jn 1: 1–2). So, one cannot now see the Father or go towards Him except through Christ (Jn 14:6), and specifically through his human nature. Using a human nature that has been assumed to the maximum of its potential (fullness of grace: Jn 1:14), the Person of the Word actualizes all his human potential (*perfect* man), and no human power or virtue is diminished (quite the contrary) because it is *through* and by means of them that the divinity appears. However, a Christ stripped of his divinity in order to make Him seem more human is not just a Christ already de–divinized; he is also a dehumanized Christ: to the same extent as his divinity is reduced or destroyed, so is his humanity.

Introduction

have a mutilated Christ, reduced at best to being an End, never a Beginning (Christ as Omega, but not Alpha).[4]

The catch–call to young people to "be themselves" runs the risk of failing to see that that is a very ambiguous expression, and a dangerous one. For the basic thing about Christianity is that man should live not his own life but that of Christ.[5] It is true that pastoral campaigns of this sort do not, in general, deny that man attains his fulfilment when he loves God; very often there is nothing basically wrong with them —but the approach, the language, is flawed and it can put the whole question out of focus.[6] Catholic pastoral action needs to be convinced that it is ineffective and dangerous to

---

[4]Rev 1:8; 21:6; 22:13. Cf. also 3:14.

[5]Many texts deal with this theme: Mt 10:39; 16:25; Mk 8:35; Lk 9:24; 14:26; Jn 12:25; 6: 57–58. See Gal 2:20 and the beautiful text of Rom 14:7. The text of Lk 14:26 uses the words *hate one's own life*. The New Jerusalem Bible translates Gal 2:20 as: "I live now not with my own life but with the life of Christ who lives in me," *The New Jerusalem Bible*, Doubleday, New York, 1985. Cf. also 2 Cor 2:15.

[6]It is true that man manages to be *himself* only by forgetting himself and going out of himself and losing (or giving up) his own life out of love. But this teaching, which belongs to the notion of love, is a discovery made by Christianity and not a truth *per se nota*. If this is not spelt out, there is a risk that young people will interpret the expression "be yourself" in a purely human way, without the supernatural connotations with which Revelation has embellished the concepts of love and man. Putting the stress more on how it sounds and on what the current fashion is than on the true content of certain concepts whose supernatural content is suppressed —this may be an attempt to win greater acceptance for a teaching which is fairly complex; but it fails to realize that, by treating it in this way, the doctrine is being mutilated (and therefore falsified to that extent), and that that approach does not in fact make it more attractive. It might at first sight seem that that approach is an effective one to introduce a doctrine so as to make it easier to practise. But it is a futile exercise because it empties the doctrine of its content and therefore of what makes it truly attractive (this is particularly important when it is young people one is dealing with). God has so arranged things that the Kingdom of Heaven is to be conquered by men of violence (Mt 11:12).

despoil the Gospel of its edge and its bite, in order to make it more acceptable to the world. Christianity is something really *new*, and it ceases to be Christianity to the degree that it ceases to be new. Once it loses what is most attractive about it, it no longer has any power to seduce adults, still less seduce young people (who are the ones most attracted by *novelty*). Hence the urgency for pastoral work with youth to stop being led by people who are old in spirit —who too often have a tendency not to believe in youth. Certain expressions (*youth council*, for example) are indicative of an attempt by older people to manipulate, to use, young people: young people get together anyway, but they would not think of doing so as a *council*.[7] It is difficult to protect these attitudes from the accusation of demagoguery; those who adopt them seem to think that their approach is pleasing to young people, and that the youth of today can neither understand nor accept anything else. They forget that young people, normally, are not at all pleased to *be themselves*; what they want, almost always, is to *be different*; this is true even of those who either have accepted defeat (drifters, drug addicts, or those who are led by sex) or protest about the world, regarding it as a joke. They fail to see that what really seduces young people is the quest for an *other* (with or without a capital letter), thinking that when they find that person they will be different and able to change the world. It is rather naive to think that young people's rebellion is always directed against the world they live in: they rebel against themselves too. Genuine young people, those who are true rebels because they are young, are never happy with themselves, and therefore the first thing they call into question is their own situation and their own

---

[7]The organization of a big youth assembly at Taize, precisely under the banner of a *Council* stemmed basically from two things: the fact that the idea of Council was very much in fashion at the time, and it was older people who planned and ran the whole affair. One has only to read its *Conclusions* to be convinced of this.

lifestyle. If one forgets this, one will try to approach young people with the naive attitude of an older person, and thereby fail to get on their wavelength. The belief that young people are incapable of accepting Christianity unless it be watered down, emptied of all supernatural content, does youth no favour: it underestimates them. One gets the impression that some people, feeling withered because of their age and being somewhat defeatist, are unable to believe in a youthful, decisive faith, however much they preach to the contrary. Theirs is an attitude very different from St John's; he really did believe in young people: *I write to you, young men, because you are strong, and the word of God abides in you, and you have overcome the evil one.*[8] The Apostle St John is convinced that young people are strong and therefore quite able to assimilate (to bear) the word of God and to overcome the Evil one; contrary to what happens to the old in spirit: they have lost confidence in their own faith.

What this book tries to do is to sketch out a theory of love, but in an unsystematic way. It sets out from the idea that the best way to understand love is to study God, because God is love (Jn 4:8). The ancient classics which deal with this subject (Plato, particularly), even though they have some excellent insights, fail to delve into the depths of this reality, which is undoubtedly the most exciting subject there is. Yet, despite the fact that it has been studied incessantly in the intervening centuries, with the added help of a full, complete Revelation, much remains to be discovered. Theology has studied the virtue of charity, or *agap,*, from all kinds of angles, but it has never made love, as such, its proper object (that is, its reference is limited to love as virtue) and therefore it has not chosen to stress

---

[8] 1 Jn 2:14.

the linkage between love and the divine life, and specifically the trinitarian mystery.[9]

In this book love will be studied as something which, first and foremost, has to do with the trinitarian *structure* of the Godhead: God is Love, and there is in Him plurality of persons because plurality of persons belongs to the very essence of love. Or, to put it another way: If God is Love, it must needs be that there is plurality of persons in Him, for love is never unipersonal; its essence consists in fact in being love of one *I* for another *I* —which, in turn and mutually, become one *Thou* and another *Thou*. This theme will be developed in this book as fundamental to the study of love; and we hope it will help to shed new light making for a better understanding of the theology of the Holy Spirit.

By taking this route, we may be able to give a deeper insight into the essence of human love. Love is the very life of God, and in its supernatural aspect human love is nothing other than that divine life infused and poured into the heart of man (Rom 5:5). The study of love at its source, God, can help towards a greater appreciation of the mystery of human love. As is easily seen with the benefit of hindsight, a profound knowledge of love is not possible without the help of Revelation. The only route to completely understanding human love is that which starts out from divine love. And, equally, man cannot know divine love unless he starts out from human love; he cannot work his way to a knowledge of uncreated Love if he knows nothing of created love. That is exactly what the *Song of Songs* does: it tries to explain both divine love and divine–human love, by pressing into service the outstanding qualities and even the

---

[9]Theology studies love as a virtue, specifically as a theological virtue. Here it will be studied simply as love, that is, as a basic reality which burst into and determines human existence. However, theology must then be called in to help understand it in all its depth.

very language of human love. A book whose main purpose is to reveal such a lofty doctrine could not do it in a different manner: *Per aspera ad astra*; man does not have any other way to reach the most sublime realities.

The Thomist explanation of God, deduced from Exodus (3:14) as *Ipsum Esse Subsistens*, is certainly the right starting–point for any sound theology. But it is easy to see that that explanation can be complemented by St John's assertion (1 Jn 4:8) that God is Love. Both definitions very accurately say what God is, but each looks at different (though all–embracing) aspects of the divine Being. However, since God is Love, and man is made in his image and likeness, one must conclude that man has been given the capacity to love (and, therefore, to be loved) as a constituent of his nature. Suitability for love must then be an element in the doctrine of man's being like unto God. This means that man must be recognized as being a person (for only a person can love) and therefore as having a dignity which is in some way infinite. What is proper to and what constitutes a person, or what confers on him his independence or, if you like, his incommunicability (as St Thomas put it) is what makes him an *I* and therefore sets him in front of a *thou*. Love can exist only in a *relationship of opposition*, for love consists in mutual *contemplation* by two persons who love one another, so that, each *facing* the other, both of them *give* and *receive* at the same time. And that oppositeness is a *total* one, an *opposition of totality*, because, though each person gives him or herself totally, he or she receives the other person also totally, as if a veritable dialectic of *contraries* were at work. This may shed some light on the Thomist characteristics of independence and incommunicability that belong to a person as person. This dialectic can be described by using correlative and corresponding concepts, such as giving and receiving, losing oneself and finding oneself,[10] speaking and listening, looking at and being looked at, desiring and being desired, etc. *Incommunicability*, therefore, has to do with that which is most intimate to, most constituent of, the person —that which makes the person to be this particular *I*, and which is the only thing he cannot give away if he is to continue to be a person. Or to put it another way: the person can give everything —except what makes him a being with a capacity to keep on giving everything. This means that only a person can love and be loved, because only an *I* can give himself or herself to a *thou* and receive, in turn, another *I*.

But man can only love in a *human way*, that is, in the manner in keeping with his nature. Even when his nature is elevated by grace and he loves, therefore, *divinely*, he continues to love in a way that suits his nature. He loves, then, in keeping with a (human) nature which, on being elevated by grace, goes absolutely beyond his own capabilities.[11] And, since human nature is made up of spirit and matter, it follows that man needs his body in order to love perfectly; this holds true even in the age to come.[12] Certainly, as long as he is making his pilgrim way on earth, there is no other way that man knows how or is able to love. Also valid here are the principles of the Scholastic theory of knowledge, according to which there is nothing in man's understanding that has not come through the senses, and

---

[10] In self–surrender by and to the other person. It is a matter of *losing oneself in the loved one*, through complete self–surrender and trust, in order to find everything once again in him.

[11] Grace does not destroy nature; it elevates it. Supernatural love is given to man by God quite gratuitously; man in no sense has a right to it. In any case, a man who loves continues to be a man.

[12] The soul, which is spiritual and is the form of the body, can exist as such separate from the body. But the separated soul is no longer a human being, and the blessed in Heaven, although they already enjoy the beatific vision, live in hope of the resurrection.

nothing that he loves that he has not first known. This means that nothing can be desired, or loved, unless it first be grasped by the understanding; and it is through the senses that the mind begins to function as a knower.

But the senses are not at the origin only of the phenomenon of human love. We have already said that man loves also through his corporality, including his senses (external and internal). Or to put it another way: if man loves primordially *with his whole soul*, clearly he does so also *with his whole heart* (with his corporality), although he does so in the unity of his unique being.[13] This being so, one must also say that the object of human love must be also in some way graspable by the senses, because it is unthinkable that human nature should fall in love with something purely spiritual — for that something purely spiritual cannot be even imagined by man. This means that man is able to love God and see God directly in heaven, face to face (provided he is elevated and assisted by special divine help), but he does so through the human nature of Jesus Christ: *Philip, he who has seen me has seen the Father; how can you say, "Show us the Father"?*[14] The formula, "in Christ, through Christ, with Christ" continues to apply in heaven. It follows that it is through the human nature of our Lord that man manages to perceive the divine nature and Person of the Word and, through them, the Father Himself.

However, it is worth pointing out that we do not mean here to question the sound doctrine that the blessed have direct vision of God in heaven, a vision which does not involve the interposition of any medium. What we are proposing as a working hypothesis

---

[13] A unique being, but one made up of spirit and matter. The expression "with his whole heart," although a metaphor, is in some sense a real one.

[14] Jn 14:9.

is that the blessed attain direct vision of the Godhead (and then enjoy it) through the human nature of Jesus Christ. By being united hypostatically to the Word, and being in the proper sense *his* nature, that nature cannot be regarded as a mere medium. It is rather like what happens when, in order to speak with another person, one looks him in the face: what one is perceiving directly is the person of the other, not just his face or his eyes. Someone who sees the Man Jesus Christ is seeing the one Person there is in Him; he is seeing the Word; and if one sees Him, one sees the Father (Jn 14:9).

There is no doubt that if one pays attention to this doctrine it becomes much easier to find new ways which will lead, eventually, to a spirituality which is based on stronger Christocentric principles,[15] and which will give one new energy to explore the why and the wherefore of the Incarnation of the Word.

As regards that matter, it is clear that the Christ–centredness of which we are speaking points directly to the appropriateness of the Word becoming flesh, once God freely decreed the creation of man and his elevation to the supernatural order. This appropriateness is based here on the fact that God, in choosing to create man and elevate him to the supernatural order, decided to make him in his own image and likeness —and therefore endowed him with a capacity to love and be loved. Here is where we can see how appropriate it was that the Word should make a human nature *his*. The incarnation became appropriate from the point when man, through God's free and kindly disposition, was destined to be intimate with God —able to see Him face to face and to speak with Him as person to person, as is proper in a relationship of love.

---

[15]The Christocentrism of spirituality (and of the theology of creation and redemption), which theoretically no one questions, does not always lead to the logical or practical conclusions which should flow from that doctrine. And of course a great deal of work remains to be done to explore that doctrine in depth.

However, for man to be able to conduct a loving conversation and have a loving relationship with God, he must first *fall in love* with Him. So, God takes a human nature and makes it his, in order to make this mutual loving relationship possible. Now indeed God can *seduce* man (and *let Himself be seduced* by him) in a divine way, and at the same time also *in a human way*.[16]

God chose to love man with a total and perfect love. Therefore, he decided to be at one and the same time his Father, his Brother, his Spouse and his Friend, in the hope that man would respond with full, reciprocal love.[17] But even though he is raised to the supernatural order, man continues to love in a manner befitting his nature or, to put it another way, his supernature; in order to *fall in love* with God he needs to perceive God in his own way of knowing. For his part, God, desiring to be known and loved by man in man's way, *with the rapture, emotion, tenderness, and sentiments proper to man when he is in love*, must needs show Himself to man as man.

---

[16]In saying this we do not mean to deny that the Redemption is a determinating and fundamental motive of the Incarnation. But medieval theologians already debated the question as to whether it would not be more appropriate, in keeping with the exigencies of the glory of God, to look for some determinating motive of the Incarnation other than that of sin. Perhaps one could conclude that both motives were present in the one plan of Divine Providence.

[17]Since man is not Love, he can only participate in it in various ways, but never exhaust it. In fact, love between parent and child, conjugal love, fraternal love, and ordinary friendship are forms of sharing in the only Love —ways given to man to attain, in some way, the totality of Love, for he has been created to love in that unlimited way. In the parable of the inopportune friend (Lk 11: 5–13) we find these various forms of love by a strange and apparent coincidence. From the parable one can clearly see that none of these forms of love excludes the other, even when (as happens in the parable) they seem to be contrasted (the desire to help his friend, yet does not want to disturb his wife or children), given that, eventually, even importunate friendship is accommodated. The same doctrine is to be found in the *Song of Songs*: 4: 9–10; 5: 1–2; 8:1.

That is only logical, for God cannot but desire that his creature love Him in the manner proper to the nature He gave him —which is the same as saying, according to the manner of loving which He Himself has taught him.[18]

Since man loves not only with his soul but also with his body, the object of his love must be in some way perceivable by the senses. Man loves when he discovers eyes different from his own, eyes into which he gazes and where he sees himself being contemplated in turn by the loved one. He loves when he finds the lips and the ear of the other person, because human love is fed by mutual sweet words and promises of love, spoken by lips of flesh and heard by ears of flesh. He loves when he feels two hearts beating together, his own and that of the person he loves, because without that experience (which happens in the embrace of love), he can only with difficulty discover what love really is. But when it is a matter of loving God, man finds all this in Jesus Christ, who is true man as well as being true God.

The man who loves does not abstract from the corporality of the person he loves, because it is through that very dimension that he comes to love the person; except that in the case in point, the other Person is not a human but a divine Person. And so, when man makes the Man Jesus Christ the object of his love (perceiving Jesus in his human nature) it is really God that he falls in love with. For it is always a person that one loves, not a mere corporal dimension, or even a nature. As love develops, *it begins* with the perception of corporality and nature, and *it ends* with love for the person with whom corporality and nature form a substantial whole.

---

[18] It must be admitted that the expression to *show Himself* does suffer from certain Docetist overtones. In fact it is not sufficient for God to appear to man in human form in order to obtain his love; he must truly be man if he is to do that. Man's heart can focus its love only on real things.

Love always focuses on the person in his totality, and therefore also on his corporality and his nature (which are proper *to him*). But the ultimate object of love —what constitutes the specific thing someone *falls in love with*— is always the person. Jesus Christ's human nature, though distinct from his divine nature, has been made its own by the Person of the Word and joined hypostatically to that Person. Therefore, when man contemplates the Man Jesus Christ and falls in love with Him, he really falls in love with God Himself, in the only way a human being can fall in love. He falls in love with the *Person* of the Word, through a love made possible the moment the Word *became flesh*. Human love is something that belongs to the spiritual order, insofar as it comes from the soul and is rooted there properly speaking; but it also belongs to the order of flesh and blood insofar as it is the entire man who is doing the loving and doing it in a manner proper to his nature. When man loves God in Jesus Christ, that love embraces everything; it *includes* our Lord's divine nature; that is no accident, nor does it derive from divine love as such: it is an exigency of the very nature of love. For, since love is totality, it embraces fully the person it is addressed to; nothing falls outside its range; the very idea of omitting anything proper to the loved person is something no lover could even conceive.

The love with which this book is concerned is perfect love, which has been granted to man through divine benevolence and free will. For, although love admits of degrees, only perfect love deserves to be called true love. It would have been possible for God not to have raised man to the supernatural order, in which case he could have loved his Creator with an ordinary creature's natural love. And, although all love tends to completeness,[19] the different forms it takes

---

[19] When it is genuine, love is a spark of the divine life placed in man. And the divine life is infinite Love.

(friendship, fraternal love, love between parent and child, and married love) each has its own nuances. God, who is infinite and perfect love or, simply Love (1 Jn 4:8), has (is) in the highest degree everything which these various forms found in man have (are) of love. But God is the only, unique Love —infinite and perfect Love— whereas creatures are only capable of receiving differing shares of that love, in a more or less elevated degree.

Since God desired to establish a relationship of perfect love with man (insofar as a created being is capable of that type of relationship), he deigned to give him the *totality* that is inherent in true love. And, although that totality can only be to the measure of a creature's capacity, it is, for all that, totality, in the sense at least that thanks to it the creature is enabled to *give himself entirely*. A created being cannot give himself in the same way as a being who is All, but he can give *all* his being. This means that divine–human love, which is a love involving total self–surrender, possesses all the perfections that the various kinds of human love can have, though in an elevated and fulfilled way. What God looks for in his creature's loving self–surrender to Him is not infinitude of being (which is impossible) but that totality or completeness which is the only fundamental condition for love to be perfect. He does not expect to be given as much as He Himself gives (that reciprocity can happen only in the bosom of the Trinity of the Divine Persons): but he does want to be given *everything* (in other words, the entire person), just as he for his part gives *everything*.

This brings us again to the doctrine that love always focuses on the person; the person is, throughout, the ultimate term and subject of attribution. In fact it is not the gifts his bride gives Him that most interest the Bridegroom, or the Bridegroom's gifts that she is most interested in: for each of them the person of the other is what truly matters. A lover finds his heart's desire in the self–giving of the loved one, so much so that he no longer looks for or desires any other thing. Love tokens serve their purpose at the start of the love relationship, heralding and preparing the ground for the encounter with the loved one; but once that encounter has come about, gifts are from then on a secondary consideration —forgotten now that what was (previously) hoped for has been fully attained (1 Cor 13: 8.13).

The relationships which God has chosen to have with man are those of perfect love. This means that He has enabled man to respond to Him with a love which, like his, is total; it embraces all the forms of love known to man —friendship, fraternal love, the love between parent and child, and married love. Divine–human love embraces all these forms to the extent that each in theory is for man a more perfect mode of loving. That is the import of the words the Bible sets on God's lips: *Therefore, I will seduce her*[20] *and bring her into the wilderness and speak tenderly to her...And in that day —says Yahweh— you will call me, "My husband," and no longer will you call me, "My Baal."*[21] Here we no longer have the normal relationship of God with his creature, but rather one that is much stronger than close friendship, such that it even excludes there being any secret the two do not share (Jn 15:15). What God has set in man's heart is the very Love that Father and Son have for each other (Jn 17:26; Rom 5:5).

---

[20] Hos 2: 16–18. The *Bible de Jérusalem* says that "il faut entendre le mot en un sens fort... La même expression est employée à propos de l'homme qui séduit une vierge," Cerf, Paris, 1973, notes c and f.

[21] As the *Bible de Jérusalem* says (cf. previous note), the word *baal* (lord) was applied to the husband. This word is found incorporated into many personal names without that implying idolatory. In later times the word *baal* was regarded as irreligious, because of its reference to the Canaanite Baals.

The *Song of Songs* speaks of love between God and man; to do so it extols poetically the qualities of love between husband and wife. Although married love is not the sum total of love, it does have features and nuances which mark it out from other forms of love; these features, for that very reason, make it the most appropriate way to describe a love which is total and intimate, a love of mutual self–surrender, involving a complete communion of lives. And, since divine–human love is absolute and ineffable, the *Song* uses poetic language —that language man speaks when he tries to express things which he can never fully manage to say. Ineffability begins at the point where God, who could have had an ordinary love–relationship with man (that proper to Creator and creature), decides to establish with him the relationship proper to perfect love.

God became man because he desired to be loved by man in a divine way and in a human way. *In a divine way*, because that is the form of love proper to God, the perfect form of perfect love, and the form which perfects man's love; and *in a human way*, because that is the form of love proper to man. Once God has become man, man can now love him in his own way —in a human way— and at the same time, also, with a perfect and total love, a love which is crazy —in a divine way. Now at last man can truly *fall in love* with God, in the sense that he can now make God the tangible, *sensible*, object of his love; he can love Him as someone like unto him: *See my hands and my feet, that it is myself; handle me, and see; for a spirit has not flesh and bones as you see that I have*, our Lord said to his disciples, after he rose from the dead; and the Gospel text adds: *And when he had said this, he showed them his hands and his feet.*[22]

---

[22] Lk 24: 39–40.

In man, divine–human love is born, develops, and reaches its consummation in both divine and human ways. It is love human-style (for it is man that is loving, and he must love in a manner suited to his nature), but grace has raised this love to the level of the infinite.[23] In Christ, man loves God *in his own human way*, and at the same time *in a divine way*; but in such a way that, because it is the true Man Jesus Christ that he loves, he loves in Him the true God.

Our Lord is particularly interested in showing his disciples that his risen body is a real body, able to use all its senses —able even to eat in their presence (Lk 24: 41–43)[24]. Jesus asks Thomas, who had resisted the testimony of the other ten apostles and remained incredulous, to put his finger and his hands into the wounds of his risen body (Jn 20:27). By means of a human body and soul, which the Word too has made his own, man loves the Person of the Lord and, therefore, God.[25] And, although it is true that the risen Lord tells Mary Magdalen not to touch Him (Jn 20:17) that must be because He *has not yet ascended to the Father*, as He Himself tells her, and

---

[23] Raised to the level of the infinite insofar as here the object of human love is infinite. In a figurative sense, insofar as man's capacity to love, when elevated by grace, surpasses anything man could do or imagine, if he had to rely on his own nature alone.

[24] The use of the sense of taste (involving the possibility of eating) is perhaps one of the most difficult qualities to understand in a glorified body. For this very reason, it is one of the most clinching proofs.

[25] Here again one comes up against the inadequacy of language. Strictly speaking, it is not a matter of man loving God *through* a human nature. The one that man in fact loves is the Person of the Word (given that it is always a person that one loves), although perceived and grasped in a human nature which, due to its being hypostatically united to the Word, belongs to the Word (is *his*) and is not distinct from Him. If one sees our Lord's eyes, for example, one is seeing the Person of the Lord. One can go a step further, although only one act of love is involved, and realize that to see the Person of the Lord is to see the Father (Jn 14:9).

she cannot yet, therefore, love Him with the true and perfect love which only the coming of the Paraclete will make possible (Jn 16:7). First must come the One who is to be sent.[26]

It would be quite difficult, if not impossible, for man to fall in love with the so-called "God of the philosophers" or the God certain theologians put forward. Man loves eagerly and tenderly, with trembling emotion; his heartbeat quickens and he is afire with passion: human love cannot but have these feelings. To love God with true and perfect love, and therefore in its very own proper manner of loving, the human heart needs God to show Himself[27] in a human nature, with a real, not just apparent, human nature, and therefore one that can be seen, heard and touched (1 Jn 1: 1–2). For, unless his senses come into play, man cannot perceive goodness or beauty or the goodness of beauty or the beauty of goodness — all things without which love cannot happen. Man firstly sees and hears and then he falls in love. After curing the man who was born blind, *Jesus heard that they had cast him out, and having found him he said, "Do you believe in the Son of man?" He answered, "And who is He, sir, that I may believe in Him?" Jesus said to him, "You have seen Him, and it is he who speaks to you." He said, "Lord, I believe," and he worshipped Him.*[28] Yet, it is not enough for man to love in a divine way and a human way. Since love is absolute reciprocity, given that God chose to have a relationship of perfect love with man, He had to become man, *in order for Him, too, to be able to love in a human way*, and not just in a divine way.

---

[26]Until Jesus ascends to the Father the Paraclete will not be sent. But only through the Holy Spirit can one love Jesus Christ with real love. On the other hand, our Lord is not speaking figuratively when he rebukes Thomas (Jn 20:27), or, much less, when he exhorts the Eleven in Luke 24:39.

[27]1 Jn 1:2; Tit 2:11; 3:4.

[28]Jn 9: 35–38.

Introduction 31

The *Song of Songs* speaks about divine–human love, which attains its fullness in man through Jesus Christ. It speaks of love in the sort of language most accessible to man; therefore it centres on married love, using the imagery and language proper to that form of love. But it does so not purely for pedagogical reasons. The fact of the matter is that divine–human love, being love which is absolute and total, includes everything to do with true love that is contained in the self–giving that is the mark of marriage,[29] and, just like married love, it too is nourished by sweet words, caresses and self–giving —on the part of both, but in this case in a divine–human way. Since married love is the kind that man most clearly sees to have these features, it seems to be the best form of love to use when speaking of perfect love, the love of total self–surrender. That is why in the human context married love is on a higher level (at least in some way) than parent–child[30] or any other love.

It is the kind of love which causes nostalgia and impatient longing when the loved one is absent, the kind that causes the lover to passionately seek the loved one; it is the kind of love that inspires anxiety and burning words, and eventually finds its fulfilment in caresses and mutual self–giving. Sometimes it is also the kind of love which some Christians feel is lacking; as they see it, if God is scarcely ever spoken of in this way, that is due to forgetting that the essence of the Good News is not a message of social justice but the Person of Jesus Christ and the Love which he came to bring

---

[29] Jesus alludes to this in the parables of the wedding and of the virgins, and in his references to the Bridegroom. John the Baptist himself (Jn 3:29) also echoes this way of speaking about divine–human love.

[30] In Mt 19: 4–5, our Lord, citing Genesis, says the following: "Have you not read that the Creator from the beginning made them male and female, and that he said, 'For this reason a man shall leave his father and mother and be joined to his wife, and the two shall become one flesh'?"

men. According to these Christians, the love that truly seduces and causes one to *fall in love* is not so much the sort of love one feels towards the beauty of a message (even the Gospel message) as the one which results from the contemplation of a person.

However, because the Christ that certain modern exegetes and theologians speak about is a mere phantasm, he is incapable of seducing anyone. That Christ, devoid of divinity and miracles, devoid even of humanity (because he has no real existence), devised as he seemingly is by the primitive Christian community, and risen only in the apostles' faith, has really vanished, has no body, no soul, and therefore cannot be the object of anyone's love. How can one love what one does not either see or hear or touch? How can one love a ghost, a figment of the imagination and the complicated minds of a few scholars? They argue that that is the only kind of Christ acceptable to man today; but no one could love it because love always focuses on real persons, not on the laboratory products of pseudo-science.

In the present age, man knows and perceives the true Christ by means of faith. But, as Spicq says, one must remember that believing and seeing are often synonymous in the Bible: "The believer is a seer. But 'seer' is an amphibological term, because the object of faith is things unseen (Heb 11:1), and the terms the Bible uses to describe sight apply both to physical perception and to reflection, deduction, or profound insight and contemplation in the strict sense. The Saviour's humanity, which is perceptible to the senses (1 Jn 1:1), is visible to the eyes of all —enemies, relations, disciples. Signs and miracles allow one to see, in this preacher of salvation, a messenger from the Father. Jesus performs many signs, because they are a support for and a guarantee of the assent of faith. For some people the occurrence of these wonders is sufficient to lead them to accept the Person of Christ (Jn 2:23; 11:45), whereas others remain rebellious or insensitive: they entirely fail to grasp their *meaning*. That is like saying that mere sight of wonders does not produce conviction; even the most unambiguous events need to be interpreted. To these events one needs to bring reflection (pondering, as St John did, when he saw the empty tomb); one needs to have a certain grasp of spiritual realities (as the Samaritan woman had), and certain moral dispositions (as the Blessed Virgin had), which sharpen the mind and leave it open to conviction by the proofs God provides."[31]

Faith, therefore, does not render the senses unnecessary; it is not a substitute for them. As Spicq says, the senses on their own, despite verifying very obvious events, would be no use. And faith for its part has need of the senses —even in the case of those who, without *seeing* the Lord, have believed (Jn 20:29; 1 Pet 1:8).

This necessary role of the senses in the context of faith is based not only on the fact that faith *comes through hearing* (Rom 10:17),[32] it also is based on the fact that, even after hearing the word or testimony of the apostles, man still needs to use all his senses (external and internal) if he is to *see* and know Jesus.

This means that faith, by giving a new supernatural vigour to the senses, provides men with a knowledge of Jesus Christ which he could never obtain by natural means. For the supernatural does not render the natural ineffective, and faith does not in any way imply the exclusion or annihilation of the senses. Man must become habituated to perceive natural beauty or goodness in persons or genuine love in those who love. Acting on his natural powers and on

---

[31] C. Spicq, *Théologie Moral du Nouveau Testament*, I, Gabalda, Paris, 1970, pp. 462 ff.

[32] The *New Vulgate* says: "Fides ex auditu, auditus autem per verbum Christi."

the dispositions of the heart that Spicq refers to, faith elevates man's understanding and heart to where they could never reach on their own; it gives them a content which they could never otherwise attain. The true knowledge of Jesus Christ man achieves in this present age is a knowledge deriving from faith, an absolutely supernatural knowledge, which belongs therefore to the sphere of mystery.[33] But this knowledge and love of Jesus Christ which man obtains not only does not prescind from the beauty and goodness of persons and natural objects (seen now from a distance and from above, but with no less sharp perception); it actually presupposes them: they are the necessary ground for the knowledge that comes through faith.

In order to know divine–human love, man needs first to know what love is. In order to fall in love with the countenance of God in Jesus Christ, man must first perceive the beauty of the human countenance. And, to appreciate what the love of total self–surrender is, he needs to know something about married love, and even to be *au fait* with the way lovers behave and with the loving things they say, with the language of love. Man grasps divine–human love, or at least begins to have an inkling of it, only if he has some natural experience of the grandeur of love (which begins with the love of friendship and extends to the consummation and mutual self–giving that is a feature of marriage).

---

[33] True, profound knowledge of Jesus Christ and therefore love for his Person, both nourished by faith, are supernatural. But they begin with natural, analogous, knowledge and love; as one can see, for example, in connexion with divine paternity, to know which man needs first to experience human paternity. In regard to this last point, and as a confirmation of what has been said, it is worth pointing out that the spread of the doctrine of *suspicion towards the father* put forward by Freud and his followers has for many Christians chilled their feeling for God as their father and themselves as His children. (See the now classic work by Henri de Lubac, *The Drama of Atheistic Humanism*.)

And, in turn, he does not really appreciate the beauty of natural love until he comes to appreciate that love after it has been raised by grace and made supernatural. When that happens, the distinction between natural and supernatural love becomes irrelevant, in the sense that, for the true lover, only love exists —nothing else— and for him the only genuine love will be love that is raised up by grace. For, since love is fullness, natural love is only a hint of that fullness: *When the perfect comes, the imperfect will pass away* (1 Cor 13:10). And, just as ordinary human love is also, in our present circumstances, accompanied by painful absences, nostalgia, and even infidelity on the part of one of the lovers, which is what happens in divine–human love, the book of the *Song* echoes these sentiments and employs them when speaking of the bride and the bridegroom in its epic account of the love between God and man.

Clearly, divine–human love cannot be less *passionate* than ordinary human love. Nor is its grandeur diminished by the fact that man always has to love *in a human way*. Because it is a perfect love, divine–human love is quite beyond anything man can attain or even conceive on his own; and it is the only way man can experience perfect love. Merely human love, no matter what heights it achieves, is always imperfect. Bearing in mind (it is worth repeating) that just as human love is a mixture of deep feelings of emotion and trembling, of tenderness and passion, of suffering and joy —feelings which can even take man out of himself, causing him to experience that *craziness* which Plato speaks of in *The Symposium* and *Phædo*—, the same happens in divine–human love; there too one finds exactly the same sentiments, although to an immensely greater degree.

It follows from this that *Christian commitment* can never be commitment to the *oppressed*; it must be total commitment to God; it is He whom man has first *promised* himself and then *commit*-

ted himself once he receives the earnest or pledge of future nuptials (Eph 1:14; 2 Cor 1:22). However, the love of God, as understood by the saints and as extolled by the almost divine poems of St John of the Cross, seems to have disappeared below the horizon of theology, to be replaced by a different notion of Christian life in which the primary (and only) thing is no longer the commandment of love, but a complicated array of sociological ideas and economic and political directives. The true Christ has been pushed aside by the *revolutionary* Christ of the Marxists or else by a cold and purely human Christ, the product of rationalist speculation in which faith plays no part, the Christ of liberal Protestantism.

Meanwhile, the heart of modern man languishes in a yearning for genuine love, desirous of a *real* and *personal* God who is capable of loving and of being loved. Man has been created with a capacity for infinite love, as St Augustine put it, and cannot live without love. Created *in the image and likeness* of that Being who is Love (1 Jn 4:8), he is therefore made for love and for being loved, infinitely, totally, because that Being who is Love is infinite Being. Therefore man needs to know (and feel) that he is loved by a loving God. Or to put it even more exactly: by a God who, since it is his office to love and his essence is love (1 Jn 4:8), is capable of loving him with an infinite "craziness." Man can never be satisfied or rest easy with the "Absolute" or any other kind of philosophical God. What he needs is a personal God, who can whisper sweet things to him from time to time, as the Bridegroom does to the Bride in the *Song of Songs*:

> *Behold, you are beautiful, my love;*
> *behold you are beautiful! Your eyes are doves.*

> ....

> *Turn your eyes away from me,*
> *they take me by assault.*
>
> . . . .
>
> *Arise, my love,*
> *my fair one, and come away;*
> *for lo, the winter is past,*
> *the rain is over and gone.*
> *The flowers appear on earth,*
> *the time of singing has come,*
> *and the voice of the turtledove is heard in our land.*

Man needs in turn to be able to say to God, fully meaning the words, what the bride says to the Bridegroom in the *Song*:

> *O that you would kiss me*
> *with the kisses of your mouth!*
> *For your love is better than wine.*
>
> . . . .
>
> *Sustain me with raisins,*
> *refresh me with apples,*
> *for I am sick with love...*

Man needs to love God in this way because it is the only way he knows how; it is what he understands by love. Love is unthinkable unless it be accompanied by passion, by wooing and loving words, by tears over the absence of the loved one, and by the infinite joy which causes him to die when, at long last, love is consummated by the presence of the Loved One.

According to some, the *Song of Songs* is merely a collection of nuptial songs which refer solely to human love. For others, the inspired poem means simply Christ's love for the Church. This present book, however, will read the *Song* convinced that it is the story of God's love *for every human being* who chooses to respond to that love. That is why it identifies in the *Song* all the kinds of things one finds in true love stories: the lovers in search of each other, powerful desires and yearnings as yet unfulfilled, absence and presence, wooing words and reproaches addressed by each to the other, love–promises, and even momentary, passing, failures in love on the part of one of the lovers.

Some may find it hard to accept that the loving relationships of God with man can follow this sort of course. However, that is how the *Song* describes them, making it the most audacious book in the Bible. It tells the story of divine–human love (of God's love with *every man, every woman*, as a person, as a real being that loves and is loved) as a love which is happening *now*, in this age which still does not know what perfect Love is. That is why we find in the sacred poem all kinds of reproaches, a veritable war of love (Sg 2:4), the anguished cries of the bride proclaiming that she is dying of love (Sg 2:5), and her invitations to the Bridegroom to seek the privacy of solitude for mutual contemplation (Sg 7: 12–13).

And so it is that the love we find in the *Song of Songs* is not only divine (that would indicate fullness and consummation) nor only human (which even if it did exist would be very defective) but is, in fact, genuine, true divine–human love, or simply true love.

First Part

"Let him kiss me with kisses of his mouth"

(Sg 1:2a)

CHAPTER I

THE DESIRE TO BE LOVED

Let him kiss me with the kisses of his mouth, or, *O that you would kiss me with the kisses of your mouth* —whichever version is used, the bride here expresses her desire to be kissed. However, it is worth pointing out that the obvious literal meaning shows that it is not so much a desire to kiss as a desire to receive the kiss of love.

One may say, therefore, that what the bride's exclamation denotes above all is her yearning to be loved, to feel loved, and to know for certain that the Bridegroom is in love with her. Although love cannot exist, does not make sense, unless it be reciprocal, what the bride desires here, *her first intention*, is to see fulfilled her longing to be loved by the Bridegroom.

We shall later see that what she in fact desires is for the Bridegroom to give Himself to her, and for her to possess Him forevermore. This is a desire whose true meaning has to do with the profound meaning of love —as will become clearer when we discuss the meaning of the "kiss" as an *intention* to consummate love.[34] The desire to be loved which impels the bride belongs to the essence of love (that is, reciprocity),[35] and it is also proper to the nature of man, made as he is for loving and being loved.

What the bride yearns for, therefore, is to feel herself desired by the Bridegroom, which is the same as saying by *the other*, the opposite term in the reciprocity of love. However, in this instance *the other* is Love itself. The bride desires to feel the kisses of the mouth of Him Who is Love and, at the same time, her Bridegroom; a Spouse in love, so much in love that he is Love entire. We must remember that here the adjectival phrase *in love* acquires primacy over the noun *Bridegroom*, at least in the sense that the latter is absolutely Love.

All this shows that the bride, more or less consciously, is following the ways of perfect love. For, in line with what we have said about the meaning of her exclamation, what she really means is that she desires *all* of Him. And so she speaks of the kiss on the mouth, the most intimate of love's kisses. Her desire that the Bridegroom express his love in that particular way, by so intimate a kiss, shows that she sees this as the best proof that He loves her completely. And if it is true that she desires above all, at this point, that the initiative be with the Bridegroom, it is equally true that she for

---

[34]By way of anticipation we can say that the kiss is one of those symbolic actions performed by man (although it is not only symbolic) which reveals the glory and wretchedness of human nature at one and the same time. Its glory, because the kiss is the gesture which best conveys the fullness of love to which man is destined (lovers *would eat one another up* if they could); its wretchedness, because, as always happens in the love–actions man performs, the kiss is simply an attempt to express total love which never achieves its purpose.

[35]Love does not only wish *to love*, but also *to be loved*, for this is precisely its essence: a reciprocal ebb and flow moving constantly from one lover to the other. Therefore, a love without a wish to be loved would simply be unimaginable.

her part also wishes to respond to Him, in reciprocity, through the same expression of love. That is how the bride sees love: unless the Bridegroom kiss her, she cannot even imagine that he loves her.[36] And there is no doubt but that this fits in with the very essence of love. For, although the bride well knows that her only end is the Bridegroom (loving Him is her true destiny), at this point she does not have a conscious conviction so much as an ardent desire to love the Bridegroom and therefore to be loved in turn by Him, for love (it is worth recalling again) is set on a basis of absolute reciprocity.

The remarkable thing here is that the bride desires to be loved by God completely, in fullest intimacy —and in the only way that she understands love. Therefore she speaks of the kiss placed on her mouth by the mouth of the Lover. What she longs for is the love of total self–surrender and absolute intimacy. Or, if one prefers to put it more simply: what the bride desires is Love.

The sacred author of the *Song of Songs* uses the language of human love to convey his meaning; for his poem he chooses the form of human love in which we can see most clearly the perfect mutual giving of lovers, the love of husband and wife. Since this is the best means available to him to convey his meaning, he could not but use it. It is just not possible to appreciate divine Love (or, simply, Love) or even to speak about it without first passing through human love (1 Jn 4:20; 4:8; 4:16; etc.). The bride knows no other way of loving, has no other route she can take to the heights of divine Love, other than that which begins with ordinary human love.

Besides, as we shall see later, the only lack of goodness that true human love suffers from is that it falls short. Its essence consists in its being simply an *attempt* (it cannot go further) to attain total

---

[36] We do not propose here to discuss the subject of grace as a means to supernaturalize the gestures and modes of love.

Love. However, just as an imperfect thing evokes the perfect, and a part implies the whole, human love is the best (and only) way available to man to understand what total Love (or, simply, Love) is and the relationship that that Love desires to have with him.

CHAPTER II

THE NOTICE OF LOVE

The bride impatiently urges the Bridegroom to kiss her because she knows that He is in love with her.

This implies that she has already received from Him affectionate and sufficient proofs of his love; otherwise she could not know that He loves her or recognize Him as her Bridegroom.

This kind of knowledge is not simply that she has a mere *notice* of his love: she has also, and, above all, *experienced* it. The bride knows that she is loved because she has already received earnests of the Bridegroom's love. *Knowing* oneself to be loved is here the equivalent of *feeling* loved, because love always makes itself known directly (it is not merely something reported); it has no need of messengers, because love by its very nature is an *intermediary*.

However, as we shall see later, the mediation of love has special features, because it is at the same time something direct, immediate. This is so because love not only *proceeds* simultaneously from both lovers; it also unites them and becomes one thing with them. Were it, for an instant, to cease to be *present* to either of them, it would be love no longer. *One-sided* love exists in a situation where one is awaiting a response; it does not reach its fullness until that moment comes, because reciprocity is part of the very essence of love. *We love one another* because *He first loved us.*[1] It is worth anticipating what we shall go on to say: in perfect Love there is no experience of waiting. Since perfect love is fullness, St John's statement that "God first loved us" should not be understood in the sense that God has been forever *waiting* for his creature to return his love; for in the eternity of infinite Being, where only the present exists, there is no room for any kind of waiting, much less any filling up of something that is already complete fullness.

Love, then, is a type of *notice* because it cannot exist unless the lover knows the loved one and knows that she reciprocates his love. But that mutual knowledge goes, as has been said, beyond even mere *notices*. In fact it is impossible for a person who loves to feel content with *knowing* that he is loved, not even when he is convinced that the message he has received comes from the loved one.[2] Love is never content with the language of *messengers*: it wants to hear from the lips of the person it loves. So, far from being reduced to mere knowledge or message, it is always accompanied by the breath and warmth caused by the presence of the loved one. As St John of the Cross said in immortal, almost divine verses which so beautifully express the impatient desire of the bride:

---

[1] 1 Jn 4:19.

[2] As one can easily see, this has important consequences for pastoral activity. Since it is not enough for man to know that God loves him, the apostle must strive (even going so far as to give up his life) to make him *feel* that love.

> *O, who will be able to heal me!*
> *Come, give yourself completely to me now*
> *From now on send me*
> *no more messengers,*
> *for they cannot tell me what I wish!*
>
> ....
>
> *Reveal your presence,*
> *and may the vision of your beauty be my death,*
> *for the sickness of love*
> *is not cured*
> *except by your presence and image!*[3]

So, the bride ardently desires to have the Bridegroom close and to receive his loving kiss. Since she knows He loves her, she tells Him to kiss her. And, since this means that divine-human love requires that the bride know the Bridegroom, and know that he loves her, it would be good for us to study more closely the various features of that knowledge.

---

[3]In the *Cántico Espiritual*:

> *¡Ay!, ¿quién podrá sanarme?*
> *¡Acaba de entregarte ya de vero,*
> *no quieras enviarme*
> *de hoy más ya mensajero*
> *que no saben decirme lo que quiero!*
>
> ....
>
> *¡Descubre tu presencia,*
> *y máteme tu vista y hermosura;*
> *mira que la dolencia*
> *de amor, que no se cura*
> *sino con la presencia y la figura!*

The notice of love, which comes from the Loved One, clearly brings knowledge of the Loved One Himself. But this notice goes in three directions —towards the past, towards the future, and towards insightfulness. This complexity of the act of (divine–human) love is due to its state of imperfection: in this present age it has not yet reached its stage of plenitude.[4]

The absence of the Loved One is what causes the notice of love to project towards the past, leading one to recall that Person and reflect on everything connected with him: *But the Counsellor, the Holy Spirit, Whom the Father will send in my name, he will teach you all things, and bring to your remembrance all that I have said to you.*[5] During this stage of love, the lover lives mainly on her memory of the Loved One, and therefore the virtue of hope infuses and moves her memory at this point,[6] maintaining, as ever, a close connexion with charity. The recalling of the Loved One, brought about by the action of the Holy Spirit, is so effective that it is able to make him *quasi–present*. It is as if that recalling had engraved on the soul the image of the Loved One. Hence the poem by St John of the Cross; in it the lover acknowledges that engraved upon his soul are the eyes of the loved one, for whose presence and contemplation the lover pines in loving nostalgia:

---

[4]Some of these three aspects, as we shall go on to see, do not derive from the present state of imperfection love labours under, but belong to the very essence of love. Naturally, they are also to be found in ordinary human love, although in ways suggesting a yet greater lack.

[5]Jn 14:26.

[6]The virtue of hope does not only look forward in confident expectation of recovering and fully possessing the Loved One. Such confidence would be impossible without previous knowledge of the Loved One, a knowledge activated in this case by memory. It is in this sense that memory is implicitly a part of hope.

> *O crystal spring,*
> *would that on your silvery surface*
> *you were suddenly to form*
> *those eyes for which I pine*
> *and which I carry graven on my soul!*[7]

This loving recollection acquires such force that, as the poet puts it, the eyes of the loved one are, as it were, *graven* deep in the heart of the enamored person. In fact, the presence of the Spirit in divine–human love causes the heartfelt memory to be much more than mere actualization. What we have called *quasi–presence* is in some way, through the influence of the Holy Spirit, a true presence (as we shall soon see at greater length) which confirms even more what we have said about the *notice* of love being in no sense a mere *notice.* So, we have here another instance of the doctrine of the *immediacy* of love (its function is not merely mediation), and of its necessary and simultaneous *presence* to the loving couple, although this is a subject which we must skirt for the moment, to be more amply developed in later chapters.

Nevertheless, as admirable and strange as it might seem, the *notice* of love also projects towards the future: *When the Spirit of truth comes, he will guide you into all truth; for he will not speak on his own authority, but whatever he hears he will speak, and will*

---

[7] In the *Cántico Espiritual*:

> *¡Oh cristalina fuente,*
> *si en esos tus semblantes plateados*
> *formases de repente*
> *los ojos deseados*
> *que tengo en mis entrañas dibujados!*

declare to you the things that are to come.[8] The *notice* of love extends into the future (thanks to the work of the Holy Spirit); if this at first sight seems strange, its explanation is to be found in the Bridegroom's delay. A person in love with Jesus Christ feels obliged to live in hope, because Christ's coming is delayed (Mt 25: 1–13; Lk 12: 35–40). His impatience born of love leads him always to be on the lookout toward the future, in watchful hope, to both interpret and *foresee* (to see with anticipation) coming events. It is here that Christian hope acquires all its meaning.[9]

Finally, the *notice* of love also tends towards ever deepening insight. Love–message that it is, it gives ever closer and fuller knowledge of the Bridegroom. And so the Spirit guides the bride towards *all the truth* (Jn 16:13) and is sent to *teach her all things* (Jn 14:26) There are no secrets between the lovers (Jn 15:15), for the current of mutual, total self–giving which links them generates in each of them a knowledge of the other that is as complete as can be in this present age, where such knowledge never reaches its fullness: *Now I know in part; then I shall understand fully, even as I have been fully understood.*[10] The bride attains this intimate knowledge thanks to the *quasi–presence* of the Bridegroom to which we referred earlier, which is effected in her by the very presence of the Spirit (Jn 14: 16–17; 1 Jn 4:16). The *notice* of love becomes so strong, so

---

[8]Jn 16:13. The prophetic function of the Spirit, which is proclaimed here as global —*the things that are to come*— and as a promise made to all the disciples, takes the Bridegroom as its first and foremost point of reference. The spirit endows the disciples with a sharp, sure sense of future events, but always with Christ as the point at which History converges, because in Him all things hold together, and all things were created through Him and for Him (Col 1: 16–17).

[9]When hope looks towards the past, it implies nostalgia; and when it looks forward, it has a sense of expectation. But it is always impatient, because it is always in love.

[10]1 Cor 13:12.

vital, that despite the absence of the Bridegroom the bride is able to hear his voice (Jn 10:27), recognizing it instantly and perfectly (Jn 10:4). This is one of the mysterious paradoxes of love: the absence that becomes presence, and that perhaps is nothing other than fullness not yet complete:

> *The voice of my beloved! Behold, he comes,*
> *leaping upon the mountains*
> *bounding over the hills.*
>
> ....
>
> *I slept, but my heart was awake.*
> *Hark! my beloved is knocking.*[11]

And, of course, once again, as is always the case with love, this knowledge is mutual: *I know my own sheep and my own know me.*[12]

So, experiencing as she does the love the Bridegroom has for her, the bride once again desires Him to show his love by means of a kiss, because love, like fire, never says *Enough!* (Prov 30:16). Love is infinite and eternal by its very nature; it knows no limits, no measures, in space, time, or intensity. The bride, mere creature that she is, is rooted in finiteness, and cannot see her desires being fully met by one caress from the Bridegroom; so she desires to receive his kiss of love over and over again. In the bosom of perfect Love, however, there is just one single kiss of love, the Holy Spirit, or *osculum suavissimum* which the Father and the Son give one another; this follows necessarily from the eternity and immensity of that kiss of love which is the Person of the Holy Spirit.

---

[11] Sg 2:8; 5:2.
[12] Jn 10:14.

CHAPTER III

THE LOVING KISS OR "OSCULUM SUAVISSIMUM"

However, the kiss is far from being a mere expression of love. The *osculum suavissimum* with which, in the bosom of perfect Love, the Father and the Son mutually seal their love, is the Holy Spirit. So, in the unique and infinite Being of the Trinity, the Holy Spirit is as it were Love itself, or He through Whom the three (the two Lovers and *their Love*) are one single thing.[1]

---

[1] *In "De Trinitate," book 6, Augustine (finally) introduces his notion of the Holy Spirit... Here he moves from previously accepted descriptions of the Spirit as the unity or communion of the Father and the Son to the designation of the Spirit as the love of the Father and the Son. In book 15 Augustine eventually gives a brilliant scriptural defense of this designation of the Holy Spirit. Although there is some precedent among earlier Fathers for naming the Holy Spirit as Love, Augustine is the first to make any significant use of this notion. From book 6 onwards, the theme of the Holy Spirit as Love comes to dominate Augustine's quest* (Juvenal Merriel, To the Image of the Trinity, A Study in the Development of Aquinas' Teaching, Pontifical Institute of Mediaeval Studies, Toronto, 1990).

But if, in perfect Love, the Holy Spirit or *osculum suavissimum* of love between the Father and the Son, is Love itself,[2] we must take it that in human love also the kiss of love is something more than an expression of love. Here, more than anywhere else, one comes up against the limitations of language (ambiguities, corruptions, etc.). There should be no need to say that we are always speaking here about genuine love; it is only in this context that what we go on to say about the kiss of love has any meaning. When love becomes corrupt, nothing connected with it, or nothing that one tries to

---

[2] God is Love (1 Jn 4:8) and therefore the whole Trinity is Love. Here we need to bear in mind, on the one hand, the doctrine of the appropriations, and, on the other, the limitations of human language. As St Augustine says, *ea dici proprie in illa Trinitate distincte ad singulas personas pertinentia, quæ relative dicuntur ad invicem: sicut Pater et Filius et utriusque donum Spiritus Sanctus: non enim Pater Trinitas, aut Filius Trinitas, aut Trinitas donum. Quod vero ad se dicuntur singuli, non dici pluraliter tres, sed unum ipsam Trinitatem: sicut Deus Pater, Deus Filius, Deus Spiritus Sanctus; et bonus Pater, bonus Filius, bonus Spiritus Sanctus; et omnipotens Pater, omnipotens Filius, omnipotens Spiritus Sanctus: nec tamen tres dii, aut tres boni, aut tres omnipotentes, sed unus Deus, bonus, omnipotens ipsa Trinitas; et quidquid aliud non ad invicem relative, sed ad se singuli dicuntur. Hoc enim secundum essentiam dicuntur, quia hoc est ibi esse, quod mangum esse, quod bonum esse, quod sapientem esse, et quidquid aliud ad se unaquæque ibi persona vel ipsa Trinitas dicitur. Ideoque dici tres personas, vel tres substantias, non ut aliqua intellegatur diversitas essentiæ, sed ut vel uno aliquo vocabulo responderi possit, cum dicitur quid tres, vel quid tria; tantamque esse æqualitatem in ea Trinitate, ut non solum Pater non sit maior quam Filius, quod attinet ad divinitatem, sed nec Pater et Filius simul maius aliquid sint quam Spiritus Sanctus, aut singula quæque persona quælibet trium minus aliquid sit quam ipsa Trinitas* (De Trinitate, VIII, Proemium). Elsewhere in the treatise, speaking of the three divine Persons, he says that *si ergo proprie aliquid horum trium charitas nuncupanda est, quid aptius quam ut hoc sit Spiritus Sanctus? Ut scilicet in illa simplici summaque natura, non sit aliud substantia et aliud charitas; sed substantia ipsa sit charitas, et charitas ipsa sit substantia, sive in Patre, sive in Filio, sive in Spiritu Sancto, et tamen proprie Spiritus Sanctus charitas nuncupetur* (De Trinitate, XV, 17. Cf. also St Thomas, *Summa Theologiæ*, I^a, q. 37, a. 1–2).

connect with it (either actions or words) has anything to do with genuine love. Mere carnal passion brings man to the condition of an animal, and in doing so takes him further and further away from God. In fact, more than an *expression* of love, the kiss is *love itself* in act and made present to the lovers, here and now, in order to bring about mutual self–surrender and possession in as full a way as possible for each. In this sense, the loving kiss denotes the presence of love even better than sexual intercourse does, because the latter contains, in addition to love, the physiological connotations of the instinct to procreate.[3] What is specific to the kiss of love is not the instinctive appetite proper to sexual intercourse, which normally leads to procreation, but the mutual self–surrender and possession of the lovers.[4]

Hence the *sacral nature* of the loving kiss, which also is, without a doubt, one of the most marvelous mysteries to be found in the world of love. The kiss is always a feature of true love, for it is more evocative of love than sexual intercourse is. It is a sign, a symbol, rather in the way that the sacraments are: not only does it *express* love, it also contains love; one can even say that *it is love*. The loving kiss denotes the presence of love to the degree that it is itself love; and it follows that the absence, or profanation, of the kiss can be a sign (intentional or otherwise) of lack of love.

---

[3]Sexual intercourse is something common to man and to animals, although there is the substantial difference that intercourse between animals is entirely a matter of instinct. The kiss on the other hand is something found only among humans.

[4]Mutual self–surrender and possession (just that) is what really constitutes the essence of the lovers' kiss (they *would eat one another* and allow each to eat the other, in their desire to have one another). Carnal union, which in principle is not excluded from the kiss of love, contains specific elements which make it essentially distinct from the kiss.

This teaching sheds light on the Gospel episode of Luke 7:36 ff. in which Jesus is invited to the house of a Pharisee. When Jesus was there, a repentant woman, who had been a sinner, came in search of Him. The woman *brought an alabaster flask of ointment, and standing behind Him at his feet, weeping, she began to wet his feet with her tears, and wiped them with the hair of her head, and kissed his feet, and anointed them with the ointment.* This woman's burning love is in contrast with the Pharisee's cold formality; his lack of love can be seen in the way he reacts to Jesus' acceptance of what the woman is doing: *Now when the Pharisee who had invited Him saw it, he said to himself, "If this man were a prophet, he would have known who and what sort of woman this is who is touching Him, for she is a sinner."* It is worthwhile recalling here what the Apostle says about true love: *love does not think evil.*[5] But the most forceful denunciation of the Pharisee's lack of love is that made by Jesus Himself: in an affectionate but heartfelt way he upbraids his host for not giving Him the kiss and for confining himself to mere good manners: *Simon, Do you see this woman? I entered your house, you gave me no water for my feet, but she has wet my feet with her tears, and wiped them with her hair. You gave me no kiss, but from the time I came in she has not ceased to kiss my feet... Therefore, I tell you, her sins, which are many, are forgiven for she loved much.*

As we have said above, sometimes it is not so much a matter of the absence of the loving kiss as its profanation, as happens when it is used as an instrument of lack of love or as a way of expressing a *love* which has nothing to do with true, genuine love. Hence the complaint, the pained complaint this time, that our Lord addresses to his treacherous disciple: *Judas, would you betray the Son of man*

---

[5] 1 Cor 13:5.

with a kiss?[6] This leads us to think that, in this case, the gravity of the deed is much greater. By using the kiss (the most–refined and delicate means of expressing love) as an instrument of lovelessness, treachery and hatred, Judas is committing the worst kind of deception, the most horrible kind of profanation. The Book of Proverbs roundly condemns this: *Faithful are the wounds of a friend; deceitful are the kisses of an enemy.*[7] And this is also what leads Jesus Himself to speak in threatening tones: *Therefore I tell you, every sin and blasphemy will be forgiven men, but the blasphemy against the Spirit will not be forgiven. And whoever says a word against the Son of man will be forgiven; but whoever speaks against the Holy Spirit will not be forgiven, either in this age or in the age to come.*[8]

The gravity of sins against the Holy Spirit lies in the fact that any falsification of love (and here lust in particular should also be included), far from being simply a lack of love, is in fact a perversion or caricature of love. The result is here the same as that produced by any perversion: love is *turned inside out*: it becomes veritable *anti–love*. True love has the power of causing the lover to forget himself; it impels him to go out of himself in search of the loved one, and give himself to her. The caricature of love, however leads the false lover to see only himself and to think of himself alone: it pushes him to seek out the other person, but only in order to use that person as a tool, as a object of pleasure, for self–indulgence. Thus, in the same way as true love thinks only of surrendering everything, so as to have nothing and be possessed entirely by the loved one, the caricature of love, on the contrary, desires to be given to and to possess everything, to abound in wealth and be the master of all he

---

[6] Lk 22:48.
[7] Prov 27:6.
[8] Mt 12: 31–32.

surveys.[9] True love sees the *other* as a person,[10] whereas for false love other people really do not exist: they are mere things, for him to take over and use as he wishes. True love wants to be poor (it is interested only in the person it loves) and to *be possessed*, whereas false love wants to be rich (no one else matters: it is interested only in things, not *persons*) and to make everything its own.[11]

So, true love also desires to possess the loved one, because its nature is such that that is the only way things can be. But no comparison is possible between it and false love. As we said above, true love desires to possess the other as person, whereas false love is only interested in the other as thing. Moreover, for true love, the essential thing, what comes first, and even what is best, is self–surrender (Acts 20:35); it is ready to give itself even though it receives nothing in return; the possession of the other comes *later*.[12] In true love the lover wants to possess the loved one because he knows that reciprocity is an essential feature of love, and that he cannot possess unless he in turn is possessed by the other; in this sense, the lover concerns himself *first and foremost* with the desires of the loved one (who wants to be possessed by him). The desires of the loved one,

---

[9]That is why it is so difficult for a rich man to enter the Kingdom of Heaven (Mt 19: 23–24; Mk 10:23).

[10]And, by extension, also *to others* to exactly the same degree that falling in love with Love necessarily brings with it love for others (1 Jn 4: 20–21). Thus, the only thing that guarantees true love for others and their consequent evaluation as persons, is true love of God.

[11]And therefore it is impossible to serve at one and the same time God and mammon (Lk 16:13). It is interesting to note that simply using the two voices (active and passive of the verb "to possess" already shows the different kinds of objects to which the concept behind the verb can be put; the expression *to be possessed* necessarily implies that the other party is a person, whereas *to possess or make everything one's own* implies that it is things that are being possessed.

[12]*We love, because He first loved us* (1 Jn 4:19).

of course, are also the desires of the one who loves, as we can clearly see if we bear two things in mind. The first is connected with the fact that love fuses the hearts of the lovers, making them a single will, with the same desires. The second is based on the very nature of love, which cannot exist unless there are two people who give themselves to one another (and therefore possess each other), for self–surrender *by one* is impossible unless there be at the same time possession *by the other*.[13]

When the bride in the *Song of Songs* expresses her desire to be kissed by the Bridegroom, what she really wants is to give herself to Him and to be His.[14] The most specific thing about love, the first intention of the lover, is his *giving* himself to the one he loves. This is what the lover yearns for most, and what fills him with happiness. That is why Jesus said, *It is more blessed to give than to receive*.[15] And so the Holy Spirit is essentially Gift. For the Holy Spirit is not *reception* but *donation*, or to put it another way: he is not *acceptio* but *spiratio*. What happens is that, on *proceeding* jointly from the Father and the Son, He necessarily becomes reciprocity, which has the virtue of turning the gift each Lover makes into reception on the part of the other. When Jesus says, in his discourse at the Last Supper, that *all that the Father has is mine*,[16] he is not saying that everything that the Father owns belongs to Him; he is referring to the fact that He has given everything that is his to the Father. Here we can clearly see that the perfect love the Son has consists

---

[13] In false love there is no bilateral relationship between persons; all that exists is a relationship between a person and a thing (or things) and therefore no bilaterality is possible. Here again we can see the notion of person as basic to love.

[14] As has already been said, she does not speak of kissing the Bridegroom, but of being kissed by Him.

[15] Acts 20:35.

[16] Jn 16:15.

in total self–giving. It is also true (and could not be otherwise) that Jesus also says in the same place, addressing the Father, that *everything that thou has given me is from thee.*[17] This in turn shows that the Father's perfect love is also total self–giving. Finally, reciprocity makes its appearance, closing the perfect circle of total love: *All mine are thine, and thine are mine,* as Jesus says at the end, speaking to the Father.[18]

It is now easier to see that true love is self–surrender, self–giving; and the selfishness of false love is veritable anti–love and a bizarre caricature of love. It is not surprising then that the *Song of Songs* opens with the first loving words of the bride which also express her burning desire for the Bridegroom: *Kiss me with the kisses of your mouth.* She desires not so much to kiss as to be kissed. For, what she desires, above all, is to give herself to Him, to give Him her all, so as to be truly His. For what love desires, even before it receives anything, is to give up everything it has. This is the tremendous mystery of love, the incredible and moving experience which brings about the miracle of its *being more blessed to give than to receive.*

---

[17] Jn 17:7.
[18] Jn 17:10.

CHAPTER IV

LOVING OR BEING IN LOVE

To make any deep progress in studying the mystery of love, one needs to call in the help of theology. Love is something which, in the last analysis, is identical with God (1 Jn 4:8), and the sphere proper to metaphysics is that of natural reason. Relying on metaphysics alone, without recourse to revelation, one probably can go no further than the fringes of the mystery and although the results can be considerable, they are not reliable and are too easily prone to error.[1] However, it is easy to see that even with the help of revelation one can never manage to know everything there is to know about love. All one can try to do is delve deeper into certain aspects of the mystery, opening up channels of research as one uncovers new dimensions of the subject. That is the primary purpose of this book:

---

[1]On the problem of the necessity and appropriateness of revelation, Cf. St Thomas, *Contra Gentiles*, 1.4; *Summa Theologiæ*, I^a, q. 1, a. 1; II^a–II^æ, q. 2, a. 4; *In Boetium 'De Trinitate'*, q. 3 a. 1.

to identify new paths it uncovers as it makes its way, leaving it to the experts to follow those paths and see if they lead anywhere.²

Setting out, therefore, with the conviction that revelation means what it says, the exclamation of the bride in this verse —*Kiss me with the kisses of your mouth*— should be taken at face value. The bride desires to receive the kiss of love, and she has no qualms about proclaiming this with ardour, because she knows that the Bridegroom is in love with her.

However, one needs to remember that it is not the same thing for man to know that God is in love with him, and for him to know simply that God loves him. The two things are not exactly the same. If man is not *in love* with God, even though he loves God in some way or other, he will never conceive of the possibility that God can be in love with him. Man truly knows —knows *by experience*— what divine love is only when he in turn has opted for God and loved him: *We, who have believed, know the love God has for us*.³ Here again we find the essential need for reciprocity in love. Man cannot know what it means to be loved by substantial Love in the manner of love proper to lovers unless he responds to that love: *He who does not love does not know God; for God is Love*.⁴ In no sense is it the same for man to say: *God loves me*, as to say: *God is in*

---

²This book is not a theological essay on love. As indicated in the Introduction, its only aim is to sketch some points to do with the mystery of love, insofar as love can be found either in God (Who is infinite Love) or in man, to whom love is given through grace. To do this it takes as its starting-point the *Song of Songs*, read in the light of faith (for it is an inspired book) and interpreted in the light of the New Testament. It is a basic assumption of this book that knowledge of the Love of God, participated in by man through the action of grace, is the indispensable and only way that leads to knowledge of the mystery of human love.

³1 Jn 4:16.

⁴1 Jn 4:8.

Loving or being in love

love with me. The consequences of these two distinct convictions (their effect on man's feelings and behaviour) are also different.

Thus the extravagant situation in which the world is today. That is why the bride's words —*Kiss me with the kisses of your mouth*— do not have much to say to the frigid Christianity of the end of the twentieth century. And the same applies to the entire book of the *Song of Songs*. There still are many believers who are convinced that God loves them, but only the saints know what it means to be in love with God.

The Dictionary of the Spanish Language notices the two meanings of the verb *enamorar* (to fall in love with), the transitive and pronominal, although it might be better to say active and passive. The first meaning is to excite the passion of love in someone, while the second is to be taken by love for a person. But which of the two meanings is the first...? Can either exist without the other...? To answer either or both of these questions satisfactorily might require the writing of several books.

Certainly, falling in love means being captivated by the person one loves. *To be taken by love for a person...* Indeed, *to be taken* also means *being seized* by the will of another. As we can see, the idea of theft (or of rapture, in this case rapture of the other person's will) is not absent from the concept of love. As we shall see in due course, here we have an instance of rapture that is consented to (even wished for, desired) by one who *suffers* it.

> *You ravish my heart,*
> *my sister, my promised bride,*
> *you ravish my heart*
> *with a single one of your glances...*[5]

---

[5] Sg 4:9.

Echoing the same kind of feelings, St John of the Cross utters beautiful *complaints* of strange sweetness because of the *latrociny* done to him:

> *Since you have wounded my heart*
> *wherefore did you not heal it?*
> *And wherefore, having robbed me of it,*
> *have you left it thus*
> *and take not the prey that you have spoiled?*[6]

The man in love feels *abducted* by the loved one: he is totally in her power. Speaking of his final victory, St Paul says: *Not that I have already obtained this or am already perfect; but I press on to make it my own, 'because Christ Jesus has made me his own.'*[7] This rapture or abduction (of which the loved one is the passive subject) does not cause him to feel victimized: in fact it fills him with happiness. Once again we find here the idea (basic to love) of being possessed or owned by someone which is precisely the first

---

[6] In the *Cántico Espiritual*:

> *¿Por qué, pues, has llagado*
> *aqueste corazón, no le sanaste?*
> *Y, pues me le has robado,*
> *¿por qué así le dejaste*
> *y no tomas el robo que robaste?*

[7] Phil 3:12. The more serious Spanish versions of the Bible customarily use the verb *alcanzar* here in the passive voice (*he sido alcanzado por Cristo Jesus*), which does not exactly translate the original (see, for example, Cantera–Iglesias, B.A.C., Madrid, 1975). The verb λαμβάνω has a more forceful meaning better translated as *agarrar, coger con las manos, asir...* (grasp, seize, take with the hands). This more forceful sense is reflected in the *Neo-Vulgate* (*comprehendere*), in the *Bible de Jérusalem* (*saisir*), and in the *New Jerusalem Bible* (*to take hold of*).

thing a person who is truly in love desires. In this sense, Love here is cast in the role of a veritable thief or abductor, who overpowers the heart of the lover, to give it to the loved one, although it might be more exact to say that what Love in fact does is to induce (or perhaps even seduce) the lover to give his heart fully and freely to the person he loves. Things having reached this point, there is no doubt but that a soul in love which was free and unmastered would feel deprived and unfortunate:

> *The day is already fading,*
> *sweet, brownish goldfinch,*
> *and so, as in a bitter dream,*
> *it leaves us both again,*
> *you without freedom, me without my master.*[8]

There, where others would desire freedom, the bride, on the contrary, wants to be taken captive. For her, true freedom consists in *giving herself freely* and totally to the one she loves. If freedom consists in being able to give oneself without being in any way forced, it never expresses itself more truly than when it in fact surrenders itself. So the freedom of love leads the lover to be left with no freedom, which is *the very thing he most ardently desires.*

---

[8]That is why the bride would rather have seen herself held captive by the Bridegroom:

> *El día ya se aleja,*
> *dulce jilguero de color trigueño,*
> *y así otra vez nos deja,*
> *como en amargo sueño,*
> *a ti sin libertad, y a mí sin dueño.*

However, this is a human way of speaking. As we shall see later, love is essentially freedom: to such an extent that love cannot exist without it. Lovers surrender to each other their will, constantly and in complete freedom, because that is what they desire and wish. However, before returning to this theme to study it in more detail (to find that this distinctive mark of love achieves its perfection only in divine love and divine–human love) it is perhaps worthwhile to stay with the theme of the theft of the will of which man in love is the passive subject.

In things to do with love the voluntary *self–emptying* by the one who loves is quite fundamental. It must be borne in mind that, for the lover, the loved one does not just come first; he is everything. That is why he allows himself to be stripped of everything he possesses, particularly of what most specifically constitutes *his life*.[9] In the *Song of Songs* the divine Bridegroom is aware that the soul in love has given Him her heart and therefore belongs to Him:

> *I come to my garden, my sister, my bride,*
> *I gather my myrrh with my spice,*
> *I eat my honeycombs with my honey,*
> *I drink my wine and my milk.*
> *Eat, O friends, and drink:*
> *drink deeply, O lovers.*[10]

When someone truly falls in love he belongs entirely to the loved one.[11] But, as always happens in true love (and only divine love,

---

[9] Mt 10:39; 16:25; Mk 8:35; Lk 9:24.

[10] Sg 5:1.

[11] In English, to say that someone is enamoured, one can speak of falling in love, which contains suggestions of having fallen under the rule of the beloved, or of having become the object of the beloved's possession.

Loving or being in love 69

or divine–human love, is love perfect and true), this possession by the other is something mutual. The Bridegroom also feels Himself to be the property of the bride, and her servant: *Before the feast of the Passover, when Jesus knew that his hour had come to depart out of this world to the Father, having loved his own who were in the world, he loved them to the end. And during supper, when the devil had already put it into the heart of Judas Iscariot, Simon's son, to betray Him, Jesus, knowing that the Father had given all things into his hands, and that he had come from God and was going to God, rose from supper, laid aside his garments, and girded Himself with a towel. Then he poured water into a basin, and began to wash the disciples' feet, and to wipe them with the towel with which he was girded. He came to Simon Peter; and Peter said to Him, "Lord, do you wash my feet?" Jesus answered him, "What I am doing you do not know now, but afterward you will understand." Peter said to Him, "You shall never wash my feet." Jesus answered him, "If I do not wash you, you have no part in me."*[12] Our Lord's last words are very significant: *If I do not wash you, you have no part in me...* It is as if he were saying, if you do not let me give myself to you, there can be no love between us. Those who are joined by the bond of love give themselves and belong mutually to one another, so much so that it is unthinkable that only one of them should be possessed by the other. In fact, the idea of mutual, equal, self–giving between Him and his disciples is a commonplace in our Lord's discourse at the last supper: *You are my friends... No longer do I call you servants, for the servant does not know what his master is doing; but I have called you friends...*[13]

---

[12] Jn 13: 1–8.
[13] Jn 15: 14–15.

Once his will has been captivated by the loved one it is natural for the lover to feel powerfully drawn to be in her presence. This is another of the key features of a person in love. The fact of the matter is that a person who is in love desires to be where his heart and his will reside. The loved one is, for the lover, his only treasure, and there his heart lies (Mt 6:21). That is where he too wants to be. The bride in the *Song* says this in all kinds of ways:

> *Draw me after you, let us make haste.*
> *The king has brought me into his chambers.*
> *We will exult and rejoice in you;*
> *we will extol your love more than wine;*
> *rightly do they love you.*[14]

> ....

> *Tell me, you whom my soul loves,*
> *where you pasture your flock,*
> *where you make it lie down at noon;*
> *for why should I be like one who wanders*
> *beside the flocks of your companions.*[15]

> ....

> *Set me as a seal upon your heart,*
> *as a seal upon your arm;*
> *for love is strong as death,*
> *jealousy is cruel as the grave.*[16]

St John of the Cross once again, and as he is in the habit of doing, says the same thing in a very beautiful way:

---

[14] Sg 1:4.
[15] Sg 1:7.
[16] Sg 8:6.

Loving or being in love

> *In search of my loves,*
> *I will go through yonder hills and river–banks,*
> *I will not pick flowers*
> *or fear wild beasts,*
> *and I will pass through the mighty and frontiers*
> *as I go.*[17]

The lovers desire to be together, so as to contemplate one another and give themselves to each other. In divine–human love, through and even despite the obscurity of faith, the bride yearns to see the divine Bridegroom:

> *I gained the hill*
> *where the fount of living water springs,*
> *and there I awaited the Loved One,*
> *for him to show me*
> *his eyes, and his lips, and his face.*[18]

---

[17] In the *Cántico Espiritual*:

> *Buscando mis amores*
> *ir, por esos montes y riberas,*
> *ni coger, las flores*
> *ni temer, las fieras*
> *y pasar, los fuertes y fronteras.*

[18] The bride ardently desires to contemplate the Bridegroom:

> *Lleguéme hasta el collado*
> *donde mana la fuente de agua clara,*
> *y allí aguardé al Amado*
> *para que me mostrara*
> *sus ojos, y sus labios, y su cara.*

The absence of the loved one causes the lover to feel a powerful, pressing need to be with the beloved again. Our Lord draws his disciples' attention to this at his farewell supper: *When I go and prepare a place for you, I will come again and will take you to myself, that where I am you may be also...*[19] *I will not leave you orphans; I will come to you...*[20] *In that day you will know that I am in my Father, and you in me and I in you...*[21] *Father, I desire that they also, whom thou hast given me, may be with me where I am...*[22] St Paul said something similar, torn by his dual love for the Lord and for his spiritual children: *If it is to be life in the flesh, that means fruitful labour for me. Yet which I shall choose I cannot tell. I am hard pressed between the two. My desire is to depart and be with Christ, for that is far better...*[23]

Certainly in divine–human love the strong desire to be together which presses those in love goes much further than a mere wish to be near the other. God and man, in their mutual love for one another, yearn (with a desire which obtains what it wants) to achieve a communion of lives which mere human love cannot even imagine: *He who eats my flesh and drinks my blood abides in me, and I in him. As the living Father sent me, and I live because of the Father, so he who eats me will live because of me.*[24]

Since the feeling of knowing oneself to be in love is the perfection of love, it also, logically, includes the ardent desire to possess the loved one, in keeping with the reciprocity which love demands. It is usually said that platonic love shares with the purely aesthetic

---

[19] Jn 14:3.
[20] Jn 14:18.
[21] Jn 14:20.
[22] Jn 17:24.
[23] Phil 1: 22–23.
[24] Jn 6: 56–57. Cf. 1 Cor 3:23; 2 Cor 5:15; Gal 2:20; Phil 3:12.

love of beauty the feature that (unlike what happens in the case of carnal love, which desires to possess the thing loved) they seek only to have the joy of contemplating the loved object.[25]

Although this is not the proper place to discuss at this point the complex problem of Platonic love, it may perhaps be helpful to make the point already that it does not seem right to identify the concepts of possession and carnal possession when discussing the mystery of love. True, the notion of possession is a more general one than that of carnal possession, and it refers to something much more perfect. In human love, carnal possession never involves more than a desire for or attempt at possession.[26] Moreover, one also needs to bear in mind that the purely aesthetic love of beauty is not the subject of this book: love in the normal meaning of the word. Love must not be confused with mere delight that the contemplation of beauty gives, as one can clearly see when one remembers that no one ever falls in love with a beautiful painting or a picturesque landscape.[27] Nor can it be identified with the satisfaction one feels when contemplating truth, or even with the attraction which the good exerts. Although it is true that love does involve the attraction of the good, the satisfaction that results from the possession of the

---

[25] Among the huge bibliography on this subject, cf., for example, Étienne Gilson, *Dante et Béatrice*, Vrin, Paris, 1974.

[26] With regard to man, and despite the fact of the *una caro*, carnal possession is not identifiable with perfect mutual possession of the lovers. Animals' incapacity to *be possessed by each other* (although their mere reproductive instinct cannot be seen as a parallel of carnal union between humans) is a clear indication that the possession that occurs in love cannot be confused with carnal union. To the objection that our Lord's words (Mt 19:6) do not simply refer to the union of the spouses' bodies *in one flesh* but to something more elevated, one can reply that that very fact indicates that possession in love is no mere fusion of bodies.

[27] The same can be said of music and poetry, no matter how much beauty a good melody or a good poem may contain.

truth and the enjoyment of aesthetic pleasure, a further element is needed, an essential, basic element: the good that attracts love, the truth grasped, and the beauty contemplated *belong here in fact to a person*; it is the person that truly attracts through love the love of another. And this is the case because, for the one who loves, that person signifies truth, radiates beauty and contains goodness; all at one and the same time and to the maximum degree.[28] This leads us to the important conclusion that, since the agent who is *exerting the attraction* here is a person, it is impossible for the one who loves not to expect his love to be reciprocated. Therefore he desires to be possessed by her and to possess her himself at one and the same time.

One also needs to bear in mind that one should not confuse in love the yearning for possession with the desire to possess (or dominate), as that desire is usually understood by man. What the true lover desires is not so much to *have* the loved one (in the sense of doing what he wants with her) as to receive her will, surrendered in a reciprocal way, *in order that love may be brought about —may come true—*: love consists, in the last analysis, in making these two wills one. The core of the matter is that the true lover knows well that he cannot be possessed by the loved one unless he in turn possesses her.

But love is a veritable battle, in which the lovers fight more to give than to possess. Or, to put it another way, it is a struggle in which both of them strive equally to give and to possess. Although, in fact, if they desire to possess, they do so in order to be able to surrender what they come to possess... The bride, for example, makes a clear reference to this point when she says in the *Song*:

---

[28] Aestheticism is an absolutely authentic feeling, but it can in no way be confused with love.

Loving or being in love

> *He brought me to the banqueting house,*
> *and his banner over me was love.*[29]

> ....

> *My beloved is mine and I am his.*
> *He pastures his flock among the lilies.*[30]

> ....

> *I am my beloved's and my beloved is mine;*
> *he pastures his flock among the lilies.*[31]

> ....

> *I am my beloved's;*
> *and his desire is for me.*[32]

The Bridegroom, clearly, desires the bride to yield to Him:

> *Arise, my love, my fair one,*
> *and come away.*
> *O my dove,*
> *in the clefts of the rock,*
> *in the covert of the cliff,*
> *let me see your face, let me hear your voice,*
> *for your voice is sweet, and your face is comely.*[33]

But He desires, above all, to give Himself to the bride and become her possession. We learn this from the following lines, which,

---

[29] Sg 2:4.
[30] Sg 2:16.
[31] Sg 6:3.
[32] Sg 7:11.
[33] Sg 2:14.

according to all the commentators, marks the climax of the sacred poem:

> *Set me as a seal upon your heart,*
> *as a seal upon your arm...*[34]

And, as is also logical, the bride's only desire coincides with the Bridegroom's most urging longings: her total surrendering to Him...

Kiss me with the kisses of your mouth is then an eager confession whereby the bride admits her desire to belong to the Bridegroom and to be with Him. With Him, rather than just close to Him. This is exactly the same desire as God feels towards man in divine–human love. So, the bride's desire and that of the Bridegroom is quite simply the desire —their only desire— to be together, which is what people in love feel.

And little more enquiry should be made as to what exactly it means to be in love. In fact, in order to discover what love is, one needs to turn to Love itself, because only someone in love can understand love, and only from the standpoint of love can one venture to speak about love. Lovers are people who *are–in–love*. But Love, however much it is cross–examined, never speaks about itself or by itself (Jn 16: 13–14), but only of the Loved One. As far as the lovers themselves are concerned: they, too, are unable to explain the mystery of their feelings: for them what remains unsaid is always more important than what they have managed to say; they never succeed in revealing about themselves what is most beautiful; they fail to explain the essence of their love. Therefore, when they speak about the Loved One or about their feelings in his regard, all they can do is babble. And what they do manage to explain, far from satisfying

---

[34] Sg 8:6.

the curiosity of the listener only serves to make him more puzzled still. What listeners hear when they ask about love is never what love is: at best they hear *something stammered*:

> *...something that they stammer
> leaves me dying.*[35]

As St John of the Cross put it. That is why the mystery of the Incarnation of the Word is nothing other than the mystery of Love, a mystery which for the Lover translates into a desire to be not only near the loved one but to be with her, sharing her life, leading to an interchange of hearts, and possessing everything in common, in mutual reciprocity. Here it must be said that, in this sense, the Incarnation of the Word is exactly what a God–in–love would do and in fact did. The mystery of the Incarnation of the Word thereby satisfies one of the most pressing requirements of love: absolute Immensity was able, out of love, to make weakness and deprivation his own, sharing the life and destiny of the loved one, in this case man. *He took our infirmities and bore our diseases.*[36] The work of Creation (the movement of creatures from nothingness to being, through the action of infinite Power and Love) is no greater a mystery than the fact that infinite Being —a Being which has need of nothing nor ever will— should make neediness and non–being his; such is his love to be with the one He loves. Only Love is capable

---

[35] The Spanish expression keeps a most beautiful and mysterious *no sé qué*:

> *...y déjame muriendo
> un no sé qué que quedan balbuciendo.*

[36] Mt 8:17, quoting Is 53:4. Cf. 2 Cor 13:4; Heb 5:2; 4:15.

of *all things*. That is why Love is the only force which truly moves the universe:

L'Amor che move il sole e l'altre stelle.[37]

---

[37] *Love, which moves the sun and the other stars.* Dante, *The Divine Comedy*, "Paradise."

CHAPTER V

THE DESIRE TO BE DESIRED

Kiss me with the kisses of your mouth. At the basis of this desire of the bride is a yearning to be desired, to be the object of a lover's loving look, and to feel that the Bridegroom is dependent upon her. For the primary desires that motivate a person to set the kiss of love on the loved one undoubtedly have to do with making the person his, with satisfying his desires to see her and contemplate her, and to give Himself, in turn, to her, to be hers entirely.

It should be borne in mind that, in true love, the yearning to be desired should not be confused with a wish to assert one's own personality. This yearning is simply a requirement of the very nature of love. Given that the law of reciprocity applies in true love, he who loves cannot desire without in turn being desired; equally, he cannot feel that he needs the other person without also feeling that she too needs him. And, just as the lover desires the loved one and needs her, so too he feels impelled to desire that she also desire him and need him. And equally, just as the need that one feels with respect to the loved one is entirely voluntary and free (like everything that is the fruit of love) to the point that the man–in–love would in no way desire to be free of this need, the same happens in the case of the desire to feel needed by the person one loves. In this sense, not wanting to feel the need of the loved one, or not desiring to be needed by her, would be equivalent to nothing less than lack of desire to love; or, to put it another way, it would be the same as not to love.

The will to be desired by the Bridegroom is clearly asserted by the bride in the *Song*:

> *I am my beloved's*
> *and his desire is for me.*[1]

However, this text, in fact, expresses not so much the bride's desire to be desired by the Bridegroom, as her total conviction that the Bridegroom really does desire her. The bride's exclamation is an explicit recognition of the fact that *all* the Bridegroom's desires are directed towards her:

> *and his desire is for me*

So sure she feels of the Bridegroom's love and so perfect, too, is the love that both lovers have. But undoubtedly we also have here, as far as the bride is concerned, a reaffirmation of her desire that this is the way things should be, which means that her words are a genuine expression of joy and rejoicing. And, as always, once more reciprocity makes its appearance: the bride feels proud to admit, at the same time, that she too belongs to the Bridegroom and that thereby she sees her own desire fulfilled:

> *I am my beloved's*
> *and his desire is for me.*

---

[1] Sg 7:11.

Also, the desire to be desired which the bride feels so pressingly is, we can see, fully satisfied. This happens because in this case the Bridegroom is God, that is, infinite and perfect Love, whose role and essence it is to love. The Gospel of St Luke, for example, explains this very well: *What man of you, having a hundred sheep, if he has lost one of them, does not leave the ninety–nine in the wilderness, and go after the one which is lost, until he finds it?*[2] This is clearly nothing other than the passionate search for the loved one, impelled by a love that is equally ardent. However, it is probably worthwhile pointing it out, before we go further, that the first thing one notices in this text is that love always has to do with the search for *one* person. The owner of the sheep has no qualms about leaving the other ninety–nine to go in search of the *one* lost sheep. Here we also see the individuality and personality that are features proper to love. For one who loves, the loved one is the *only one*; she is his all:

> *My dove, my perfect one, is only one,*
> *the darling of her mother,*
> *flawless to her that bore her.*[3]

The desire that impels the lover is a passionate desire. According to the text, ninety–nine sheep the owner leaves alone in the desert so as to be able to search for the one that is lost. This is clearly a way of saying that love is ready to run whatever risks are necessary: the owner does not mind leaving the ninety–nine in the wilderness, that is, in a dangerous area where anything may happen which implies a real risk for the flock and for himself. So, his plan to search for the lost sheep does not seem to make much sense, leaving as he does the ninety–nine to their fate, to go in search of just one sheep.

---

[2] Lk 15:4.
[3] Sg 6:9.

However, we should remember that in morals of this type it is normal to put the emphasis on just one aspect, ignoring others, which one sets aside for the moment. Here our attention is clearly being directed to the lost sheep (which is truly the *only* sheep, as far as the owner is concerned), leaving to one side considerations about the other sheep. But although that is the case, the main point the text seeks to teach goes in another direction.

All the indications are that the text is ready to agree that the business of love is a *bad business*, at least in the way that worldly logic distinguishes good and bad business. Whatever one may say, it is clear that we have here a risk of losing ninety–nine sheep in an attempt to recover one sheep —not the sort of thing that current ideas are likely to approve of. However, it is also clear that the text is making the point that *when it is love that is at stake, one must be ready to lose all*:

> *If a man offered for love all the wealth of his house,*
> *it would be utterly scorned.*[4]

For there is nothing to compare with love. On the contrary: love demands forgetting about, *despising*, other things in exchange for its self–surrender. The only thing that love seeks is *the person* who is trying to find it. This brings us again into the channels of logic and even —making an innocent play on words— of *pure logic*, because the logic of love is always more logical than strictly worldly logic. However, we are not really talking about two distinct logics, for, in the last analysis, the logic of love (or the logic of God) is the only true logic. And, although it is true that usually it does not appear this way, that is not due to anything other than the corruption of nature, which is responsible for man's not always perceiving the true

---

[4]Sg 8:7.

nature of things with sufficient clarity and transparency.[5] It must be admitted, however, that the presence of these two perspectives leads one to think at times that there are indeed two distinct and even opposed logics: that of love and that of the world. Accordingly, love would be ruled by rules of its own which are quite different from those which govern worldly wisdom and something it cannot grasp. And so the logic of love, compared with that of the world, seems to the latter to be *illogical* on two scores. In the first place, it seems to be a logic closed in on itself, because love has its own rules and seeks no justification other than its own. It is truly certain that only love can understand love and in the last analysis one loves because one loves: *Causa diligendi Deum Deus est*, said St Bernard.[6] There is every reason, then, for saying that, in this sense, if one really does not love, not only is love left without reasons to justify it, but itself actually becomes incomprehensible.[7] This in turn leads

---

[5] The same can be said about the New Testament texts that counterpose God's wisdom and worldly wisdom. The fact that to the eyes of the world —and even sometimes also to Christians themselves— worldly wisdom always seems more logical than divine wisdom is due to the state of fallen nature man finds himself in, and therefore to his tendency to follow the mistaken choices proposed by his will —choices which lead him to perceive that which is not, rather than that which is.

[6] St Bernard, *De diligendo Deo*, I, 1.

[7] In saying this we do not imply that love is an *irrational* tendency; the whole thrust of this book goes in the opposite direction. What we mean here is that true love is grasped only by the person who loves. Indeed, it is worldly logic that regards true love as irrational. That is why it is only when the Church let herself be led astray by worldly ideologies that it became possible for so many Catholic Curias (diocesan and archdiocesan) to bring in *de facto* divorce, by granting virtually all annulment petitions submitted to them. In this way, although divorce is not recognized doctrinally, it is recognized in fact. The basic problem stems from the fact that people no longer believe in the possibility of true love, a love capable of totality and an enduring love, a love that is ready to give itself entirely and forever. The *wisdom* of the world cannot understand the *madness* of the love of God.

to the second aspect of love's apparent lack of logic: love is no longer something which seems unjustifiable: it even seems *absurd and preposterous*, if not crazy: *For since, in the wisdom of God, the world did not know God through wisdom, it pleased God through the folly of what we preach to save those who believe. For Jews demand signs and Greeks seek wisdom, but we preach Christ crucified, a stumbling block to Jews and folly to the Gentiles.*[8] According to this, the natural logic of human wisdom, and even the logic of those miracles the world would like to witness, not only is not always identical with divine logic, it quite frequently has very little to do with it. The supreme act of love, or the greatest which man has ever experienced —the death of Christ on a gibbet— was a *stumbling block to Jews and folly to Gentiles.* That was what the world thought of the most extraordinary paradox that infinite Intelligence and Love could devise. However, in spite of everything, against everything worldly logic and wisdom might say, the Bible carefully, precisely, adds that *the foolishness of God is wiser than men, and the weakness of God is stronger than men.*[9]

The bride, therefore, sees her yearning to be desired by the Bridegroom come true.

> *Open to me, my sister, my beloved,*
> *my dove, my perfect one,*
> *for my head is wet with dew,*
> *my hair with the drops of night.*[10]

According to the Gospel narrative of the lost sheep, the owner of the sheep goes in search of the one that has strayed and he does

---

[8] 1 Cor 1: 21–23.
[9] 1 Cor 1:25.
[10] Sg 5:2

not cease in his endeavor *until he finds it.* That is why St John of the Cross said:

> *In search of my loves,*
> *I will go through yonder hills and river–banks,*
> *I will not pick flowers*
> *or fear wild beasts,*
> *and I will pass through the mighty and frontiers*
> *as I go.*[11]

And in fact the Bridegroom hastens in his impatience:

> *leaping over the mountains,*
> *bounding over the hills.*[12]

He searches tirelessly; nothing can get in his way, so keen is he to find his bride. Hence his anxiety:

> *gazing in at the windows,*
> *looking through the lattice.*[13]

---

[11] In the *Cántico Espiritual*:

> *Buscando mis amores*
> *iré por esos montes y riberas,*
> *ni cogeré las flores*
> *ni temeré las fieras*
> *y pasaré los fuertes y fronteras.*

[12] Sg 2:8.
[13] Sg 2:9.

When the owner of the sheep eventually finds the lost sheep, he puts it on his shoulders and brings it home: *And when he has found it, he lays it on his shoulders, rejoicing. And when he comes home...*[14] The gesture of bringing the sheep back on his shoulders, once he has found it, is full of tenderness. Clearly the intention here is to stress the intimacy and intensity of love. One gets the impression that the owner of the sheep now loves the lost sheep more intensely; clearly, if it had not strayed and been looked for and found, it would never have been the object of the loving tenderness it was shown by being brought home on the shoulders of its owner. There is a parallel to this in the parable of the prodigal son, when the father lovingly embraces his son on his return home (Lk 15:20).

Finally when the Shepherd of the sheep comes home, having recovered the object of his love, a festival of rejoicing is held. That is not surprising because —as the father of the prodigal son also said— *this your brother was dead, and is alive; he was lost, and is found.*[15] Here the same thing happens, once the bride has been found and regained once more: *And when he comes home, he calls together his family and his neighbours, saying to them, "Rejoice with me, for I have found my sheep which was lost."*[16] The nuptial feasts and banquets are the prologue to the consummation of love. The *Banquet of the Kingdom of Heaven* will be nothing other than the definitive consummation of love... *You are sad now, but I shall see you again, and your hearts will be full of joy, and that joy no one shall take from you:*[17]

---

[14] Lk 15: 5–6.
[15] Lk 15:32.
[16] Lk 15:6.
[17] Jn 16:22.

Come then, my beloved,
my lovely one, come...[18]

....

I come to my garden, my sister, my bride,
I gather my myrrh with my spice,
I eat my honeycomb with my honey,
I drink my wine with my milk.
Eat, O friends, and drink:
drink deeply, O lovers![19]

The festival of joy is celebrated because lovers' comings and goings have reached their end. All the searching, all the absences, all the sighing have given way to the enduring mutual presence of the lovers. The bride's desire —which the Bridegroom shares— is at long last achieved: *Jesus knew what they wanted to ask Him; so he said to them, "Is this what you are asking yourselves, what I meant by saying, 'A little while, and you will not see me, and again a little while, and you will see me.' Truly, truly, I say to you, you will weep and lament, but the world will rejoice; you will be sorrowful, but your sorrow will turn into joy. When a woman is in travail she has sorrow, because her hour has come; but when she is delivered of the child, she no longer remembers the anguish, for joy that a child is born into the world. So you have sorrow now, but I will see you again and your hearts will rejoice, and no one will take your joy from you."*[20]

But the texts always end up saying the same thing: the festival of the joy of love is not celebrated *until home is reached.* It is

---

[18] Sg 2:10.
[19] Sg 5:1.
[20] Jn 16: 19–22.

celebrated at home, the destination and place of rest, and not on the road, for that is still a place of fatigue and pilgrimage. *Life is a bad night spent in a bad inn*, Saint Teresa of Ávila used to say. For the parable of the lost sheep, too, joy is incomplete until they arrive back home: *...And when he comes home, he calls together his friends and his neighbours, saying to them...*[21] So, there is no celebration until they reach their destination. Until then the bride is still anxiously seeking the Bridegroom and desiring to be desired by Him. Until then, the searching and anxiety continue, and one goes on walking until the very end of the way is reached, in a tireless pilgrimage.

> *If you are heading toward the hillock,*
> *allow me to accompany you, pilgrim,*
> *let us see if he whom I love*
> *gives us of his wine to drink*
> *as we reach the end of the road together.*[22]

For the time being, therefore, the bride lives in a state of yearning and nostalgia for the Bridegroom. Her exclamation —*Kiss me with the kisses of your mouth*— is also a recognition of the fact that she does not yet already fully possess Him. But, at the same time, she knows that her desire to be desired will be fully answered by

---

[21] Lk 15:6.

[22] In the original:

> *Si vas hacia el otero,*
> *deja que te acompañe, peregrino,*
> *a ver si el que yo quiero*
> *nos da a beber su vino*
> *en acabando juntos el camino.*

The desire to be desired

the Bridegroom. Like the *man of desires*, or the man who is the object of desires, as the Bible describes the prophet Daniel,[23] she too knows that she is ardently desired. In fact, the Bridegroom Himself candidly admits that he is following the tracks of his bride, seeking his loved one: *Behold, I stand at the door and knock, if any one hears my voice and opens the door, I will come in to him and eat with him, and he with me.*[24] Here God is describing Himself as a beggar who knocks on the door of man's heart seeking the alms of love. If his knock is heard and the door opened to Him, he enters immediately with the haste proper to a lover who has at long last, after intense searching, found his loved one.

When that happens, *he who enters by the door is the shepherd of the sheep.*[25] And the sheep listen to his voice (Jn 10:3) because they know it well (Jn 10:4). As the text suggests, the fact that the sheep know their owner's voice clearly implies that they have had a long and loving contact with him. His voice and his words have always been for them voices and words of love: *I have given them the words which thou gavest me, Father, and they have received them...*[26] *I have given them thy word; and the world has hated them because they are not of the world...*[27] *I have called you friends, for all that I have heard from my Father I have made known to you...*[28] The

---

[23] Dan 9:23. The *Vulgate* and the *New Vulgate* here give *vir desideriorum* as what the angel Gabriel calls Daniel. But all authors agree that the text describes the prophet as the object rather than the subject of desires; in this case, Daniel is the object of the desire and predilections of God; hence the RSV's *you are greatly beloved*.

[24] Rev 3:20.

[25] Jn 10:2.

[26] Jn 17:8.

[27] Jn 17:14.

[28] Jn 15:15.

sheep know very well that the Shepherd's whistle has always been for them a loving whistle, and his words have never been but the message of love which he came to bring to all men: *I have made known to them thy name, and I will make it known, that the love with which thou hast loved me may be in them, and I in them.*[29] The bride in the *Song* is used to hearing the voice of the Bridegroom and to listening to his wooing words; that is why she recognizes it instantly:

> *The voice of my beloved!*[30]
> *My beloved speaks to me and says to me,*
> *"Arise, my love,*
> *my fair one, and come away;*
> *for lo, the winter is past,*
> *the rain is over and gone..."*[31]

It should not be forgotten that the new commandment, the only commandment, really, which the Master left his disciples is the commandment of love (Jn 13:34; 15:12). Unfortunately, official catechesis does not always keep this in mind, and so it tends to smother the sheep with an excess of messages which all too often have little to do with the kind of nourishment they actually need. It is a terrible punishment with which God seems to be chastising, time after time, present–day Christians. These messages usually refer more to the earthly city than to the heavenly one, and they give the impression that official catechesis, despite what the Letter to the Hebrews says, is convinced that Christians have already found their lasting city and do not need to wait for another to come (Heb 13:14, *a sensu*

---

[29] Jn 17:26.
[30] Sg 2:8.
[31] Sg 2: 10–11.

contrario).³² All this helps to give the impression that the official Church is too bent on cultivating its image as an Institution *preoccupied with man*. It is as if, in its desperate attempt to flee from accusations of contributing to the alienation of man, to *disincarnationism*, and to always being on the side of the *bourgeoisie*, it has fallen into the trap set by its enemies. It ought to have realized that neither fear nor inferiority complexes ever make good counsellors. It would have been better if the Church had not been so concerned about the running away from the world's accusations, which are almost always unfounded, and always ill–intentioned. When the Church listens to these criticisms, even to the point of accepting them as justified, not only is she doing what the world wants but she is running the risk of being rightly criticized. The Church should not forget that the only way open to her *to be truly concerned about man*, is to concentrate, strictly and faithfully, on the goals and means that her Founder has laid down for her.

---

³²Even catechesis on the dogma of hell (which should never be omitted) should be given from the point of view of love, insofar as the only comprehensible explanation of hell is that of love voluntarily rejected and lost. But official catechesis today makes no mention of hell, for the same reason as it also tends not to speak about true Love. Nowadays it is quite common for the sheep of Christ's flock to be forced to draw their nourishment from fodder which is not likely to provide it: ecology, pacificism, racism, political systems, politics, the rights of man, irenic ecumenism, social justice... The fact that a new State, for example, is or is not recognized by the Vatican may be important from certain points of view, but it is of no importance at all to souls, whatever anyone may say. As regards the *social teaching* of the Church, it might be useful to stop to consider whether the immense library of documents containing it, constantly growing, has produced the results one might expect from such a high input of energy; surely not, perhaps because, quite often, the problems this material deals with are more to do with economic science than with moral judgments which are the Church's competence. Be that as it may, certainly the true needs of souls are not always catered to along the route of social teaching.

The sheep know their Shepherd and they in turn are known to Him. As always happens with love, knowledge is mutual: *I know my own and my own know me;*[33] so much so that love is in fact impossible without this reciprocity: *Now I know in part; then I shall know fully, even as I have been fully known.*[34] For St John the likeness or equality which love creates between lovers depends also on mutual knowledge: *We are God's children now; it does not yet appear what we shall be, but we know that when He appears we shall be like Him, for we shall see Him as He is.*[35] This reciprocity, which also involves intimate and definitive knowledge,[36] is the outcome of a situation in which both those lovers give themselves *entirely and reciprocally* to one another. That is why the Shepherd calls each of his sheep by name (Jn 10:3), as befits something so eminently *personal* as love, and which therefore is endowed with the attributes or characteristics proper to personality: unicity, individuality and incommunicability: *Ego vocavi te nomine tuo; meus es tu.*[37] Indeed, our Lord Himself tells us that this mutual knowledge is absolutely intimate and complete, in the sense that it extends to the very depth

---

[33] Jn 10:14.

[34] 1 Cor 13:12.

[35] 1 Jn 3:2.

[36] In the text quoted above from 1 Cor 13:12, St Paul contrasts the imperfect knowledge we now have (which he describes as *partial*) with the perfect knowledge one has in heaven, which is the knowledge proper to genuine love.

[37] Is 43:1. It is interesting to note that the relationship of property seems to depend here on prior intimate and personal knowledge: *I have called you by name, you are mine* as if the calling of Israel, an absolutely special and unique calling, and one which in turn stemmed from a knowledge and election which were equally singular and exclusive, was the determining factor in Jacob's belonging to Yahweh. Perhaps what we have here, once again, is a reassertion of the demands of reciprocity which are proper to love: I knew you, I chose you, I gave myself to you, and I belong to you; now you should remember that you too belong to me.

of the personality of those in love: *I know my sheep and my sheep know me, as the Father knows me and I know the Father.*[38]

The mutual, intimate knowledge that the Bridegroom and bride have of each other is a vitally important theme in the *Song of Songs* as it is proper to the love described in that book. Sometimes the bride responds to the urgings of the chorus and describes the Bridegroom (Sg 5: 9–16). But the entire sacred poem abounds in descriptions which each of the lovers makes of the other:

> *How beautiful you are, my love;*
> *how beautiful you are! Your eyes are doves.*[39]

> ....

> *You are beautiful, my beloved, truly lovely,*
> *Our couch is green.*[40]

Often, too, wooing words are spoken:

> *As a lily among brambles,*
> *so is my love among maidens.*[41]

> ....

---

[38] Jn 10: 14–15. The text, which is certainly quite profound, seems to imply that our Lord's knowledge of his sheep is of the same type as the knowledge that exists between Him and the Father. This is not surprising if you remember that, according to John 6:57, just *as the living Father sent me, and I live because of the Father, so he who eats me will live because of me*; and that, according to John 17:26, Jesus Himself, on the most solemn of all occasions, addresses the Father in these words: *That the love with which thou hast loved me may be in them, and I in them.* And so it is: a *total* mutual love must be concomitant with a mutual knowledge which is also *total*.

[39] Sg 1:15.
[40] Sg 1:16.
[41] Sg 2:2.

> *An apple tree among the trees of the wood,*
> *so is my beloved among young men.*[42]

The desire to be loved by the loved one is paralleled by the desire the lover feels for her. Therefore, as in everything to do with love, both desires are equal in magnitude and both refer always to totality.[43] The bride wants the Bridegroom to desire her without limits; nor is there any limit to her desires of Him.[44]

The fact that the creature should desire to be desired by God is yet another mystery within the great abyss of mystery that Love is. Certainly the creature could never manage to desire such a thing were she not convinced that God is in love with her and were she not

---

[42] Sg 2:3.

[43] In the *Summa Theologiæ* II^a–II^æ, q. 27, a. 5, St Thomas poses the question, *utrum Deus possit totaliter amari*. To which he replies by saying *cum dilectio intelligatur quasi medium inter amantem et amatum, cum quæritur an Deus possit totaliter diligi, tripliciter potest intelligi. Uno modo, ut modus totalitatis referatur ad rem dilectam. Et sic Deus est totaliter diligendus: quia totum quod ad Deum pertinet homo diligere debet. Alio modo potest intelligi ita quod totalitas referatur ad diligentem. Et sic etiam Deus totaliter diligi debet: quia ex toto posse suo debet homo diligere Deum, et quidquid habet ad Dei amorem ordinare, secundum illud Deut. 6,5:* "*Diliges Dominum Deum tuum ex toto corde tuo.*" *Tertio modo potest intelligi secundum comparationem diligentis ad rem dilectam, ut scilicet modus diligentis adæquet modum rei dilectæ. Et hoc non potest esse. Cum enim unumquodque in tantum diligibile sit in quantum est bonum, Deus, cuius bonitas est infinita, est infinite diligibilis: nulla autem creatura potest Deum infinite diligere, quia omnis virtus creaturæ, sive naturalis sive infusa, est finita.*

[44] The phrase of St Bernard, to the effect that there is no other way of loving God than that of loving Him *sine modo*, goes back in fact to St Augustine: *Ipse ibi modus est sine modo amare*, although some say it in fact belongs to his friend Severinus (cf. Étienne Gilson, *Introduction a l'Étude de Saint Augustin*, Paris, 1982, pg. 180). St Bernard's words are taken from *De diligendo Deo*, 1. For St Augustine, cf. *Epistola 109*, 2. St Thomas explains the matter admirably in *Summa Theologiæ* II^a–II^æ, q. 27, a. 6, "Respondeo dicendum."

also convinced that He ardently desires her. Therefore, blessed are they who are daring enough to come, offering their heart in order to assuage the burning thirst God feels: *Then the King will say to those at his right hand, "Come, O blessed of my Father... For I was thirsty and you gave me drink..."*[45] The fire of hell is in reality the fire of an infinite thirst for love which someone chose not to quench. How sad it is, as so often happens, that man should fail to understand this...! For this is a thirst which only they can understand who themselves feel a similar thirst; or, to put it another way, it can be understood only by those who also love, who are thereby the only ones disposed to come forward to assuage that thirst. Therefore, the great love–thirst that is God (Jn 19:28)[46] summons especially those who have a similar thirst, knowing that they are ready to respond to his call.[47] That is why those who do not thirst, or those who do not love, never manage to know God (1 Jn 4:8).

On the other hand, those who truly thirst do not much mind feeling at the same time miserable and ragged. They know that the Master, who has not come to call the just, but sinners (Mt 9:13; Mk 2:17; Lk 5:32), has not minded leaving the ninety–nine sheep in the wilderness to go in search of the one that was lost (Lk 15:4). And they also know that those called and anxiously sought out to attend the great banquet are *the poor and maimed and blind and lame*, no less.[48] Not the perfect, but the thirsty, they alone are invited, despite the fact that they must come bearing the burden of their wretchedness and even of their deformity. No matter how many come, no matter how miserable they may be, there will always

---

[45] Mt 25: 34–35.
[46] Cf. Jn 4:7.
[47] Cf. Jn 7:37; Rev 21:6; 22:17; Is 55:1.
[48] Lk 14:21.

be room, as the parable of the great banquet also tells us, when after following his instructions the servant has gathered in the poor and maimed and blind and lame, and he says to his Master: *Sir, what you commanded has been done and still there is room...*[49]

---

[49] Lk 14:22.

CHAPTER VI

THE DESIRE TO BE CONTEMPLATED

We have already pointed out[1] that the bride's desire to receive the Bridegroom's loving kiss includes another desire, which in fact is already part of the very act of love, the desire to be the object of His loving gaze. The bride wants the Bridegroom's eyes to rest on her eyes, as is usually the case between lovers.

Loving contemplation is part of love, and it often happens that the loving look of the lovers is the first step in love and even what initiates the process:

And Jesus looking upon him loved him and said to him...[2]

Here we can clearly see the look which evokes love, the love which follows, as its fruit so to speak, and, finally, a dialogue which is sometimes also followed by the loving kiss:

---

[1] Cf. the previous chapter.
[2] Mk 10:21.

> *To me came my Lover*
> *before the sun rose on the hillcrest,*
> *and, when he gazed upon me,*
> *I felt in his eyes that*
> *which only a kiss can cure.*[3]

The loving look is able to disconcert and move the lovers, and is in fact equivalent to the silent offering which each of them makes of himself/herself to the other. In the *Song*, the loving look of the bride causes the Bridegroom to say:

> *Turn away your eyes from me,*
> *for they take me by assault.*[4]

With these words the Bridegroom addresses the bride, once again, in a special language which, precisely because it is so profoundly human, is most appropriate to those in love. What He in fact desires is that she do exactly the opposite of which He asks her

---

[3]In the original:

> *Vino hasta mí el Amado*
> *antes que el sol naciera por el teso,*
> *y, habiéndome mirado,*
> *sentí en sus ojos eso*
> *que solamente sana con un beso.*

Clearly the look can be something prior to and even something which conditions love. However, the look of love is already part of the entire love–process, possibly the point at which it begins. Certainly, it is difficult to conceive a look, which is then followed by love, as being completely unconnected with the complex phenomenon of loving feelings. Clearly love always begins with *contemplation*, but that *loving contemplation* is already part of the very act of loving.

[4]Sg 6:5.

to do.[5] The truth is that the Bridegroom burns with a desire to continue to contemplate the bride's eyes:

> *How beautiful you are, my love...!*
> *Your eyes are doves behind your veil...*[6]
>
> ....
>
> *You have ravished my heart*
> *with a glance of your eyes.*[7]

That is why he also expressly tells her:

> *Let me see your face, let me hear your voice,*
> *for your voice is sweet, and your face is comely.*[8]

This kind of language, with its alternating of apparently contradictory expressions,[9] is typical of love. Clearly these contradictions do not exist for the lovers. The fact of the matter is that love is ineffable, and therefore it has to use all kinds of recourses and forms

---

[5]One of the oddest, strangest and most characteristic recourses of language is that of *a sensu contrario* expressions. Although these expressions mean the opposite of what they literally say, they do however have a special force and can even have nuances which make them extremely interesting. Because of this, they are not only perfectly intelligible but also leave no room at all for ambiguity or confusion. The detailed study of this subject would lead right into some of the most interesting questions in the philosophy of language.

[6]Sg 4:1. Cf. 1:15.

[7]Sg 4:9.

[8]Sg 2:14.

[9]If taken literally they are in fact contradictory.

of expression, and still never explain itself adequately. The inexpressible tries desperately to express itself in all kinds of ways, even contradictory ones, and yet it never manages to *put into words* and explain itself fully.[10]

Also, these things the Bridegroom says show his desire to contemplate the face of the bride and the happiness it gives Him, but they also contain a profound and strange mystery. In spite of the fact that the Bridegroom has now managed to look upon his bride, she however has not yet removed the veil from her face. It is the Bridegroom Himself Who tells us this:

> *Your eyes are doves behind your veil...*[11]
>
> ....
>
> *Your cheeks are like halves of a pomegranate, behind your veil.*[12]

That the bride does not clearly see the Bridegroom, or yet possess Him fully, must be due to the fact that love has not yet reached its perfection: *For now we see in a mirror dimly, but then face to face. Now I know in part; then I shall understand fully, even as I have been fully understood.*[13] Love is present, undoubtedly, but because it is as yet intermingled with faith and hope (1 Cor 13:13), it is still something that needs to be sought out (1 Cor 14:1) and it needs to temper its urges by the exercise of patience (1 Cor 13:4). But what is truly surprising about all this is the fact that the (mo-

---

[10]Only in the bosom of infinite Love is the *reciprocal saying* of their love between the Father and the Son expressed in complete infinitude. Therefore, the Holy Spirit, with respect to the divine essence, is equal to the Father and to the Son.

[11]Sg 4:1.

[12]Sg 6:7.

[13]1 Cor 13:12. Cf. 1 Cor 13: 9–10; 1 Jn 3:2.

mentary) imperfection of love also affects, in some way, the Bridegroom. For it is not given to Him, either, to contemplate the face of the bride other than *through a veil*; we even find Him forced to go in search of her, eagerly, despite obstacles, in an effort to get a better view of her, as she herself confesses:

> *My beloved is like a gazelle, or a young stag.*
> *Behold, there he stands behind our wall*
> *gazing at the windows,*
> *looking through the lattice.*[14]

Here again we see *reciprocity* as a fundamental feature of love, and it is even probable that this is something hinted at by the texts here. Obviously the Bridegroom's knowledge of the bride is not distinct from the perfect knowledge that God has of all things and therefore of each human being. But it is also clear that the lack of fullness which seems to apply here to love in some way affects one lover as much as the other. Love is imperfect in the present circumstances *for both*, because it is one and the same for both.[15]

Hence the impression of inadequacy one can sometimes get from classical teaching on contemplation. This is true as regards both *active* and *passive* contemplation, to use the complicated terminology of mystical theologies, which take account of the greater or lesser role (or even no role) that human activity performs in contempla-

---

[14] Sg 2:9.

[15] Love is the bond which joins two persons who love one another, being, as it is, breathed or *spirated* by both. It is true that the Holy Spirit has already been poured into man's heart (Rom 5:5), but only as the first fruit or as an earnest of a future fullness (Eph 1:14; 2 Cor 1:22). The attribution to God of an imperfect love is theologically inadmissible, although it is clear that God can love creatures with different degrees of intensity. Certainly, one has to bear in mind that, since created love is equivalent to a relationship, it depends not only on God but also on the creature.

tion. Starting out always, as is logical, from the necessity of grace, man here either contributes a laborious effort or else is simply swept up by a divine impetus which does all the work. We might recall here St Teresa's famous examples of the waterwheel and the rain: whereas the wheel draws the water out of the well little by little and by dint of effort, the rain makes water fall on the earth copiously and without anyone having to work. By concentrating on the role which grace plays in contemplation, to a greater or lesser degree, in order to determine the role which man plays, they forget that in the loving activity of contemplation *two people are involved*. According to classical doctrine, whatever degree of perfection of contemplation is involved, practically always it is man, and only man, who does the contemplating. The undeniable fact of the specific need for grace in contemplative prayer is responsible for the doctrine speaking (quite correctly) of the elevation and help man needs in order to achieve contemplation. But at the same time the doctrine usually forgets that God's role here is not only one of healing and elevating: his is also a *specifically contemplative* role. According to the universal, unchanging rules of love, neither of the lovers simply offers himself to the loved one, in a purely passive way, in order to be contemplated. That would not make sense nor would it fit in with the notion of love, which is always something involving reciprocity: it is a *spiration* by both. Neither lover is satisfied or set at ease by offering himself purely passively to the other, to be contemplated; rather, he wants to contemplate the object of his love, or at least to rejoice in his awareness (which necessarily implies perception) of the contemplation which the other is actively engaged in.

The evidence that all this is clearly implied may make it seem unnecessary to attempt any clarification of the doctrine on the subject. However, the practical consequences of this kind of thinking can do a great deal of harm, as we shall go on to show. Moreover, it should also be remembered that love puts little value on what is implied or tacit: it wants things to be expressed clearly. It is proper to the nature of love to express itself clearly in one way or another, and therefore neither lover is content with supposing (or even with knowing) that his love is returned by the loved one: he does everything he can to have her manifest that she loves him. The entire *Song of Songs* is nothing other than a hymn to a love which tries to express itself in every possible way. It is an incontrovertible truth that the lovers need to see one another, to contemplate, speak to, listen to, and caress one another *reciprocally*. In fact, from the moment that love is a *spiration*, or breathing–out, of the heart by both lovers (an exhalation which contains the *entirety* of the persons of both) all interpretations and suppositions cease to have any meaning: and so it is that love only exists to the extent that it is expressed or manifested. There is no love without an *I love you*, without a glance full of meaning, a loving caress, a sigh, at least, from the heart of one of the lovers, and all this in the hope of the other's response. That is why the Spirit always manifests Himself in a way perceptible to the senses (although often one does not know where he is coming from or where he is going to), blowing and letting his voice be heard (Jn 3:8; Acts 2: 2–4), speaking, guiding and revealing (Jn 16:13), teaching and reminding (Jn 14:26), moving men to utter the words of God (Jn 3:34), bearing witness (Jn 15:26), praying for and with man with sighs too deep for words (Rom 8:26). It is not surprising, therefore, that when he is neither seen nor known he cannot be received (Jn 14:17). As the great mystics have been given to see, far from God's confining Himself in contemplative prayer to the role of a static being, an object of contemplation, he reveals Himself rather as someone who gives Himself and communicates Himself, which is the same as saying that it is in contemplation above all that he reveals Himself as someone who contemplates, who speaks, who whispers, who caresses —in other words, who loves. In the last analysis, as required by the rules of love, man also is the object of contemplation; the Bridegroom expressly says so to the bride in the *Song*:

> *Let me see your face, let me hear your voice,*
> *for your voice is sweet, and your face is comely.*[16]

Nothing else would make sense. Since reciprocity is the basic rule of perfect love, the lover in love needs to *see and feel* that he is loved by the other in the same way that his love is returned. Man cannot fully fall in love with God unless he first experiences divine love: *We love, because he first loved us.*[17] And God's mad outpouring of love for man is made manifest in Jesus Christ: *In this the love of God was made manifest among us, that God sent his only Son into the world, so that we might live through Him. In this is love, not that we loved God but that he loved us and sent his Son to be the expiation for our sins.*[18] St John adds an even more intriguing assertion: *By this we "know" that we abide in Him and he in us: because he has given us of his Spirit.*[19]

St John of the Cross does not put too much stress on what might be called the *contemplative attitude* of God in prayer, nor on what we have been describing here as *reciprocity* in love. But this does not in any way mean that he ignores this doctrine; it is really all a matter of terminology and viewpoint and emphasis. The part God plays

---

[16] Sg 2:14.

[17] 1 Jn 4:19.

[18] 1 Jn 4: 9–10.

[19] 1 Jn 4:13. According to this, it is precisely the presence of the Spirit that causes man *to know and feel* the wonderful interchange of divine–human love (and therefore of lives).

The desire to be contemplated 105

in contemplative prayer is described by the Saint in the form of a rigorous and correct exposition of the need for grace, to be supplied by God, counter–balanced by the absolute requirement of pure faith and putting no reliance on the senses, on man's part. However, as is only logical, the mystic poet reveals his great intuitiveness, on this point too, in a passage of his *Spiritual Canticle*: clearly, the eyes of the Lover, to which the Saint refers, are not desired only in order to contemplate them in a fully absorbed loving look: they are, above all, desired in order to be contemplated by them. And that is why, in the *Song*, the bride contemplates the eyes of the Bridegroom; but, at the same time, the Bridegroom, who has fallen ardently in love, also contemplates in utter absorption the bride's eyes:

> *How beautiful you are, my beloved,*
> *how beautiful you are!*
> *Your eyes are doves.*[20]

This is how the poet puts it:

> *O crystal spring,*
> *would that on your silvery surface*
> *you were suddenly to form*
> *those eyes for which I pine*
> *and which I carry graven on my soul!*[21]

---

[20]Sg 2:15.

[21]In the original:

> *¡Oh cristalina fuente,*
> *si en esos tus semblantes plateados*
> *formases de repente*
> *los ojos deseados*
> *que tengo en mis entrañas dibujados!*

This is expressed even more clearly in two beautiful stanzas of his *Canticle*:

> *That one golden hair*
> *which you regarded fluttering on my neck,*
> *you gazed at it upon my neck,*
> *and you were captivated,*
> *and one of mine eyes wounded you.*[22]

> *When you were gazing at me,*
> *your eyes left on me the imprint of their grace;*
> *because of this you loved me greatly*
> *whereby my ejes deserved to adore*
> *that which they saw in you.*[23]

Important consequences derive from this as far as the life of prayer is concerned. The fact is that the theology of prayer is too

---

[22]In the original:

> *En solo aquel cabello*
> *que en mi cuello volar consideraste*
> *mirástele en mi cuello*
> *y en él preso quedaste*
> *y en uno de mis ojos te llagaste.*

[23]In the original:

> *Cuando tú me mirabas*
> *tu gracia en mí tus ojos imprimían;*
> *por eso me adamabas*
> *y en eso merecían*
> *los míos adorar lo que en ti vían.*

often *one-sided*: prayer of petition, prayer of supplication, prayer of adoration, thanksgiving... Here God almost always is cast in the role of someone *whom man addresses* and addresses merely as Creator and Lord. Very little emphasis is put on the fact that prayer is also dialogue, and still less on the fact that God manifests Himself in prayer as a Bridegroom, as a companion, and as a friend (Jn 15:15). The result is that the pedagogy of prayer tends to make it out to be a duty; and the practice of prayer can even become tedious, because one forgets (as incredible as it might seem) that prayer is not just a dialogue but also and above all *a true meeting of lovers*, with all that that implies.

The infinite distance that lies between the divine lover and the human lover does not suspend the basic laws of love. And therefore divine–human love —the most perfect love given to a creature to experience, in this world and in the next— must not be spoken of as if it were a mere shadow of genuine love. In fact the Word became flesh in order to bridge this infinite distance, and to make it possible for there to be a true love–relationship between God and his creature. Or to put this in another way: *to make this love a real and true love*, with all the consequences that it implies. The larval remnants of Manicheism, which always find a place in Christianity, are surely the source of the belief that the form of love proper to man —composed as he is of body and soul— is something as prone to imperfection as the corporeal ingredient of the (one) human nature. But human nature, even though it is lower than angelic nature,[24] is not on this lesser level because of the matter which forms part of its make–up: it is lower simply because it was created to be like that. In fact, the Word of God was able to take on a human nature without ceasing to be the Word. This is the reason for the tendency

---

[24] Although not as low as one might think, according to Ps 8:6 and Heb 2:7.

to think that, in the order of love also, Jesus Christ's human nature has only a medicinal or elevating role as far as man is concerned. St Thomas, for example, says that *Matters concerning the Godhead are, in themselves, the strongest incentive to love and consequently to devotion, because God is supremely lovable. Yet such is the weakness of the human spirit that it needs a guiding hand, not only to the knowledge, but also to the love of Divine things by means of certain sensible objects known to us. Chief among these is the humanity of Christ.*[25] Once again the Saint has got it right, although it might have been better to put the accent not so much on the *weakness of the human spirit* as on the inbuilt needs of human nature. In other words, the human nature of Jesus Christ is not merely a medicine for man: it is the only route for him to take, the true, absolute *conditio sine qua non* for reaching the Father: *No one comes to the Father, but by me.*[26] The weakness of human nature is not due in this case to any imperfection (here we might think, perhaps, of some sort of moral imperfection) but simply to the fact that it was made like that (with its own inbuilt limitations): that is just its nature.[27]

So, there is nothing remarkable about the fact that the bride should desire to be contemplated by the Bridegroom just as she de-

---

[25] *Ea quæ sunt divinitatis sunt secundum se maxime excitantia dilectionem, et per consequens devotionem: quia Deus est super omnia diligendus. Sed ex debilitate mentis humanæ est quod sicut indiget manuduci ad cognitionem divinorum, ita ad dilectionem, per aliqua sensibilia nobis nota. Inter quæ præ cipuum est humanitas Christi.* In *S. Th.*, II^a-II^æ, q. 82, a. 3, ad 2.

[26] Jn 14:6. Cf. also Mt 11:27.

[27] The word *weakness* should not be used when something is acting in conformity with its nature. If it were, all creatures (including angels) would be *weak*, or imperfect, given that there is only one perfect, infinite Being. To reach the Father, man does not need the human nature of Christ because man is imperfect, *but simply because he is man*. This in no way takes from the role of Christ's human nature in the work of redemption: unfortunately man is also a sinner.

The desire to be contemplated 109

sires to contemplate Him. The rules and laws of love, which, as we know, also involve a veritable *struggle* between the lovers (Sg 2:4), forever set the two of them in a relationship of equality and reciprocity. That is why the bride says:

> *My Lover, I have walked*
> *upon the path in your orchard of lemon*
> > *blossoms,*
> *and then I hid myself*
> *behind the lemon tree*
> *to see if I could kiss you first.*[28]

Yet love is a combat in which each lover struggles to achieve an ever greater self–surrender to the other:

> *He has taken me to his cellar,*
> *and his banner over me is love.*[29]

The Bridegroom takes the bride to the intimacy of a secluded place. There, each one tries to surrender everything he or she possesses to the other; there, each lover clearly feels that it is better to give than to receive (Acts 20:35) and that losing oneself in the arms

---

[28] In the original:

> *Amado, he recorrido*
> *de tu huerto de azahares el sendero,*
> *y, luego, me he escondido*
> *detrás del limonero*
> *para poder besarte yo primero.*

[29] Sg 2:4.

of the loved one is the best way, the only way, to find true, abundant life. Therefore the Bridegroom, who is not prepared to be bested in matters of love, hastens to reply and to put forward the very same argument. That is why the Bridegroom answers the bride with almost the same words that she had previously used. And this answer is one of love since each one wishes to come out winner because he has been more generous in this self–surrender contest:

> *Beloved, I have searched*
> *for the path in my orchard of lemon blossoms,*
> *and then I waited for you*
> *behind the lemon tree*
> *to see if I found you first.*[30]

---

[30]In the original:

> *Amada, yo he buscado*
> *de mi huerto de azahares el sendero,*
> *y, luego, te he esperado*
> *detrás del limonero*
> *a ver si te encontraba yo primero.*

CHAPTER VII

THE SELF-SURRENDER OF THE BRIDEGROOM TO THE BRIDE

The bride's desire to receive the kiss of love from the Bridegroom includes, as we have already said, the desire that the Bridegroom should give Himself to her.[1] A kiss, which is the way love most typically uses to express itself,[2] implies a certain submission of the lover to the loved one;[3] this is nothing but a consequence of the total and absolute personal *self-surrender* which takes place in love. As the bride says in the *Song*:

> *My beloved is mine...*[4]

---

[1] Cf. chapters I and V.

[2] Cf. chapter III, particularly note 3.

[3] In this case, submission of the one who kisses to the one who receives the loving kiss. Due to the essential feature of *reciprocity*, inherent in love, submission and belonging can be attributed to either of the two lovers, because they in fact belong to one another. This chapter has to do with the bride's desire (become a reality) to possess the Bridegroom; the following chapter will deal with the theme of the bride's belonging to the Bridegroom.

[4] Sg 2:16.

The possession of the loved one, in participated love, takes place in a "logical" second moment, for the lover's self-surrender must come first.[5] However, this obviously applies to either of the lovers. According to our Lord, *It is more blessed to give than to receive*,[6] which probably also means that the giving of oneself is the first intention of the one who loves. Here the preference can be temporal and that is what happens, in fact, the more imperfect the love is.[7]

The *lordship and possession* which man acquires, also with respect to God, once God has given Himself as a gift of love,[8] is a central idea in New Testament revelation, although this is a point that is not always made strongly enough. St Paul asserts it quite formally in his first letter to the Corinthians: *All things are yours, whether Paul or Apollos or Cephas or the world or life or death or the present or the future, all are yours*.[9] And, even though he goes on to say that *you are Christ's, and Christ is God's*,[10] as the reciprocity of love requires, the very clear assertion that *all are yours* is not diminished in any way if the context of the New Testament is

---

[5]In the bosom of perfect and infinite Love, the Father and the Son *breathe* the Holy Spirit at the same time, without there being any logical "first" or "second" in the procession of the third Person.

[6]Acts 20:35.

[7]Take, for example, love not yet responded to, and love of enemies. Since love is dependent on two persons, it can be imperfect on the part of one of the lovers, even when the other's surrender is total and perfect.

[8]Although without affecting the fact that God is the Creator and Lord, whereas man is a creature. The perfect identity and clear distinction of each of the *persons* are essential in love. This is not only an obstacle to love, but a necessary condition for love to happen: *Do you know what I have done to you? You call me Teacher and Lord; and you are right, for so I am. If I then, your Lord and Teacher, have washed your feet...* (Jn 13: 12–14).

[9]1 Cor 3: 21–22.

[10]1 Cor 3:23.

taken into consideration.[11] The dignity love has conferred on man, in the new economy of grace, sets him as far away as possible from that famous *alienation* where some say that Christianity has put him. It is precisely now, through the action of love, that man, far from being lessened, has truly turned into the master *of the world, of life, of death, of the present and of the future.*[12]

Each of the lovers is aware that the other belongs to him. One must realize that this belonging is not a mere consequence of the love–process, nor something incidental to it: it is something fundamental that belongs to the essence of true love; in the last analysis it is nothing but the result of the fact that each of the lovers gives

---

[11]On the contrary: it is precisely by virtue of belonging to Christ that man has become the lord and master of everything. Here again the requirement of reciprocity that love involves comes into play. This is what St John of the Cross came to say, although in another context: *Por la nada al todo*. Through nothing to everything: We come to possess everything by ways of total dispossession.

[12]Although this is not the place for it, there is plenty of scope for study to establish the basis for human dignity by following this route. Apropos of Hebrews 2: 6–8, St Thomas (*Comm. Ad Hebræos*, Cap. II, Lect. II) and some Fathers too, think that Jesus Christ was made *lower than the angels* because he underwent his passion and death, and not because he assumed a human nature. Irrespective of how this disputed text is interpreted (cf. also I^a, q. 20, a. 4, ad 2, where the saint clearly distinguishes what refers to nature from what refers to supernature), it is clear that it does also show that human nature, as a result of the act of divine love which the Incarnation of the Word involved, has been elevated in a most sublime way and *crowned with glory and honour* in the highest heaven. According to St Thomas, although God assumed human nature, he did not do so in any sense because he loved man more but because man needed it more; nevertheless, if one takes into account his own teaching that things are better the more they are loved by God (which in turn cannot but mean that they have received greater benefits from Him; I^a, q. 20, aa. 3–4), one should perhaps conclude that, according to this, man has been loved in a very special way: from the moment that God became not angel but man, it seems conclusive that man received much more grace from God; the fact that he stood in need of it in no way diminishes the greatness of the gift.

himself entirely to the other. The desire to have the other at one's disposal, which is but the desire to possess the other, is something implicit in and consubstantial with the desire to belong to him; this makes it, for that very reason, inseparable from the loving act. The lover knows that he cannot surrender himself to the possession of the loved one unless she in turn makes herself over to him to be possessed by him. In true love surrender never occurs without reception:

> *My beloved is mine and I am his.*[13]

It is an undisputed truth that love desires the good of the loved one. According to traditional doctrine, the assertion that the essence of love consists in desiring good for someone, is a commonplace. St Thomas says: *This belongs properly to the nature of love, that the lover wills the good of the one he loves*;[14] elsewhere he says, for example, that *it is the nature of love that the lover desires and seeks the good of the one he loves...*[15] or that *love consists principally in this, that the lover desires the good of his loved one.*[16] But the fact that at the same time it is also true that love (he who loves) desires his own good and his own delectation seems to raise a curious aporia. This was a subject which already seriously worried St Augustine;[17]

---

[13] Sg 2:16.

[14] *Hoc enim est proprie de ratione amoris, quod amans bonum amati velit.* In *Contra Gentiles*, I, 91.

[15] *Si hoc habet amoris ratio quod amans velit aut appetat bonum amati...* In *loc. cit.*

[16] *In hoc enim præcipue consistit amor, quod amans amato bonum velit.* In *Contra Gentiles*, III, 90.

[17] Étienne Gilson, *Introduction a l'Étude de Saint Augustin*, Paris, 1982, pp. 178 ff.

he asked whether one and the same will could tend at the same time towards two different objects: his own good and the good of his good. The Saint solved the problem by arguing that love, as Denis had already said, is a power which tends towards unity (unitive power) and to make the two lovers one; and, logically, there can be no opposition within something which is a single thing. Yet, one would need to stress the aporia even more, as far as created love is concerned, using the following argument: given that love is a *vis unitiva*, since God is not a good but the Supreme Good, and given that man should love Him in an unlimited way (created beings are merely particular beings), how can one describe as love a relationship in which man has only the role of a subordinate being, even to the point of counting for nothing at all...? To which St Augustine replied by saying that one needs to bear in mind that in reality the only true way valid for man is to renounce himself and lose himself: it is only then, the saint says, when he possesses the Absolute Good, that man has need of nothing else and his desires are fully satisfied.

The first aporia, which refers to the fact that the lover desires the good for the loved one and also for himself is resolved by St Thomas in I^a, q. 20, a. 1, ad 3. Starting out from the idea that love (in God as well as man) is a unitive force, the saint points out, however, that with respect to God all composition is excluded, because the good which he desires for himself is not something distinct from Himself.[18] As the Angelic Doctor sees it, when someone loves himself he desires good for himself and therefore tries to appropriate it in so far as possible; whereas, when someone loves another, he desires good for that other, and therefore he treats that person as if she were himself,

---

[18]This is how he replies to objections to the effect that since love is a force which links and unifies and is therefore opposed to the simplicity of God, it has no place in Him.

referring good to the other as he would to himself; that is why love is called a *force which unites*, because it gathers the other to oneself, causing the lover to treat the loved one as he would treat himself.[19]

It may be necessary to go closer to this mystery, bearing in mind that Love, which is identical with infinite Being and with the Supreme Good, is a *personal Being*, in which there is, also, a plurality of persons without that plurality being an obstacle to the perfect simplicity and absolute unicity of its essence. As St Thomas says, working out from the evidence, divine love does not need to desire anything outside itself. However, that truth does not prevent one from thinking that perfect Love or infinite Being, due precisely to the plurality of divine Persons found in it, is also *love of one for another*. And so it can be said that, even though divine Love has no need to go outside itself, we do find in it a *thou* and an *I*, perfectly differentiated as Persons and totally given over, the one to the other.[20]

Probably, by working out from this consideration which takes account of the nature proper to love, we may be helped to find the solution of the aporia according to which the lover, in addition to seeking the good of the person loved, also seeks his own good. For we could say, with St Augustine, that love tends to make the two lovers one; or else, as St Thomas says, that love is a unitive force which

---

[19] *In hoc vero quod aliquis amat alium, vult bonum illi. Et sic utitur eo tanquam seipso, referens bonum ad illum, sicut ad seipsum. Et pro tanto dicitur amor vis concretiva: quia alium aggregat sibi, habens se ad eum sicut ad seipsum.*

[20] On the other hand, creatures, due to the limitation of their nature, need absolutely to go outside themselves in order to find the *other* and in order to love; for it is absolutely impossible for any creature to be at one and the same time an *I* and a *thou* distinct as such in one and the same nature. As regards the manner in which God loves creatures, cf. St Thomas, *Summa Theologiæ*, Iª, q. 20, a. 2, ad 1 and "Respondeo."

brings together (or joins) the loved one and the lover, causing the lover to refer to the loved one as if she were himself. But one thing we can be sure about is that even though love *tends* to make the two lovers one, *they will undoubtedly always continue to be two and not one*. And it is equally certain that, however much the lover refers to the loved one *as if she were himself*, they will always continue to be two distinct persons: the lover and the loved one. Therefore it may perhaps not be necessary to insist so much on an identification (or sameness) of wills or of persons which anyway can never be, no matter how much effort is made, it would seem. Only in the bosom of perfect Love, which is uncreated Love, are the Persons fully identical in the sameness of a single essence (and therefore of a single will), while yet remaining perfectly distinguished as the Persons they are.

So it seems appropriate, when discussing love (and even more so when it is creaturely love) to lay the stress more on the relative opposition and perfect differentiation which is found between the *I* and the *thou* of both lovers. Although it is true that love is a unitive force, and even the greatest such force that one can conceive, there may perhaps be no need to regard the two lovers *as if they were one*, or even to think that the lover ever manages to treat the loved one *as if she were himself*.[21] Bearing this in mind, it is probable that there is no need either merely to put the accent on the fact that the love–union brings about an identification between the lovers, when it may be appropriate to stress also, as we have been saying, their perfect differentiation and opposition. Uncreated love should serve as a point of reference for explaining created love, given that in the last analysis the latter is a participation in the former. However,

---

[21] In fact the *as if* does not entirely solve the difficulty. The expression itself is suspect, due to the ambiguity of its meaning; and, anyway, the two lovers still remain two.

even though the analogy fits so perfectly here, given that it is his own Love that God has placed in man's heart (Rom 5:5; Jn 17:26; etc.), one must avoid confusing the two. In uncreated Love, the Lovers and the Love with which they love one another are fully identical (in the simplicity and unicity of the divine essence), but they still do remain distinct as Persons. In the case of creatures, that kind of identification is impossible, although the differentiation of persons (since it is essential in love) is not affected.

And so it may be said that the good which the lover desires for himself is in fact the loved one, to the point that she and no other is for him his entire good. As far as the good of the loved one is concerned..., the lover of course desires this, and the more perfect his love the more he strives to obtain it for her; therefore, the very thing he tries to give the loved one is *everything he has and everything he possesses*, which is the same as saying that he desires to give her his own person. So, rather than insist on the fact that the lover desires good for himself and for his loved one, perhaps it would be more exact to say that the lover desires the loved one (who is for him his own good) at the same time as he desires to give himself to her entirely (which is to desire for the loved one all good, all goodness possible). So, it is not necessary to turn the two wills into one, which is something that can happen only in God. Nor is there any contradiction in the fact that, apparently, the same will tends towards two different ends; because what in fact happens in the mysterious reality of love, is that *there exist in it always two lovers who desire, reciprocally and at the same time, to give and to receive.* From the moment that love is a *spiration* by each of the two, there is brought about, necessarily, in one and the same act of love, a desire to surrender oneself and a desire to receive the other.

The second aporia St Augustine poses starts out from the fact that love tends towards unity and to making the two lovers one; yet it is difficult to describe a relationship as love (in this case, divine–human love) in which man has a subordinate role, counting for virtually nothing. Something can be said about this, too. It is clear that, in divine–human love, God continues to be the Creator and man the creature. However, if one thinks deeply about the matter, it is unlikely that this should constitute an obstacle to love between God and man. It is even possible that in the way the problem is posed we may have gone further than the nature of the love-relationship strictly requires. The truth is that the fact that, in divine–human love, man's continuing to be a creature (it could not be otherwise) does not lessen his condition as God's *partner*. As we have already stressed, in love it is essential for each of the lovers to retain unaltered their condition as unique persons (as happens in the Trinity itself). In love the union of the lovers is as important as their total differentiation and even their relative *opposition*. The perfect identification of the lovers, and of the love wherewith they love one another, in the sameness of a single essence is something proper and exclusive to perfect, infinite Love. The fact that it does not happen like that in the creature, as is obvious, would imply diminishment and subordination for the creature only to the extent that its creaturely condition would also imply such a diminishment. However, it would never occur to anyone to think that the creature, simply because he is a creature, finds himself in a situation of diminution and subordination. The fact that God and creatures are on absolutely different planes can be seen as nothing but awesome, *for what is truly adorable and beautiful is that God is God and things are things*. What really matters, in true love, is that the lovers give themselves totally to one another. Man, who has been called by grace to experience Love by participation, can never at any point cease to be a creature nor has he any reason to do so. Besides, the ineffable fact that man is able to love God by contemplating Him face to face, to relate to Him in the bilateral intimate relationship of a *thou and I*, and to participate in the very life of God, is precisely what the mystery of his gratuitous elevation to the supernatural order is all about. It is a mystery which consists precisely in the fact that man, in his creaturely condition, has been raised by grace to a relationship of intimacy with his Creator by participating in divine Love and in divine life. That kind of love–relationship, far from putting man in a situation of diminution or subordination, or leaving him as it were reduced to nothing, raises him to that relative and incredible condition of *equality* in which love sets those who love one another. Once they are placed in this position, the lovers fully enjoy the fruits of a relationship which is at one and the same time a love of friendship, of fraternity, of paternity–filiation and, of course, conjugal love; or, to put it another way: they enjoy love in all its forms and modes, because theirs is an authentic love–relationship which unfolds itself in totality. This love–relationship and it alone is the subject of this book. And it should not be forgotten that it is precisely by means of love, through the contrast with the *other* as loved one, that the person actualizes all his potentialities to manifest himself as the person he is: so that in the Trinity the Father would not be the Father without the Son, or the Son the Son without the Father, nor would either of them be without the Holy Spirit, nor the Holy Spirit be without the Father and the Son.

The problem of the surrender and loss of one's own life, whereby man would seem to be reduced to nothing, leads St Augustine to say, as we already mentioned above, that the possession of absolute Good in fact eliminates the need for anything else. According to the saint, given the possibility that Good is within one's grasp, losing one's life is the only way of saving it, and renouncing it is the only way of gaining it. So, it is probably possible to tease this matter out a little further. For perhaps it is not just a matter of possessing absolute Good (thereby eliminating any need of anything else), but of something more. Although the Scriptural texts do speak about losing one's life, they are careful to add that that is the only way to go *to find one's life again*. For example, St Matthew says: *He who finds his life will lose it, and he who loses his life for my sake will find it.*[22] Here we seem to have a veritable dialectic of losing and finding (thesis/antithesis), where the middle term, which resolves the dialectic (synthesis) is nothing other than love: *He who loses his life "for my sake" will find it*. For it should never be forgotten, if one wants to find a solution to this problem, that we are dealing with a question of love. And given that, in love, both lovers, through the action and grace of reciprocity, give themselves entirely to one another, it can be taken that each makes a gift to the other of his own life along with all that he has and has received. *Hence, according to this, each gives the other the life which he has received as a gift from that other*. And so our Lord says that *he who loses his life for my sake "will find it."* It is as if love makes it possible for each of the lovers to give the other everything he has received from him, in addition to that which is proper to himself: *He who had received the five talents came forward, bringing five talents more, saying: "Master, you delivered to me five talents; here I have made five talents more."*[23] Therefore, the mutual indwelling and union of lives (the fruit of love) of which our Lord speaks in the discourse at Capernaum (Jn 6: 56–57) are as complete as the differentiation

---

[22] Mt 10:39. Parallel texts: Mt 16:25; Mk 8:35; Lk 9:24.
[23] Mt 25:20.

and identity of the two lovers: *He who eats my flesh..."abides in me, and I in him."*[24] The texts refer to the union and intimacy that are obtained between the lives of the lovers as clearly as they define and distinguish the persons: *In that day you will know that I am in my Father, and you in me and I in you.*[25] So, as we said earlier, divine love, far from leaving the creature in an ill–defined or almost non-existent position, raises him instead to a position of nearness to and intimacy with God —one could almost say a position of *equality*— such as only Love could devise: the texts never tire in telling us this: *And when I go and prepare a place for you, I will come again and will take you to myself, that where I am you may be also.*[26] Or: *Behold, I stand at the door and knock; if any of you hears my voice and opens the door, I will come in to him and eat with him, and he with me.*[27]

Since divine–human love is true love, and the most perfect kind of love that can exist after Supreme Love, it must include the condition of total and reciprocal self–surrender that is proper to the loving act. And so the divine lover gives himself into the possession of

---

[24] What our Lord does in John 6:57, where he says that anyone who eats Him "will live because of Him," is to establish a relationship of similarity between, on the one hand, the life of the Father and the life that He receives in dependence on that of the Father and, on the other, the life of the disciple and Jesus' own life: *As the loving Father sent me and I live because of the Father, so he who eats me will live because of me.* An ineffable dependence and intimacy in which the persons who love one another continue, nevertheless, to be distinct, loving persons.

[25] Jn 14:20. It is interesting to notice here the accumulation and counterposing of the various personal pronouns one to another and with respect to the Person of the Father. The loving union leaves intact the separate identity of the persons (both in created love and in uncreated Love) without in the latter case this being an obstacle to the simplicity of the divine essence (Jn 17:22).

[26] Jn 14:3.

[27] Rev 3:20.

man, creating a situation of belonging that is as genuine as the love that God professes to the creature in love who responds to him. It is clear that the New Testament —which contains the good news of the gift God has made man of his Love— speaks of nothing else, and we find it even earlier in Old Testament revelation, in the *Song of Songs* particularly.

The eucharistic discourse at Capernaum (Jn 6: 26–59) is a proclamation of the loving surrender of God to man. This sounded so incredible, due to its excessive generosity, the fruit of a love no less excessive, that it scandalized most of those present (Jn 6: 60.66). From the discourse we can see that, just as food is assimilated and turned into part of his own body by the person who eats it,[28] Jesus offers Himself to the man who loves Him: *My flesh is food indeed, and my blood is drink indeed.*[29] But the scandal caused by the eucharistic mystery, which has never been absent down the centuries, has acquired greater virulence in our own days, due, surely, to a cooling of charity (Mt 24:12) caused, in turn, by a lack of faith: it is impossible to believe in the kind of madness love is capable of if one no longer believes in love. As we have pointed out so often, only lovers are capable of truly believing in love, and only those who generously open their hearts can accept that anyone could give himself in the way Christ does in the Eucharist. So, to the extent that Christians have been abandoning faith in the real presence, they have been also abandoning belief in the possibility that God could love man to the extent of making Himself over to him.

A similar example of how God gives Himself to man, to be his in love, is found in the episode of the washing of the feet on the night of

---

[28] Assimilated food becomes not just the property of the eater but actually part of him.

[29] Jn 6:55.

the last supper.[30] The narrative begins with a solemn declaration by Jesus which shows how very aware he is of his own dignity: *Knowing that the Father had given all things into his hands, and that he had come from God and was going to God, he arose from supper, laid aside his garments...* We can clearly see here the evangelist's intention to contrast the dignity and majesty of the Master, on the one hand, with his attitude of abasement and self-surrender, on the other; but we can also see that, for the evangelist, it is not so much a matter of inexplicable contrasts as of the logic proper to love, which causes the lover to give himself totally to the loved one. Besides, it is our Lord Himself Who points out (applying the teaching to himself) that, in the new doctrine of love which is now going to be preached, dignity and pre–eminence take the form of service: *You know that the rulers of the Gentiles lord it over them, and their great men exercise authority over them. It shall not be so among you; but whoever would be great among you must be your servant, and whoever would be first among you must be your slave; even as the Son of man came not to be served but to serve, and to give his life as a ransom for many...*[31] *Which is the greater, one who sits at table, or one who serves? Is it not the one who sits at table? But I am among you as one who serves.*[32] It is not in any way surprising, therefore, that Love should place in the Master's heart an ardent desire to substitute for the old master–servant relationship a new relationship of intimate, trusting friendship, in which secrets can no longer exist once everything is surrendered by one to the other: *No longer do I call you servants, for the servant does not know what*

---

[30] Jn 13: 2–15.
[31] Mt 20: 25–28.
[32] Lk 22:27. Cf. Lk 12:37.

his master is doing; but I have called you friends, for all that I have heard from my Father I have made known to you.[33]

In fact, the attitude of service and self–surrender of the Bridegroom towards the bride goes much further than that. He makes Himself poor in spite of being rich (2 Cor 8:9), he empties Himself, becoming a slave (Phil 2: 7–8) and, as if that were little, he even consents to being made sin on her behalf even though He has never known sin (2 Cor 5:21).[34]

So, aware of all this, the bride in the *Song*, not content with expressing her yearning to be with her Bridegroom (Sg 8:6), makes bold to proclaim that she too has a burning desire (it has already come about) for the Bridegroom to be with her. This surely is a joyful recognition that He belongs to her; she proclaims that He is with her, in deepest intimacy, ready to serve her:

> *My beloved is to me a bag of myrrh,*
> *that lies between my breasts.*
> *My beloved is to me a cluster of henna blossoms*
> *in the vineyards of Engedi.*[35]

The Bridegroom, for his part, consistent with his attitude of total self–surrender and belonging to his bride, joyfully proclaims to other creatures his great desire to care for her and serve her and lovingly protect her. Given as he is to her with all his affection, to be held and owned by her, he has no desire other than to serve her and make her happy. Hence his warning to others to respect

---

[33] Jn 15:15.

[34] Cf. Is 53: 5–12; 1 Jn 3:5; Rom 8:3; Gal 3:13.

[35] Sg 1: 13–14.

the intimacy of his beloved and not to disturb the joy of her free self–surrender:

> *I adjure you, O daughters of Jerusalem,*
> *by the gazelles or the hinds of the field,*
> *that you stir not up nor awaken my beloved*
> *until she pleases.*[36]

Until she pleases... Because all in love is freedom; because each lover feels a deep and passionate longing for only those things that the other yearns for: even as far as renouncing the joy of being together, if that is what the other wants. This stanza of the *Song*, so beautifully composed by the sacred writer, which evokes the image of the Bridegroom imposing silence on creation with an imperative, hissing whisper, has been paraphrased by St John of the Cross in two of the most subtle and ardent verses of his *Spiritual Canticle*:

> *You birds that fly with ease,*
> *lions, stags, skipping fallow deer,*
> *hills, valleys, river–banks,*
> *waters, winds, heats,*
> *and watchers that fill the nights with fear.*[37]

---

[36]Sg 2:7. Cf. 3:5, 8:4.

[37]In the original:

> *A las aves ligeras,*
> *leones, ciervos, gamos saltadores,*
> *montes, valles, riberas,*
> *aguas, aires, ardores*
> *y miedos de las noches veladores:*

> *by the sweet lyre*
> *and songs of sirens I conjure you*
> *to cease your wrath.*
> *Do not even echo on the wall,*
> *that the bride may sleep more securely.*[38]

However, modern man is incapable of thinking that God could love him to the extent of surrendering Himself to him and belonging to him. No longer believing in true love, he no longer believes in the ineffably beautiful and magnificent things that have been given to him. That is why he has put out of his mind the words of the Lord that promise him these unbelievable things: *Truly, I say to you, that he who believes in me will do the works that I do; and greater works than these will he do, because I go to the Father.*[39] And so modern Christianity has replaced the search for God with the search for man. Nowadays the various Churches devote themselves to social work of different kinds, to helping the underprivileged... or to activities which benefit those who run them.[40] However, even in Antiquity, Diogenes the Cynic scoffed at man's search for man. So,

---

[38] In the original:

> *por las amenas liras*
> *y cantos de sirenas os conjuro*
> *que cesen vuestras iras*
> *y no toquéis al muro*
> *porque la esposa duerma m s seguro.*

[39] Jn 14:12.

[40] Consider, for example, the huge and profitable business set–ups the Protestant churches have in wealthy countries and the many Catholic Institutions and parishes that are dedicated, with a zeal worthy of a better cause, to activities which have social, political and money–making aims, where the supernatural horizon is no longer anywhere to be seen.

even if contemporary Christianity succeeded in finding man with the help of its modern lantern, the search would have proved fruitless. That kind of man, found by pursuing paths which are not those of Love, would be completely *elusive* and inaccessible, because only love can provide the possibility of possessing another person since love is the only thing capable of making that person give herself in joyful freedom.

The Christian *had his way* with God to do as he liked when he loved Him and searched for Him, because he believed in Him. *Truly, I say to you, if you have faith as a grain of mustard seed... nothing will be impossible to you.*[41] The bride in the *Song* anxiously sought the Bridegroom:

> *Upon my bed by night*
> *I sought him whom my soul loves;*
> *I sought him, but found him not;*
> *I called him, but he gave no answer.*
> *"I will rise now and go about the city,*
> *in the streets and in the squares;*
> *I will seek him whom my soul loves."*[42]

That was why she was perfectly correct in saying:

> *My beloved is mine and I am his.*[43]

And even:

> *I am my beloved's*
> *and his desire is for me.*[44]

---

[41] Mt 17:20.
[42] Sg 3: 1–2.
[43] Sg 2:16. Cf. 6:3.
[44] Sg 7:11.

Man can believe that God is able to surrender Himself and become man's possession as long as he believes that he too, in his turn, can belong to God... and that such a thing is worthwhile. But, as we said earlier, only faith can give man access to that ineffable reality, as indeed to all other realities, because *nothing is impossible for him who believes*. So, believing in God —*credere Deo*— is the equivalent of loving God. And loving God is possessing Him; and possessing Him is having all things: *Deus meus et omnia*. We can say of love what St Augustine says of prayer: that it is man's strength and God's weakness. The saint must surely have had in mind that, through prayer, man in a way has God's power available to him; which is undoubtedly even more true of love. For love, which according to Dante is a force capable of moving the sun and the stars, is also the only true weakness that God has. But it is clearly a rather special kind of weakness, because if, according to the Apostle, *the weakness of God is stronger than men*,[45] it is reasonable to think, without fear of contradiction, that nothing and no one will prevail against this force which moves the universe: *Love never ends; as for prophecies, they will pass away; as for tongues, they will cease; as for knowledge, it will pass away...*[46]

The possession of God by man is an essential consequence of love. However, it should not be forgotten that, due to man's still being *in via* while in this present age, love has not yet achieved in him its perfect climactic stage. The Bridegroom seems to delay (Mt 25:5) and even sometimes to become a fugitive, as the bride in the *Song* well knows. Really what we have here are the rules of the game of a love which only attains its consummation in Heaven. One gets the impression that the Bridegroom would like to see the bride

---

[45] 1 Cor 1:25.
[46] 1 Cor 13:8.

dissolve in her eagerness, in her nostalgic longing over the absence of her Lover. Perhaps because otherwise the flame of love would be quenched...? or because love needs to be set alight by yearning and desires before enjoying the perfect happiness that the consummation of that love brings...? or because it is necessary, perhaps, for the creature always to pass through the imperfect prior to savoring the perfect...?[47] Whatever the answer, man does suffer when he has been overtaken by true Love; his heart is wounded because God has not yet given Himself entirely to him, as St John of the Cross expresses it so movingly in his *Canticle*:

> *O, who will be able to heal me!*
> *Come, give yourself completely to me now*
> *From now on send me*
> *no more messengers,*
> *for they cannot tell me what I wish!*[48]

And yet..., even though it is still only an earnest, yet in a fuller way the more perfect one's love is, Love's self–surrender to man is already a sweet reality. Perfect joy has already begun here, in some way, for those whose thirst is insatiable because it is total Love they seek. The Carmelite saint–poet was able to write those verses because (in some ineffable way) he already possessed the Bridegroom;

---

[47] Cf. 1 Cor 13:10.

[48] In the original:

> *¡Ay!, ¿quién podrá sanarme?*
> *¡Acaba de entregarte ya de vero;*
> *no quieras enviarme*
> *de hoy más ya mensajero*
> *que no saben decirme lo que quiero!*

which explains why the bride in the *Song* speaks not merely of hopes but of something that has already come about when she says that:

> *My beloved is mine and I am his.*[49]

---

[49] Sg 2:16.

CHAPTER VIII

THE SELF-SURRENDER OF THE BRIDE TO THE BRIDEGROOM

Just as the Bridegroom gives Himself entirely to the bride, in genuine divine–human love, the bride also gives herself completely to the Bridegroom. As it has been said so often, everything in love is reciprocal: there is no surrender, no reception, by one of the lovers that is not offset by a corresponding reception or surrender by the other.

It should be noted, however, that we are not dealing here with a requirement or condition imposed by either of the lovers, or by both at the same time, for conditional clauses have no place in true love. What we have is, rather, something to do with the inner nature of a reality (that of love) which cannot exist except by way of a *spiration* or procession from each of the two.

The surrender by the lover —in the case we are examining now we refer to the bride— to the loved one is undoubtedly the most beautiful and characteristic feature of love. At the very least it is the ingredient which provides most joy, as our Lord Himself tells us:

It is more blessed to give than to receive.[1] This sends off in another direction the discussion of the primary ("first intention") objectives that love pursues: whether it is the good of the loved one or that of the lover (perhaps both at the same time), or whether it is the loved one himself. Whatever conclusion one arrives at, it is certainly clear that the feeling that makes the lover really happy, and what he therefore most desires, is his own readiness to give himself to the loved one.

So, it would seem that in love, at least as far as intentions go, self-surrender is prior to acceptance (or reception). This could lead to the conclusion, if one accepts this first statement as correct, that the good of the loved one is the first thing sought by the lover, even to the point where he seems totally to forget his own good.[2]

According to this, love would be much more a struggle to *surrender* than a struggle to *accept*, and it could even seem much closer to the first than to the second.[3] Of course, in the bosom of the Trinity the Holy Spirit is not reception but *Gift*, mutual surrender and giving; however, because this giving is truly *mutual*, each of the Lovers is receiving the other in turn.

And yet, there is no absurdity involved in saying that love is a struggle, and only someone who knows very little about love could be surprised by that statement. Leaving aside the most blessed and unfathomable serenity of trinitarian Love, love as practiced by crea-

---

[1] Acts 20:35.

[2] The root of the problem lies, as always, in the need to distinguish between infinite Love and participated love. It is well known that, given the plurality of Persons that live in God, He does not need to go outside Himself to desire the good of the loved one.

[3] Reciprocity demands that, in true love, surrender never occurs without possession. What it is said here has to do mainly with what one might call the lover's "first intention," without going into unnecessary technicalities.

tures (even divine–human love) is truly a struggle in which both lovers contend ardently to give themselves more to the other. However, it should be noted that the effort each makes does not have to do so much with giving *more* than the other as with giving *everything* to the other:

> He brought me to the banqueting house,
> and his banner over me
> was love.[4]

The explanation of the meaning of this struggle or contest must be sought in the fact that in this present age love is still in a state of *via*. Because the love–relationship has not yet reached its perfection or consummation, both lovers vie in their attempt to give themselves more and more, until they reach the point of giving everything. In the realm of divine–human love, there is no difficulty involved in understanding this as far as man is concerned; with respect to God, one must bear in mind that because the human party does not give itself entirely, He too is impeded from giving Himself entirely, for that is the way the law of reciprocity in love works. Therefore, when love eventually reaches its point of consummation, at least insofar as that is possible in this life, a situation of peace and repose is created, one which no man alien to it can possibly grasp.

> Arise, my love,
> my fair one, and come away;
> for lo, the winter is past,
> the rain is over and gone...[5]

---

[4] Sg 2:4.
[5] Sg 2: 10–11.

St John of the Cross says the same thing, paraphrasing the text, in the last stanza of his *Ascent of Mount Carmel*:

> *Lost to myself I stayed,*
> *my face reclining on the Beloved;*
> *everything ceased and I abandoned myself,*
> *throwing my cares*
> *among the lilies to lie forgotten.*[6]

But, as it has been said above, that moment has not yet arrived. Everything leads one to think that love is consummated definitively in Heaven, or perhaps, when one reaches its outskirts, at the moment of death, as the last words spoken by our Lord during his mortal life seem to confirm: *When Jesus had received the vinegar, he said, "It is finished"; and he bowed his head, and gave up his spirit.*[7] If one reads

---

[6] In the original:

> *Quedéme y olvidéme,*
> *el rostro recliné sobre el Amado,*
> *cesó todo y dejéme,*
> *dejando mi cuidado*
> *entre las azucenas olvidado.*

[7] Jn 19:30. Love reaches its culmination, in this present age, through something which is the greatest proof of love man can possibly give: death (Jn 15:13). However, self–surrender or the giving of one's life, which is consubstantial with love, and the death of the body, which is a consequence of sin, should not be put on the same plane. It is important to note the ambiguity of the word "death," an ambiguity which must be due to the fact that it expresses two distinct New Testament concepts: that of the improperly called death of the body, which should really be called death of man and which refers to the separation of soul and body, with the consequent destruction of the latter; and the concept of eternal death, or damnation, which is what the texts see as real death. But, with or without the death of the body, the lover is always ready to give his life to the loved one.

the last stanza of the *Ascent of Mount Carmel* very carefully, it is difficult to avoid the double impression that it could only have been composed at the moment of death... or for the moment of death, and that that is the only context in which it makes sense.

Hence the bride in the *Song* feels overwhelmed by love right up to the moment of death by the love which ravishes her, on the one hand, and because that love has not yet attained its perfection, on the other:

> *Sustain me with raisins,*
> *refresh me with apples,*
> *for I am sick with love.*[8]

The bride feels that she is dying of love because love tends towards death insofar as it tends to its own perfection or consummation. Therefore *dying of love* —an expression that should not be thought of in purely metaphorical sense— is the only kind of death that makes sense for man, since he has been created for nothing other than love. In his farewell speech on the night of the Last Supper, Jesus refers rather to his *departure* than to his death. But the disciples cannot follow Him now, the reason being that their love has not yet matured. Peter —who with good sense has perceived somehow that it is the surrendering of one's own life which is at stake here—, in his presumption, thinks that he is able to go that far; Jesus hurries to open his eyes and to make him understand the hard reality: *Simon Peter said to Him, "Lord, where are you going?" Jesus answered, "Where I am going you cannot follow me now; but you shall follow afterward." Peter said to Him, "Lord, why cannot I follow you now? I will lay down my life for you." Jesus answered,*

---

[8] Sg 2:5.

"Will you lay down your life for me? Truly, truly, I say to you, the cock will not crow, till you have denied me three times."[9]

> *Should you see me again*
> *yonder in the valley, where the blackbird sings,*
> *do not say that you love me,*
> *for, upon hearing it, I may die,*
> *were you ever to repeat it.*[10]

Turned in this way into the consummation of love and of a life of love, death becomes an offering made with absolute freedom. For, since love is essentially freedom, it is also the necessary condition for any kind of true freedom (2 Cor 3:17). Therefore, only when death means an act of perfect love can it be accepted in the most complete freedom: *The Father loves me, because I lay down my life, that I may take it again. No one takes it from me, but I lay it down of my own accord. I have power to lay it down, and I have power to take it again.*[11] Man's death becomes free, and it even results in a gain (Phil 1:21), precisely to the extent —and only to the extent— that it is an expression of love. In this way, through the action and grace of love, sin and death are at last destroyed forever: *Death is swallowed up in victory. O death, where is thy victory? O death,*

---

[9] Jn 13: 36–38.

[10] In the original:

> *Si de nuevo me vieres*
> *allá en el valle, donde canta el mirlo,*
> *no digas que me quieres,*
> *no muera yo al oirlo*
> *si acaso tú volvieras a decirlo.*

[11] Jn 10: 17–18. Cf. vv. 11 and 15.

where is thy sting?[12] However, what is involved here is no mere destruction of death. For what is really incredible, what far exceeds anything human imagination could devise, is the fact that death is transformed into a principle of life and a love–offering in freedom: the amazing thing, too wonderful for words, that comes across from the texts is that death has not only been destroyed: it has been totally *swallowed up in victory...!*

This explains how man in love with God can face death with serenity and even desire death, *dying because he does not die*, in the well–known phrase of St Teresa. Once the fear that death caused has been destroyed by the power of love (Heb 2: 14–15),[13] the bride can face death with eagerness and also with nostalgia:

> *But how, O life, can you go on living,*
> *since your life is not where you are,*
> *and since the arrows which you receive*
> *from the conceptions of the Beloved formed*
> $\qquad\qquad\qquad\qquad\qquad$ *within you*
> *they deal you death?*[14]

That is how St John of the Cross put it in his *Spiritual Canticle*. St Paul, for his part, writing to the Philippians says: *I am*

---

[12]1 Cor 15: 54–55. Cf. also 2 Tim 1:10.

[13]Cf. 1 Jn 4:18.

[14]In the original:

> *Mas ¿cómo perseveras,*
> *¡oh vida!, no viviendo donde vives*
> *y haciendo porque mueras*
> *las flechas que recibes*
> *de lo que del Amado en ti concibes?*

hard pressed between the two. My desire is to depart and be with Christ, for that is far better...[15] The out–dated and false existentialist ideologies were, however, correct, though in a way very different from what they would have thought, when they spoke of man as a being–for–death. The truth is that man has been called to share in a death which, far from meaning the end of everything, is in fact the climax or perfection of love and the beginning of real life: *Do you not know that all of us who have been baptized into Christ Jesus were baptized into his death? We were buried therefore with Him by baptism into death, so that as Christ was raised from the dead by the glory of the Father, we too might walk in newness of life.*[16] So, only from this perspective is one able to conquer the fear of death, and only in this way can one come to see death as something beautiful: *Precious in the sight of the Lord is the death of his saints.*[17] Thanks to this, as it has been already said, the Christian reaches the end of his life by making his own a death which is consummation, rather than the end of everything: *I have fought the good fight, I have finished the race, I have kept the faith. Henceforth there is laid up for me the crown of righteousness, which the Lord, the righteous judge, will award to me on that Day, and not only to me but also to all who have loved his appearing.*[18] The only meaning death has for the bride in love is the long–awaited arrival of the Bridegroom; she will greet Him with shouts of joy, even if his coming happens at the dark midnight hours brought about by her bodily agony: *At midnight there was a cry, "Behold, the bridegroom! Come out to meet him!"*[19] The Bridegroom, awaited for a long time with anxious

---

[15] Phil 1:23.
[16] Rom 6: 3–4.
[17] Ps 116:15.
[18] 2 Tim 4: 7–8.
[19] Mt 25:6.

vigilance and yearning, arrives at last. No one should be surprised at the bride's impatience urging him to hurry, to come to her and be with her before the night descends:

> *Make haste, my beloved,*
> *and be like a gazelle, or a young stag*
> *upon the mountains of spices.*[20]

....

> *Until the day breathes*
> *and the shadows flee,*
> *turn, my beloved, be like a gazelle,*
> *or a young stag*
> *on the mountains of the covenant.*[21]

Nor should he be surprised at her great impatience to be with her Bridegroom, to be as close to Him as possible:

> *Set me as a seal upon your heart,*
> *as a seal upon your arm.*[22]

But the most profound meaning of the love–struggle has to do not so much with the amount —greater or lesser— one gives as with giving all: this can be clearly seen from New Testament revelation taken as a whole. Our Lord says it very emphatically, for example, in the account of the poor widow's offering in the temple: *Truly, I tell you, this poor widow has put in more than all of them; for they*

---

[20] Sg 8:14.
[21] Sg 2:17.
[22] Sg 8:6.

*all contributed out of their abundance, but she out of her poverty put in all the living that she had.*²³ These last words: *all the living that she had* confirm that the loving gift of everything refers to his own life which the lover gives up: *Greater love has no man than this, that a man lays down his life...*²⁴

However, an important point needs to be made here: *the loving gift the lover makes of his own life refers more to the life of the loved one than to his own.* For the true life of the lover is that of the loved one, insofar as this is what truly constitutes *his life* —the life of the lover—, as the Apostle tells us: *For you have died, and your life is hidden with Christ in God. When Christ Who is our life appears, then you also will appear with Him in glory.*²⁵ The statement that the life of the Christian is hid (or lost) in Christ is a clear reference to the interchange of lives that love makes possible. If a person has truly been in love then it is a fact that he has, a long time ago, already given his life to the loved one: *He who eats my flesh and drinks my blood abides in me, and I in him. As the living Father sent me, and I live because of the Father, so he who eats me will live because of me.*²⁶ So, since one cannot give what one has not got, we need to bear in mind also that the only thing which the lover possesses, his very life in fact, is the actual person of the loved one. This is something which necessarily follows from the

---

²³Lk 21: 3–4.

²⁴Jn 15:13. The Gospel passages which speak about self–surrender, self–denial and losing one's life for love's sake, clearly refer to the giver's surrender of absolutely everything, including that which is most precious and intimate. If they speak of *giving* or *losing* one's life, we can take it that that is because the gift of life is the one which man most values and that which epitomizes and includes everything else.

²⁵Col 3: 3–4.

²⁶Jn 6: 56–57.

marvellous interchange that love, with its demand of absolute reciprocity, imposes on the lovers. Love, as it has been said repeatedly, and as one can see from the parable of the talents (Mt 25: 14–30),[27] *not only implies the giving up of all that is one's own, but also the giving up of what one receives in exchange*: which means that it is equivalent to the surrendering of absolutely everything one has. If that were not the case, love would be reduced to a mere interchange of things, whereby each would acquire what the other had, so that really things would end up as they began. *All that the Father has is mine*,[28] said the Lord. And this should be understood as applying in a double sense: because the Father has given them to the Son (and therefore they are now his) and because the Son has in his turn given them to the Father (as he could do, because they were his). Bearing in mind also that the readiness to give more than one actually possesses (a feature of perfect love) acquires special relevance when what one receives is of greater value than what one gives away. This is precisely what happens to man in divine–human love: he always gets more than he gives. However, due to the fact that *God's gift is authentic and real*, and that man therefore makes his own what he receives, man is enriched in such a way that he can in his turn offer God's heart and the infinite Love which has been made over to him. Only when Christ becomes truly *his life*,[29] does the Christian attain the possibility of offering God a wonderful gift of infinite value. At the apex of perfect love, where everything is received at the same time as everything is surrendered, no one owes anyone anything once what is possessed belongs to the lovers equally. Each of the lovers

---

[27] *Master, you have delivered to me five talents; here I have made five talents more*, one of the servants says.

[28] Jn 16:15.

[29] Cf. Gal 2:20.

gives the other everything that is his and also what he receives from the other: one heart and one soul (Acts 4:32). That is when man is truly a *partner* of God.

In the relationship of divine–human love, the first thing the creature surrenders is himself, as lover; and it is only later that he has the possibility of giving the Loved One to the Loved One Himself, as the most precious of his treasures. In the case of God, on the other hand, the giving of existence and grace is what comes first, to be followed by his generous self–offering to man in loving intimacy and equality. However, because it is a veritable contest of love, everything happens as if each of the lovers were fighting to give himself and to be the first to do so. That is why the bride says:

> *My Lover, I have walked*
> *upon the path in your orchard of lemon*
> *blossoms,*
> *and then I hid myself*
> *behind the lemon tree*
> *to see if I could kiss you first.*[30]

To which the Bridegroom, more in love with his bride than ever and completely determined, as always, to take no defeat at the hands of his bride, immediately replies:

---

[30]In the original:

> *Amado, he recorrido*
> *de tu huerto de azahares el sendero,*
> *y, luego, me he escondido*
> *detrás del limonero*
> *para poder besarte yo primero.*

The self–surrender of the bride to the Bridegroom 145

> *Beloved, I have searched*
> *for the path in my orchard of lemon blossoms,*
> *and then I waited for you*
> *behind the lemon tree*
> *to see if I found you first.*[31]

But the bride will eventually admit that she is defeated. She does so joyfully, of course, because it is really adorable that God should be God. She very well knows that the entire initiative lies with the Bridegroom: *We love, because he first loved us.*[32] Therefore, and bearing in mind the possibility of not being true to the gift she has received, she says to the Bridegroom:

> *Tell me then, sweetheart,*
> *where will you lead your flock to graze,*
> *where will you rest it at noon?*
> *That I may no more wander like a vagabond*
> *beside the flocks of your companions.*[33]

The bride wishes to know with all certainty where the Bridegroom is: where he leads his flock to graze, where he rests at noon... She does not want to expose herself to a dangerous wandering here

---

[31] In the original:

> *Amada, yo he buscado*
> *de mi huerto de azahares el sendero,*
> *y, luego, te he esperado*
> *detrás del limonero*
> *a ver si te encontraba yo primero.*

[32] 1 Jn 4:19.
[33] Sg 1:7.

and there which would probably end in her getting lost. Or to put it in a poetic way:

> *If I should flee from your side*
> *search for me again, friend,*
> *and, when you have found me,*
> *take me back to the path,*
> *there where you first met with me.*[34]

The Virgin Mary, mother and model of the Church, experienced these feelings at the foot of the cross more than any other believer ever has. Since no one has ever shared in as elevated a degree as she in the death of her Son, the whole question of her earthly death ceases to have any relevance. It is at the foot of the cross that she truly dies, accepting the will of the Father and offering her Son's life, which is her own. This thereby reveals the deepest meaning of Simeon's prophecy (Lk 2:35): the apparently meaningless reference to a sword that will pierce her soul cannot but be to a painful and terrible death, as distant from bodily death as the distance between piercing the body and piercing the soul with a sword.

It is possible that this aspect of the mystery of love, one that is not always sufficiently stressed, may make it easier to solve certain aporias and difficulties. One often tends to think, for example, that the good servants referred to in the parable of the talents were

---

[34] In the original:

> *Si huyera de tu lado*
> *búscame tú de nuevo, compañero,*
> *y, luego de encontrado,*
> *retórname al sendero,*
> *allí donde me hallaste tú primero.*

concerned only about being careful to give back what they had received; whereas the truth is that they gave back double: the five talents received as well as the five gained; the two received as well as the two gained. So man is enabled, by the grace of love, to give God infinitely more than what belongs to him: his own things and what he has received from God in the form of a love–gift.[35] Love enables man to give God something which he could never have owned or given, since it has an infinite value, namely, God Himself, Who now belongs to man because God has given Himself to man with all his love. No shadow now survives of that condition of subordination and inequality which some detected, not without certain worry, in the divine–human love–relationship.

Modern man, who tends to be always so anxious to obtain his rights, has completely forgotten that it is much better to lose them altogether, just as he has forgotten our Lord's words about it being much better to give than to receive, or about the poor being the only ones who are truly blessed or happy. But it is true that love, which leads one to despoil oneself of one's I completely, and which walks hand in hand with absolute poverty, is the only route that can lead man to perfect joy. The old world of God and man has become now the world of man and no one else. The only thing is that man is now a being en route to nothingness, as modern ideologies tell us, and he can find no horizon other than that which he can devise for himself. The Church herself, who like a modern Martha seems

---

[35] This is in no way at odds with the fact that man has received from God everything he possesses. In one way he does have it as truly his own, because when God gives he really does transfer ownership; and therefore the servant could have kept and *buried* it for himself, as the wicked servant in the parable did in fact. But now he gives up freely and voluntarily, out of love, that which belongs to him and that which, being proper and intimate to God, has been given him through God's love for him.

to be too concerned with earthly things, has a certain difficulty in recalling and savoring the things *quæ sursum sunt*. It is possible therefore that, given the anguish of the present time, the moment has come to revive the dialogue between the Bridegroom and the bride and sing again the love songs of the past, the moment when the bride tells the Bridegroom once again:

> *While strolling around the meadows*
> *your eyes met my eyes;*
> *they looked at each other in silence,*
> *and they wounded each other*
> *with the mutual wound of love they caused.*
>
> *The sun was peering*
> *and wakening the flowers with a kiss;*
> *yet, noticing I was listening to you*
> *in sweet rapture,*
> *he decided to delay his rising more.*[36]

---

[36] In the original:

> *Pasando por los prados,*
> *tus ojos con los míos se encontraron;*
> *miráronse callados,*
> *y heridos se quedaron*
> *en la llaga de amor que se causaron.*
>
> *El sol que se asomaba*
> *despertaba las flores con un beso;*
> *y, al ver que te escuchaba*
> *con un suave embeleso,*
> *decidió demorarse más por eso.*

The self–surrender of the bride to the Bridegroom 149

> *I will hasten*
> *there where your mouth may ask me;*
> *there where, proud,*
> *the eagle nests;*
> *there where all things have forgotten us:*
>
> *my Lover, to the misty*
> *slopes of craggy mountains,*
> *with foxes dens*
> *and silver peaks*
> *in the silence of forgotten snows...*[37]

Perhaps the beginning of a new age is approaching for the world. An age in which people will rediscover —or remember once more— that the loss of everything is the greatest gain, and that the frantic search for rights does not mean very much. There is more joy in giving than in receiving. Who has a right to be loved? Since when has love resorted to imposing conditions? Does love not draw nourishment from freedom at its purest? Not even the Supreme Good constrains the creature to love Him, because love loves because it wants to, and it is love only to the extent that it is also

---

[37] In the original:

> *Iréme presurosa*
> *allí donde tu boca me lo pida;*
> *allí donde, orgullosa,*
> *el águila se anida;*
> *allí donde ya todo nos olvida:*
>
> *Amado, a las brumosas*
> *laderas de montañas escarpadas,*
> *con cuevas de raposas*
> *y simas plateadas*
> *en silencio de nieves olvidadas...*

freedom. If God did not give man his Love *because he chose to*, what then would he have given him? In the new Age of the world the Church will once again speak of love. And once again we shall see saints, poets, dreamers, people forgetful of self, the poor and all other kinds of true lovers. It will be an Age in which men, tired of speaking among themselves and with themselves, will once again turn to speak to God. Life will have found its meaning, and the world will at last remember why it was created. Then the bride will hear once more the voice of the Bridegroom, and she will again take up with Him her dialogue of love. Meanwhile, all other created things, rejoicing, yet at the same time envious, will sing a canticle which to some will sound like a loving complaint and to others a hymn of praise:

> *With their silent talk*
> *in the tranquil night, the stars*
> *complained to my Lover:*
> *He willed to make them fair,*
> *but never out of love to die for them.*[38]

---

[38] In the original:

> *En el hablar callado*
> *de la noche serena, las estrellas*
> *quejáronse al Amado:*
> *que quiso hacerlas bellas,*
> *pero nunca de amor morir por ellas.*

Second Part

"Your love is better than wine"

(Sg 1:2b)

CHAPTER I

THE INTOXICATION OF LOVE

With a more than joyful exclamation the bride proclaims that her relationship with the Bridegroom is like an intoxication of love, only more intense and heady than that caused by wine:

Your love is better than wine...

This intoxication is a rapture caused by great joy and enthusiasm which can develop into a paroxysm, quite capable of taking a person out of himself. It is a phenomenon which seems to have something to do either with madness or at least with those kinds of madness which cause in man a frenzy of joy and an optimistic view of life.

It is interesting that love can cause feelings akin to intoxication, and sometimes also to madness, by drawing man out of his enclosed inwardness, placing him as it were out of himself, and giving him an exultant view of reality.[1] This already brings us to the question

---

[1] Cf. Acts 2: 12–16.

of checking whether these feelings really are anomalous or whether it might not be more correct to say that the anomaly consists in not feeling like this. It is true, though, that everyone seems to be agreed that there is such a thing as a *madness of love*, which in fact is utter normality;[2] indeed, there are those who say that if love does not make one drunk then it is not fully love.

The views of people in all ages support the idea that love is a feeling of inebriation to the point of exultation, a feeling which really can take a human being *outside of himself*[3] and raise him to incredible heights, through a powerful and mysterious dynamic which gives him a new vitality. The Bible, too, always sees love as essentially a real superabundance: *Before the feast of the Passover, when Jesus knew that his hour had come to depart out of this world to the Father, having loved his own who were in the world, "he loved them to the end."*[4] Regarding the Spirit we are told that He is always given *without measure* (Jn 3:34). And perhaps this is why love is so often associated with the ideas of wine and intoxication, as the Bridegroom Himself tells the bride in the *Song*:

---

[2] According to some, this is one of the many tricks of language. In the whole question of love, this *madness of love* should be regarded as a normal state, and a loving relationship which did not cause intoxication should really be described as anomalous.

[3] There is an interesting connexion between the concept of someone *being mesmerized* into himself, which always includes ideas of stupor, of innervation, and being closed in on oneself, and the New Testament texts which refer to those people who, due to their failure to understand what love is all about, seek their own life and then lose it. Intoxication, on the contrary, takes man *out of himself*. So there seems to be a connexion between selfishness and being mesmerized into oneself, on the one hand, and intoxication and love, on the other.

[4] Jn 13:1.

> *How much better is your love than wine.*[5]
>
> . . . .
>
> *I come to my garden, my sister, my bride,*
> *I gather my myrrh with my spice,*
> *I eat my honeycomb with my honey,*
> *I drink my wine with my milk.*
> *Eat, O friends, and drink:*
> *drink deeply, O lovers.*[6]

And indeed our Lord Himself refers to wine when he talks about the definitive banquet which will take place in the Kingdom: *I tell you I shall not drink again of this fruit of the vine until that day when I drink it new with you in my Father's kingdom.*[7]

One can therefore rightly say that to speak of a love that is abundant and most fruitful, something which allows of no measurement because it reaches "to the end," is the same thing as simply speaking of love. So, love is always superabundant, exultant and intoxicating. It admits of no measures or deadlines[8] nor of any possibility of anything being kept back for oneself.[9] In this sense the *intoxication of love* is a metaphor–reality as rich in meaning as that of the *death of love*. And there is the interesting point, apropos of metaphors, that something happens in divine–human love which, in some way, is contrary to what happens in purely human love: whereas in the latter case the metaphors usually go beyond reality, in the former

---

[5] Sg 4:10.
[6] Sg 5:1.
[7] Mt 26:29.
[8] Cf. Lk 6:38; 1 Cor 13:8.
[9] Cf. Mk 10:21; Lk 21: 1–4.

they always fall short of what they try to express. Particularly sublime are St John of the Cross' stanzas in his *Spiritual Canticle* which allude to the intoxication of love:

> *Following your footprints,*
> *the maidens run along the way*
> *touched by the spark,*
> *and by the taste of your spiced wine,*
> *flows forth the Divine balsam.*
>
> *In the inner cellar,*
> *of my Beloved have I drunk, and, when*
>   *I went forth*
> *over all this meadow,*
> *then I knew naught,*
> *and lost the flock which I used to follow.*[10]

In the first of these stanzas three images appear of elements which play a part in producing an abundance and exaltation of love: the spark, spiced wine and a divine balm. They all conspire to stir up the young maidens who follow the path in the footsteps of the

---

[10] In the original:

> *A zaga de tu huella*
> *las jóvenes discurren al camino*
> *al toque de centella*
> *al adobado vino;*
> *emisiones de bálsamo divino.*
> *En la interior bodega*
> *de mi Amado bebí, y cuando salía*
> *por toda aquesta vega*
> *ya cosa no sabía*
> *y el ganado perdí que antes seguía.*

Bridegroom. It seems as though the poet wanted to describe the manner (eager, yet vacillating) in which virgins go in search of the Bridegroom: love has made them drunk, dazed, as it were, by the intoxication that love has brought about in them.

The second stanza is even more expressive, in the sense that it speaks clearly of an intoxication which in this case has also been caused by love. The bride has been drinking in the secret cellar of the Beloved to such an extent that on leaving it she has no idea what she was doing.

So, love is undoubtedly a form of intoxication, because it gives man a feeling of exaltation and a new degree of vitality which are impossible to measure. This kind of exaltation is accompanied by a feeling of joy —exultation— of parallel intensity which puts man *outside of himself.* In this sense love causes an effect that is the opposite of that of sin, because sin closes a man up inside his I, causing him to be *engrossed in himself* even to the point of denaturalizing him (insofar as the human creature is created to go outside himself and give himself). And so the Apostle says: *None of us lives to himself, and none of us dies to himself. If we live, we live to the Lord, and if we die, we die to the Lord; so then, whether we live or whether we die, we are the Lord's.*[11]

If it is correct, as it seems to be, that man is made to live in a state of constant *exaltation* and exultation, the only way to describe coldness of soul or lukewarmness is as an anomaly, with much more serious and dangerous consequences than those of a mere psychopathy: *I know your works: you are neither cold nor hot. Would that you were cold or hot! So, because you are lukewarm, and neither*

---

[11] Rom 14: 7–8.

cold nor hot, I will spew you out of my mouth...[12] But I have this against you, that you have abandoned the love you had at first.[13]

Our Lord, on the contrary, always revealed Himself to have sufficiently passionate soul to be able to speak very strongly, sometimes in a way that might seem excessively violent: *I came to cast fire upon the earth; and would that it were already kindled! I have a baptism to be baptized with; and how I am constrained until it is accomplished! Do you think that I have come to give peace on earth? No, I tell you, but rather division...*[14] *If any one thirst, let him come to me and drink...*[15] John the Baptist, for his part, contrasts his mission, which is that of a mere precursor, preparing the way and doing penance (baptism of water) with that of the Messiah which, on the contrary, will set everyone aflame with the fire of the Spirit (baptism of fire): *I baptize you with water for repentance, but he who is coming after me is mightier than I, whose sandals I am not worthy to carry; he will baptize you with the Holy Spirit and with fire.*[16]

In contemporary society, alcohol, sex and drugs are among the substitutes people use in a vain attempt to quell the need they feel for *exaltation* and a passionate joy —things they miss so much that they feel tormented. The problem lies in the fact that this kind of exaltation and intoxication, which is caused and nourished in man by a love for which he has been created, can only be satisfied by the very thing that causes it in the first place. There is a certain parallel here with the phenomenon observed by biologists whereby laboratory rats subjected to vitamin–ration experiments desperately

---

[12] Rev 3: 15–16.
[13] Rev 2:4.
[14] Lk 12: 49–51.
[15] Jn 7:37.
[16] Mt 3:11.

search their excrement for substances held back from them which they need for their survival.

The problem has grown worse in recent times, due to the fact that Church catechesis has dropped the subject of the *ardour of charity*. No one can deny that the love of God and the love for God have been relegated to a more than modest secondary place in preaching (when they have not disappeared from it completely). In a parallel way, love for one's neighbour has had to yield its place to a purely natural concern for others. However much this concern is wrapped up in lots of pompous terminology —commitment to the underprivileged, the Church of the third world, preferential options for the poor, solidarity with the working classes and the oppressed, incarnation with the world—, it finds it very difficult to disguise its dependence on purely human ideologies and even ideologies which are quite opposed to any type of transcendence. Once again the mistake has been made of forgetting that there can be no genuine concern for others unless one first has a genuine concern for God. Hence the distressing feeling that this current style of preaching so often causes in those who hear it, the feeling that this cliche is being abused.[17] In reality, the fact that the theme of Love has disappeared from Church catechetical programs is one of the most noteworthy phenomena of modern times, paralleled only by the substitution of social injustice for the theme of sin, or the transformation of

---

[17] When a kind of fear of the world leads a person to capitulate, stressing, for example, that *theology is also anthropology*, the ground is being prepared for the argument that theology is anthropology. And, although probably what is meant is that theology, being the science of the Godhead, is also concerned with man *qua* creature called to have a special relationship with his Creator, it is still true that theology and anthropology are distinct sciences (as genuine anthropologists would no doubt firmly hold). The only certain thing here is that man, and the science of man, depend entirely on God and on the science of God. It is difficult to avoid the impression that the background to all these ideas is really Rahnerian idealism.

eschatology into a mere concern for building up the earthly city. The second half of the twentieth century has witnessed the appearance of a *bland* sort of Catholicism,[18] with very little religious content, to become eventually a kind of welfare Program, more suited to a World Organization for the Development and Advancement of Peoples. It is easy to see that religion is turning into sociology.

But the point has already been made that man cannot live without love or without the feeling of intoxication that love causes. It may well be that this absence has brought about the appearance, in contemporary Catholicism, of a host of *charismatic* Movements which are in a way reminiscent of the phenomenon of the *Spirituals* in the high Middle Ages and of the illuminati of Joachim de Fiore. Their common denominator is based, though this is not expressly said, on the idea that the world has entered another new Age of the Spirit. And, as always happens in the background of historical phenomena, these Movements also arise in an attempt to answer a pressing need. Once Catholicism was emptied of the fire of the Spirit, to become a kind of socio–political World Organization for Welfare and Advancement, the vacuum just had to be filled; the ever increasing religious hunger experienced by a desacralized society had to be satisfied. The situation certainly continues to be grave. Whether Movements of this sort will or will not achieve what they set out to do raises dangerous questions for Catholicism at the start of the twenty–first century. It does not seem an exaggeration to suggest that a new failure would lead to the appearance of an age of greater materialism and virtually total unbelief. But what makes this subject seem extremely delicate is the fact (not sufficiently real-

---

[18]In Protestantism, dechristianization began to set in much earlier and the situation is much more serious, except in certain confined sectors in which a more intense faith seems to be practiced than is the case in Catholicism in general.

ized) that the legitimation of these renewal Movements poses grave problems, which it is not appropriate for us to deal with here. The definitive answer to this whole question cannot be found unless one manages to develop a clear, systematic, and healthy *charismatic theology* which is truly Catholic and free from Protestant infiltration. If desired, some examples might be given, just to mention them, in passing as it were: the counterposing of *law* and *freedom*, proposed by those who claim a certain kind of freedom promoted by the action of the Spirit, apparently not always well understood and whose definitive solution is dependent on clear rulings of the Magisterium; the authentication of the Spirit by clear identification, and definition, of the way charisms work, in order to make it possible to distinguish them from mere naturally provoked psychological phenomena; the connection between love and charisms (or between charity and charisms): although St Paul seemed to provide the final answer on this, new ambiguities have arisen which need to be addressed. To all this should be added the urgent need to clarify the thinking of these Movements on such subjects as the priesthood (both the ministerial priesthood and that of the faithful); the laity and its role in the Christian Community; the sacraments (specifically the Eucharist); the relationships between the ordinary faithful and the Hierarchy; the Magisterium and its proper normative role and scope vis-à-vis the freedom supposedly conferred by the Spirit... and so on and so forth —quite a long list of things.

Perhaps one day people will see the need to return to the original springs of pure water. Therefore, returning to the central theme of this chapter (the intoxication of love), it is encouraging to note that the bride feels herself in love because of the graces and beauty of the Bridegroom —hence her shout of enthusiasm and the words she addresses to Him: *Your love is better than wine!* The Bridegroom's love is more intoxicating and unnerving than the fruit of the vine because the Bridegroom is quite wonderful and sublime. Here is where one can see particularly clearly both the poverty of a totally insufficient language and the bride's frustration at not being able to describe the Bridegroom. It is not so very difficult to describe man's feelings of astonishment at the sight of beauty, but it is almost impossible to paint the features of beauty itself. The bride does the best she can with metaphors —perhaps one of the main tools of the poet— in her effort to describe the Bridegroom with some degree of accuracy. Indeed, this is the reason why the *Song* is written in poetry. It is a sacred poem, but still a poem:

> *How beautiful you are, my beloved, Truly lovely!*[19]
>
> ....
>
> *As an apple tree among the trees of the wood,*
> *So is my beloved among young men.*[20]
>
> ....
>
> *My beloved is all radiant and ruddy,*
> *distinguished among ten thousand.*
> *His head is the finest gold;*
> *his locks are wavy,*
> *black like a raven.*
> *His eyes are like doves*
> *beside springs of water...*[21]

The bride uses the language of poetry because poetry is the tool the human being employs when the ineffable has to be expressed.

---

[19] Sg 1:16.
[20] Sg 2:3.
[21] Sg 5: 10–12.

It is, as it were, a last resort to which one must go to make up in some way for the inadequacy of ordinary language. And, although poetry too falls far short of achieving its objective, it is still a great advance and therefore fully justified. In fact, the inadequacy referred to here is due not so much to words and concepts as to human nature itself. Man's inability to grasp the totality of Goodness and Beauty (and therefore to speak about them, both to himself and to others) is nothing but an aspect of his inability fully to understand the infinity of Being. However, poetry is not just a resort. For, just as it is said that philosophy was born of man's sense of *wonder* and awe in the face of the reality of being, one can also say that poetry arose out of a similar feeling of wonderment in the face of goodness and beauty. However, one should add that in the case of poetry the sense of *wonder* should be taken in its highest degree of sublimity and intensity. For there is here something much more than a simple sense of awe. The truth is that poetry has quite a lot to do with a reality —love— which the bride confesses in the *Song* to have caused her a much more intense feeling of intoxication and joy than that caused by wine. This explosion of joy and enthusiasm is a feeling powerful enough to take a man out of himself, far surpassing the state of intoxication and even, in a way, madness. The madness of love is not in any way a mere metaphor —particularly so when it is caused, as in this case, not by an encounter with the beauty and goodness of things but by a certain apprehension of supreme Goodness and Beauty.

The apparently simple question the choir of the *Song* puts to the bride is one of the most difficult of all questions ever put to man over the entire course of history. It concerns nothing less than the question of *what* God is and *what he is like*. So much so that a whole line of thought running especially from Denis to St Thomas

Aquinas has taken it for granted that the only way an answer can be found is by way of negation:

> *What is your beloved more than another beloved,*
> *O fairest of women?*
> *What is your beloved more than another beloved,*
> *that you thus adjure us?*[22]
>
> . . . .
>
> *Which way did your lover turn*
> *so that we can help you seek him?*[23]

But, as is has been said, one can also try to speak of the Bridegroom by resorting to poetry —prescinding for the moment from philosophical method, such as the use of the way of negation, and taking instead an indirect route: the language that describes beauty. St John of the Cross, in his *Spiritual Canticle*, tries to use poetry to speak of the Beloved, just as the *Song* does:

> *Scattering a thousand gifts,*
> *he passed through these woods in haste,*
> *glancing around as he went,*
> *clothing them with the beauty*
> *that reflected from his face.*[24]

---

[22]Sg 5:9.

[23]Sg 6:1.

[24]In the original:

> *Mil gracias derramando*
> *pasó por estos sotos con presura*
> *y, yéndolos mirando,*
> *con sola su figura*
> *vestidos los dejó de su hermosura.*

> *The creatures all around me*
> *speak of your thousand gifts,*
> *yet they wound me even more.*
> *Something that they stammer*
> *leaves me dying.*
>
> *Reveal your presence,*
> *and may my seeing your beauty be my death,*
> *for nothing can cure*
> *the pain of love*
> *but the presence and image of the lover!*[25]

One can see that, unlike the *Song*, which tries to describe the Bridegroom by using metaphors (5: 10–16), St John of the Cross is content, rather, to allude more to the figure of the Lover and to his own yearning to contemplate him. It is as if he had given up an attempt which he knew in advance was impossible and would only result in stuttering:

---

[25]In the original:

> *Y todos cuantos vagan*
> *de ti me van mil gracias refiriendo*
> *y todos más me llagan*
> *y déjame muriendo*
> *un no sé qué que quedan balbuciendo.*
>
> *¡Descubre tu presencia,*
> *y m teme tu vista y hermosura;*
> *mira que la dolencia*
> *de amor, que no se cura*
> *sino con la presencia y la figura!*

> *...something that they stammer*
> *leaves me dying.*
>
> *O crystal spring,*
> *would that on your silvery surface*
> *you were suddenly to form*
> *those eyes for which I pine*
> *and which I carry graven on my soul!*
>
> *Rejoice, my Love, with me,*
> *and let us go to behold in your beauty*
> >> *ourselves reflected:*
> *by mountain and by hill,*
> *where the pure water runs,*
> *we will enter deeper in the thicket.*[26]

Although theological language is more exact and more accurate, the language of poetry, on the other hand, evokes feelings which no science can achieve that begins with a principle which in every other respect is quite on the mark: *Si intelligis non est Deus.*

---

[26] In the original:

> *...y déjame muriendo*
> *un no sé qué que quedan balbuciendo.*
> *¡Oh cristalina fuente,*
> *si en esos tus semblantes plateados*
> *formases de repente*
> *los ojos deseados*
> *que tengo en mis entrañas dibujados!*
> *Gocémonos, Amado,*
> *y vámonos a ver en tu hermosura*
> *al monte o al collado*
> *do mana el agua pura;*
> *entremos más adentro en la espesura.*

Clearly both forms of talking about God are as necessary as they are complementary and as each is insufficient each on its own. The truth of the matter is that the philosopher has nothing to fear from the poet, nor the poet from the philosopher. True philosophy and true poetry, like the justice and peace the psalmist speaks about, always end up at the same point greeting each other with the kiss of friendship. Thus, genuine poetry always ends up talking about God, for the object of poetry is Beauty —and just as surely theology cannot survive without using a transcendental which, like all transcendentals, in the last analysis is identical with God.[27]

Yet, whether one uses philosophy/theology or does without it, it is undeniable that if anyone were to dare speak of God without allowing himself to be led by the hand of the Spirit —and without, therefore, the fire of true Love—, he would be embarking on a pretty risky enterprise. Only *the Spirit searches everything, even the depths of God.*[28] And the Spirit, Who is as it were the heart of a God Who is Love, is for that very reason pure Love. It is not for nothing that the first fruit of the Holy Spirit is charity (Gal 5:22).[29]

Hence the importance of not confusing the function of charity with that of charisms. St Paul makes a clear and careful distinction between the two (1 Cor 12:28–14:36), putting special stress on both the primacy of charity and the uselessness of charisms when they are not imbued with charity. And yet the clarity of this centuries–old

---

[27] Cf. Hans Urs von Balthasar's complaints in this regard in *The Glory and the Cross*, where he tries to systematize all theology from the point of view of aesthetics. The fact that poetry has nothing to do with scientific language does not mean it has nothing to do with truth. Although poetic truth has its own language, its object is none other than being, insofar as it is beautiful: the reality of beauty *and the beauty of reality*.

[28] 1 Cor 2:10.

[29] Cf. 2 Cor 6:6; 1 Tim 4:12.

teaching has not been able to prevent the appearance, in the bosom of modern Catholicism, of two tendencies which put at risk both the absolute primacy of love and its authentic and true meaning. One can detect here that the spirit of confusion is once more stalking the true believers.

The first tendency consists in moving the accent from charity to justice. Starting from the gratuitous assumption that these two virtues are opposed to one another, and that the Christian concept of charity is even more antiquated than it is obsolete, they have tried to forget that the true concept of Christian charity has always necessarily included that of justice.[30] But to assume that charity can be separated from justice is an absurdity similar to thinking that true justice can ever exist without love.[31] Worthy of note are certain so–called modern pastoral programs of *commitment* and of *options for the poor* and the underprivileged which have subtly replaced the proclamation of the *new commandment* and which often seem to inspire feelings of aggression. The intoxication of love has been supplanted, both in pastoral catechesis and in the life of many Christians, by a feeling of hatred which is justified in turn, it is argued, by claims of social justice and by the fact that charity is no longer effective. Now the Church is less an ἐκκλεσία of men and women who love one another, and more an Organization devoted to asserting rights and one which does not even exclude recourse to violence.

---

[30] Apropos of a text of St Augustine, Gilson says that *the so–called modern ideal of justice has nothing to do with a heightened form of justice but rather with a debased form of charity.* Étienne Gilson, Introduction a l'Étude de Saint Augustin, Vrin, Paris, 1982, p. 179.

[31] In the simplicity of the divine essence, charity and justice merge into one and the same thing; but in man, charity includes justice while at the same time surpassing it. Whereas justice seeks equality for the other, *giving him what is his due*, charity desires, for the other, this *and also everything else*.

The intoxication of love 171

The second tendency, much less frightening but quite as dangerous as the first, opts instead for putting the emphasis on charisms and for centering worship around the Spirit. This modern worship in some way echoes the medieval dreams of those who proposed a new Age of the Holy Spirit, an age which was going to take the place of the Age of the Son. Those illuminati failed to remember that the only reason why the Holy Spirit is sent to man is to lead him to Jesus Christ, so that then, from Christ, man can find his way to God once and for all. Also they forget the fundamental fact that, after the revelation of God One and Three, any cult offered to the Spirit which is not perfectly centred and framed within an overall Trinitarian context, makes no sense at all: *Our fellowship (communion) is with the Father and with his Son Jesus Christ*, said the Apostle St John.[32]

St Paul, following a doctrinal line which is quite clear in the New Testament, already referred to the possibility that charisms, if not informed by charity, could be of no use whatsoever (1 Cor 13: 1–3). The truth is that the presence of the Spirit can never be authenticated by the presence of charisms, but only by the presence of fruits. This is shown by the fact that our Lord Himself (as St Paul would later do) clearly warns of the danger of certain charisms which, because they have nothing to do with charity, are totally foreign to both the presence and the action of the Spirit: *On that day many*

---

[32] 1 Jn 1:3. Our Lord clearly establishes a direct relationship of his disciples with Himself and with the Father (Mt 10:40; Lk 10:16). It is also important to bear in mind that the strength given by the Spirit has no other purpose than that of bearing witness to Jesus Christ (Acts 1:8). Moreover, the Spirit never speaks for Himself (Jn 16:13) or gives glory to Himself; He speaks of and glorifies only Jesus Christ (Jn 16: 14–15). Genuine worship of the Holy Spirit *centres the way of Christian life entirely on Jesus Christ*, so that it ends at the Father: with Christ, and in Christ, through the Holy Spirit, to the Father.

will say to me, "Lord, Lord, did we not prophesy in your name, and cast out demons in your name, and do many mighty works in your name?" And then will I declare to them, "I never knew you; depart from me, you evil doers."[33] It is interesting that the reply our Lord gives to the users and dealers in charisms who claim their rights is the same as that given the foolish virgins: *Truly, I say to you, I do not know you* (Mt 25:12). If one bears in mind, too, the meaning the Bible usually gives to the verb *to know*, one might arrive at the conclusion that this reply has a lot to do with a clear accusation of a lack of love: *We never knew each other* cannot but mean here, in fact, that we never loved each other, insofar as we were always total strangers and aliens to one another. It would be dangerous to forget that the devil, like the wise men and magi of the Pharaoh (Ex 7:11), is also capable of showing that he has certain charisms and can work signs and wonders.

Everything seems to indicate that the modern fad for charisms is really just another symptom of man's hunger for genuine love. When man feels the need for real food (material or spiritual) he searches desperately for anything that will do in its stead. The overproduction of social doctrine and the excessive socio–political involvements and concerns of many Pastors have left little time or space for speaking about God. This led to the growth of Marxism and of oriental religions in the first instance, and then to the re-awakening of Islamic fundamentalism —all of which is simply one consequence caused by a Christianity that has grown old and allowed its charity to cool. The changing of the accent from charity to justice —as if one could exist without the other, and as if they were even opposed to one another— has led to forgetting all about God; and the doctrine of love has lost its relevance. By choosing to think

---

[33] Mt 7: 22–23.

that it is necessary to be just before being lovers, Christians have forgotten that justice without charity is a mere chimera. They have failed to realize that, whenever one tries to give another person *what is his due* but one does not love him, one ends up thinking that what belongs to another *is nothing but what each person finds it impossible to make his own*. With the result that human life is no longer seen as an intoxication of love: it has become a kind of mad forum for claiming rights to which everyone flocks to make speeches and claim what is his. A frenzy has taken the place of feelings of intoxicated joy. The drug problem, like so many others, is simply a further sign of the frustrating search for some lenitive to fill the vacuum left by the absence of God.

However, the purpose of the good news of the Gospel was nothing other than to proclaim and provide man with perfect joy. And precisely because this good news is the good news of love, the ecstasy of intoxicating joy (which is now consubstantial with man, raised as he is by grace) is intimately linked to love by our Lord Himself: *As the Father has loved me, so have I loved you; abide in my love. If you keep my commandments, you will abide in my love, just as I have kept my Father's commandments and abide in his love. These things I have spoken to you, that my joy may be in you, and that your joy may be full.*[34] So it is not surprising that St Paul should classify joy as the second of the fruits of the Holy Spirit, after charity (Gal 5:22), or that St John should say, in his first letter, that the only reason he wrote it was to share complete joy with his disciples (1 Jn 1:4).

Almost at the very end of his earthly life, our Lord spoke in these terms to his disciples: *I tell you I shall not drink again of this fruit of the vine until that day when I drink it new with you in my Father's*

---

[34] Jn 15: 9–11.

kingdom.³⁵ These words seem to refer to something which had been part of his life up to then and which, after a brief interruption, we will see continued with his disciples in the definitive consummation of the Kingdom. Clearly the delay will not be a long one, and must surely refer only to the days he will spend in the tomb, because really his idea is to be with them always (Mt 28:20) and never to leave them. All this seems to indicate a total continuity between the intoxicating joy which has begun here on earth and that which will be consummated in heaven. Escrivá de Balaguer, the founder of Opus Dei, used to say that *God has reserved the happiness of Heaven for those who have managed to be happy on earth*. Here it is confirmed again that the virtue of hope, on which the Christian lives in this present life, is not in any sense a virtue to do with promises about the future; it is not something alien to joy. The Christian's joy is not something that has been promised for later, while he has to wait resigning himself to his present lot —the old Marxist accusation—: it is *something that he has already been given*, although only by way of a pledge or earnest.³⁶ The view of existence already depicted in the *Song of Songs* is a completely different one. Here can be seen the bride beseeching the Bridegroom to take her with Him and to bring her into his chambers, which is where joy will be consummated. But a carefully reading of the text also makes it clear that she is thinking of something that is happening now, because she makes the point that the quality of the Bridegroom's

---

[35] Mt 26:29.

[36] The possession of perfect joy as pledge or earnest, which results from a similar possession of the Holy Spirit, refers simply to the fact that its consummation and definitive stage will take place in heaven. But this does not mean that the Christian's joy now is superficial, or measurable purely in human terms. The perfect joy of the Christian is a joy in keeping with this present age, but it is a perfect joy.

The intoxication of love 175

love, which bewitches her to such degree, is better than that of wine:[37]

> *Draw me after you, let us make haste.*
> *The king has brought me into his chambers.*
> *We will exult and rejoice in you;*
> *we will extol your love more than wine.*[38]

The perfect happiness caused by intoxicating love will find its definitive culmination in the Kingdom, where the followers of the Lamb, according to the promise made to them (Mt 26:29), will drink with Him the fruit of the vine:

> *If you are heading toward the hillock,*
> *allow me to accompany you, pilgrim,*
> *let us see if he whom I love*
> *gives us of his wine to drink*
> *as we reach the end of the road together.*[39]

But this does not mean that that intoxication has not already begun while we are on our way. For one always makes one's way in this life hand in hand with the Lover:

---

[37] The second half of the verse is in the present tense.
[38] Sg 1:4.
[39] In the original:

> *Si vas hacia el otero*
> *deja que te acompañe, peregrino,*
> *a ver si el que yo quiero*
> *nos da a beber su vino*
> *en acabando juntos el camino.*

*My Beloved, we are walking
through green and tranquil countrysides;
and, while we gaze at each other,
you fill them with flowers:
nards, lemon blossoms, and white lilies.*

*Come near me,
while the North wind blows on the fields.
Leave the flock to find its way,
and whisper to me
if by chance you have been wounded by my love.*

*The voice of my Lover is
like a sweet cooing of doves,
like a rosy dawn
tinged with a thousand hues
when the sun rises on the mountains.*[40]

---

[40]In the original:

*Amado, caminamos
por las campiñas verdes y serenas;
y, mientras nos miramos,
de flores tú las llenas:
de nardos, de jazmines y azucenas.
Acércate a mi lado
mientras el cierzo sopla en el ejido,
y deja ya el ganado,
y cuéntame al oído
si acaso por mi amor estás herido.
Es la voz de la amada
como un arrullo dulce de paloma,
como un alba rosada
que mil colores toma
cuando el sol por los montes ya se asoma.*

> *The voice of my Bridegroom is*
> *like the fleeing wake of a ship:*
> *like the murmuring air,*
> *like a soft whispering,*
> *like the flying of a night fowl.*[41]

---

[41]In the original:

> *Es la voz del Esposo*
> *como la huidiza estela de una nave:*
> *como aire rumoroso,*
> *como susurro suave,*
> *como el vuelo nocturno de algún ave.*

CHAPTER II

CHRISTIAN JOY

Although Chesterton used to say that joy is the greatest secret the Christian has, few people nowadays would dare to give this statement anything more than literary validity. The modern Christian intellectual world does not outrightly deny what Chesterton says (it could not do so), but it certainly does not openly subscribe to it. It rather seems as if this is a subject which definitely belongs to the past; there is no point discussing it nowadays.

Irony apart, any attempt to speak about joy these days would show that one had forgotten that the world is no longer interested in jokes. It is as if life had become much more serious, in every sense of the word. Man's problems today are so many and so great that even the Church feels it should put on a worried look, and it often even adopts pastoral attitudes which some people —exaggerating, obviously— have dared to call *edgy*.

It is worthwhile, however, pointing out that the problems that confront the Church today are not those which some people naively would think. There still are those who think that the main problem facing the Church is the loss of God, with the desacralization of Christianity that this brings in its trail. Yet a considerable part of contemporary theology has striven to emphasize the need to play down ideologies which have a supernatural tinge. If man today is only interested in a God–for–man, this leads him to put the accent more on anthropology than on theology. On the other hand, the *reactionaries* have once again shown that they are incapable of taking on board the new approaches and it is not surprising to find some of them showing a certain lack of seriousness daring to say that an *economic* God is nothing but a *cheapened* God.

Hence the change in tone that one finds over a considerable area of Church catechesis. According to some, the Christian message has found its right channel of expression in a scientific theology, perhaps for the very first time one that is truly suited to man's needs. As these enthusiasts see it, we have seen the last of both the old–fashioned sugary language, with its promises of future blessings in Heaven, and the no less outdated threatening and berating language harping mainly on sin, punishment, and hell. Theology has been rescued from the vague realm of the supernatural —an ethereal world, difficult to grasp—, and Pastoral care (now properly counselled by *human* sciences) has finally been set on grave and serious lines. People have at long last come to realize that, whereas God is really just a debating theme, an object for speculation, man on the other hand is something real, here–and–now, with it all hanging out, in a crucible of real problems and burning issues. And so, just as the first Marxist philosophers saw the need to turn philosophy into political action, so, along the same lines, quite a number of modern theologians have seen the urgency to make theology face real problems at last, although by that they mean problems which hinge entirely on man. Anyway, once personal sin has disappeared from the horizon of man's concerns, it is not surprising either that morality has been reduced to the so–called *social teaching of the Church* or that charity has had to yield pride of place to social justice.

At the present point in history it is interesting to see a coincidence of two apparently contradictory social phenomena: on the one hand, over–emphasis on the rights of man as an individual; on the other, an expansion of the social element such as has never been seen before.

This craze for the social as distinct from the individual has had marked impact within the Church. After the Second Vatican Council, for example, Priests' Councils, Pastoral Councils and also Episcopal Conferences have had a considerable impact on the pastoral policy and work of Bishops and parish priests (although, as regards the latter, the phenomenon has perhaps been less noticeable). The net effect of this is that the work of Pastors has become more consolidated, more uniform, at the expense of being less personal and responsible.[1] But it is not all that clear that the well–known antinomies of person/community and individual/society have at last been overcome in favor of the person.

By divine institution, the Church is at once a flock and a Body (the Body of Christ), as the New Testament texts clearly state —so much so that no other human grouping has ever existed in which the social element has had greater importance or such a high degree of consistency. It is also clear, at the same time, that each of these metaphors (Body and flock) has a truly unique meaning and originality.

---

[1] Many further examples could be given, and the practical problems raised have already been the subject of studies but there is still room for further study.

As regards the metaphor of the flock it should be noted that, despite what a certain pejorative meaning of the word might suggest, it is not a matter here of numbers or mere individuals assembled together, but of true *persons* who enjoy, besides, a divine filiation which makes them sons and daughters of God. These sheep of this flock are known personally to the Shepherd (that is the point: he is not a stranger to the sheep),[2] so much so that he calls each by his or her name,[3] and gives up his life for them.[4]

The same happens with the metaphor of the body, as regards the members of the Mystical Body. The personality and dignity *of each of the members* of this Body is affirmed by St Paul in the first Letter to the Corinthians, in texts noted for their clarity and eloquence: *You are the body of Christ and individually members of it...*[5] *If all were a single organ, where would the body be...?*[6] *The parts of the body which seem to be weaker are indispensable...*,[7] etc.

It is absolutely certain therefore that the *personal* element has as much strength and importance as the *social* element —although in practice, the perfect mixing and balance of the community and personal elements within the content of the whole and to the benefit of the person seems still very far from being a reality for some.

Joy and a festive sense of life are characteristic features of Christianity. If they were to disappear, even for a moment, from the horizon of the Christian life, that would be a very serious matter. But, during the second half of the twentieth century particularly, the sheer magnitude of problems and a general denunciation of social

---

[2] Cf. Jn 10:5.
[3] Cf. Jn 10: 3.14.
[4] Cf. Jn 10:11.
[5] 1 Cor 12:27.
[6] 1 Cor 12:19.
[7] 1 Cor 12:22.

injustice seem to have relegated the theme of Christian joy to a secondary place. Even preaching has become somewhat edgy, perhaps due to focussing almost exclusively on such subjects as the so-called *option for the under-privileged*. It is not surprising that any attempt to speak about Christian joy is regarded as out-of-date and inappropriate, and even a betrayal of the purer essences of the Christian message. One would hope that after the fall of communism and once Marxism is fully discredited, a more serene, a more objective era will be ushered in which a return to genuine supernatural values will be possible.[8]

But without the proclamation of joy the Christian message cannot be passed on. *I bring you good news of a great joy which will come to all the people; for to you is born this day in the city of David, a Saviour, Who is Christ the Lord.*[9] In the last analysis *the Kingdom of God does not mean food and drink but righteousness and peace and joy in the Holy Spirit.*[10] All Jesus' teachings point in this direction: *These things I have spoken to you, that my joy may be in you, and that your joy may be full.*[11] That is why He came; there was no other reason: *I will see you again and your hearts will rejoice, and no one will take your joy from you.*[12] The bride in the *Song*, who is as much in love with the Bridegroom as she is experienced in the joys of true love, is well aware of this; that is why she proclaims, addressing the Bridegroom: *Your love is better than wine...*

---

[8] It is well known that Marxism is incompatible with joy. This may explain why the *theology of liberation*, when it held sway, was always nasty and aggressive.

[9] Lk 2:10.

[10] Rom 14:17.

[11] Jn 15:11.

[12] Jn 16:22.

The best explanation so far given for Christian joy is perhaps the story told in chapter VIII of the *Little Flowers of St Francis*:

"On a winter day St Francis was journeying from Perugia to St Mary of the Angels. Brother Leo was with him and the bitter cold tormented both of them. St Francis called out to Brother Leo who was a short distance in front:

—Brother Leo, though the friars minor are setting a high example of holiness and uprightness and good edification, yet write down and note well that therein is not perfect happiness.

A little further on, he called to him again:

—Brother Leo, though a friar minor give sight to the blind and straighten a twisted body, drive out demons, give hearing to the deaf, make the lame walk and the dumb speak, and even raise the four days dead, write down that this is not perfect happiness. And, again, he loudly called:

—Brother Leo, though a friar minor should know the speech of all peoples, all sciences and Scriptures, and how to prophesy, and show not only what is yet to be, but even what lies in the heart of others, write down that this is not perfect happiness. A little further on, as they were still walking, he called out once more:

—Brother Leo, little lamb of God, though a friar minor speak with the tongue of angels, know the courses of the stars, the virtues of herbs, and the secret of earth's treasure, and understand the qualities and peculiarities of fish, beasts, men, roots, trees, stones and waters, write down clearly, and carefully note, that this is not perfect happiness.

And after a little while he called again:

—Brother Leo, though a friar minor should know how so earnestly to preach that he should bring all unbelievers to faith, write that here is not perfect happiness.

So the conversation continued for two miles. But Brother Leo, very baffled by all this, said:

—Father, I beg you in God's name, tell me where lies perfect happiness?

The saint replied:

—We shall come to St Mary of the Angels thus drenched in rain, stiff with cold, defiled with mud and afflicted with hunger, and knock at the door; and if the porter comes angrily and asks: 'Who are you?' we reply: 'We are two of your Brethren.' And if he should contradict and answer: 'No, you are a pair of vagrants who go about everywhere, seizing on the alms of the poor,' and should not open to us, but make us stand in the snow and rain, cold and hungry until night; and if then we patiently endure submissively and without complaint to much wrong and rejection, humbly and charitably thinking that the porter truly recognizes us, and that God stirs his tongue against us, then Brother Leo, write down that there lies perfect happiness. And if we continue knocking, and the porter comes out angry at our persistence, and cruelly heaps blows on us saying: 'Be off, basest rogues, go to the poorhouse. Who are you? Certainly you shall not eat here.' And if we endure patiently and accept his abuse with love wholehearted, Brother Leo, write that there lies perfect happiness. And if we in all ways afflicted, with hunger pressing, cold tormenting us, and night approaching, go on knocking, calling and pleading with tears that he should open to us, and he, stirred thus, should say: 'These are persistent trouble-makers. I will deal with them,' and coming out with a knotted cudgel, and seizing us by the hood he will fling us down in the mud and snow, battering us all over with his cudgel; if we bear such ills and abuse with joy, bearing in mind the sufferings of the blessed Christ, write, Brother Leo, that there lies perfect happiness."

As one can see, St Francis does not say that perfect joy consists in owning or controlling natural things, or even certain supernatural things, as many might think: "Even if the friar minor knew the courses of the stars and the qualities of every herb, and had revealed to him all the treasures of the earth, and knew the nature of birds and fish and all animals and men, and the properties of trees, stones, and roots and waters... Even if he knew all the scriptures and could prophesy... Even if he could raise to life someone who had been four days dead... Even if he could preach so well as to be able to convert all unbelievers to faith in Christ..."

Many Christians make the mistake of thinking that it is enough to renounce things in order to discover the way to perfect joy. However, it has been well proven that the lack of things —*qua* mere lack—, even if voluntary, is not what causes happiness. We are not talking here about poverty, even when it is voluntarily embraced, but of *Christian poverty*, which is completely different and much more radical than mere poverty. The rich young man in the Gospel is shown that he is still lacking in something, and he is invited to sell all he has and give it to the poor; this is followed immediately by an invitation: *Come, follow me.*[13] The poverty which produces blessedness is none other than Christian poverty (Lk 6:20; Mt 5:3), which adds an essential element —love— to what would otherwise be mere meaningless deprivation. The invitation is to give up one's house, brothers and sisters, father and mother, children and lands,

---

[13] Lk 18:22. The material side of poverty (want, privation) is also much more real in Christian poverty than in ordinary poverty. It should be remembered that poverty as a supernatural virtue calls for self–surrender and renunciation (inspired by love) both of natural goods and of supernatural goods, and even of all that one has to live on. Cf. Lk 14:33; 21:4; etc. Cf. also A. Gálvez, *El Amigo Inoportuno*, Shoreless Lake Press, New Jersey, 1995, pp. 113 ff.

but *for my sake and for the gospel*.¹⁴ St Francis of Assisi understood very clearly that the path of perfect joy is that which leads one to share the life and destiny of the Beloved; that is why he says in the *Little Flowers*: "Higher than all the goods, graces and gifts of the Holy Spirit that Christ gives his friends stands that of overcoming oneself and bearing with a will, out of love for Christ, pains, hurts, insults and contradictions; for we cannot glory in all the other gifts of God, and therefore the Apostle says: 'What do you have that you have not received from God? And if you have received it from Him, why, then, do you boast as if it were your own?' But we can boast of the cross of tribulations and afflictions, because that is truly ours; and so the Apostle says: 'I do not want to boast of anything but the cross of our Lord Jesus Christ.'"

Strictly speaking, the text of the *Little Flowers* does not explain what perfect joy is; it confines itself to pointing out the path and means that take you to it. That is all it could do, for this feeling (like that of love, which is its most direct cause) is both ineffable and incommunicable: *He who has an ear, let him hear what the Spirit says to the churches. To him who conquers I will give some of the hidden manna, and I will give him a white stone, with a new name written on the stone which no one knows except him who receives it*.¹⁵ Since the only real sadness is that caused by not being holy, the only true joy is that of holiness; or to put it another way, it is not possible to know anything of perfect joy (this is something one

---

[14] Mk 10:28.

[15] Rev 2:17, quoted by St Thomas in *Super Evangelium S. Ioannis Lectura*, I, lect. 15. There the Saint, commenting Jn 1:39, says that *mystice autem dicit "venite, et videte" quia habitatio Dei, sive gloriæ, sive gratiæ, agnosci non potest nisi per experientiam: nam verbis explicari non potest; Ap II, 17: "In calculo nomen novum, etc." Et ideo dicit "Venite, et videte." "Venite," credendo et operando, "et videte," experiendo et intelligendo.*

can know only through experience) unless one truly shares in the sufferings and death of the Lord.

Here one enters again the strange world of Christian paradoxes. The path which leads man to perfect joy, here and now, is that of suffering in Christ; the *Little Flowers* tells us this in a way that is as poetic as it is exact. *Blessed are those who mourn.*[16] But the paradox is solved when one remembers that it has to do not so much with suffering for the sake of suffering as with sharing the life and destiny of the Loved One. For true joy is never the outcome of the search for suffering and the search for joy; it is something which results from being with the Loved One, as the Baptist also says: *He who has the bride is the bridegroom; the friend of the bridegroom, who stands and hears him, rejoices greatly at the bridegroom's voice; therefore this joy of mine is now full.*[17] So, joy is never found by him who is bent on finding it; it is found only by true lovers, who are precisely those who feel as indifferent and unconcerned about joy as they are eager and impatient to locate those whom they love. The perfect *beatitudo* of the blessed in Heaven consists, without a doubt, in the satiative contemplation of the truth; yet it is even more certain that such contemplation aims only to the perfect possession of the Beloved —how could it be otherwise?— without it, *nulla beatitudo*.[18] For the Baptist, as it has been said, the secret consists in being with the Bridegroom (sharing, therefore, his fate) and hearing his voice, which is what happens to the bride in the *Song*:

---

[16] Mt 5:4; Lk 6:21.

[17] Jn 3:29.

[18] Although it may seem to be a question of terminology and where the stress is laid, this is an important problem.

> *The voice of my beloved! Behold, he comes,*
> *leaping over the mountains,*
> *bounding over the hills.*[19]
>
> ....
>
> *Come, my beloved, let us go forth into the fields,*
> *and lodge in the villages;*
> *let us go out early to the vineyards,*
> *and see whether the vines have budded,*
> *whether the grape blossoms have opened*
> *and the pomegranates are in bloom.*
> *There I will give you my love.*[20]

And therefore the bride also says:

> *The voice of my Bridegroom is*
> *like a fleeing wake of a ship,*
> *like the murmuring air,*
> *like a soft whispering,*
> *like the flying of a night fowl.*[21]

That is why there is no sorrow for the bride except the absence of the Bridegroom, because it is then that joy is put out and the world becomes submerged in night:

---

[19] Sg 2:8.

[20] Sg 7: 12–13.

[21] In the original:

> *Es la voz del Esposo*
> *como la huidiza estela de una nave,*
> *como aire rumoroso,*
> *como susurro suave,*
> *como el vuelo nocturno de algún ave.*

> *At night he left for the hill,*
> *at night he followed the road,*
> *at night I was left, in unknown land,*
> *at night I was left without my friend...*[22]

Joy, then, is something one finds rather than something one seeks. A true lover is not so much interested in pursuing his own interest as in being with the loved one,[23] and even (if that were possible) he is less interested in his own salvation than in the well–being of his beloved: *For I could wish that I myself were accursed and cut off from Christ for the sake of my brethren.*[24] He who loves is very far from seeking joy above all else; and so he chooses in its place what brings him closer to the love of the loved one, unhesitatingly, taking no account of obstacles: *Looking to Jesus the pioneer and perfecter of our faith, who instead of the joy that was set before Him endured the cross, despising the shame, and is seated at the right hand of the throne of God.*[25] And one must not forget that the complete gift the lover makes of himself to the loved one includes also the gift of his own joy (which would be the equivalent of a renunciation), and he receives in return the joy of the other (for love involves total reciprocity), thereby —and only thereby— making his joy complete:

---

[22] In the original:

> *De noche se marchó hacia la montaña,*
> *de noche se marchó por el sendero,*
> *de noche me quedé, por tierra extraña,*
> *de noche me quedé sin compañero...*

[23] It should be kept in mind that the last end of man does not consist so much in the *perfecta beatitudo* as in the possession of God; nevertheless the latter leads to the former.

[24] Rom 9:3.

[25] Heb 12:2.

These things I have spoken to you, that my joy may be in you, and that your joy may be full.[26]

When St Paul speaks of the fruits of the Spirit (Gal 5:22), he puts joy second on the list, immediately after charity. This may be because love comes first always and joy is its most direct effect. Man does not love because he is happy; he is happy because he loves. How could he be happy without love, and what would be the object of and reason for his happiness? And so it is that man can renounce joy (Heb 12:2), but there is no way he can renounce love. However, on surrendering his joy for love's sake (the only reason that could justify such renunciation) he finds it again (and now it is complete), for love never exists without joy. Joy is what gives meaning to the wedding day:

> *Go forth, O daughters of Zion,*
> *and behold King Solomon,*
> *and the crown with which his mother crowned him*
> *on the day of his wedding,*
> *on the day of the gladness of his heart.*[27]

According to this, happiness (or perfect joy) is not so much the result of seeing (or contemplating) as of possessing, although you cannot have the second without the first. And this matter cannot be dismissed as a mere problem of words or expressions; the order of the concepts, let us say it again, is of the utmost importance, possibly with practical consequences for the life of the faithful. The contemplation of the truth (even though it be of the First Truth) can only attain its full meaning if it is in possession of the Bridegroom,

---

[26] Jn 15:11.
[27] Sg 3:11.

and therefore the *beatific vision*[28] consists in nothing other than the definitive, consummated nuptials of Heaven. For the *Song*, as we have seen, *the day of gladness of heart* is in fact *the day of the wedding*, and none other. This shows that it is not a matter only of seeing but of hearing, of possessing and of mutual self–giving.[29] And so the Bridegroom says to the bride:

> *Let me see your face, let me hear your voice,*
> *for your voice is sweet, and your face is comely.*[30]

And the bride says the same thing, addressing the Bridegroom:

> *I held him, and would not let him go*
> *until I had brought him into my mother's house,*
> *and into the chamber of her that conceived me.*[31]

For love is not only mutual gazing and contemplating: it is also consummation and possession:

---

[28] Possibly a rather poor and not very felicitous expression. *You have sorrow now, but I will see you again and your hearts will rejoice, and no one will take your joy from you.* These words of our Lord (Jn 16:22) must be understood in the context of the definitive return of the Bridegroom, when his disciples will possess Him. In fact our Lord goes on: *In that day you will ask nothing of me* (Jn 16:23), which leads one to think that he is referring to the consummated and definite nuptials which will take place in the Kingdom.

[29] As one can readily see, it is not a problem of doctrine which nobody has ever contested, but of stress or terminology. One cannot always manage to find the right expressions to convey clearly and precisely what one means.

[30] Sg 2:14.

[31] Sg 3:4.

> *O that his left hand were under my head,*
> *and that his right hand embraced me!*[32]

The proclamation of Christian joy should never be afraid of making this known; otherwise it is either incomplete or it is not the true proclamation of the Good News. God is Supreme Truth as well as Supreme Love. And if it is true that man has been called to the contemplation of the First Truth, it is also true that he has been made by and for Love. Jesus came to bear witness to the truth (Jn 18:37), but to a truth which is at the same time a Person (Jn 14:6), of whom therefore witness can also be borne in turn (Jn 5:33). Persons contemplate one another exactly to the same extent as they love one another and also mutually surrender to one another —as happens in the bosom of the Trinity, where the Son is the Idea or *Verbum mentis* of the Father, the same as the Holy Spirit is the *spiratio amoris* Who proceeds from the Father and the Son.

---

[32] Sg 2:6.

CHAPTER III

CONTEMPLATION AND POETRY

Full of emotion, the bride declares to the Bridegroom that the loves he causes in her are better than wine. With this she seems to be giving rein to a feeling of happiness caused by a love which she says is more intoxicating than wine. This happiness takes the form of a state of excitation and exaltation, caused by a certain exuberance of life, which in turn becomes a feeling that all her vital energies are fully active and that all the deepest and most private desires of her heart have at last been fulfilled. Clearly these are feelings which nicely satisfy her eagerness to live. The book of Ecclesiasticus says that *wine is like life to men, if you drink it in moderation. What is life to a man who is without wine? It has been created to make men glad.*[1] The intoxication which wine causes is, in a way, a sort of foretaste of the fullness of eternal life insofar as it in some way

---

[1] Sir 34:27, according to most modern translations. The *New Vulgate* gives the text in 31: 32–33.35, with some variations of translations.

satisfies the desire and love–nostalgia that man experiences. Our Lord seems to be referring to the fullness of something which begins in this life, when, addressing his disciples, he tells them that *I shall not drink again of this fruit of the vine until that day when I drink it new with you in my Father's kingdom.*[2] The degree to which man yearns for this state of completeness is something that can be seen, for example, in the immoderate use of alcohol and in the resort to drugs so widespread nowadays despite the devastating effects these substances can have.

For the bride of the *Song*, the best and only drug that can indeed meet the demands of the restless human heart is love. Apparently, she finds love so wonderful that, far from causing destruction and annihilation, it leads to the fullest kind of life and delivers everything man can desire. While all the things that God has created leave the heart of man empty, only love is able to fill it to an overflowing point: *Whoever drinks this water will be thirsty again; but no one who drinks the water that I shall give him will ever be thirsty again...*[3]

If that is the case, once it is established that love is much better than wine, one might ask the bride to explain concretely, in a more exact way, what are these effects that love causes and that are so delightfully perturbing? The bride has simply said that the loves of the Bridegroom are better than wine: that does not tell us very much about them. We know, of course, in advance, that she will not find it easy to reply —if reply she can.

One possible way to approach the subject would be to set it in the context of prayer, more specifically contemplative prayer. Prayer is the most suitable place to resolve the very special kind of love–combat which takes place between the Bridegroom and the bride

---

[2] Mt 26:29.
[3] Jn 4: 13–14.

(Sg 2:4); it is where, in general, the love–relationships between the two most frequently occur. But this approach does not provide an entirely satisfactory solution. For, unfortunately, although one can talk as much as one likes about ordinary prayer, it is not possible to do that with contemplative prayer, yet that is the most elevated and proper form of prayer. To explain what contemplation is one would need to avail oneself, as usual, of human concepts and language —yet these are absolutely inadequate to the purpose proposed. If despite that one tries to carry on the task, one runs the risk of meandering off into tangential themes and ending up discussing entirely different things. This is exactly what happens to St Teresa of Avila in her *Way of Perfection*.

St Teresa rather naively begins her book saying that she is going to explain what contemplation is and then she goes on to discuss at length the preconditions for contemplation. These are, according to the saint, of two kinds —positive and negative. As one might suppose, the positive ones consist in the virtues proper to the Christian life, without which one cannot even conceive of any sort of contemplation. It is quite reasonable, therefore, for the mystical doctor to apply herself to describing these virtues at great length. But although it is a very interesting subject, it is not to the point: if one discusses the preconditions for something, that is not the same as explaining the thing itself; it is simply a preliminary step.

The Christian virtue of obedience, for example, should not be confused with charity, no matter how much true obedience is a sign of the presence of charity and, indeed, a necessary pre–condition for it. The same could be said of poverty,[4] and, in general, of any virtue.

---

[4] St Paul told the Corinthians that Jesus Christ had become poor *for them*, so that they might be enriched by his poverty (2 Cor 8:9).

St Teresa, after speaking about the virtues, finishes her book with some beautiful considerations on the Our Father, leaving the reader edified, certainly, but not satisfied, because she has not done what she promised.[5]

St Paul is more exact when he describes charity in his famous chapter XIII of the first Letter to the Corinthians: *Though I command languages both human and angelic... Though I should give away to the poor... Love is always patient and kind...* It is interesting to note that the argument used in chapter VIII of the *Little Flowers of St Francis* (dealing with Christian joy)[6] is the same one as the Apostle uses when speaking of charity. Perfect joy does not consist, for St Francis, in the friars minor working miracles and making prophecies, or in understanding all the natural sciences, or in converting all infidels or in other things like that. St Paul, for his part, who explains at the start of the chapter what charity is not, seems to devote the first two verses to the supporters of a radical and therefore off-centre spirituality (to the extent that it is disincarnated and has not got its feet on the ground).[7] The third verse, on the other hand, seems to refer to those who, as defenders of a horizontal and purely human theology, are all keen on turning the Church into

---

[5]The accounts given in her *Life* which tell of her mystical experiences do not clarify the matter either, insofar as mystical phenomena should not be confused with a divine–human love which can indeed occur without them (although, when they are present and are genuine, they are a clear indication of the presence of that love). The subject seems to be dealt with in more depth in the *Interior Castle* (though that may not at first sight seem to be so), which is probably her most important work and the best treatise on prayer ever written.

[6]Cf. chapter II of this second part, *Christian Joy.*

[7]Which is the position of those who forget that God became man in Jesus Christ, for the glory of the Father and the good of all mankind: *the man Christ Jesus* of 1 Tim 2:5.

some kind of social welfare institution or patron of political causes.[8] So, according to these three verses, as the Apostle sees it, love is not necessarily connected with charisms (not that of tongues, or that of prophecy, or any other charism),[9] and certainly not with faith (even if one has faith enough to move mountains), and not even with the generous gift of one's possessions or of one's life. St Paul then goes on to expound in the following verses, now in a descriptive style, having excluded what charity *is not*, certain features or properties[10] of genuine love. This is clearly the best method to follow, because by explaining and analysing the main qualities of something, one is best able to understand what that thing is. Besides, it is important to note here (especially insofar as it touches on certain currents of spirituality which have come very much to the fore in the Church in recent times) that the Apostle does not forget to stress also (and he must be doing this to emphasize that they are on a lower level than charity) that charisms are passing things; therefore, they are designed to disappear eventually; and he even seems to imply the same with regard to the theological virtues of faith and hope.[11]

---

[8]In this category one should put political activists of the Church (liberationist theologies, and all theologies which are political or godless) as also a sizeable group of *experts* and pastoral hangers-on: sociologists, psychologists, ecologists, theorists, catechists, experts on the laity, and a swarm of charism manipulators, and many others. They all tend to share, in addition to enthusiasm for purely human disciplines and recourse to psychological sentimentalism (which leads them to use methods and procedures which lack any supernatural bearing), a lack of confidence in the interior life which is so acute that they systematically fail to practice it. If the people referred to in the previous section, or out-and-out spiritualists, usually forget that Jesus Christ is Man, the people we refer to here forget that He is God.

[9]Cf. Mt 7: 22–23.

[10]One can easily see that the Apostle could not have intended to provide a full list.

[11]On this last-mentioned aspect cf. 1 Cor 13:13.

The descriptive method[12] is also used by the bride in the *Song* when she tries to sketch a portrait of the Bridegroom (5: 10–16). Certainly, the path here always has to take turns, like the courses of rivers which meander when the nature of the terrain will not let them do otherwise. Perhaps that is why St Paul paints a picture to show the qualities of true love: *Charity is patient and kind; charity is not jealous or boastful; it is not arrogant or rude. Charity does not insist on its own way; it is not irritable or resentful...* The Bride in the *Song*, for her part, has recourse to metaphor to describe the Bridegroom to her companions:

> *My beloved is all radiant and ruddy,*
> *distinguished among ten thousand.*
> *His head is the finest gold;*
> *his locks are wavy,*
> *black as a raven.*
> *His eyes are like doves*
> *beside springs of water*
> *bathing themselves in milk,*
> *perching on a fountain–rim...*[13]

At any rate it soon becomes obvious that, despite all the descriptions and metaphors, it simply is not possible to draw a good likeness of the Bridegroom or to explain what love is. The only thing these efforts manage to make clear is that all they do is increase the hunger and the desires experienced by eager lovers, as St John of the Cross so beautifully describes in his *Spiritual Canticle*:

---

[12]Here it is not a matter (as when the *Little Flowers* was dealing with perfect joy) of describing a way to attain something, but rather an attempt to explain what that something (in this case love) is.

[13]Sg 5: 10–12.

> *The creatures all around me*
> *speak of your thousand gifts,*
> *yet they wound me even more;*
> *something that they stammer*
> *leaves me dying.*[14]

One finds here again the glory and the misery of human language. So, according to the poet, there is a *something that they stammer*; for the only thing human language can utter, in the face of the ineffable and awesome,[15] is babble, stammering, and even stuttering caused by amazement. That is all one could expect, because the love–relationship is anything but a narrative designed to be declaimed to the gallery. In fact, that relationship takes place in the secret intimacy created by an *I* and a *thou*, an intimacy which develops in the silence that follows our voluntary distancing from other things and our earnest searching for solitude. Lovers find everything in their love for one another and in their reciprocal self–surrender and possession, and they desire absolutely nothing more. Because the love–relationship *cannot transfer* into the exterior, and it does not exist in any way outside the thou/I binomial, it cannot be described in words. The love–dialogue between the lovers is essentially a secret

---

[14]In the *Cántico Espiritual*:

> *Y todos cuantos vagan*
> *de ti me van mil gracias refiriendo*
> *y todos más me llagan*
> *y déjame muriendo*
> *un no sé qué que quedan balbuciendo.*

[15]The more than brilliant construction of the last line of the stanza —with its repetition of *qué* (*un no sé qué que quedan balbuciendo*) one after the other and the allusion to a very mysterious and suggestive stammering— conveys the idea of a stuttering and as it were intoxicating language, caused by amazement and wonder.

dialogue and it ends within itself, in the sense that in it everything that one has is for the other —nothing else matters, for the words of love enunciated by each lover are addressed exclusively and solely to the other: *To him who conquers I will give some of the hidden manna, and I will give him a white stone, with a new name written on the stone which no one knows except him who receives it.*[16]

The *Song of Songs*, using a most beautiful poetic language, attempts to express this intimacy that the lovers so ardently desire; thence the charm uttered by the Bridegroom and the invocation of the Bride:

> *I adjure you, O daughters of Jerusalem,*
> *by the gazelles or the hinds of the fields,*
> *that you stir not up nor awaken love*
> *until it pleases.*[17]
>
> ....
>
> *Come, my beloved, let us go to the fields.*
> *We will spend the night in the villages,*
> *and in the early morning we will go to the vineyards.*
> *We will see if the vines are budding,*
> *if their blossoms are opening,*
> *if the pomegranate trees are in flower.*
> *Then I shall give you*
> *the gift of my love.*[18]

St John of the Cross glosses this in his *Dark Night*:

---

[16] Rev 2:17.
[17] Sg 2:7; 3:5; 8:4.
[18] Sg 7: 12–13.

*In darkness and quite safe,
by the secret stairway, in disguise,
O moment of delightful chance!
in darkness and in concealment
my house being now at rest.*[19]

In the *Spiritual Canticle* he stresses the same idea:

*In solitude she lived
and in solitude she has built her nest
and in solitude now her beloved guides her
alone, who likewise
in solitude was wounded by love.*[20]

In the light of this doctrine, the words our Lord addresses to the Apostles acquire an unsuspected relevance: *No longer do I call you servants, for the servant does not know what his master is doing;*

---

[19] In the original:

*A oscuras, y segura
por la secreta escala disfrazada
¡oh dichosa ventura!
a oscuras y en celada
estando ya mi casa sosegada.*

[20] In the original:

*En soledad vivía
y en soledad ha puesto ya su nido
y en soledad la guía
a solas su querido
también en soledad de amor herido.*

but I have called you friends, for all that I have heard from my Father I have made known to you.[21] This seems to indicate that he has made his disciples sharers in the mysterious, ineffable and eternal dialogue of love which takes place between Him and the Father. What it says is that he has given them all his Love, or the fullness of the Spirit: *That the love with which thou hast loved me, Father, may be in them, and I in them,*[22] thereby implementing the incredible mystery of God giving man nothing less than *all his Love*. Now we can understand better the words of Jesus: *Nevertheless I tell you the truth: it is to your advantage that I go away, for if I do not go away, the Counsellor will not come to you; but if I go, I will send Him to you.*[23] If love is the most intimate and personal thing there is in the heart of someone who loves, no one can know it except himself and, of course, the one who has become the object of that love (the one to whom he has given his love) in a gift that is both strictly personal and unique: *For what person knows a man's thoughts except the spirit of the man which is in him? So also no one comprehends the thoughts of God except the Spirit of God. Now we have received not the spirit of the world, but the Spirit which is from God, that we might understand the gifts bestowed on us by God... For who has known the mind of the Lord so as to instruct him? But we have the mind of Christ.*[24] What does this mysterious statement, so full of possibilities, mean: *we have the mind of Christ*?

---

[21] Jn 15:15.
[22] Jn 17:26.
[23] Jn 16:7. Cf. Rom 5:5.
[24] 1 Cor 2: 11–12.16.

The so-called *theologies of the laity* try to rescue lay people from the situation of submission or prostration in which, according to some, they have been kept up to now by the policy of the Hierarchy. One cannot help thinking that the defenders of the *advancement of the laity* seem to have forgotten that lay people, as true members of the People of God, have no need of being given their place by means of a new redemption. They are already redeemed and elevated. All Jesus Christ's faithful,[25] whether members of the Hierarchy or not, have been called to enjoy, from now on, the greatest possible intimacy with God. Those who push for certain kinds of *advancement* seem to have forgotten that every Christian, by the very fact of being a Christian, has been called to the divine–human nuptials which, although they are destined to reach their fullness in the Fatherland, have already begun here on earth, albeit in the form of an earnest and first–fruits.

It is a pity to find the great themes of theology being sometimes marginalized. Initiatives for the *advancement of the laity*, in addition to seeming to forget that the ecclesiastical Hierarchy is of divine institution, tend to suffer from a mistaken view of the role of the ministerial priesthood. They see the ministerial priesthood as

---

[25]Lay people do not need to be *promoted* or advanced to some new position. They are simply Christ's sheep, the part of the People of God that has not been made a part of the Hierarchy. It is as simple and as important as that. And, although it may be argued that this is a negative definition, it is probably the most accurate and exact definition of the laity possible. If one prefers, one can say that the laity is simply the People of God, whereas those consecrated by the sacrament of Order are members of the People of God who have *additionally* been established as Hierarchy. It is difficult not to feel that it is only some clerics, not lay people, who press for certain advancements which really only turn normal Christians into a new breed of sacristans. Basically this is another form of clericalism, more subtle, disguised, which eventually leads to the abuse of intervening in the rightful field of the laity.

something *up there*, in a position of superiority, whereas the laity are away *down below*, in a clearly inferior position. The truth is that, although it is correct that Hierarchy is composed of the ministerial priesthood (and the other members of the Mystical Body are ordinary faithful), we need to remember the New Testament notion of Christian authority. The priest is someone *set apart*, rather than someone on a higher level: *ex hominibus assumptus et pro hominibus constituitur*.[26] He has been put there to serve his brethren, and with the express instruction to regard himself as the last of all.[27] The Letter to the Hebrews, which recognizes that the priesthood is an honour,[28] does however remind us that he who is instituted in the ministerial order *should deal gently with the ignorant and wayward, since he himself is beset with weakness. Because of this he is bound to offer sacrifice for his own sins as well as for those of the people*.[29] It is difficult not to get the impression that underlying many attempts to advance the laity there is at times a triumphalist and authoritarian notion of the ministerial priesthood.

The feelings that love gives rise to (just as we saw in connexion with perfect joy, which is the direct effect of love) are indescribable and incommunicable because they are quite ineffable. As far as divine–human love is concerned, if one has to try to describe it, it may be useful to call in the aid of poetry (in this case mystical poetry). In the last analysis *The Song of Songs* is a work of poetry, and everyone knows that poetry, with its ability to evoke and hint, can reach areas of comprehension which are inaccessible to ordinary language. However, one needs to bear in mind that to speak about

---

[26] Heb 5:1.
[27] Cf. Mt 20: 26–27; Mk 10: 43–45; etc.
[28] Heb 5:4.
[29] Heb 5: 2-3.

mystical poetry is not the same as to speak about religious poetry, because even if all mystical poetry is religious poetry, not all religious poetry is mystical poetry. Mystical poetry should be, first and foremost, poetry and then it should have the characteristics proper to mysticism.

Poetry —which should not be confused with verse, either— is language's last, greatest attempt at describing the indescribable. Poetic language, because it is language, has to do with being, here apprehended as beauty in order to be described in a beautiful way. Poetry embarks on its task to lend a hand, as it were, once metaphysics has done its bit to grasp what being is. Recognizing that it is impossible for man fully to grasp being as reality, as truth and as goodness, poetry tries to approach being via the path of beauty, expressed in this case by means of language. Of course, poetry, even less than other disciplines which study being, does not claim completely to explain it, nor does it work by way of definitions. Fully conscious of its limitations, it is content with making evocative suggestions and with sketching out possible paths and horizons; it makes no attempt to achieve goals and heights which exact sciences have already shown to be inaccessible.

However, this does not mean that poetry has nothing to do with truth. Since, as we have just said, poetry too looks at being, it should not be regarded as in any sense foreign to reality. Beauty (like truth and goodness) is simply another aspect of a reality which man can never plumb and which, therefore, he feels he must try to grasp by looking at it from all possible angles. However, poetry does have its own way of saying things, of expressing the truth. It is not interested in the first meaning of words, which experience, anyway, has shown to be incapable of expressing the ineffable. However, if the words poetry uses are concerned with beauty, they should be recognized as also having a connexion with truth and, therefore and in the last analysis, with being.

Mystical poetry reaches its high point in the sixteenth century with St John of the Cross. When the great Italian and Spanish Renaissance poets devised new forms of poetry, certain writers devoted themselves to rewriting the inspired verses of Petrarch, Bosc n and Garcilaso to give them a *divine reference*. But St John of the Cross was the only one who managed to write mystical poetry at the same level as the work of those great masters —and no one since then has put him in the shade. His *Spiritual Canticle*, for example,[30] seems to be not so much a systematic gloss on the Song of Songs as a work made up of stanzas written by the poet on different occasions (for the spiritual solace and benefit of his nuns), which draw their inspiration from the sacred book:

> *You shepherds, as you make your way*
> *to the sheepfolds in the hills,*
> *if by any chance you should see*
> *him whom I most love,*
> *tell him that I sicken, grieve and die.*[31]

It is easy to detect the verses of the Song which inspired the stanza:

---

[30] *Songs between the Soul and the Bridegroom.*

[31] Slight changes are made to this and other Spanish texts to make them more intelligible to the modern reader, without affecting the sense of the original.

> *Pastores los que fuéredes*
> *allá por las majadas al otero,*
> *si por ventura viéredes*
> *aquel que yo más quiero,*
> *decidle que adolezco, peno y muero.*

> *I adjure you, O daughters of Jerusalem,*
> *if you find my beloved,*
> *that you tell him I am sick with love.*[32]
>
> ....
>
> *Tell me, whom my soul loves,*
> *where you pasture your flock, where you make it lie down*
> *at noon;*
> *for why should I be like one who wanders*
> *beside the flocks of your companions.*[33]

Both the sacred writer and the Carmelite poet seem to refer here to one of the most characteristic features of the passion of love: the inexplicable joy which overcomes the lover when he feels he is dying of love. Love is so strong, so sharp a feeling that it makes a person who *suffers* from it think that this superabundance of joy and life is more than he can take. However, as is typical of the inexplicable and mysterious paradoxes of love, this dying of love is not the anguished death that brings one's life to an end, but an incredible and, as it were, infinite exultation of joy *which wells up to eternal life.*[34] The mention of death here is a direct allusion to the mystery of the tremendous force of love. The *I die because I do not die* of St Teresa of Avila and St John of the Cross,[35] or the common expression *dying of love*, are an example of the strange connexion which seems to exist between death and love: *Greater love has no man than this, that a man lays down his life for his friends.*[36] One

---

[32] Sg 5:8.

[33] Sg 1:7.

[34] Jn 4:14.

[35] On the originality of this verse, see Dámaso Alonso, *Poesía Española*, Gredos, Madrid, 1981, p. 237.

[36] Jn 15:13.

possible explanation might have to do with the fact that love feels an irresistible impulse to express itself unambiguously (Jn 3:34), and moreover, and particularly, because it feels an absolute need to go to the very end (Jn 13:1):

> *For love is strong as death,*
> *jealousy is cruel as the grave.*
> *Its flashes are flashes of fire,*
> *a flame of Yahweh himself.*[37]

The burning desire to speak about the ineffable leads poetry to use the beauty of language in an attempt to create feelings evocative of mysterious and inexplicable realities. We should note, for example, in the last verse of St John's stanza, a wonderful graded range of feelings:

> *tell him that I sicken, grieve, and die.*[38]

To sicken or be ill, to grieve, and suffer even more, so as eventually to arrive at death through love when you can bear it no longer: for a moment it seems that the barriers and limitations of language have been overcome and that one has managed to say *something*

---

[37] Sg 8:6.

[38] In the original:

> *decidle que adolezco, peno y muero.*

about what love is capable of.³⁹ And although one cannot say that this is all or even much of what could be said, clearly a certain advance has been achieved which is now difficult to better.

Moreover, if one examines the tenses the saint uses in the stanza, one will notice that they hint at the idea of a future which, although it is undoubtedly conditioned and uncertain, is still a happy one if it comes to be, as one might hope it will:

> *You shepherds, as you make your way...*
>
> *if by any chance you should see...*⁴⁰

These words, signifying conditionality, which the bride addresses to the shepherds, cannot be more accurate, and they embrace at one and the same time the two meanings of uncertainty and of fortunate happiness.

> *if by any chance...*⁴¹

Language is not slow to use the beauty of sounds when it tries to speak about dying of love. This is the kind of death which the

---

[39] And hence, on the basis of the nature of the thing or its mode of operation, managing in some way to convey what the thing is in itself.

[40] In the *Cántico Espiritual*:

> *pastores los que fuéredes...*
>
> *si por ventura viéredes...*

[41] In the *Cántico Espiritual*:

> *si por ventura...*

inexplicable and mysterious love of the Bridegroom is able to cause in the bride (by force of its presence and the ensuing feeling of joy). The words evoke a kind of tinkling of bells in the background.

> *Should you see me again*
> *yonder in the valley, where the blackbird sings,*
> *do not say that you love me,*
> *for upon hearing it I may die*
> *were you ever to repeat it.*[42]

This evocation of tinkling sounds also seems in some way to refer to the intimacy of that loving dialogue that takes place in contemplation:

> *Your words of love are*
> *like a cloth made of soft threads*
> *upon a bed of flowers;*
> *come to my side and say them*
> *amid the roses and lindens of my garden.*[43]

---

[42]In the original:

> *Si de nuevo me vieres,*
> *allí en el valle, donde canta el mirlo,*
> *no digas que me quieres,*
> *no muera yo al oírlo*
> *si acaso tú volvieras a decirlo.*

[43]In the original:

> *Son tus dichos de amores*
> *como una tela de suaves hilos*
> *en un lecho de flores;*
> *ven a mi lado, y dilos*
> *en mi jardín de rosas y de tilos.*

It is worth noting that the important thing here is the *feelings awakened* by the words, and not what the words themselves mean. This feature of awakening feelings, which is proper and specific to poetry, allows it to arouse different feelings (in nature as well as in depth) in different readers. Yet, the sensibility and aptitudes of the readers are also to some extent responsible for that disparity of feelings. Hence the usefulness of poetry. For, once the point has come where it seems that everything that could be said has been said (a point which normally comes quite quickly), that is when man feels a more urgent desire to know more —particularly when the matter has to do with such key things as love or contemplative prayer. This is where poetry is able to say more than prose, because of its ability to reach further than ordinary language. This is why the *Declarations* or explanations which St John of the Cross provides (in prose) for his own poetry are so instructive yet so disappointing. The reader usually gets the impression of not finding everything he expected —not in the sense that the teaching contained in the prose text is not profound and sublime, but because the poetry, which preceded it, seemed to *promise* much more. And there is no doubt but that it did, since poetry is much more insinuating, suggestive and evocative than is the language of prose. No one is in any doubt that the saint *said much more* in his short poetical work than in all his weighty prose treatises.

As far as the dialogue in contemplative prayer is concerned, we have already seen the bride adjure the Bridegroom to come to her side and tell her his *words of love*. There is no need to stress that contemplative prayer is the ideal venue for the dialogue of love between God and man. Once involved in the intimacy of that dialogue, the lovers seek privacy and silence, for as everyone knows, love desires to give itself entirely and not to be disturbed by any other thing.

Therefore, the Bridegroom in the *Song* adjures all other creatures not to disturb the bride in any way, so that she can devote herself calmly to the task of love with her whole heart, with her whole mind and with all her strength:[44]

> *I adjure you, O daughters of Jerusalem,*
> *by the gazelles or the hinds of the field,*
> *that you stir not up nor awaken love*
> *until it pleases.*[45]

That is the way it is put, in a veritable torrent of poetry, in the *Song of Songs*. Everything depends on what she wants and as long as she wants it; for love, as always, essentially involves free will. And St John of the Cross, in his turn, glossed these verses in wonderful stanzas, so evocative of beauty and bursting with almost divine music that no one has surpassed them:

> *You birds that fly with ease,*
> *lions, stags, skipping fallow deer,*
> *hills, valleys, river–banks,*
> *waters, winds, heats,*
> *and watchers that fill the nights with fear:*[46]

---

[44] Cf. Mt 22:37; Mk 12:30.

[45] Sg 2:7; 3:5.

[46] In the original:

> *A las aves ligeras,*
> *leones, ciervos, gamos saltadores,*
> *montes, valles, riberas,*
> *aguas, aires, ardores*
> *y miedos de las noches veladores:*

> *By the sweet lyre*
> *and song of sirens I conjure you*
> *to cease your wrath.*
> *Do not even echo on the wall,*
> *that the bride may sleep more securely.*[47]

It is striking how beautifully he speaks of the intimacy of a dialogue of love which takes place in silence and solitude, away from everything else. How is it possible to describe contemplation as an incredible exaltation of life, of mutual giving, of vying generosities, of indescribable happiness..., all of which takes place in a setting which shuts out everything else for the simple reason that the lovers are entirely sufficient one for another (they keep nothing back, nor are they distracted by anything else) in their total mutual self–giving? We already know that the dialogue and self–surrender of love that occurs in contemplation can never be explained through prose, or even through poetry. But this does not prevent the mysterious feeling of beauty which poetry causes in the human being, conveying something more than presentiment of some great marvel. Poetry can provoke more profound and more intense feelings than ordinary prose. Anyone with literary ability, with the scalpel of criticism in his hand, can dissect the first of these two stanzas, for example, and offer an expert's opinion. He will probably notice that the poet has achieved this strange and beautiful effect by piling nouns on top

---

[47]In the original:

> *por las amenas liras*
> *y cantos de sirenas os conjuro*
> *que cesen vuestras iras*
> *y no toquéis al muro*
> *porque la esposa duerma más seguro.*

of one another, so that they seem to be tripping over each other, without verbs or any other words to separate them. Yet the great truth is that poetry is a mysterious tool which helps to explain, in some way or another, something which in itself is inexplicable. The miracle of poetry rides roughshod through the most basic rules of grammatical structure; this can be seen, for example, in the last stanza of Miguel Hernández' elegy for Ramón Sijé (which also in fact deals with the dialogue of love). The special grammatical and poetic features of this passage consist in the extraordinary beauty which the poet achieves particularly in the last line, simply by the repetition of one word, placed at the beginning and at the end:

> *To the winged souls of the roses*
> *of the creamy almond tree I call you;*
> *for we have to talk about many a thing,*
> *my friend, my soul, my friend.*[48]

This is how the poet expresses himself. Of course, as one can easily perceive, beauty is something more ethereal and mysterious than mere grammatical cleverness can achieve. In this stanza there is a strange evocation, more likely to be grasped by those who have experience of love, and not explicable in terms of the language used by the author, of the desire to *talk about many a thing* with one's soul–companion. For it is well known that people in love always

---

[48] In the original:

> *A las aladas almas de las rosas*
> *del almendro de nata te requiero,*
> *que tenemos que hablar de muchas cosas,*
> *compañero del alma, compañero.*

want to be together, to talk and talk, and thereby attain the mysterious and intimate dialogue of love which will eventually find its consummation in mutual self–surrender.

In some sense we can apply to contemplative prayer what St Paul, quoting the prophet Isaiah, said about his own experience of Heaven: *no eye has seen, nor ear heard, nor the heart of man conceived, what God has prepared for those who love Him.*[49] In the last analysis contemplation is a foretaste of Heaven, and that is why no one has really managed to write a treatise on it.[50]

But it is perhaps worth pointing out again, to avoid anyone being misled, that contemplation is not merely a dialogue: it is also, above all, communion, whereby lovers interchange their lives (this is another of the very special and important effects of love):

> *I should lead you,*
> *I should take you into my mother's house,*
> *and you would teach me!*
> *I should give you spiced wine to drink,*
> *juice of my pomegranates.*[51]

St John of the Cross says this very beautifully, once again, in one of the stanzas of his poem, the *Dark Night*. In it the poet speaks about the union of the Bridegroom and the Bride, a union which has become a true communion and almost a transformation of lives:

---

[49] 1 Cor 2:9.

[50] Some people regard St Teresa of Avila's *Mansions* or *Interior Castle* perhaps the best treatise on prayer written so far. St John of the Cross deals with the subject more explicitly in his prose work.

[51] Sg 8:2.

> *O night that guided me!*
> *O night more lovely than the dawn!*
> *O night that has joined*
> *the Beloved with his lover,*
> *lover transformed into the Beloved!*[52]

Dámaso Alonso already noted the masterly alternation of the *a* and the *o* in this stanza, especially in the last two verses, and the wonderful effects this has on the reader. But quite apart from stylistic devices (which are not the same thing as the poetry itself, just as the description of a dissected corpse cannot explain the nature of man), poetry clearly has a role to play in any attempt to say something more about a reality which is already ineffable on the purely natural level and which, when it reaches the supernatural level (as is the case here), is absolutely beyond man's ability either to attain or to describe.

> *The king has brought me into his chambers.*
> *We will exult and rejoice in you;*
> *we will extol your love more than wine.*[53]

The communion and exchange of lives, which is the most important effect of love, logically leads to mutual possession. When this

---

[52] In the *Noche Oscura*:

> *¡Oh noche que guiaste!*
> *¡Oh noche amable más que el alborada!*
> *¡Oh noche que juntaste*
> *Amado con amada,*
> *amada en el Amado transformada!*

[53] Sg 1:4.

happens, both lovers give themselves to be the total and absolute possession of the other:

> *My beloved is mine and I am his,*
> *he pastures his flock among the lilies.*[54]
>
> ....
>
> *I am my beloved's and my beloved is mine;*
> *he pastures his flock among the lilies.*[55]
>
> ....
>
> *I am my beloved's*
> *and his desire is for me.*[56]

It is impossible to describe things like these, because their greatness transcends the purely human sphere, but poetry can give us some help to put things in place. For someone living in a post–Christian world which has forgotten God, and in a Church in crisis which seems to have marginalized the supernatural world and allowed charity to grow cold, poetry provides us anew with encouragement in the form of a beauty which transcends the world around us. And with that beauty comes true goodness and genuine truth. At this point man feels immersed in a powerful thrill of emotion, which is what happens precisely at the point when he realizes that the reality of being (goodness, truth and beauty) still exists in the universe and is in fact the only thing that is truly real. Man then discovers once more that the world is not entirely the kingdom of

---

[54] Sg 2:16.
[55] Sg 6:3.
[56] Sg 7:11.

lies, and that perfect joy is the exclusive patrimony of those who hunger for justice, the patrimony of the clean of heart, of the poor, of those who mourn, and of those who bear peace within their own soul and spread it to others. By elevating man above himself, mystical poetry also makes him realize what true love really is. For, what the whole thing is about is true love, that ineffable reality which man, mysteriously, seems bent on destroying. To the ancient question which philosophers and theologians have always posed —Why is being better than non–being?— one can certainly in all justice add another: How can hatred be better than love, and how can it be possible to hate love...? But, in the meantime, God and man together continue to seek solitude and oblivion, in order to be able to give themselves into the joyful and total possession one of another:

> *My Lover, I would like*
> *to enjoy your supper in the fresh air of*
> *the garden,*
> *for it is spring time*
> *and the mountains are now filled*
> *with rosemary, thyme, and mint.*
>
> *Let us join hands*
> *and go to see the green meadows,*
> *the orchards of apple trees,*
> *the groves of pomegranate trees,*
> *the silver poplars in the river banks.*[57]

---

[57]In the original:

> *Amado, yo quisiera*
> *al aire del jardín gustar tu cena,*
> *pues es la primavera*
> *y el monte ya se llena*
> *de romero, tomillo y hierbabuena.*

Contemplation and poetry 221

> *My Lover, we will climb*
> *the mountains of the rosemary and rockrose,*
> *and then we will drink,*
> *the two of us, from the abundant spring,*
> *its fresh, clear, and murmuring waters.*[58]

This attempts to echo the impassioned utterance that the bride of the *Song*, across the darkness of the centuries, has been sending out:

> *Come, my beloved, let us go forth into the fields,*
> *and lodge in the villages;*
> *let us go out early to the vineyards,*
> *and see whether the vines have budded,*
> *whether the grape blossoms have opened*
> *and the pomegranates are in bloom.*
> *There I will give you my love.*[59]

The thrill which man feels through the beauty evoked by poetry is nothing other than the emotion that overcomes him in the face

---

> *Juntemos nuestras manos*
> *y vámonos a ver los verdes prados,*
> *los huertos de manzanos,*
> *los bosques de granados,*
> *las riberas de chopos plateados.*

[58] In the original:

> *Mi Amado, subiremos*
> *al monte del tomillo y de la jara,*
> *y luego beberemos*
> *los dos, en la alfaguara,*
> *el agua rumorosa, fresca y clara.*

[59] Sg 7: 12–13.

of the mystery of being and, in the last analysis, the mystery of God. Encountering beauty is the equivalent of encountering truth and goodness, which is the same as saying being; for being is simply God, when being possesses the fullness of the infinite. Once one has scaled the peak and found beauty, it is easy to find goodness and truth there also, if one just looks a little to the right and left. Just as these transcendentals are identical with being, in their supreme degree they become one thing with that Being Whose essence it is to exist, Who possesses them in all fullness, or, rather, Who is them but to an infinite degree. Therefore, poetry does not even have to expressly mention Him Who, besides, has a Name above all other names; and therefore mystical poetry is not afraid to use profane forms when speaking of infinite Beauty. For man only needs to cross the threshold of the world of beauty to sense that he has come very near to God. This can be seen, for example, in these fragments from the last chapter of *The Lord of the Rings*, Tolkien's great epic poem:

"It was evening, and the stars were glimmering in the eastern sky as they passed the ruined oak and turned and went on down the hill between the hazel–thickets. Sam was silent, deep in his memories. Presently he became aware that Frodo was singing softly to himself, singing the old walking–song, but the words were not quite the same.

> *Still round the corner there may wait*
> *A new road or a secret gate;*
> *And though I oft have passed them by,*
> *A day will come at last when I*
> *Shall take the hidden paths that run*
> *West of the Moon, East of the Sun.*

Contemplation and poetry 223

"And as if in answer, from down below coming up the road out of the valley, voices sang:

> *We still remember, we who dwell*
> *In this far land beneath the trees,*
> *The starlight on the Western Seas.*

"Frodo and Sam halted and sat silent in the soft shadows, until they saw a shimmer as the travellers came towards them.

"There was Gildor and many fair Elven folk; and there to Sam's wonder rode Elrond and Galadriel. Elrond wore a mantle of grey and had a star upon his forehead, and a silver harp was in his hand, and upon his finger was a ring of gold with a great blue stone, Vilya, mightiest of the Three. But Galadriel sat upon a white palfrey and was robed all in glimmering white, like clouds about the Moon; for she herself seemed to shine with a soft light. On her finger was Nenya, the ring wrought of mithril, that bore a single white stone flickering like a frosty star...

"Then Elrond and Galadriel rode on; for the Third Age was over, and the Days of the Rings were passed, and an end was come of the story and song of those times. With them went many Elves of the High Kindred who would no longer stay in Middle–earth; and among them, filled with a sadness that was yet blessed and without bitterness, rode Sam, and Frodo, and Bilbo, and the Elves delighted to honour them.

"Though they rode through the midst of the Shire all the evening and all the night, none saw them pass, save the wild creatures: or here and there some wanderer in the dark who saw a swift shimmer under the trees, or a light and shadow flowing through the grass as the Moon went westward. And when they had passed from the

Shire, going about the south skirts of the White Downs, they came to the Far Downs, and to the Towers, and looked on the distant Sea; and so they rode down at last to Mithlond, to the Grey Havens in the long firth of Lune.

"As they came to the gates Cįrdan the Shipwright came forth to greet them. Very tall he was, and his beard was long, and he was grey and old, save that his eyes were keen as stars; and he looked at them and bowed, and said:

—All is now ready.

"Then Cįrdan led them to the Havens, and there was a white ship lying, and upon the quay beside a great grey horse stood a figure robed all in white awaiting them. As he turned and came towards them Frodo saw that Gandalf now wore openly upon his hand the Third Ring, Narya the Great, and the stone upon it was red as fire. Then those who were to go were glad, for they knew that Gandalf also would take ship with them.

"But Sam was now sorrowful at heart, and it seemed to him that if the parting would be bitter, more grievous still would be the long road home alone. But even as they stood there, and the Elves were going aboard, and all was being made ready to depart, up rode Merry and Pippin in great haste. And amid his tears Pippin laughed.

—You tried to give us the slip once before and failed, Frodo, —he said—. This time you have nearly succeeded, but you have failed again. It was not Sam, though, that gave you away this time but Gandalf himself!

—Yes, —said Gandalf—; for it will be better to ride back three together than one alone. Well, here at last, dear friends, on the shores of the Sea comes the end of our fellowship in Middle–earth.

Go in peace! I will not say: do not weep; for not all tears are an evil."

As can be seen, once more we find, side by side, beauty, love, death, and painful, final farewells. The majestic and gentle beauty of the poetic language combines here with the no less impressive beauty of the situation described in the poem. Which is the more impressive? It would be difficult to say, just as it would be difficult to say also as regards other similar pages of world literature which have achieved immortality. That is what happens in Bernanos' *Diary of a Country Priest*, whose last words before dying, which virtually mark the end of the famous diary —"grace is everywhere"— led Charles Moeller[60] to say that they were the most beautiful statement to be found in twentieth–century literature. The same applies to the concluding dissertation of the Chronicler Cide Hamete Benengueli in Cervantes' great work when he turns to his pen, after describing the death of Don Quixote, and says to it, with sadness and at the same time with joy: "Here shall thou remain, hung upon this rack by this brass wire. I know not if thou beest well cut or not, O pen of mine, but here thou shall live for long ages to come, unless some presumptuous and scoundrelly historians should take thee down to profane thee."

We find the same in the Bible, for it could not occur otherwise: *Because I have said these things to you, sorrow has filled your hearts. Nevertheless I tell you the truth: it is to your advantage that I go away, for if I do not go away, the Counsellor will not come to you; but if I go, I will send him to you... A little while, and you will see me no more; again a little while, and you will see me... So you have*

---

[60]Charles Moeller, *Literatura del Siglo XX y Cristianismo*, I, Gredos, Madrid, 1961, 3¦ parte, cap. III.

sorrow now, but I will see you again and your hearts will rejoice and no one will take your joy from you.[61]

However, a new element appears here: the incredible novelty of divine–human love, which is the only love that can make final farewells become momentary ones. For this love alone, and not purely human love, is the one that endures forever (1 Cor 13:8). That is how the poetry of the Bible manages to add something essential which was lacking in purely human love and literature: the joy caused by an expected and desired eternity without which human joy could never have been joy. Without this hope of eternal joy, human poetry would have been a veiled shadow, forever condemned to try to dissemble and hide (but never succeed in doing so) the bitterness of the human heart.

And so the sacred author also has recourse to poetry, making the Bridegroom say, quite rightly, regarding Himself:

*I am the root and the offspring of David,
the bright morning star.*[62]

A Bridegroom Who feels as in love with his bride as he does has no qualms about turning to her and saying to her:

*How fair and pleasant you are,
O loved one, delectable maiden.*[63]

....

---

[61] Jn 16: 6–7.16.22.
[62] Rev 22:16.
[63] Sg 7:7. Cf. 6:4.

> *Turn away your eyes from me,*
> *for they hold me captive.*[64]

Here we have the incredible mystery of the love of God for man. If he had kept that in mind, man would never have needed to go in search of his own grandeur, because none has addressed such ardent loving praise to the human being as God Himself has:

> *Who is this that looks forth like the dawn,*
> *fair as the moon,*
> *bright as the sun,*
> *terrible as an army with banners?*[65]

That is why the bride is, and will always be, unable to heed those who urge her to give an account of her love. She feels unable to speak about her Bridegroom's love, to explain what goes on in the intimacy of the love–dialogue of contemplation. That is why she has recourse to poetry, in order to give some sort of answer to the eager demands of her enquirers:

> *What makes your lover better than other lovers,*
> *O loveliest of women?*
> *What makes your lover better than other lovers,*
> *to put us under such an oath?*[66]

In the end, the best she can do by way of reply is to invite her companions to follow her. For, in the presence of something that is

---

[64]Sg 6:5.
[65]Sg 6:10.
[66]Sg 5:9.

so wonderful and ineffable that she can find no words to describe it, the only course open is for them to travel the road together, so as to reach the great goal to which really all are called: *"We have found Him of whom Moses in the Law and the prophets wrote, Jesus son of Joseph, from Nazareth." Nathanael said to him, "From Nazareth? Can anything good come from that place?" Philip replied, "Come and see."*[67] And that is the way her companions understand it:

> *Whither has your beloved gone,*
> *O fairest among women?*
> *Whither has your beloved turned*
> *that we may seek him with you?*[68]

Moreover, the journey will be more bearable and pleasant when the wayfarers keep each other company. Who knows? perhaps it is a journey that can only be taken together:

> *If you are heading toward the hillock,*
> *allow me to accompany you, pilgrim,*
> *let us see if he whom I love*
> *gives us of his wine to drink*
> *as we reach the end of the road together.*[69]

---

[67] Jn 1: 45–46.
[68] Sg 6:1.
[69] In the original:

> *Si vas hacia el otero,*
> *deja que te acompañe, peregrino,*
> *a ver si el que yo quiero*
> *nos da a beber su vino*
> *en acabando juntos el camino.*

The best way of following the route back to the Father's house is that of going in the company of others, for a Christian should never cease to rely on his brethren's help. As the great Gandalf said in Tolkien's epic: "Yes, for it will be better to ride back three together than one alone."

CHAPTER IV

CONTEMPLATION AND FAITH

God has poured his Love into the human heart (Rom 5:5), although in this life man only possesses it in the form of an earnest or first–fruits (Rom 8:23; 2 Cor 1:22; 5:5). However, even though it takes this imperfect form, it is still true that divine–human love is a happy reality within man's reach.

But, although divine–human love in this life is something provisional, something imperfectly possessed, that is true only insofar as the fullness of love has yet still to come, as love has not yet reached its definitive consummation. The whole point about an earnest or first–fruits is that it is a reality partially or provisionally possessed, always with reference to the fullness still to come.[1] It is clear that

---

[1] The concept of earnest or first–fruits implies two fundamental ideas: the sparsity and imperfection of a present, on the one hand, and the promise of a future of perfection and fullness, on the other. What happens is that here the sparsity is so abundant and rich that it can be regarded as small only when compared with the totality that its definitive possession guarantees.

divine love, poured into man, is a reality that can flood the human heart with ineffable feelings, even now. As the bride says in the Song, speaking in a context which clearly refers also to the present age: *Your loves are better than wine.*

A love which involves permanent absence, or total lack of knowledge of the loved one, is inconceivable, because one cannot love what one does not know. But a love which has not yet reached its ultimate perfection must necessarily be nourished by nostalgia and memories (which presuppose previous contact or friendship with the loved one). On the other hand, if the mystery of hope as a theological virtue is nothing other than the mystery of the tension between the *not yet* and the *already*, clearly that also means that the *already* exists now. St John of the Cross, the mystic of the *Nights* and the nothings, of pure faith and of spiritual nakedness, is also the mystical poet of the *Spiritual Canticle*, able to write in the last stanza of his *Dark Night* that almost divine farewell, which he places on the lips of the bride:

> *Lost to myself I stayed,*
> *my face reclining on the Beloved;*
> *everything ceased and I abandoned myself,*
> *throwing my cares*
> *among the lilies to lie forgotten.*[2]

---

[2]In the original:

> *Quedéme y olvidéme,*
> *el rostro recliné sobre el Amado,*
> *cesó todo y dejéme,*
> *dejando mi cuidado*
> *entre las azucenas olvidado.*

To realize how divine love can flood the human being with ineffable feelings, one need do no more than read the *Song of Songs*. As regards feelings of joy and gladness, one can go, for example, to the discourse at the last supper, where Jesus says to his disciples, among other things, that *you have sorrow now, but I will see you again and your hearts will rejoice, and no one will take your joy from you... Hitherto you have asked nothing in my name; ask, and you will receive, that your joy may be full.*[3] As the Apostle also says, *the kingdom of God does not mean food and drink, but righteousness and peace and joy in the Holy Spirit.*[4] So, divine love gives man an incredible superabundance of feelings and of life: *The fruit of the Spirit is love, joy, peace, patience, kindness, goodness, faithfulness, gentleness, self-control; against such there is no law.*[5] Which is what Jesus Himself said earlier, in mysterious words of unsuspected depth: *I came that they may have life, and have it abundantly.*[6]

Love can exist with a mutual presence of the lovers which is not yet complete, or with a knowledge and possession which are not yet total for either of them. But all that is only the path to something which is called to find its fulfilment in perfection: *Now I know in part; then I shall understand fully.*[7] The earnests and first-fruits which for the time being constitute the basis and background of divine–human love are affected in the same sort of way as happens with the problem of the knowledge of God which man is able to attain in his present situation. For, the principle that *si intelligis non est Deus*, which applies to the knowledge about God that man has, is not meant to stress a radical lack of knowledge of God on

---

[3] Jn 16: 22.24.
[4] Rom 14:17.
[5] Gal 5: 22–23.
[6] Jn 10:10.
[7] 1 Cor 13:12. Cf. 1 Jn 3:2.

man's part, but rather that no matter how much he knows about God there is still much more to know (of course, it also does emphasize the absolute transcendence of God with respect to human knowledge). This says quite a lot about how much further man's knowledge has to go, but it says very little about the allegedly little knowledge of God that man already possesses. On the other hand, if *now we see in a mirror darkly, but then face to face*, according to the Apostle,[8] that must mean that man can see even now, albeit in an imperfect way or as if in a dark mirror.

Perhaps the key to the question lies in what the Apostle goes on to say: *Faith, hope, love abide, these three; but the greatest of these is love.*[9] So, charity is *already* a fact, insofar as it is in fellowship with hope and faith. In this way the present reality of love is recognized —for the time being an imperfect reality since it still relies on faith and hope (because of the absence of the beloved), and at the same time there is the hint that we await a future in which love will be perfectly consummated. Indeed, that perfect love was already expressly promised: *Then face to face.* Certainly, at least one thing is very clear: the beautiful reality of divine–human love already exists, drawing its nourishment from hope and immersed in the obscurity of faith.

All this can be transferred, in the practical sphere, to putting us on guard against certain over–sentimental attitudes which tend to disregard essential elements —faith and hope— in the genuine divine–human love. Catholic liturgy is in fact very much at risk from attitudes of this sort, which sometimes express themselves in very peculiar forms.

---

[8] 1 Cor 13:12.
[9] 1 Cor 13:13.

Liturgical action, for example, has ceased to look *to God* as its principle objective; instead it has turned almost entirely *towards man*. It is no longer a matter of honouring God in the first place, but of attracting man, or even of entertaining him. Liturgical ceremonies have lost their religious unction and become more like a *show*. As far as the Mass is concerned, the consecration has ceased to have pride of place; this is now held by the readings and things surrounding them. Much importance is given to the multiform activity of a legion of *ministers* who are coming and going and doing things right through the ceremony: so much is going on that the *principal celebrant* could disappear from the scene without his absence attracting much attention.[10] The faithful in fact have become used to giving the same importance to a Mass as to so–called *liturgies of the word*.[11] Also, people no longer try so intently to participate in our Lord's death, as to participate actively in the ceremony (a very different thing indeed). No longer is it so important to take part in the banquet of the Lord's Body in a dignified way;[12] what really matters now is taking part in the entire ceremony, receiving

---

[10] In the old solemn pontifical Masses which used to be celebrated in cathedrals prior to Vatican II, and whose ceremonial was explained in enormous detail in the manuals, a large number of ministers were involved in addition to the Bishop: Assistant Priests, Deacons, Sub–deacons, assistants at the throne, Masters of ceremonies, thurifiers, torch–bearers, candle–bearers, etc. But it was plain to see (as it still is in the eastern liturgies) that the whole ceremony had a decidedly sacred atmosphere, always hinging on the person of the Bishop and above all on the Eucharist; Latin and Gregorian chant contributed not a little to this atmosphere.

[11] *Liturgies of the word*, led by deacons, and more frequently everyday by lay people, are termed by many as *masses without consecration*. The alarming aspect of this fact is that the simple faithful do believe it so, which proves how ubiquitously spread out confusion is.

[12] 1 Cor 11: 23–29.

communion at all costs, whether worthy or not.[13] And so you find, for example, the book of the Gospels being carried in procession with pomp reminiscent of the way the Ark of the Covenant used to be carried around —all with the valid desire, undoubtedly, to emphasize the presence of Christ in his Word— and then, in the very same ceremony, the Eucharist is sadly treated, not at all with the respect and reverence it deserves. The odd thing is that the content of the homily is not always on a par with the fastuous ceremonies that precede it —rather like what happens with nuts, which make a lot of noise but produce little to eat.[14]

They do not want to remember that genuine love is based, above all, on faith and hope: *As it is, these remain: faith, hope and love, the three of them; and the greatest of them is love.*[15] And, although the Lord already issued a warning about the danger of taking easy paths,[16] his disciples seem to have forgotten it. The crisis of faith which has let loose an unbridled hedonism among Christians has led to a general lack of appreciation of supernatural values and has created a vogue for an easy, empty type of Christianity. And this is how the kneeling before the world (an expression coined by Maritain) and the horror of appearing not to be integrated in the new and only

---

[13]Loss of awareness of the need to be in the state of grace in order to receive Communion has played a big part in people's loss of faith in the real presence of Christ in the Eucharist. And the same might be said of the indiscriminate and often unnecessary multiplication of *eucharistic ministers*; or of the easy access given to all and sundry to use the eucharistic Sacrament any way they want, which has turned the tabernacle into something very like a *self-service* machine.

[14]Also, one can see that lack of faith in the real eucharistic presence also infallibly leads to unbelief in the presence of Christ in his Word.

[15]1 Cor 13:13.

[16]*Enter by the narrow gate, since the road that leads to destruction is wide and spacious, and many take it; but it is a narrow gate and a hard road that leads to life, and only a few find it* (Mt 7: 13–14).

set of values that the System of this world admits has come to pass among Christians.[17] As far as Pastors are concerned, many of them have chosen to ignore the real problems, in order to devote their whole attention to those questions only which the *media* and the world put the emphasis on at any particular time; they give the impression that they are more concerned with projecting an image of modernity and rapport with the world than with attending to the needs of the faithful. Yet again one can clearly see that the old temptation to present a *reasonable* Christianity, a Christianity accessible to and accepted by the world —a chimera, which goes right back to the mysterious world of the Gnosis— is one of the most subtle of all temptations, always trying to entrap the disciples of Jesus Christ.

St John of the Cross, in the course of a commentary on Psalm 19:3,[18] once again stresses the need for faith to enlighten and guide everyone in this world. According to the saint, when the psalm says that *et nox nocti indicat scientiam*, he is referring to life in this world; this life is deep night and it is illuminated in turn by the other dark, though infallible, night of faith. Faith, actualized by

---

[17]The *de facto* legalization of divorce and the *de iure* legalization of contraceptives, the putting out of mind the idea of God's providential care and the consequent fear of having a large family, the fall–off and even disappearance of the practice of receiving the sacraments, the disintegration of the family and the unavailability of Christian education for children, horror at the notion of sacrifice (and the immediate effect of this, scandal at the cross), the forgetting of prayer, ignorance of the true meaning of the Mass, the discredit of the so–called passive Christian virtues (such as humility, obedience or poverty), the absence of genuine catechesis, and the crisis of confidence in the Hierarchy are a few further examples. However, this has not prevented many official statistics, in true triumphalist style, from proclaiming, without a trace of a blush, that the Church is going through a splendid period.

[18]*Ascent of Mount Carmel*, III, 5.6.

charity and good works (the other virtues), is in fact what leads to sharing in our Lord's cross and to the perfection of the Christian life that results from that sharing.

There are those who put too much emphasis on what they claim are *charisms* more or less spectacular, evidencing a presence of the Spirit which is not always paralleled by a serious life of virtue. So it may be necessary to recall that St Paul identifies the fruits of the Spirit as *love, joy, peace, patience, kindness, goodness, faithfulness, gentleness, self-control,*[19] and that the Apostle goes on to add that *those who belong to Christ Jesus have crucified the flesh with its passions and desires,*[20] adding in the next breath as a logical consequence that *if we live by the Spirit, let us also walk by the Spirit.*[21]

But it is clear that walking according to the Spirit does not mean, in any sense, walking on trodden paths. The way of the cross has never seemed an easy way, especially if one remembers that the best guide to help us follow it is that offered by the dark night of faith: *et nox nocti indicat scientiam.* The Church can easily find herself in a fairly delicate situation if she forgets the danger that easy paths imply. Avoidance of difficulty, particularly in terrain where there is no other path than the steep and narrow path of the cross, can be a dangerous trap: *Enter by the narrow gate; for the gate is wide and the way is easy, that leads to destruction, and those who enter by it are many. For the gate is narrow and the way is hard, that leads to life, and those who find it are few...*[22] *Strive to enter by the narrow door; for many, I tell you, will seek to enter and will not*

---

[19] Gal 5: 22–23.
[20] Gal 5:24.
[21] Gal 5:25.
[22] Mt 7: 13–14.

*be able.*²³ Easy ways have never proved themselves to be the right ones for Christians.

The practice whereby children *preach* the homily in special children's Masses, for example (by the system of asking each child his opinion on the Gospel pericope of the day or some such method), can add a certain novelty and keep children's attention, and maybe bring up some amusing, naive anecdotes; but experience shows that these methods can easily make people regard them as always being a guaranteed success. And, what is worse, the true effectiveness —almost *ex opere operato*— of preaching is displaced by blind confidence in a kind of *ex opere operantis* system, a purely human one, whose usefulness is very questionable. By not putting much reliance on the actual graces which preaching can produce —and preaching should, in turn, be backed up by prayer and the good example of the preacher—, one tries to use instead purely human pedagogic methods, devoid of supernatural content, which one imagines to be much more effective. It is true that actual graces are by no means incompatible with teaching methods which make it easier for such graces to be communicated; but it is one thing to smoothen out paths and quite another to use spells which one regards as little less than infallible talismans. Putting the emphasis on human methods with little or no supernatural content, as if they were the universal panacea for pastoral success, is only one step away from believing that the supernatural does not work. One has heard of pastors, to give an example, who are convinced of the inefficacy of the Gospel unless it is explained to people in the form of *renewing one's life*. Besides, strange as it may seem, children also need to practice a certain asceticism in the liturgical context: it is good for them to feel things drag a little. Some people think that in order to get a sense

---

²³Lk 13:24.

of the sacred, the faithful must at all costs be distracted by more or less well–organized *entertainment*; but this approach really does not seem well–founded. The acting out of the Gospel pericope of the day by the children to whom it is addressed —another method currently used to spirit away the homily— may be an interesting experience from the artistic or theatrical point of view, but it is very doubtful and questionable whether it is good pastoral practice in the context of a Mass. Children, like other members of the faithful, are sheep who form part of Christ's flock, and they need to hear the preaching of the word of God —in line with the *fides ex auditu*— from the mouth of the priest.[24] The fact is that it is not an easy job to prepare and then preach the homily (independently of who the congregation is): it takes study and prayer, commitment and the witness of a good life. It is the last–mentioned item, above all, which leads some preachers to put these difficulties to one side, particularly when innovations also have the advantage of giving their promoters a certain aura of being revolutionary and avant–garde.

No one denies the need and desirability of celebrating Mass for particular groups of people on special occasions, as is done in religious communities, seminaries, schools, hospitals, barracks, and on days of recollection, retreats and in other circumstances which may arise. However, it is no longer very clear that children derive any benefit by regularly attending celebrations designed specially for them. In addition to being called to be reared in a Christian home, children also need to feel themselves part of a religious community or family —the parish, for example, and in the last analysis, the Church— which, as everyone knows, is —like the natural family—

---

[24]The homily (like all catechesis) must be adapted to the mentality of the congregation (in this case, children) yet be serious and profound. Adapting the language of the Gospel to the listener has nothing to do with such things as superficiality, commonness, and blandness: cf. Col 4:6.

also made up of a providential and heterogeneous assembly of children, mature people and the aged.[25] A *family* in which there were only children or only old people would look like something forced, something rather artificial —the same sort of atmosphere as one finds in a hospice or old people's home.

It is clear that Masses *adapted* to suit young people —often far too adapted— run the risk of diluting the sacred and solemn character of the liturgy. Also, the widespread use of methods and arrangements devoid of supernatural content can reach the stage of turning them into an infantile show, in the worst sense of the word. And all this is being done because, on the one hand, people forget that children possess a faith they received at baptism which in general does not have any complexes or doubts; on the other hand, it seems to be taken for granted that they are incapable of assimilating the rich content of Christian truths. And so they are taught a body of doctrine which is in fact nothing but a religion *for children* in the very worst sense.

The designing of ceremonies to make them *accessible* to children, with the good intention of making it easier for them to play a part in them, can also cause the sacrificial character of the Mass to fall into oblivion. What this does is make participation in the cross and death of our Lord seem something far too distant, if not forgotten altogether. And the result of this is that children do not even come to know of the existence of this fundamental basis of the Christian life (Gal 2:19). The modern world vigorously rejects any attempt

---

[25] Modern pleasure–seeking society, in addition to destroying the family, has striven to drive the old out of the home. But the venerable figure of the grandfather, or *paterfamilias* of a family, while he may have only moral authority, is still beneficial to young people and infants, as part of a pedagogical and educational system, in the last analysis invented by God, in the natural institution that the family is.

to give children the idea of suffering, even though it is a Christian suffering. For contemporary child–pedagogy, it is an axiomatic truth that they must at all cost be kept away from anything connected with sacrifice; with the result that they are prevented from growing up to be true men and true Christians. Afterwards, no weight is ever given to the fact that, due to the destruction of the family, children are deprived of the joy of living in the bosom of a true home and are at the mercy of all kinds of suffering.

The temptation to seek easy paths, and the search for God which does not feel obliged to follow the dark, rocky road of faith, have always been there, but they come more to the fore in times when people lose sight of the supernatural dimension of things. At such times it can happen that one no longer knows what one is looking for, and even Pastors may leave the real problems to one side and turn to questions which may be futile or marginal but which happen to enjoy certain acceptance among the people at large.

In the last decades of the twentieth century, the official Church in the United States has considered it necessary to deal with a problem which, although widespread throughout the world, seems to concern North American society in a particular way. The problem we refer to is known by the unpleasant name of *machismo*, and it has to do with an alleged despotic exercise of power by man over woman. Official Churches tend to be alert to the way the wind blows in their societies, so it is not surprising that the North American Church should have decided to concentrate its efforts in eradicating machismo. In this way the official Church once again, by echoing this theme which is aired a lot in the media, has shown that it is in tune with the modern world or —to put it another way— the world of its time. The happy objective in this instance is none other than to give women the pre–eminent place that they undoubtedly deserve. As if the Church, who rightly calls the Virgin Mary *Mater Ecclesiæ* and *Regina Cœli*, had ignored women and never taken them into consideration...

But unfortunately it is not always the case that the themes the mass media bring up to date are in fact the most important ones, and it may not be going too far to say that very often the only object pursued by the *media* is that of drawing attention away from the real problems. Since this is not the right place for a sociological analysis of the subject, perhaps it is sufficient to point to the possibility that, if anyone ever did conduct an analysis —with all due objectivity and serenity— perhaps the results would show that the campaign against machismo is simply a new kind of witch–hunt.

Of course, no one denies that modern society is affected by the disease of machismo, just as it is affected by many other vices and defects. Some of them, we know, are talked about more than others; others are the subject of a strange silence (when they are not actually praised and defended).[26] But it should also be accepted that modern society (like every society in crisis and even though one would prefer not to admit it) is also affected by the phenomenon which one might term, somewhat euphemistically, the matriarchal society, which is just the opposite of what is widely bandied about.

It is clear that the role of woman in society is so important and so large that it does not need to be stressed. Nor is there any need for women to try to take over everything men have been doing up to now, in order to have their dignity and value acknowledged by all. Once it is accepted —obviously there is no question about it— that women are neither inferior nor superior to men, it is no longer necessary to show that women's excellence is helped and even enhanced when women show themselves to be *real women*, with no

---

[26]Which is what is happening now with homosexuality and concubinage, for example.

need to become judges, tractor drivers or lieutenant–colonels. And although it is undeniable that women are perfectly capable of doing these and similar things, it is equally true that they have no need of them in order to make their exceptional qualities quite obvious. On the other hand, there is the danger, when they do get involved in such things, that they will cease to do other, more important things that only they can do. One way or another, the current witch–hunt against *machismo* is having serious repercussions within the Church.

No one would dare deny that the Church has always recognized the exceptional role played, over the centuries, by women both in the Church and in society —with the Blessed Virgin Mary in the lead, proclaimed as she is as the greatest of all purely human beings, be they men or women. It is impossible to count the women who, within the Church and over the past two thousand years, have devoted their lives to mankind through prayer and penance or through charitable works, especially in the sphere of education. Not to mention the role played by women as educators and trainers of the children of God in the bosom of Christian homes or the undeniable fact, to cite only one example from ordinary life, that women have always given men an example of fortitude and spirit of sacrifice, despite their totally unjustified label of the *weaker sex*. Nor is there anything to compare with the incredible heroism, for the most part ignored, of the millions of mothers who have lived on this earth. Clearly, the decisive influence of women on the life of the Church from its foundation right down to modern times, and in the evolution of society —an influence quite on a par with that of men— is an undeniable fact, but one that statistics fail to notice.

All this, however, is being relegated very much to a secondary plane, as if people hoped it would be put totally out of mind. Those who are behind the struggle against *machismo* argue that women should also carry out functions within the Church which have hitherto been seen as exclusive to men. This is clearly going to have important consequences; and it will perhaps create certain dangers, which have to do not so much with whether women carry out certain liturgical functions (such as distributing holy communion, acting as readers or preaching),[27] *as with the possibility that the key and untransferable role which women are called to perform in the Church may be marginalized, forgotten, or even abolished.* It is odd, for example, that they would have us believe that a woman is more important when she gives out the Eucharist than when she devotes herself to such things as the contemplative life, or works of charity or mercy, or the education of her children and looking after her husband in the context of a Christian home (which, besides, could not survive, or could survive only with so much difficulty, without a woman's self–sacrifice and heroic work).

The truth is that the *machismo* approach gives the impression of being a bogeyman, a monster created by the feminist movement and not at all a sociological fact —and one whose aim is not to dignify women but to destroy women as persons and as the essential basis of the family. And it is even more surprising how ecclesiastics, naively supporting this ploy, can let themselves be convinced that this is a serious *problem.* Perhaps we might apply here —given that the phenomenon is becoming common practice within the Church— what Gilson said about certain neo–Thomists who, on the epistemological problem of knowledge, felt overcome by the need —a really serious matter, according to them— to reconcile St Thomas with Descartes and Kant: "After Kant, whose doctrine was the radical

---

[27]When the Church considers it opportune, in view of particular needs and circumstances, she clearly has good reasons for doing so, which all the faithful should respect.

negation of their dogmatic metaphysics, they asked themselves how their own dogmatism could be justified by the critique. It would seem that, for them, the history of philosophy is an undifferentiated whole, so that whenever one philosophy asks a question, all other philosophies must ask the very same question. This is why we see so many Thomists and Aristotelians seeking to obtain from Aristotle and St Thomas answers to problems which were brought about by the abandonment of classical realism. They are engaged in what could be called a 'naive realism,' one in which it is sufficient proof that there actually is a critical problem to say: *some one has posed it.*"[28] This gets right to the nerve–centre of the question, for many people let themselves be drawn into relatively unimportant questions or ones which have little to do with their own sphere of activity —in this case the ecclesiastical sphere— and they fail to attend to really vital matters which brook no delay. For example, in the face of the pressing problem of shortage of priests, it does not make sense to debate about the ordination of women when at the same time there is no genuine concern over the true state of seminaries or the level of training of the clergy; or when the idea of priesthood is being allowed to be destroyed; or when there is no truly supernatural program able to attract young people who are even ignorant of Christian ideals. There are many, perhaps due to fear of offering true solutions or fear of adopting too great a commitment, who are unaware that it is quite some time since modern medicine stopped using remedies such as hot poultices. Once launched on its Quixotic campaign to eradicate *machismo*, the North American Church has lost no opportunity to make it the subject of Conferences and a goodly number of enlightening exhortations, undoubtedly with the

---

[28]Étienne Gilson, *Réalisme Thomiste et Critique de la Connaissance*, Vrin, Paris, 1986, p. 175.

good and praiseworthy intention of showing that it is quite in tune with the world and sincerely wants to solve its problems. But in the meantime other pressing matters remain to be dealt with: racial hatred and injustice, the seminaries and the crisis of vocations, the moral degeneration of the clergy, consecrated souls leaving their communities, the disorientation of religious (both men and women), liturgical anarchy, Masses and preaching devoid of supernatural content, the *financial exploitation* of parishes, the tragic withering away of Catholic schools and the consequent danger to catechesis, the loss of the sense of sin and the virtual disappearance of the sacrament of penance, the desacralization of the Eucharist, the crisis of faith, the corrupting of dogma and moral teaching, the intrusion of Protestant theology, the fierce hedonism that imbues the environment, the tensions cleaving conservative and liberal Catholics, loss of prestige by the Hierarchy, and even the danger of schism within the national Church itself, to cite a few examples.

It may be that underlying all this is the undeniable fact that Christians have forgotten, that in the present state of the pilgrim Church in which they all find themselves, *all genuine love is a crucified love.* As was said above, following St Paul, true charity is always, in this present economy, found in the company of faith and hope: *Faith, hope and love abide, these three; but the greatest of these is love.*[29] Everyone can see that in the present age charity cannot exist without the darkness of faith and without the needs and absences which necessitate hope. Or to put it in another way: every disciple who would aspire to fall in love with the Lord needs to share in the cross. No one can speak of love unless he is ready to share in the destiny of the one he loves. And, since that was the destiny of the Master, the only road open to his disciples is that of

---

[29] 1 Cor 13:13.

the cross. *Whoever does not bear his own cross and come after me cannot be my disciple.*[30] Love cannot happen unless it involves the desire to stay with the loved one, to live like him, and even to share his fate, making a reality of that *I for you and you for me, for my life is your life and your life is mine.* That is why Jesus said: *As the living Father sent me, and I live because of the Father, so he who eats me will live because of me.*[31] So, it is necessary to live by drawing nourishment from hope and being guided by faith, because for the Christian that is the only way successfully to pass through the vicissitudes of the long, dark night of our earthly pilgrimage. Because what is at issue here is pilgrimage —the pilgrim Church—, and not some goal already attained and reached: *So that is how I run, not without a clear goal; and how I box, not wasting blows on air. I punish my body and bring it under control, to avoid any risk that, having acted as herald for others, I myself may be disqualified.*[32] The crown is given to the victors once they have won the battle. The temptation to take the easy paths is the great danger that has always threatened Christians, even Christians with good will: *The road that leads to destruction is wide and spacious, and many take it.*[33] St John of the Cross sums this teaching up very beautifully in the stanzas of his *Dark Night*:

> *O night that guided me!*
> *O night more lovely than the dawn!*
> *O night that has joined*

---

[30] Lk 14:27.

[31] Jn 6:57.

[32] 1 Cor 9: 26–27.

[33] Mt 7:13.

> *the Beloved with his lover,*
> *lover transformed into the Beloved!*[34]

According to this, the saint does not think that the *Night* is really so bad. Undoubtedly many Christians would prefer to have a Christianity *prêt-à-porter* and easy to live, thinking maybe that this would also be more acceptable to the world. The Carmelite poet, however, is convinced that the *Night* is the only sure guide, and the only one able to bring the Lover and the loved one together. For him, the *Night*, since it is *more lovely than the dawn* is even more bearable and attractive than the latter. If it turns out that the saint was right, then we would have to conclude that many people nowadays are mistaken, which would, in turn, explain why the world rejects the debased form of Christianity which it is being offered.

Because the Beloved has to be sought during the *Night*, faith —given its darkness— is very reliable. In the heavenly Jerusalem night will be no more: *I saw no temple in the city, for this temple is the Lord God the Almighty and the Lamb. And the city has no need of sun or moon to shine upon it, for the glory of God is its light, and its lamp is the Lamb... Its gates shall never be shut by day and there shall be no night there... Night shall be no more...*[35] But in the meantime, there are no trodden paths, gaily lit to make the search easier:

---

[34]In the original:

> *¡Oh noche que guiaste!*
> *¡Oh noche amable más que el alborada!*
> *¡Oh noche que juntaste*
> *Amado con amada,*
> *amada en el Amado transformada!*

[35]Rev 21: 22–23.25; 22:5.

> *Upon my bed by night*
> *I sought him whom my soul loves;*
> *I sought him, but found him not.*[36]

The Christianity of the easy paths and broad ways (which the Master tells us lead to perdition) is the Christianity of the gnosis. The real truth is that the bride will never find the Bridegroom without experiencing considerable difficulty, and only after a hazardous search which may take a long time and will very often seem impossible and meaningless:

> *Tell me then, sweetheart,*
> *where will you lead your flock to graze,*
> *where will you rest it at noon?*
> *That I may no more wander like a vagabond*
> *beside the flocks of your companions.*[37]
>
> ....
>
> *I will rise now and go about the city,*
> *in the streets and in the squares;*
> *I will seek him whom my soul loves.*
> *I sought him, but found him not.*
> *The watchmen found me,*
> *as they went about in the city.*
> *'Have you seen him whom my soul loves?'*[38]

St John of the Cross used to gloss these passionate, filled–with–pain stanzas of the *Song*. In his *Espiritual Canticle*, he himself also

---

[36] Sg 3:1.
[37] Sg 1:7.
[38] Sg 3: 2–3.

speaks of this search for the Bridegroom: painful to the same degree as it is a passionate and a longing one:

> *Whither have you hidden yourself,*
> *O Beloved, leaving me to lament?*
> *Like the stag you have fled,*
> *having wounded me;*
> *I went after you, calling, and you were gone.*[39]

And of course no one, while still in this world, can claim that his search is over. The Spirit is too vast and too transcendent for anyone to say that he already has Him in his pocket: *The wind (spirit) blows where it wills, and you hear the sound of it, but you do not know whence it comes and whither it goes.*[40] The Spirit is absolutely free (2 Cor 3:17), and therefore no one can boast that he has already made Him his own: *So, if they say to you, "Lo, he is in the wilderness," do not go out; if they say, "Lo, he is in the inner rooms," do not believe it.*[41] The search will always involve suffering, and it always has to be made along the way of the cross and with faith as one's only guide: *Wretched man that I am! Who will deliver me from this body of death?...*[42] *Do you not know that in a race all*

---

[39] In the original:

> *¿A dónde te escondiste,*
> *Amado, y me dejaste con gemido?*
> *Como el ciervo huiste*
> *habiéndome herido;*
> *salí tras ti clamando, y eras ido.*

[40] Jn 3:8.
[41] Mt 24: 25–26.
[42] Rom 7:24.

the runners compete, but only one receives the prize? So run that you may obtain it. Every athlete exercises self-control in all things. They do it to receive a perishable wreath, but we an imperishable. Well, I do not run aimlessly, I do not box as one beating the air; but I pummel my body and subdue it...*[43]

Since love is communion of lives, following the Beloved has to mean sharing his destiny. This means that the disciple has to follow the way of the cross, has to share it: *You know the way where I am going... I am the way, and the truth, and the life.*[44] That is why the *Song* repeats:

> *I arose to open to my beloved...*
> *I opened to my beloved,*
> *but my beloved had turned and gone.*
> *I sought him, but found him not;*
> *I called him, but he gave no answer.*
> *The watchmen found me, as they went about*
>   *in the city;*
> *they beat me, they wounded me,*
> *they took away my mantle,*
> *those watchmen of the walls.*[45]

This sums up, in a poetic but exact way, what the life of the true disciple[46] is like; he will always feel the need to live on hope alone, and to get used to calling and getting no reply:

---

[43] 1 Cor 9: 24–27.

[44] Jn 14: 4.6.

[45] Sg 5: 5–7.

[46] 2 Tim 3:12: *All those who desire to lead a godly life in Christ Jesus will be persecuted.*

> *My beloved had turned and gone.*
> *I sought him, but found him not.*
> *I called him, but he gave no answer.*

And that is not all. For, along with the inner anguish caused by the absence of the Beloved and the apparent failure of one's search, there are also external trials and sufferings:

> *The watchmen found me, as they went about*
> *in the city;*
> *they beat me, they wounded me,*
> *they took away my mantle.*[47]

But undoubtedly, the worst trial of all is the absence of the Beloved that the bride feels; this is what makes her feel she is dying:

> *I adjure you, O daughters of Jerusalem,*
> *if you find my beloved,*
> *that you tell him I am sick with love.*[48]

And her sorrow becomes even more poignant when she realizes that she herself is to blame for the Beloved's absence. *There is but one sorrow: that of not being saints...* Yet man does have an even greater sorrow —that of not feeling pain over the absence of God. Sad nostalgia over the absence of the loved one is still a feeling, and indeed a beautiful feeling; but the coldness of a heart which feels indifferent to love, or to the absence of love, is nothing less than an anticipation of future condemnation.

---

[47] That is why the Apostle could quite rightly say: *We were attacked at every turn, fighting without and fear within* (2 Cor 7:5).

[48] Sg 5:8.

So, one way or another, it has to be admitted that the human condition on earth, *in this valley of tears*, is a sad one. And so the bride, who is fully aware that she is capable of abandoning the Bridegroom, tearfully begs Him in advance to take the initiative if that should happen, to seek her out and bring her back again to the fold:

> *If I should flee from your side,*
> *search for me again, friend,*
> *and, when you have found me,*
> *take me back to the path,*
> *there where you first found me.*[49]

That, in fact, is what he does. The Bridegroom is even more in love than the bride, and he is the first to go in search (Lk 15: 4–6; Mt 18: 12–14). And there is here something so wonderful (as is everything to do with love) that because it is so awesome, it is able to wipe away the sorrow the bride feels over the absence of the Beloved: for, since reciprocity is an essential part of love, the Beloved too has to undertake the search. That should not appear odd if one remembers that, as the bride does not yet fully possess the Bridegroom, neither does he yet possess the bride —which means that absences must be felt by the Bridegroom too; he too must pass through the *Night*, as the *Song* so beautifully gives us to understand:

---

[49] In the original:

> *Si huyera de tu lado,*
> *búscame tú de nuevo, compañero,*
> *y habiéndome encontrado*
> *devuélveme al sendero,*
> *allí donde me hallaste tú primero.*

Contemplation and Faith 255

> *Hark! My beloved is knocking,*
> *"Open to me, my sister, my love,*
> *my dove, my perfect one;*
> *for my head is wet with dew,*
> *my locks with the drops of the night."*[50]

And so, once again, we come to the same conclusion as regards what constitutes the true vocation of the Christian: to share his Lord's cross: *Do you not know that all of us who have been baptized into Christ Jesus were baptized into his death?*[51] That is why the Bridegroom even goes as far as to ask the bride, with a trembling and eager voice, to open to Him, *because his head is wet with dew and his locks with the drops of the night.* Because sharing means nothing less than having the same thing, experiencing the same thing, suffering the same thing, and rejoicing over the same thing: *If we have been united with Him in a death like his, we shall certainly be united with Him in a resurrection like his.*[52]

Love's quest, in this present age, is nothing other than following the way of the cross. This applies to both the bride and the Bridegroom, because love is shared and reciprocal, and the consummation of perfect love cannot take place until one at long last reaches the Fatherland: *Where I am going you cannot follow me now..., but you shall follow afterward.*[53] Hence our Lord's warning about the danger of easy paths, which are nothing but false paths. And for this reason too, contemplation, in this life, never happens except in and through faith; for there is still always something interposed between the Bridegroom and the bride: the windows, the lattice,

---

[50] Sg 5:2.
[51] Rom 6:3.
[52] Rom 6:4.
[53] Jn 13:36.

the veil of the bride. For the time being, as the Apostle said, *we see only reflexions in a mirror, mere riddles.*[54] Thus the bride:

> *My beloved is like a gazelle, or a young stag.*
> *Behold, there he stands behind our wall,*
> *gazing at the windows,*
> *looking through the lattice.*[55]
>
> ....
>
> *How beautiful you are, my love,*
> *how beautiful you are!*
> *Your eyes are doves, behind your veil.*[56]

And it could not be otherwise, for even the bride herself would not wish it: because the Bridegroom suffered, she too desires to suffer and die, in order to share his entire destiny. To live as He lived, to suffer and to rejoice as He suffered and rejoiced, to die as He died, so that we may be in everything as He was and may always be with Him. In reality the *Night* of faith that this life is, does not make sense any other way. But then that Night becomes *more lovely than the dawn*, since it is always accompanied by hope and encouraged by love. That is why those theologies which spirit away the cross are not true theologies, and why contemplation which in one way or another avoids the obscurity —and thereby the *risk!*— of faith is nothing but deception. But the Night of faith can be turned into a happy Night, if it is animated and guided by the fire of a love which for the time being must involve, above all, a quest:

---

[54] 1 Cor 13:12.
[55] Sg 2:9.
[56] Sg 4:1. Cf. 4:3; 6:7.

Contemplation and Faith

> *On the happy night,*
> *all in secret, since none saw me,*
> *nor I beheld aught,*
> *without light or guide,*
> *save that which burned within my heart.*[57]

But neither the darkness of the night, nor the windows nor the lattice, nor the veils nor the distances, are able entirely to drown the voice of the Bridegroom. Like a true lover's lament, it is a voice which does not cease to be heard even when the Bridegroom seems to have gone far away:

> *The voice of my Bridegroom is*
> *like the fleeing wake of a ship,*
> *like the murmuring air,*
> *like a soft whispering,*
> *like the flying of a night fowl.*[58]

---

[57]In the original:

> *En la noche dichosa*
> *en secreto que nadie me veía*
> *ni yo miraba cosa,*
> *sin otra luz ni guía*
> *sino la que en el corazón ardía.*

[58]In the original:

> *Es la voz del Esposo*
> *como la huidiza estela de una nave:*
> *como aire rumoroso,*
> *como susurro suave,*
> *como el vuelo nocturno de algún ave.*

*Come near me
while the North wind blows in the fields;
and leave the flock untended,
and let us make our nest
strewed with lilies and roses.*[59]

---

[59]In the original:

*Acércate a mi lado
mientras el austro sopla en el ejido,
y deja ya el ganado
y hagámonos un nido
de lirios y de rosas florecido.*

CHAPTER V

CONTEMPLATION AND HAPPINESS

The bride feels so happy over the love the Bridegroom professes to her that she exclaims in delight: *Your loves are better than wine*; she does not hesitate to use a comparison in which one can sense that she feels it is a love absolutely intoxicating:

> *The king has brought me into his chambers...*
> *We will exult and rejoice in you;*
> *we will extol your love*
> *more than wine.*[1]

She now clearly realizes that it is for this that she has been created, and that happiness is the object and goal of her life. Jesus told his disciples as much: *These things I have spoken to you, that my joy may be in you, and that your joy may be complete...*[2] *But now, Father, I am coming to thee; and these things I speak in the*

---
[1] Sg 1:4.
[2] Jn 15:11.

*world that they have my joy fulfilled in themselves.*³ Clearly, for the bride, total happiness is the Bridegroom and only the Bridegroom: He is everything to her; he is what she dreams about all the time:

> *My beloved is to me a bag of myrrh,*
> *that lies between my breasts.*
> *My beloved is to me a cluster of henna blossoms*
> *in the vineyards of Engedi.*⁴

And this is because happiness is the goal of man's existence: he has been created to possess happiness. This statement leads to a question as to how this is going to take place: in what consists the essence of the happiness to which the human being is called?

About this transcendental theme, truly decisive for human existence, there is a long tradition of teaching which begins with Aristotle⁵ and, passing through St Augustine⁶ and St Thomas,⁷ comes

---

³Jn 17:13.

⁴Sg 1: 13–14.

⁵On Aristotle, see, for example, *Nicomacean Ethics*, X, 6 and 7.

⁶"Neque enim et nos videndo angelum beati sumus; sed videndo veritatem, qua etiam ipsos diligimus angelos, et his congratulamur" (*De Vera Religione*, 55, 110). There are lots of quotations and nuances in this connexion, as well as interesting ideas on the so-called *Augustinian intellectualism* in Étienne Gilson, *Introduction a l'Étude de Saint Augustin*, Paris, 1982, chap. I. Pieper does not agree with Gilson on the Augustinian primacy of the will on this point; he defends the saint's intellectualism in regard to the essence of a happy life primary (Josef Pieper, *El Ocio y la Vida Intelectual*, Rialp, Madrid, 1962, p. 289).

⁷"Beatitudo est bonum perfectum naturæ intellectualis, apprehensum per intellectum" (*S. Th.*, Iª, q. 26 a. 1); "Visio Dei per essentiam est tota essentia beatitudinis" (*S. Th.*, Iª, q. 1 a. 4); "Beatitudo nihil aliud est, quam gaudium de veritate" (*S. Th.*, Iª–IIæ, q. 3 a. 4); "Beatitudo consistit in contemplatione veritatis et maxime Dei" (*S. Th.*, IIª–IIæ, q. 176 a. 1 ad 1); "Felicitas contemplativa est actus sapientiæ acquisitæ" (*II Sent.*, d. 41 a. 1).

right down to our own time, according to which happiness consists in a contemplation of the truth that satiates. A contemplation which, in all logic, is nothing other than direct vision of the Supreme Truth.[8]

Clearly, if there is no contemplation of God as Supreme Truth —perhaps someone would prefer to say, simply, without contemplation of the Bridegroom— there can be no happiness for the bride, for it is God Who is the Supreme Truth. Love is unthinkable without contemplation of the loved one, for that is precisely the point at which love *begins*.[9]

> *My beloved is all radiant and ruddy,*
> *distinguished among ten thousand.*
> *His head is the finest gold;*
> *his locks are wavy,*
> *black as a raven...*[10]
>
> ....
>
> *How beautiful you are, my beloved, truly lovely.*
> *Our couch is green.*[11]

One can only desire (love) what is delightful, and one cannot appreciate something as delightful unless one contemplates it. No

---

[8] St Thomas, as is his custom, nuances his thought elsewhere: "Beatitudo est fruitio Dei" (*S. Th.*, I*, q. 95, a. 4); "Ad beatitudinem tria requiruntur: scilicet visio Dei, comprehensio, et delectatio" (*S. Th.*, I*–II*, q. 4, a. 3). It would be interesting to explore what exactly the saint means by *fruitio* and *comprehensio* here: is he referring to a *fruitio* and a *comprehensio veritatis*? Or perhaps a *fruitio* and *comprehensio Dei ut Veritas*? Or simply a *fruitio* or *comprehensio Dei*?

[9] As one might suppose, this last statement (to the effect that contemplation is simply the initial stage of love) anticipates the approach we propose to take to this question.

[10] Sg 5: 10–11.

[11] Sg 1:16.

one can *fall in love* unless there first exists the wonderful stone that can cause the lover to fall: the lover is thereby captivated and bewildered by the charm and enchantment that befalls him. So, the first thing in love is the contemplation in amazement of the beauty of the loved one:

> *Scattering a thousand gifts,*
> *he passed through these woods in haste,*
> *glancing around as he went,*
> *clothing them with the beauty*
> *that reflected from his face.*[12]

Love achieves its total consummation only through perfect, total contemplation: *Now we see in a mirror dimly, but then face to face. Now I know in part; then I shall understand fully, even as I have been fully understood...*[13] *Beloved, we are God's children now; it does not yet appear what we shall be, but we know that when he appears we shall be like Him, for we shall see Him as he is.*[14] Until she has sight of the Bridegroom no happiness is possible for the bride; hence St John of the Cross' anguished complaint at the start of his *Spiritual Canticle*. The saint even thinks that the Bridegroom has hidden Himself, since the saint does not feel his presence; this hurts him

---

[12]In the original:

> *Mil gracias derramando*
> *pasó por estos sotos con presura*
> *y yéndolos mirando*
> *con sola su figura*
> *vestidos los dejó de hermosura.*

[13]1 Cor 13:12.
[14]1 Jn 3:2.

and he sets out in an anguished quest that will lead him to where the Bridegroom (who by now is the saint's heart) may be found:

> *Whither have you hidden yourself,*
> *O Beloved, leaving me to lament?*
> *Like the stag you have fled,*
> *having wounded me;*
> *I went out after you, calling, and you*
> *were gone.*[15]

From what one can gather from the doctrine of *beatitudo* as contemplation of the truth that satiates, provided that this is a contemplation of Supreme Truth —and Supreme Truth is identical with God—, we must conclude that the object of this contemplation is God Himself, no less. However, once it is established that we are talking about contemplation of the Godhead, we can still try to get our concepts more exact by asking a series of questions: are we discussing here the doctrine of contemplation of God as Supreme Truth or simply the contemplation of God? What can we say, following a more mystical approach, about contemplation of the Bridegroom by the bride? And why is so much stress put on the classical teaching that contemplation which satiates, in which *beatitudo* consists, refers to God as Supreme Truth? Why does St Thomas say that *beatitudo* consists in delighting in the truth and that it is a perfect

---

[15]In the original:

> *¿A dónde te escondiste,*
> *Amado, y me dejaste con gemido?*
> *Como el ciervo huiste*
> *habiéndome herido;*
> *salí tras ti clamando, y eras ido.*

good of an intellectual nature grasped by the mind? And one further question: if it should happen that one manages to establish that *beatitudo*, or the supreme happiness of man, is rooted in total love, is the concept of vision (or contemplation) enough to explain what perfect or consummated love is, or does the concept of possession also need to be brought in? Or, to put it another way, does the concept of contemplation which satiates include or not include the concept of possession? This last point is a key one, which one needs to bear in mind if one accepts that supreme happiness consists in consummated love, for which (mutual) possession is utterly essential.

It is undeniable that the beatific vision either signifies in itself what is beatitudo for man, or leads to *beatitudo*. But what we want to discover now is whether the mutual and reciprocal self-surrender between God and man —consummated, perfect love between them both—, which seems to be for man the source of *beatitudo*, is adequately explained by the concept of vision (contemplation) or whether the concept of possession is also needed. For, although it does seem clear, at least at first sight, that the concept of possession necessarily presupposes that of vision (you cannot have loving possession, or therefore love, unless you see or contemplate the thing possessed), it is not quite so evident that the concept of vision necessarily requires that of possession.

The key point in the matter arises when one takes into account that man is not solely intelligence but also will —or, if one prefers, heart. Man has been created to know, but perhaps even more so to love; the latter not being possible without the former. In fact, given that man has been made in the image and likeness of God, and given that God is Love (1 Jn 4:8), it seems legitimate to think that the human being has been created by Love to love and to be loved.[16] And of course, no one loves with his intellect alone. It is inconceivable that the Bridegroom or the bride in the *Song* would feel fulfilled until each attained possession of the other:

I am my beloved's and my beloved is mine.[17]

As far as satiating contemplation of the truth is concerned, St Thomas says that *beatitudo* cannot consist simply in seeing Christ's humanity.[18] Accepting that the saint is once again correct, one might think that his statement must be based on the fact that, once man has been elevated to the supernatural order, perfect happiness is not possible for him unless he contemplates God. However, it is possible that this subject will warrant further research.[19] Sight of Christ's humanity is not sufficient for *beatitudo* because perfect happiness is not possible without perfect love. And Christ's humanity is not the Person of the Word, although it is hypostatically united to the Person. But love always has as its object and terminus a person: the loved one, who as such is a person different from the lover. No one ever falls in love with a body or a soul or even both together, but rather with that subtle entity, difficult to describe —the person.

---

[16] The true meaning of the doctrine of man being in the image and likeness of God is something quite difficult and complicated to work out; some of the answers suggested are not always very convincing. One can agree, for example, that man is like God, one and three, because of the three faculties of his soul (memory, intelligence and will), but it is difficult to avoid the impression that that explanation only avoids the issue. There seem to be better grounds for locating man's likeness to God in his ability to love.

[17] Sg 6:3. Cf. 2:16; 7:11.

[18] *Beatitudo non consistit in visione humanitatis Christi: I Sent.*, d. 1, q. 1, 3m.

[19] The intellectualism of the ancient world had a profound influence on all subsequent thought. For Aristotle, only the wise man was the perfect man; for Plato, only philosophers had the competence to govern nations.

However, man cannot perceive the person except via that person's body and soul; so, these two fundamental parts of man's make-up are very important to what we are discussing. Certainly, the terminus or object of love which is always the person is necessarily seen by the loving *I* as *the other*; in other words, there is a kind of relationship of opposition.[20] Accordingly, it is through (in) the Person of Christ that man comes to the Godhead —*through Christ, with Christ and in Christ*— and even to the very person of the Father, as the Master Himself tells his disciples: *I am the way, and the truth, and the life; no one comes to the Father, but by me. If you had known me, you would have known my Father also; henceforth you know Him and have seen Him... He who has seen me has seen the Father.*[21]

If one is ready to accept that man perceives the other through corporality and soul —of the other, of course, but also through his own,[22]— which seems fairly clear, one can better grasp the need for

---

[20]Both unity (or identity) and distinction play a key role in love. Love tends to make persons (who as such are totally distinct) into one single thing. And participated or created love is a reflection and image of what happens in the bosom of Infinite Love, the God Who is Three and One.

[21]Jn 14: 6–7.9. ...*Neither height, nor depth, nor anything else in all creation, will be able to separate us from the love of God 'which is in Christ Jesus our Lord'* (Rom 8:39). The Spanish edition of *Cantera–Iglesias* has a less than happy translation of this last passage, in which it also adds editorial explanations in brackets: *Ni el [alto] cielo ni el [abismo] profundo, ni ninguna otra criatura podrá (sic) separarnos del amor que Dios [nos tiene] en Cristo Jesús, Señor nuestro.* The *Bible de Jérusalem* is better: ...*Ne pourra nous séparer de l'amour de Dieu manifest, dans le Christ Jésus notre Seigneur.* And the *New Jerusalem Bible* parallels this: ...*Will be able to come between us and the love of God, known to us in Christ Jesus our Lord.* Finally, the *New Vulgate* gives an exact translation: ...*poterit nos separare a caritate Dei, quæ est in Christo Iesu Domino nostro.*

[22]Even though they already enjoy the beatific vision, the souls of the blessed are not yet in a definitive estate, at least in the sense that they are still waiting for

Christ's humanity, once God has freely determined to raise human nature to the supernatural level. Therefore, if it happened, as Duns Scotus says, that the decree of Incarnation came prior to man's committing sin, the Incarnation of the Word would no longer depend so much on sin —and the need for Redemption to follow— as on pure Love.[23] The Word becomes flesh in order to redeem man, but also to enable man to love Him supernaturally, and also in the manner suited to human (albeit elevated) nature.

Given that man has been made in the image and likeness of God Who is Love —which is the same as saying that he has been made to love and to be loved—, it seems reasonable to conclude that man cannot attain the beatitude that is his final end other than by the consummation of a perfect love. The human heart is not going to feel satisfied until the point comes where it is consumed in the fire of an infinite Love for which it was created. Therefore St Augustine said that, man having been made for God, his heart cannot rest easy until it rests in Him. But love, in turn, is not satiated or satisfied by the contemplation of the loved one, for what the lover yearns for is to possess the loved one. And, even more, to be possessed by him, for, as our Lord Himself tells us, self–surrender (giving) is more blessed than receiving (Acts 20:35). Just as in the bosom of the Trinity, or substantial Love, the Holy Spirit is essentially Gift, a mutual self–

---

the resurrection of their bodies in order to attain the full consummation of perfect love.

[23] The usual explanation given for why the just of the Old Testament were kept in the bosom of Abraham was their need for a Redemption which still had not been accomplished. But, although this is a true explanation, it suffers from being somewhat legalistic, whereas its roots lie deeper, in an ontological explanation: without the humanity of Christ, according to what we have just said, supernatural *beatitudo* is not possible for man. The only one Who can, by and through his assumed humanity, open for man the *Portæ Æternales* is the Person of the Word.

giving between Persons —*Qui ex Patri Filioque procedit*—, so also participated love must consist in a mutual and reciprocal self–giving which also takes place between persons. And, while it is true that contemplation can be imagined merely as meaning reception, love on the other hand cannot be understood essentially as anything other than something given.[24] Both the Bridegroom and the bride of the *Song* ardently extol the glory and beauty which each *contemplates* in the other. But even the most superficial reading soon shows that the poem hinges more on mutual possession than on reciprocal contemplation. Besides, that supposed (mere) contemplation, as one can see from the obvious meaning of the *Song*, would be something quite alien and strange to both the outlook and the intention of its author.

Of course it is perfectly true that the bride is eager to see the Bridegroom in order to enjoy contemplating Him. What love would not ardently desire to contemplate the loved one...?[25]

> *Haste away, my love,*
> *be like a gazelle,*
> *a young stag,*
> *on the spice–laden mountains.*[26]

St John of the Cross speaks about this in some of the most beautiful stanzas in his *Canticle*:

---

[24] Although, since everything to do with love is reciprocal, the self–giving by each of the lovers becomes necessarily, for each of them, a receiving.

[25] In the Trinity, the intellectual procession —the procession of the Word— takes place first, with a priority that is merely intentional, not temporal; the *spiratio* (active and passive) of the Holy Spirit comes after, although that "after" is also merely intentional.

[26] Sg 8:14.

Contemplation and Happiness

> *Bring my sufferings to an end,*
> *for none but you can remove them,*
> *and let my eyes behold you,*
> *since you are their light;*
> *and for thee alone I wish to have them!*
>
> *Reveal your presence,*
> *and may the vision of your beauty be my death,*
> *for the sickness of love*
> *is not cured*
> *except by your presence and image!*[27]

But in some way contemplation suffices, because love is not fulfilled unless the lover gives himself entirely to the loved one and also possesses her in reciprocity. Without that mutual self–surrender, either there is no love or perhaps it is something so imperfect that it scarcely merits the name. And if there is no love, neither is there any chance of man's being happy. Nor does the concept of contemplation seem to include anything as essential to love as the concept of reciprocity, apropos of which the texts speak both clearly and elegantly:

---

[27] In the original:

> *¡Apaga mis enojos,*
> *pues que ninguno basta a deshacellos,*
> *y véante mis ojos,*
> *pues eres lumbre de ellos*
> *y sólo para ti quiero tenellos!*
> *¡Descubre tu presencia,*
> *y máteme tu vista y hermosura;*
> *mira que la dolencia*
> *de amor, que no se cura*
> *sino con la presencia y la figura!*

> *O my dove, in the clefts of the rock,*
> *in the covert of the cliff,*
> *let me hear your voice,*
> *for your voice is sweet,*
> *and your face is comely.*[28]

As one can see, the Bridegroom also seeks the bride most eagerly, as she does Him —in the clefts in the rocks, in the slits in the cliffs, or looking in at the windows or the lattice— for He also desires most eagerly to see the face of his beloved and hear her voice. How could it be otherwise?

> *See how he comes*
> *leaping on the mountains,*
> *bounding over the hills...*[29]
>
> ....
>
> *Come from Lebanon, my promised bride,*
> *come from Lebanon, come on your way.*
> *Look down from the heights of Amanus,*
> *from the crests of Sanir and Hermon,*
> *the haunts of lions,*
> *the mountains of leopards.*[30]

But certainly it is the Good Shepherd who diligently searches for the lost sheep, is it not? *And when he has found it, he lays it on his shoulders, rejoicing. And when he comes home, he calls together*

---

[28] Sg 2:14.
[29] Sg 2:9.
[30] Sg 4:8.

his friends and his neighbors, saying to them, "Rejoice with me, for I have found my sheep which was lost."[31]

> *I come to my garden, my sister, my bride.*
> *I gather my myrrh with my spice,*
> *I eat my honeycomb with my honey,*
> *I drink my wine with my milk...*
>
> ....
>
> *Open to me, my sister,*
> *my love, my dove, my perfect one;*
> *for my head is wet with dew,*
> *my locks with the drops of the night.*[32]

And for the Bridegroom, too, the quest is painful and difficult, as well as passionate. To prove this we have the parables or allegories of the lost sheep and the Good Shepherd,[33] as well as the mystery of the cross. That is why the Bridegroom complains so bitterly to his bride, and why he tells of his tribulations: *my head is wet with dew and my locks with the drops of the night...*

It is worthwhile checking to see how in the last part of the sermon at the last supper —a sermon made up of farewells and final messages— in the priestly prayer our Lord addresses to the Father, his words show a wonderfully balanced approach to this whole question: *This is eternal life, that they know thee the only true God, and Jesus Christ Whom thou has sent...*[34] *I in them and thou in me,*

---

[31] Lk 15: 5–6.

[32] Sg 5: 1–2.

[33] Cf. Mt 18: 12–14; Lk 15: 4–6; Jn 10: 1–17.

[34] Jn 17:3. The purpose of this verse seems to be to stress the contemplative aspect of love and particularly of *beatitudo*.

that they may become perfectly one, so that the world may know that thou hast sent me and hast loved them even as thou hast loved me. Father, I desire that they also whom thou hast given me, may be with me where I am, to behold my glory which thou hast given me in thy love for me before the foundation of the world... I made known to them thy name, and I will make it known, that the love with which thou hast loved me may be in them, and I in them.[35] And so St John of the Cross also sings in his poem to the love that suffers to the point of death on account of the Bridegroom's absence and the soul's yearning to be one with Him:

> *You shepherds, as you make your way*
> *to the sheepfolds in the hills,*
> *if by any chance you should see*
> *him whom I most love,*
> *tell him that I sicken, grieve and die.*[36]

---

[35] Jn 17: 23–24.26. On the other hand it is mainly in verse 24 that the intention seems to be to stress both the contemplative aspect of love as well as that of mutual possession: our Lord wants the disciples to contemplate his glory but to do so by being with Him: *I desire that they also, whom thou hast given me, may be with me where I am.* For its part, verse 23 alludes to a consummation of mutual love in unity, whereas verse 26 refers to the merging produced by unitive love which makes the lovers one single thing in a mutual and reciprocal possession.

[36] In the original:

> *Pastores los que fuéredes*
> *allá por las majadas al otero,*
> *si por ventura viéredes*
> *aquel que yo más quiero,*
> *decidle que adolezco, peno y muero.*

This is but a distant echo of a verse of the ancient *Song* whose resonance has been heard down the centuries, and which now has been taken up and made his own by the poet.

> *Tell me, you whom my soul loves,*
> *where you pasture your flock,*
> *where you make it lie down at noon;*
> *for why should I be like one who wanders*
> *beside the flocks of your companions?*[37]

The only thing that can lead man to true *beatitudo*, once he has been raised by grace to the supernatural order, is perfect love sharing in God's own life, not just contemplation.[38] The demands of the human heart cannot be satisfied by purely intellectualist or voluntarist approaches. It is man in his entirety —with his intellect and with his will, therefore— that has been made by Love to love and be loved. If the accent is moved to either of the two extremes, stressing one aspect at the expense of the other, that may lead to harmful consequences as far as asceticism and Christian pastoral practice are concerned. Excessive emphasis on the will robs love of its content, and exaggerated intellectualism leads to a love which has no purpose, no object. The doctrine of satiating contemplation of the truth must bear in mind that now Truth is a Person (Jn 14:6; 17:17; 5:32) Who has made his own a human nature in order to be able to be loved in the only way that man can love. And a person cannot be

---

[37]Sg 1:7.

[38]The contemplation that satiates the blessed, that is their *beatific vision*, which the doctrine speaks about, presupposes love; this is something which is beyond doubt. But what we want to do here is draw attention to the need to get the concepts very clear so as to avoid any possible regrettable approach from the wrong angle when dealing with these matters.

regarded as merely the ultimate object of contemplation: a person is the first and last intention of possession and self–surrender. The capacity to contemplate *another* person —and to be contemplated by that person— leads to a capacity to possess that person —and be possessed in turn. The God Who is love knows and loves Himself, although in such a way that, in his absolute simplicity, infinite Intelligence and infinite Will are identical; so that the Father is not Father without the Son (*generatio intellectualis*), nor can either of them be without the Holy Spirit (*spiratio amoris*). Similarly, man, made as he is by God in his image and likeness, has been endowed with an intellect capable of knowing... and a will capable of loving what he knows. And in this case what is known and loved is God Himself: the definitive object and last end of human intelligence and human *love*. To say that there is no love without knowledge and will is the same as to say that there is no love without contemplation and without reciprocal self–surrender and possession. So, given that man has been made for love, he cannot attain his final beatitude unless he gives himself to the object of that love and unless he in turn obtains possession of it.[39] The process works in such a way that first there has to be knowledge of the thing worthy to be loved, and only then does love for the thing develop. And we need not concern ourselves here with whether the priority involved is one of time, or has nothing to do with time, or is merely a priority of reason or nature. So, we can conclude, with a reasonable prospect of being right, that what really is to be found at *the very end* of everything —the only true end— is love, not just contemplation.

Even if everyone seems to agree as to the conclusions, we need to stress how important it is to get the concepts right and not to

---

[39] Hell does not consist in the last analysis in absolute privation of knowledge of God, but in total lack of love of God.

leave important aspects of any question in a state of vagueness or oblivion. Sleight of hand is one of the methods the System uses when it wants to dispense with a doctrine. If there is some teaching that one cannot openly deny, one passes over it in silence. Another method is to cast doubt on it, insinuating for example that the subject is *debatable*. In recent times it is fairly easy to find this method (the background to it is distinctly Rahnerian) being used in official documents issued by certain ecclesiastical Curias.

There is no doubt but that following Jesus becomes much more attractive if one sets out from the base that perfect love is the source of man's ultimate happiness. It is always easy to follow a person with whom one is deeply in love, no matter where she goes. And love (it is worth saying again) only happens between persons, which is the same as saying that it is a wonderful interchange between an *I* and a *thou* who give themselves to each other and possess each other. Truth can be the object of love, and even of special love, but no one *falls in love* with truth, unless it be perceived also as a *person*. This happened only in the case of Jesus Christ, the faithful witness (Rev 1:5), Who could say of Himself that He was the truth (Jn 14:6) and had come into the world in order to bear witness to it (Jn 18:37). The ancient world could never have even suspected that the Truth was capable of becoming flesh (Jn 1:14) to show his love for men and to be able to be loved by them. God knows that, even though man does not usually offer his heart to a mere abstraction, he can do that to a person who is going to give his own heart in return. In this way, both lovers, by mutual self-surrender, attain to the perfect joy of total beatitude. Man needs to contemplate in Jesus Christ both true God and true Man. For without the divinity of our Lord his Person would disappear, and love would be deprived of its proper object. And without his humanity it would be totally impossible for man to love Him, insofar as he could not from then on let Himself be seduced and ensnared by another *heart* (Phil 3:12) which in turn is also ensnared: could love, for the human being, mean anything other than that? When St Thomas says that contemplation of the Humanity of Christ is not the object of man's *beatitudo*, he does so because he is thinking that the fleshly (human) heart of Jesus Christ belongs to a Person Who is in fact divine —whereas love, which is the only thing that can make man completely happy, always has another person as its object and terminus. That other person is divine in the case of the supernatural love, perfect, definitive, complete, total, to which man is called and raised. But man can only gain access to the divinity of that Person, with Whom he has fallen in love, through the human, fleshly heart of that same Person, for that is the only form of loving available to him.[40] And so the journey ends and the cycle is at last completed: through the human nature of the Lord, letting oneself be guided by the hand of the Spirit, to the Person of Christ, there to reach the Godhead and in it the Father.

The theology of prayer is also helped considerably by this approach to the question. Given that prayer is the best place for an intimate relationship with the Lord, it should be remembered that the intimacy of friendship is founded on and made possible by a love which only takes place between persons. The loving dialogue and encounter, which prayer ultimately becomes, culminate in a mutual self–surrender —and for that to happen man needs to see God as the *other*, Whom he loves and by Whom he is loved. The main thing is that, in order to love, man needs to see the loved one, to speak to, listen to, caress and even, quite often, contend with the one he loves:

---

[40]This might provide a good way to establishing the basis for a theology of the Heart of Jesus.

> *He has taken me to his cellar,*
> *and his banner over me is love.*[41]

And all this has to happen in absolute reciprocity and in a manner which is totally foreign to and far removed from what happens in mere contemplation. So, all the forms of meditation or of Eastern self–concentration which some people want to import into Christianity as methods of prayer are doomed to fail. They start out from an erroneous notion of Christian prayer and have very little to do with it. In supernatural prayer, man does not try to get inside himself in order to find himself; he does the exact opposite: he tries to go outside himself to find the Person he loves. The solipsism of reflection or auto–concentration is poles apart from the passionate quest for the other (which is what the process leading to love involves). The bride in the *Song*, who is very *au fait* with the true paths of love, has come to be convinced that she will never find true happiness unless she go outside of herself in order to be with the Bridegroom:

> *On my bed at night I sought*
> *the man who is my sweetheart:*
> *I sought but could not find him!*
> *So I shall get up and go through the city;*
> *in the streets and in the squares,*
> *I shall seek my sweetheart.*[42]

And from that point on, her only desire is to be with Him. Not to be with herself, or to find herself, but to be with the Bridegroom

---

[41] Sg 2:4. On prayer as contention or struggle see, for example, Spicq, *Théologie Morale du Nouveau Testament*, I, Gabalda, Paris, 1970, p. 217, note 3. Cf. also M. D. Molini,, *Le Combat de Jacob*, Cerf, Paris, 1967.

[42] Sg 3: 1–2.

and to possess the Bridegroom. That is why St John of the Cross says in his *Spiritual Canticle*:

> *O, who will be able to heal me!*
> *Come, give yourself completely to me now*
> *From now on send me*
> *no more messengers,*
> *for they cannot tell me what I wish!*
>
> *Since you have wounded my heart,*
> *wherefore did not heal it?*
> *And wherefore, having robbed me of it,*
> *have you left it thus*
> *and take not the prey that you have spoiled?*[43]

The bride is no longer soothed or satisfied with messengers or reports: she ardently desires the presence and gift of her own Spouse. The messengers are unable to tell her what she wants to hear..., because her yearning is in fact to hear it from the lips of the Bridegroom Himself:

---

[43] In the original:

> *¡Ay!, ¡quién podrá sanarme?*
> *¡Acaba de entregarte ya de vero;*
> *no quieras enviarme*
> *de hoy más ya mensajero,*
> *que no saben decirme lo que quiero!*
>
> *¿Por qué, pues has llagado*
> *aqueste corazón, no le sanaste?*
> *Y, pues me le has robado,*
> *¿por qué así le dejaste*
> *y no tomas el robo que robaste?*

Contemplation and Happiness   279

> *...for they cannot tell me what I wish.*[44]

This is true even though the messengers are most diligent and no matter how full and extensive the news is: all that it does is make her yearnings worse, increase her restlessness and nostalgia. The more she hears about the Bridegroom, the better she gets to know Him, the greater is her hunger to be with Him. For, really, as she says herself, trying to explain why she is so discontented:

> *...something that they stammer*
> *leaves me dying.*[45]

In everything to do with the Bridegroom what remains to be said is always much more than what has been said. The beauty still to be seen is always greater than what has already been contemplated. And the road still to be travelled is much more attractive than the road one has already travelled with Him. The more one enjoys the Bridegroom's love and the more one is given by Him —earnests or first–fruits, for the time being—, the more one knows and desires what still remains to be had: *Fire never says, "Enough,"*[46] and God is truly a *devouring fire.*[47]

---

[44] In the original:

> *...que no saben decirme lo que quiero.*

[45] In the original:

> *...y déjame muriendo*
> *un no se qué que quedan balbuciendo.*

[46] Prov 30:16.
[47] Deut 4:24.

In the verses of St John of the Cross, as is true of the entire *Song* and of the New Testament, the love–relationship between God and man (and man's ultimate beatitude to which it leads) can only happen through a relationship of mutual self–surrender and possession. This leads infallibly not to a mere union of both as lovers (being together) but to a true communion and true interchange of lives.[48] And so the bride in the *Song* expresses in ardent verses her desire to be with the Bridegroom:

> *Draw me after you, let us make haste.*
> *The king has brought me into his chambers.*
> *We will exult and rejoice in you;*
> *we will extol your love more than wine.*[49]

The Bridegroom means absolutely everything to her. He is her very life. Therefore she cannot imagine life other than being with Him. It means giving herself to Him and having Him as her own. How could either lover be content with merely contemplating the other?

> *My beloved is to me a bag of myrrh*
> *that lies between my breasts.*
> *My beloved is to me a cluster of henna blossoms*
> *in the vineyards of Engedi.*[50]

The love the bride feels for the Bridegroom is very far from being satisfied by mere contemplation. That is why she also says, referring to her Bridegroom:

---

[48] Cf. Jn 6: 56–57; Gal 2:20. Here one is already very far from mere contemplation, which would not at all satisfy the bride.

[49] Sg 1:4.

[50] Sg 1: 13–14.

> *O that his left hand were under my head*
> *and that his right embraced me!*[51]

And the Bridegroom, feeling as she does, responds in the same language, in perfect reciprocity:

> *How sweet is your love, my sister, my bride!*
> *how much better is your love than wine.*[52]
>
> ....
>
> *Your neck is the Tower of David*
> *built on layers,*
> *hung round with a thousand bucklers,*
> *and each the shield of a hero.*[53]

St John of the Cross will say the same thing in his *Canticle*, where he too uses ardent, poetic language:

> *The bride has now entered the pleasant garden,*
> *as she had long desired,*
> *and she rests in delight,*
> *her neck reclining*
> *on the gentle arms of her Beloved.*[54]

---

[51] Sg 2:6.
[52] Sg 4:10.
[53] Sg 4:4.
[54] In the original:

> *Entrado se ha la esposa*
> *en el ameno huerto deseado*
> *y a su sabor reposa*
> *el cuello reclinado*
> *sobre los dulces brazos del Amado.*

> *In the inner cellar,*
> *of my Beloved have I drunk, and, when*
> > *I went forth*
> *over all this meadow,*
> *then I knew naught,*
> *and lost the flock which I used to follow.*[55]

He says he *knew nothing* after having drunk *in the inner cellar of my Beloved*, referring to the infinite and indescribable intoxication caused by perfect love, which, as the *Song* also says, is smooth and better than wine: *Your loves are better than wine.*

Therefore, it seems we may deduce from what has been said that man's ultimate destiny is not contemplation or even *beatitudo* or *fruitio*,[56] but the love which is fulfilled with the possession of God. That is the only way that man can be flooded with a complete happiness; yet that happiness is less important to man than the possession of God. So, both of them —God and man— seek each other, like the Bridegroom and the bride in the *Song*, in order to offer themselves to each other as the food of love. All that concerns the lover is the loved one, and only then, when she at last is his, does he feel happy. This is what the bride in the *Song* delicately hints at, referring to the Bridegroom:

---

[55] In the original:

> *En la interior bodega*
> *de mi Amado bebí, y cuando salía*
> *por toda aquesta vega*
> *ya cosa no sabía*
> *y el ganado perdí que antes seguía.*

[56] St Thomas reserves the term *beatitudo* exclusively for divine happiness, to differentiate it from merely human happiness.

> *With great delight I sat in his shadow,*
> *and his fruit was sweet to my taste.*[57]

The Bridegroom, for his part, says the same to his bride:

> *I say I will climb the palm tree*
> *and lay hold of its branches.*
> *Oh, may your breasts be like clusters of the vine,*
> *and the scent of your breath like apples.*[58]
>
> ....
>
> *I come to my garden, my sister, my bride,*
> *I gather my myrrh with my spice,*
> *I eat my honeycomb with my honey*
> *I drink my wine with my milk.*
> *Eat, O friends, and drink: drink deeply, O lovers.*[59]

And the bride likewise tells the Bridegroom:

> *Your loves are greater than wine.*[60]

André Gide said in his *Diary* that *the terrible thing is that one can never get drunk enough.* And yet the height of intoxication is possible for man, but only when it is love that causes it. Even more, the great intoxication of happiness and complete joy, which begins in this life, is in fact the end to which man is destined. The culmination

---

[57] Sg 2:3.
[58] Sg 7:9.
[59] Sg 5:1.
[60] Sg 1:2.

will come later, when the bride drinks in the Kingdom the wine of the Bridegroom's winery, after both have travelled together the path of earthly pilgrimage:

> *My Beloved, we will climb*
> *the mountain of the cumin and the rue*
> *and when we finally arrive,*
> *the road already ended,*
> *we will joyfully drink your wine.*[61]

Is it possible for man to live without this love...? Perhaps it is, but only if he is ready to spend his life in the greatest sadness. That would be the worst kind of sadness; not just because it is an absence of happiness but because it means absence of supreme happiness. The happiness the bride of the *Song* feels, and her desire to see that happiness reach its fullness, cause her such pain and suffering that she desires death, as St John of the Cross says:

> *tell him that I sicken, grieve, and die.*[62]

---

[61]In the original:

> *Amado, subiremos*
> *al monte de la ruda y del comino,*
> *y cuando al fin lleguemos,*
> *cumplido ya el camino,*
> *alegres beberemos de tu vino.*

[62]In the original:

> *decidle que adolezco, peno y muero.*

Contemplation and Happiness

Love always means feeling, emotion, tenderness, trembling, enchantment, rapture, madness and joy. And how could supernatural love, or divine–human love, ever lack the qualities which even mere human love possesses? Grace presupposes nature: it uses it, heals it, and raises it up without ever destroying it. Therefore, the bride desires the kisses of the Bridegroom's mouth: *kiss me with the kisses of your mouth.* Yes, for she does not even mind death if it is through death that she will attain, for ever more, the enduring love–kiss of the Bridegroom.

> *I ascended to the stars,*
> *burning with love in sweet fire,*
> *so that, if I should find you there,*
> *I might ask you with a soft plea:*
> *Give me a kiss of love, may I die thereafter...!*[63]

---

[63] In the original:

> *Subí hasta las estrellas,*
> *consumido de amor en dulce fuego,*
> *por, si te hallaba en ellas,*
> *pedirte en suave ruego:*
> *¡Dame un beso de amor, muera yo luego...!*

CHAPTER VI

LIVING THE LIFE OF THE OTHER

According to the Lord, eternal life consists, for man, in knowing the Father, the only true God, and his envoy, Jesus Christ: *This is eternal life, that they know thee the only true God, and Jesus Christ whom thou has sent.*[1] This knowledge is ordained to (divine–human) love and to possession of one another, in line with what was said in the previous chapter: *I made known to them thy name, and I will make it known, that the love with which thou hast loved me may be in them, and I in them.*[2]

In order to attain this eternal life one needs to eat the flesh of the Lord and drink his blood: *Truly, I say to you, unless you eat the flesh of the Son of man and drink his blood, you have no life in you; he who eats my flesh and drinks my blood has eternal life, and I will raise him up at the last day. For my flesh is food indeed, and my blood is drink indeed.*[3] This brings about a mysterious interchange whereby God and man each live in the other. As the Lord says, *He*

---

[1] Jn 17:3.
[2] Jn 17:26.
[3] Jn 6: 53–55.

who eats my flesh and drinks my blood abides[4] *in me and I in him... He who eats me will live because of me.*[5] St Paul also insists on that mysterious presence of God in man: *Do you not know that you are God's temple and that God's Spirit dwells in you...?*[6] *God's hope has been poured into our hearts through the Holy Spirit, who has been given to us.*[7] This is a mutual presence which leads to a no less mysterious interchange of lives.

Only those who read the texts superficially will miss the depth of the problems that are posed here. So, with respect to the questions which may arise, the first thing to say is that they admit of no easy answer. For example: what is meant by living because of someone else or living the life of another...? What does this interchanging of lives really mean...? What is being referred to when speaking of losing one's own life, out of love, or renouncing one's life, out of love...?[8] How can each of the lovers become the other, and up to what point do they both keep their own identity —if in fact they do— ...? What is St Paul referring to when he tells the Colossians that Christ is their life...?[9] In what sense is reciprocity here a basic exigency of love...?

Ignoring the empty–headed view which says that these are just ways of speaking, and accepting that language does carry intrinsic and distinctive meaning, one can readily conclude that these ques-

---

[4]The Greek verb μένω means to stay or be fixed in a place, involving the idea of duration. *The New Jerusalem Bible* translates it as *to live in* but it also accepts it can mean *to be in*. The *New Vulgate* uses *maneo* (to stay, to abide) as the translation.

[5]Jn 6: 56–57. Cf. also Col 3:4.

[6]1 Cor 3:16.

[7]Rom 5:5. Cf. 1 Cor 6: 15–20; 1 Jn 3:24; 4: 9.13.

[8]Cf. Mt 10:39; 16:25; Mk 8:35; Lk 9:24; Jn 10: 11.15; etc.

[9]In Col 3:4.

tions all bring up the whole problematic question of love. Nor is it difficult to appreciate that they constitute the internal structure of the entire New Testament and are the foundations of Christian spirituality.

The transfusion of lives and the transformation of one person into another that love brings about were summed up poetically by St John of the Cross in one of the stanzas of the *Dark Night*. What he has to say provides helpful clues —and poses some interesting questions:

> *O night that guided me!*
> *O night more lovely than the dawn!*
> *O night that has joined*
> *the Beloved with his lover,*
> *lover transformed into the Beloved!*[10]

It is worth noting the expression the saint uses. He says *lover transformed into the Beloved* and not the contrary, because that would make no sense. However, this idea does also call for certain explanations and nuances, as we shall see in some detail later. The first thing that needs to be made clear is that this transformation does not mean loss of personality on the part of either of the lovers. That would be something contrary to the essence of love. The inviolability and independence of the I of each of the lovers is

---

[10]In the original:

> *¡Oh noche que guiaste!*
> *¡Oh noche amable más que el alborada!*
> *¡Oh noche que juntaste*
> *Amado con amada,*
> *amada en el Amado transformada!*

a necessary condition for love to exist. As we have been stressing in earlier chapters, the I is always defined as in *opposition* to the thou which is the other,[11] and therefore it can be said quite definitely that an I has never existed on its own. What makes it possible for the person to give himself is the fact that he is *person*, and he can give himself only so long as he is *person*, for love always necessarily is found between personal beings that relate to each other on *I–thou* terms. The so–called *incommunicability* of the person refers to his total independence and autonomy vis–...–vis others —not being mixed with other(s)— which is what makes it possible for a person to relate to others as a complete rational being. So, one can say that each person is a complete (or closed) universe, but able freely to open himself to other universes. This independence is precisely what defines the person as free and what allows him to give himself if he so wishes, because only an I is capable of surrendering and renouncing everything..., everything except that very possibility of self–surrender which flows essentially and necessarily from his condition as personal being. Therefore, love not only does not imply fusion into a new entity, with resultant loss of personality by either of the lovers, but on the contrary it means being woven onto the mesh of a certain *opposition*. In love there are two persons who face each other as an *I* and a *thou*, reciprocally, in a relationship which even has certain features of a *struggle* or contest (though of an absolutely special type):

---

[11]In substantial Love, each of the Persons possesses the one divine essence in absolute fullness. However, *qua* divine Persons, the Father would not be the Father without the Son, nor would the Son be the Son without the Father, nor would they be without the Holy Spirit —and the Spirit would not be the Spirit without the Father and the Son.

*He brought me to the banqueting house,
and his banner over me was love.*[12]

The Prophets also were acquainted with this idea:

*In maturity he wrestled against God.
He wrestled with the angel and beat him
he wept and pleaded with him.*[13]

This struggle has nothing to do with a conflict of wills which, not being in agreement, pursue opposed or different interests. And given that what happens here is precisely the contrary,[14] one might ask whether it is a matter of mere opposition (but of a special kind) between two wills. To which one must reply: not necessarily between two wills, but between one I and another I which, as such, are absolutely distinct: *As the Father has life in Himself, so he has granted the Son also to have life in Himself.*[15]

The *incommunicability* or independence of the person means that love is resolved in the last analysis in the *I–thou* relationship;[16] everything else is forgotten; it is *as if* the two lovers were the only thing that existed in the world.[17] This is simply a consequence of

---

[12] Sg 2:4.

[13] Hos 12: 4–5. Cf. following footnote.

[14] Remember the struggle between Jacob and the angel (Gen 32: 25–33).

[15] Jn 5:26. However, it is easy to see how, when it is the creature who is loving or being loved, there always are two distinct wills.

[16] In love, due to reciprocity, each I is at the same time a thou for the other. The I, seen *from in front* by the other, becomes thereby a thou.

[17] In some other places of this book, this extremely important theme, as well as the problems it might bring about, are treated at full length.

the fact that each gives everything entirely to the other. As St John of the Cross says in the last stanza of the *Dark Night*:

> *Lost to myself I stayed,*
> *my face reclining on the Beloved;*
> *everything ceased and I abandoned myself,*
> *throwing my cares*
> *among the lilies to be forgotten.*[18]

As the Apostle teaches, in expounding his instruction on the Mystical Body, *all the members of the body, though many, are one body*.[19] However, he also says that *the body does not consist of one member but of many*,[20] going on to add that *God arranged the organs in the body, each one of them, as he chose*,[21] and that *you are the body of Christ and individually members of it*.[22] From the Book of Revelation one can see that the prize consists in a manna that is *hidden* to all except the conqueror himself and the Spirit, and also

---

[18] In the original:

> *Quedéme y olvidéme,*
> *el rostro recliné sobre el Amado,*
> *cesó todo y dejéme,*
> *dejando mi cuidado*
> *entre las azucenas olvidado.*

[19] 1 Cor 12:12. Here we are not in any way questioning the unity and solidarity of all Christians in the Mystical Body of Christ (Rom 12:5); we are trying to achieve a deeper appreciation of the essence of divine–human love, or, simply, love. The one and only Mystical Body of Christ is made up of individual members who are persons.

[20] 1 Cor 12:14.

[21] 1 Cor 12:18.

[22] 1 Cor 12:27.

a new name known only to each of them: *He who has an ear, let him hear what the Spirit says to the churches. To him who conquers I will give some of the hidden manna, and I will give him a white stone, with a new name written on the stone which no one knows except him who receives it.*[23] So, in love everything happens in such a way that at the end there is only the lover, the loved one and the love that they profess to each other. In his *Spiritual Canticle*, St John of the Cross insists on this idea in a beautiful way:

> *In solitude she lived;*
> *and in solitude she has built her nest;*
> *now in solitude her Beloved guides her*
> *alone, who likewise*
> *in solitude was wounded by love.*
>
> *Let us rejoice, my Beloved,*
> *and in your beauty see ourselves reflected:*
> *by mountain and by hill,*
> *where the pure water runs;*
> *let us enter deeper into the thicket.*[24]

---

[23] Rev 2:17.

[24] In the original:

> *En soledad vivía*
> *y en soledad ha puesto ya su nido*
> *y en soledad la guía*
> *a solas su querido*
> *también en soledad de amor herido.*
> *Gocémonos, Amado,*
> *y vámonos a ver en tu hermosura*
> *al monte y al collado*
> *do mana el agua pura;*
> *entremos más adentro en la espesura.*

> *Then we shall climb up high*
> *to the lofty caves of the rock,*
> *well hidden from the view;*
> *and there we shall enter,*
> *and revel in the first wine of the pomegranates.*[25]

Although the Apostle says of himself: *It is no longer I who live, but Christ who lives in me,*[26] he clearly is not referring to his being being lost in the Godhead. Rather, what he is doing is stressing the opposition of personalities, because, in addition to what he has just been saying about being crucified *with Christ,*[27] he explicitly makes the point that it is the Master Who lives in him: *it is Christ who lives "in me."* What the Apostle means is that his life has been transformed into that of Christ; he does not intend his words to have any other meaning than that which our Lord previously indicated.[28] Apart from that, reciprocity as a quality of love also requires the specification or individuality of those who love, which is as remote as could be from loss or fusion of the lover in the loved one or vice versa. It is important to bear in mind that without the defined profile of the I of each lover no love can possibly exist.

---

[25] In the original:

> *Y luego a las subidas*
> *cavernas de la piedra nos iremos,*
> *que están bien escondidas,*
> *y allí nos entraremos*
> *y el mosto de granadas gustaremos.*

[26] Gal 2:20.

[27] Gal 2:19.

[28] In Jn 6: 56–57. What has to be done now is to explain the true meaning of the transformation of lives which takes place.

Reciprocity in love (including divine–human love) puts the lovers in a situation which tends to ignore any differences which may exist between them. At the same time as it keeps the I of each lover unchanged, love finds its consummation in the self–surrender which each makes to the other. This self–surrender, being *reciprocal* and *total*, puts the lovers on the logical plane of equality to which mutual possession leads: since each gives the other *what he has*, and more so and principally *what he is*, it follows that they tend to become in some way equal. Only love can work the wonder of harmonizing identity and distinction: identity, in the measure in which the lovers tend to become one single thing, through the attraction of love; and distinction, because each of them is only that lover to the extent that he sees the other as *other* and defines himself as *I*.[29] However, only in substantial Love does there coexist perfect identity of nature of the lovers and total distinctness of the Persons.

Reciprocity as a quality of love can give rise to problems as regards how to explain the interchange of lives. From the moment that either of the lovers lives the life of the other (or lives by the other), what meaning can reciprocity continue to have? If divine–human love means that the creature lives the life of Christ, by being changed into Him, how is it possible to continue to talk of an in-

---

[29]That is why the lover goes out of himself to draw near to the other. The voluntary isolation that solipsistic selfishness produces is the very opposite of love. Whereas the expression *I love you* makes complete sense, that is not the case with *I love*, which on its own means practically nothing. The concepts of love of self, love of enemies, and love of things are nothing but expressions of the all–embracing and extensive meaning of a divine and shared love which never imposes limitations on itself. As the Book of Proverbs says, fire never says *Enough!* (Prov 30:16). He who has been caught in the nets of love loves all things, and he loves them forever, because he sees in all of them vestiges and presence of the loved one. Giving one's life for one's enemies is an immense proof of love (Rom 5:8), though not as great a proof as that shown by one who gives his life for his friends (Jn 15:13).

terchange of lives, which would, one would think, always have to happen on a certain level of equality?

Clearly, in this special relationship of friendship which God has chosen to establish with man, the creature is the one destined to be raised up to share in the divine life (2 Pet 1: 3–4). It is through incorporation into Christ that the human being is born to supernatural life and matures in that life.[30] But this does not mean that man has nothing to contribute, and that all he can do is let himself be absorbed by the Godhead. Although man cannot give God anything positive that He does not already have, he does through grace enjoy the possibility of making the gifts he has received bear fruit and of generously handing them back to God. The parables of the talents and the pounds (minas) are quite relevant here.[31] From them one might deduce that grace enables man to give back more than he received. Of course he can give God his will and his love, once he has *really* been given the gift of freedom, without which he could not love. Once man is created by God as a person and as a free being, he also has the possibility of surrendering himself. But as well as that, since every love–relationship consists in mutual self–surrender and reception (and it is the aspect of gift which is considered the most important),[32] it may still be asked whether man has anything which he can give as specifically his own: is there really anything

---

[30] Cf. Rom 6: 3–11; Gal 3: 27–29; 2 Pet 1: 3–4.

[31] Mt 25: 14–30; Lk 19: 12–27. According to these parables, those who are given talents or pounds do not confine themselves simply to giving back what they have received; they give back double the amount, as a result of the business they have conducted: *You delivered to me five talents; here "I have made five talents" more.* They are therefore rewarded, whereas the one who limited himself to giving back only the talent or pound he received is condemned. This is because strict justice without love counts for nothing in a being that has been created for love.

[32] Cf. Acts 20:35.

man has not received from God, anything he can therefore give Him as exclusively his own? And the reply, though it may seem strange, is surprisingly, Yes. For man does have the possibility of giving his wretchedness and his nothingness as things which are specifically and exclusively his. That God is ready to accept and to make his own the burden of man's misery and sins (and has in fact done so) is shown by the agony in the garden, and the passion and death of our Lord.[33] According to the Apostle, He Who knew no sin God *made to be sin, so that in Him we might become the righteousness of God.*[34] Jesus Christ made man's sin and wretchedness his own by taking them voluntarily upon Himself: *Quod non est assumptum non est sanatum.* Also, if man had just shed his sin and misery (supposing he could have done so), that would not perhaps have been the best solution; nor would it have been the right solution for God to destroy misery and sin with a decree of his will. It was more appropriate to the plan of salvation that what was freely desired and willed should be freely *surrendered.* And because nothing can be freely given unless there is someone willing to receive it freely, so it came about that God intervened through Jesus Christ. In Him God receives the sins of mankind; and in Him it is made possible, by means of his voluntary self–surrender, that man should detach himself of his wretchedness, surrendering it out of love and freeing himself of it. Only in Him Who possesses the fullness of the Spirit, by being true God and true Man, can total reception and absolute self–surrender be perfectly made one. And so the Prophet says, re-

---

[33]The baptism of Jesus in the Jordan by the Precursor has a similar meaning, as one can deduce from Matthew 3: 13–17 and the other Synoptics. The Baptist's reluctance to baptize the Messiah is very significant, given that his was a baptism of penance and public repentance for sins and by receiving it Jesus would look like a sinner.

[34]2 Cor 5:21.

ferring to the Messiah, that *he has borne our griefs and carried our sorrows... wounded for our transgressions, he was bruised for our iniquities. Upon him was the chastisement that made us whole, and with his stripes we are healed... The Lord has laid on him the iniquity of us all.*[35]

Despite the fact that this teaching is so fundamental to Christian spirituality, it has been pushed to one side in recent times. Our Lord's attitude (taking upon Himself faults which he did not commit and making Himself responsible for them) contrasts with the way a lot of contemporary Catholic pastoral activity is orientated.[36] What might be termed fault displacement tends to be very much the fashion, but it is nothing other than turning one's back on our sense of personal fault. Although there are many who still do recognize the existence of sin, there is quite a general tendency to regard it as something that *other people* commit. Preachers and lecturers, not to mention those who draft documents in the alchemy laboratories of ecclesiastical offices, have become quite used to issuing broadsides and anathemas addressed (usually) not to themselves (that would hurt) or to those who are listening to them (that would be too close to the bone). Whatever one may say, the preaching and teaching given by some of the clergy and even by certain ecclesiastical organisms have served to encourage this situation. The change of direction with respect to revealed dogmas is fairly easy to see. Jesus Christ consents to make the sins of men his own and is ready to be taken for a sinner, but many modern preachers treat their listeners as if they were irreproachable Christians, people with inalienable rights and

---

[35] Is 53: 3–6.

[36] It has become increasingly necessary to carry out a study of the contrast, more often than not so obvious, between the directives of modern Pastoral practice and the most pure essentials of the New Testament.

victims almost always of injustice done by others.[37] The world has once again become divided into separate compartments of good people and bad people, according to Manichean criteria, whereby the blameworthy are always those who suit: bourgeoisie and working class, committed Christians and uncommitted Christians, conservatives and progressives, warmongers and pacifists, capitalism and Third World, rich countries and oppressed countries (or countries of the North and colonized countries), etc. When these systems of classification are applied as suits, a person only needs to belong to some particular structure to become automatically good or evil. However, the demagoguery of these pastoral planners goes even further, because they usually start out from the assumption that their listeners are always good and it is other people who are bad, or else the blame must be laid squarely at the feet of structures.

Along with feelings of guilt, other personal attitudes, such as feelings of repentance and love of God, also disappear. Once one has decided that the blame is to be put either on others or on structures, the personal I is liberated and it no longer feels any duty to accept guilt for anything. This means the destruction of any chance of loving God: once any vestige of personal feeling has been uprooted, it is very likely that not a trace of love of God has survived.

However, any attempt to rid Christian spirituality of its eminently *personal* character is doomed to fail, because that spirituality is grounded essentially on love–relationships. And if one wants to

---

[37] This pastoral approach, which is basically demagogical and politicized, tends to be followed particularly in certain European and Hispano–American countries where Marxism is still rather influential (especially among the clergy). In countries like the USA, on the other hand, the dominant tendency is to see parishes as money–making units (though that is never admitted), and preaching tends to be banal and insipid. The disappearance of the sense of sin as a personal fault is common to all these approaches.

put even more stress on reciprocity as a quality of love, it is worth noting that as far as divine–human love is concerned there are very many scriptural texts that refer to the subject. In the *Song*, for example, it is the dominant note, although on certain points it is given special stress:

> *My beloved is mine and I am his.*[38]
>
> ....
>
> *I am my beloved's and my beloved is mine.*[39]
>
> ....
>
> *I am my beloved's,*
> *and his desire is for me.*[40]

The very way the book is arranged, in the form of a dialogue in which Bridegroom and bride alternate with light counterpoints by the choir, acts as a kind of backdrop to a situation of equality between the lovers as lovers:

> *I will rise now and go about the city,*
> *in the streets and in the squares;*
> *I will seek him whom my soul loves.*[41]

Her quest is such an anxious one that she even feels afraid she will go astray and not manage to find the Bridegroom. And so she asks the Bridegroom Himself to guide her and lead her to where He is:

---

[38] Sg 2:16.
[39] Sg 6:3.
[40] Sg 7:11.
[41] Sg 3:2.

> *Tell me, you whom my soul loves,*
> *where you pasture your flock,*
> *where you make it lie down at noon;*
> *for why should I be like one who wanders*
> *beside the flocks of your companions.*[42]

But the Bridegroom, in turn, seeks the bride in the same way:

> *Arise, my love, my fair one,*
> *and come away...*[43]
>
> ....
>
> *Open to me, my sister, my love,*
> *my dove, my perfect one...*[44]

The New Testament, for its part, is quite explicit and has much to say: *Behold, I stand at the door and knock; if anyone hears my voice and opens the door, I will come in to him and eat with him, and he with me...*[45] *Abide in me, and I in you...*[46] *He who abides in me, and I in him, he it is that bears much fruit...*[47] *No longer do I call you servants, for the servant does not know what his master is doing; but I have called you friends, for all that I have heard from my Father I have made known to you...*[48] *If the world hates you, know that it has hated me before it hated you...*[49] *If they kept my*

---

[42] Sg 1:7.
[43] Sg 2:10.
[44] Sg 5:2.
[45] Rev 3:20.
[46] Jn 15:4.
[47] Jn 15:5.
[48] Jn 15:15.
[49] Jn 15:18.

word, they will keep yours also.⁵⁰ And it is even clearer in Christ's priestly prayer to the Father: *That they may all be one; even as thou, Father, art in me, and I in thee, that they also may be in us...*⁵¹ *Father, I desire that they also, whom thou hast given me, may be with me where I am...*⁵² And there are these strange and profound words which our Lord uses elsewhere: *A disciple is not above his teacher, nor a servant above his master; it is enough for the disciple to be like his teacher, and the servant like his master.*⁵³

But what exactly do these mysterious words mean, living in the other and living by the other? The first thing to be borne in mind is that almost everyone is able to intuit to some extent the things that refer to love, and the real difficulty arises only when one starts to look for explanations. Be that as it may, it is clear that we have here a communion of lives and of goods which goes far beyond mere co-sharing. But to say this is not to say much.

In his priestly prayer addressed to the Father, our Lord says that *all mine are thine, and thine are mine.*⁵⁴ This can be applied certainly to human love and even more so to divine–human love, provided one does not forget the analogy involved. Up to this point the subject seems to present fewer difficulties than the idea of living through or by the other, or the no less strange idea of living in the other. That what each of the lovers possesses belongs to the other is not too difficult to understand, given that love is, as we know, always mutual giving and self-surrender. However, the point must be made at the start that we are not dealing here merely with voluntary co-possession of goods, but with a total giving in which

---

⁵⁰ Jn 15:20.
⁵¹ Jn 17:21.
⁵² Jn 17:24.
⁵³ Mt 10: 24–25.
⁵⁴ Jn 17:10.

it is the lovers who give themselves unreservedly to each other. The *Song* expresses it very clearly:[55]

> *My beloved is mine and I am his.*[56]

The lovers give to each other, not just *everything they have*, but also *everything they are*. So, one can quite properly say that each gives himself to the other, which brings in the idea of a certain mutual immanence. Due to the fact that the texts clearly say that each is in the other, or that each lives by the other, it does not seem justifiable to reduce love to a mere reciprocal possession of the person of the other (in the sense that I belong to you and you belong to me): *Abide in me, and I in you. As the branch cannot bear fruit by itself, unless it abides in the vine, neither can you, unless you abide in me. I am the vine, you are the branches. He who abides in me, and I in him, he it is that bears much fruit, for apart from me you can do nothing.*[57]

So, what does *abide in* really mean, or what is the nature of this apparent mutual inherence? Having established that no fusion or mixture of nature takes place,[58] and that the individuality of the persons is preserved intact, clearly we have to look elsewhere for the answers to this question.

It can be taken as definite that certain expressions are not just figures of speech. For example, expressions such as: Christ as the life of the disciple (Col 3: 3–4), the disciple living because of Christ

---

[55] In the bosom of the Trinity there is the same, identical, divine nature, which is communicated to the Son by the Father.

[56] Sg 2:16. Cf. 6:3; 7:11; 8:6.

[57] Jn 15: 4–5. Cf. 1 Jn 4: 9.16.

[58] Unicity of nature and distinction of Persons is found only in God.

(Jn 6:58) and both abiding in one another. The least that can be said here is that the disciple makes the master's life his own, in the sense that he shapes his behaviour —actions, words, thoughts— to that of Christ: *he who says he abides in him ought to walk in the same way in which he walked.*[59] If love brings about a communion of affections and of ideas —a consequence of the lovers' mutual self-giving— it must also lead to identity of conduct, as well as identity of destiny: *As the Father has sent me, even so I send you.*[60] A person who is in love not only desires to be with the person he loves but also and above all he wants to be like her (which here means act like her):[61]

> *Draw me after you, let us make haste.*
> *The king has brought me into his chambers.*
> *We will exult and rejoice in you.*[62]

> ....

> *Come, my beloved, let us go forth into the fields,*
> *and lodge in the villages.*[63]

To be together, of course. To achieve that, neither the bride nor the Bridegroom hesitates in running in search of each other. But the bride does not stop there: she also, particularly, desires *to be like the Bridegroom*:

---

[59] 1 Jn 2:6.

[60] Jn 20:21. Cf. Rom 6: 3–5.

[61] Which does not in any way exclude the pristine sense of *being like her*. The lover desires to make his own the loveliness he sees in the loved one, and in that sense to be like her and even to be identified with her insofar as is possible. Besides, the principle that action follows being also applies here.

[62] Sg 1:4.

[63] Sg 7:12.

> *O night that guided me!*
> *O night more lovely than the dawn!*
> *O night that has joined*
> *the Beloved with his lover,*
> *lover transformed into the Beloved!*[64]

It is in this sense that it is correct to say that the Christian is another Christ. Identification of lives does not mean copying or imitating actions and thoughts; what God desires in fact is not that people see in the disciple someone whose behaviour is similar to Christ's; he wants them to see Christ Himself: *Take me as your pattern, just as I take Christ for mine.*[65] God's plan is that the Person and life of Jesus should shine in the soul and in the body of the disciple, not only in his actions: *So that the life of Jesus may also be manifested in our bodies. For while we live we are always being given up to death for Jesus' sake, so that the life of Jesus may be manifested in our mortal flesh.*[66] The disciple's goal, therefore, is to be like He was, which is even more than *living as he did*.[67] This means that the disciple not only acts and feels in every way like Jesus (Phil 2:5; 1 Cor 2:16), but that his entire being (body and

---

[64] St John of the Cross, *Noche Oscura*:

> *¡Oh noche que guiaste!*
> *¡Oh noche amable más que el alborada!*
> *¡Oh noche que juntaste*
> *Amado con amada,*
> *amada en el Amado transformada!*

[65] 1 Cor 11:1; 4:16. But reality always goes beyond what a mere imitation would be.

[66] 2 Cor 4: 10–11. Cf. Phil 1:20; 1 Cor 6:20.

[67] 1 Jn 2:6. Clearly, for St John, living like Jesus and abiding in Him are one and the same thing: if one lives like Him, one abides in Him.

soul) is possessed and influenced by the Spirit of Jesus Himself: *As many of you as were baptized into Christ have put on Christ.*[68]

Because the Spirit of the Lord is the hinge on which his whole life turns, the disciple is seen by the world as another Christ, for he and Christ live exactly the same life: *because I live, you live also.*[69] The disciple, then, looks like Christ, but he remains other: he looks in fact like *another* Christ.[70] If, on the one hand, love demands perfect distinction of persons, on the other, testimony makes no sense unless it refers to *another*, the one of whom testimony is borne. The proof of this lies in the fact that the true disciple —the saint— evokes in his person the presence of God, which causes his own person to fade into the background. Therefore, genuine Christian witness is something given more by a person's life than by what he says, because its true purpose is to manifest personal life and not just to say things about it. Witnessing does not consist principally in transferring information or knowledge, but in presenting and dynamically communicating a life —in this case, Jesus'— so that it may be shared; and to do this the witnessing must be animated by the strength of the Spirit (Acts 1: 7–8).[71]

If the disciple lives through Christ and has put on Christ, he does so because he is really living *in* Christ, which is the same as saying, if we listen to the texts, that Christ really lives *in* him. Granting

---

[68] Gal 3:27.

[69] Jn 14:19.

[70] The English language expresses this more exactly than Spanish does.

[71] St John stresses that Christian witness is not simply a reporting of events, but something which hinges on someone who has seen, heard and touched —and who now passes this experience on to others— not just to inform them, but to have them share it and enjoy it along with him, with the very same joy as he himself has (1 Jn 1: 1–4).

the fact that the persons are absolutely different from one another[72] and that it is absurd to think of any mixture of natures, one must acknowledge in divine–human love a real presence or inherence of Jesus (and even of the whole Trinity) in the disciple.[73] According to our Lord, *If a man loves me, he will keep my word, and my Father will love him, and we will come to him and make our home with him.*[74] St Paul echoes our Lord's teaching: *Do you not know that your bodies are members of Christ?... Do you not know that your body is a temple of the Holy Spirit within you, which you have from God? You are not your own.*[75] As regards the Apostle's profound words in Galatians 6:17, *Henceforth let no man trouble me; for I bear on my body the marks (stigmata) of Jesus*, whatever their exact meaning is, they clearly refer to a special presence of the Lord in the soul of the disciple, a presence which can also be seen in his body.[76] Speaking of the presence of God and his Love in the disciple is not using metaphors or referring to mere feelings: it refers to realities which man alone could never have thought up: *God's love has been poured into our hearts through the Holy Spirit who has been given*

---

[72] It is worth emphasizing once again that this point is essential in love. Without the mysterious dialogue and the ineffable transference between the *I* and the *thou*, love has no meaning and cannot even be imagined.

[73] The difficulty involved in fully explaining this matter is another consequence of the impossibility of really understanding what essential Love is and how it is shared in by a created being (the divine–human analogue).

[74] Jn 14:23. Cf. Jn 6:56; etc.

[75] 1 Cor 6: 15.19. Cf. Gal 2:20.

[76] *If your eye is sound, your whole body will be full of light* (Mt 6:22). This seems to be the most logical explanation of this difficult verse. The word *eye* here must be taken as a synonym of spirit or soul, as Matthew 20:15 seems to confirm. This emphasis on the *physical* clearly indicates that the presence of our Lord in his disciple is much more than something merely moral.

to us.[77] Since Christian anthropology embraces both soul and body, God's presence in his creature does not mean presence only in the soul —the texts do not support that sort of reduction— but in the whole man: *Always carrying in the body the death of Jesus, so that the life of Jesus may also be manifested in our bodies. For while we live we are always being given up to death for Jesus' sake, so that the life of Jesus may be manifested in our mortal flesh.*[78] Besides, the very logic of love requires that he who loves desire to be in and with the one he loves, not just with the body or with the soul of that person.

Forgetting this doctrine has given rise to too many *spiritualizing* interpretations of the *Song of Songs*. Theologies of Platonic tendency, always ready to be scandalized by things to do with the body, have adopted positions which are in fact far removed from a genuine *supernatural* interpretation of the *Song*. But if one accepts that the sacred book is a song celebrating the loves between God *and man*, as it undoubtedly is, it should not surprise anyone that it is written in the way it is.

The same can be said as regards the claim (which many make) that the book is really a song extolling the relationship between Christ and his Church. That interpretation seems to be mere verbal quibbling when one remembers that in the last analysis the Church is made up of individual men and women, and in the order of reality they are all that exist. Besides, when true and perfect love is at issue, as in the case of divine love, what can love of a collectivity mean? Clearly, that love either translates ultimately into a genuine affective feeling —involving real self-surrender— towards each of

---

[77]Rom 5:5.
[78]2 Cor 4: 10–11.

the *persons* that make up the group, or else one must admit that it is quite meaningless.

The great misfortune of Catholic theology is that it has been afflicted by two serious illnesses at the same time, illnesses which are undoubtedly closely connected: invasion by Protestant theology, and the reduction of theology to sociology.[79] Individualist subjectivism has caused the objective reality and entity of grace, with the true presence of the Lord that it causes in the Christian, to be replaced by feelings. This has given rise, for example, to indefinite deferring of important sacraments like confirmation and baptism, on the excuse that the candidate needs to be mature enough *to know* what he is going to receive and *to ask for it himself*. At one fell swoop, centuries of Catholic teaching on the sacraments of Christian initiation are done away with. Once the teachings about the objective reality of grace and the *ex opere operato* effectiveness of the sacraments have been thrust aside, the only thing that matters now is what the person

---

[79] At one point when this book was being written, I happened to listen to Spanish State radio (controlled by the Socialist government); in the course of a *religious* program, the following, apparently well–intentioned, exhortation could be heard:

—My friend, you are entitled to have beliefs or not have them; but do try to understand your neighbour.

Clearly, apart from the words sounding rather pretentious, the first thing that comes to mind is the following difficulty: if one tries to understand one's neighbour when one does not have any beliefs, what reason is there to understand him, particularly when, as implied, he is not a very agreeable person? Clearly, as is also logical, before reaching this point one would need to know exactly what the speaker (in this case an ecclesiastic) meant by *understanding your neighbour*. Here, once again, is an instance of the generalities and ambiguity one meets when dealing with common–places. Of course, in this case, it may have been simply a question of articulation (the neighbour may not have been able to pronounce words clearly). But, that aside, the main thing is that theology is being replaced by an odd sort of sociology: it does not matter whether you believe or not: the only thing that matters is understanding your neighbour.

knows, desires or does by and for himself. As regards the Eucharist, when all that remains of it is pure subjectivism, it no longer matters very much if one receives it with no particular disposition of soul; especially when it is assured that the Eucharist is a mere symbol whose only purpose is to develop feelings of solidarity within the community.

But the life of Christ in the disciple —which means that the disciple lives in Christ and through Christ— implies something else as well, which also stems from the logic of love. It implies that the disciple cannot live without Jesus, because the Lord is for him his whole life, the only meaning of his existence: *Because you have died, and now the life you have is hidden with Christ in God. But when Christ is revealed —and He is your life— you, too, will be revealed with Him in glory.*[80] St John of the Cross refers to this subject in his *Spiritual Canticle*:

> *But how, O life, can you go on living,*
> *since your life is not where you are,*
> *and since the arrows which you receive*
> *from the conceptions of the Beloved formed*
> > *within you*
> *they deal you death?*[81]

---

[80] Col 3: 3–4.

[81] In the original:

> *Mas ¿cómo perseveras,*
> *¡oh vida!, no viviendo donde vives*
> *y haciendo porque mueras*
> *las flechas que recibes*
> *de lo que del Amado en ti concibes?*

> *Since you have wounded my heart*
> *wherefore did not heal it?*
> *And wherefore, having robbed me of it,*
> *have you left it thus*
> *and take not the prey that you have spoiled?*[82]

The disciple who is in love thinks so much and so continuously about the Beloved that he forgets himself, to the point that he *no longer lives his own life*; he lives the life of the other more than his own. In fact one could say that the life of the other is his only life: *He died for all, that those who live might live no longer for themselves but for him who for their sake died and was raised.*[83] St John of the Cross, as we have just seen, expresses this poetically when he says that his own life is no longer where he lives:

> *But how, O life, can you go on living,*
> *since your life is not where you are...?*[84]

---

[82]In the original:

> *¿Por qué, pues, has llagado*
> *aqueste corazón, no le sanaste?*
> *Y, pues me le has robado,*
> *¿por qué así le dejaste,*
> *y no tomas el robo que robaste?*

[83]2 Cor 5:15.

[84]In the original:

> *Mas ¿cómo perseveras,*
> *¡oh vida!, no viviendo donde vives...?*

And even more so when *the Other* is continuously stealing his life away, so that eventually he causes his death through love:

> *...and since the arrows which you receive*
> *from the conceptions of the Beloved formed*
> *within you*
> *they deal you death?*[85]

This is the same feeling as the bride of the *Song* experiences:

> *Sustain me with raisins,*
> *refresh me with apples;*
> *for I am sick with love.*[86]

The laments and complaints of love make no sense at all, of course, to anyone who does not know how to love and has never experienced these feelings. Are these laments due to sorrow or to joy? Are these complaints caused by pain or does the pain lie in the fact that the wound and pain are not even more acute? Is it the pain of one who feels himself dying because of love, or is the reason for his tears the fact that he is still alive and is not dying as soon as he would like? Hagiographers and saints have tried to describe these sentiments in poetry, or had recourse to grammatical constructions whose deepest meaning will never be explained. Is

---

[85] In the original:

> *¿...y haciendo porque mueras*
> *las flechas que recibes*
> *de lo que del Amado en ti concibes?*

[86] Sg 2:5. Cf. 5:8.

there really any other way to speak about this subject? The New Testament texts are there for everyone to interpret as best he can, led by the light of the Spirit. As regards poetry... Poetry will always be something one resorts to; despite its inadequacy it can at least hint at —whisper, as it were— what can never be articulated, much less explained... But it is something that true lovers will understand, at least insofar as their hearts can take it in. For, the heart can be said to have its reasons which the mind does not understand. The Apostle recognizes this love–death and transformation into the Beloved as happening to himself: *It is no longer I who live, but Christ who lives in me.*[87] And he also refers to it as happening to others (here his language is amazingly beautiful): *none of us lives to himself, and none of us dies to himself. If we live, we live to the Lord, and if we die, we die to the Lord; so then, whether we live or whether we die, we are the Lord's.*[88] All this —what both the Old and the New Testaments have to say— is simply a reflection of the Master's teaching: *He who finds his life will lose it, and he who loses his life for my sake will find it.*[89] For the bride feels so acutely that her life is the Bridegroom that she is afraid that the very words the Bridegroom addresses to her may cause her death–through–love:

---

[87] Gal 2:20.

[88] Rom 14: 7–8.

[89] Mt 10:39. Cf. Mt 16:25; Mk 8:35; Lk 9:24; Jn 12:25.

> *Should you see me again*
> *yonder in the valley, where the blackbird sings,*
> *do not say that you love me,*
> *for, upon hearing it, I may die,*
> *were you ever to repeat it.*[90]

As always happens, and as reciprocity in love dictates, the Bridegroom harbours the same feelings towards the bride. And therefore he turns to her to say:

> *Turn away your eyes from me,*
> *for they take me by assault.*[91]

The fact that the disciple who is in love cannot live without his Master, because by divesting himself of his own life in favor of Him he no longer has that life, helps us to understand better St Paul's warning to the Colossians. The Apostle tells them to learn to savor the things of heaven and gives them a reason why: *For you have died, and your life is hid with Christ in God.*[92] If the Colossians have renounced —or lost— their life for love's sake, then they are, logically, dead. But in this case, and contrary to what one might think, we are dealing with a death that really is the way leading to

---

[90] In the original:

> *Si de nuevo me vieres,*
> *allá en el valle, donde canta el mirlo,*
> *no digas que me quieres,*
> *no muera yo al oírlo*
> *si acaso tú volvieras a decirlo.*

[91] Sg 6:5.
[92] Col 3:3.

true life. So, the Apostle reminds his disciples that, far from having ended their life, they have only just begun to possess it in all its fullness: their life is in Christ, albeit in a hidden way.

And why *hidden* exactly? To explain these words of the Apostle we would need to go into all the nooks and crannies of love, because that is where many of the characteristic features of love seem to lie. Like all true love, divine–human love is something that outsiders know nothing about —or at least they know nothing of its deepest fabric—, although it is also true that love never passes totally unnoticed. Lovers usually seek out solitude, hidden places, because it is only there that the mystery of the dialogue and mutual self–surrender of *I* and *thou* can take place:

> *Come, my beloved,*
> *let us go forth into the fields,*
> *and lodge in the villages;*
> *let us go out early to the vineyards,*
> *and see whether the vines have budded,*
> *whether the grape blossoms have opened*
> *and the pomegranates are in bloom.*
> *There I will give you my love.*[93]

And St John of the Cross, in his *Spiritual Canticle*:

---

[93] Sg 7: 12–13.

> *Let us rejoice, my Beloved,*
> *and in your beauty see ourselves reflected:*
> *by mountain and by hill,*
> *where the pure water runs;*
> *let us enter deeper into the forest.*[94]

The holy Carmelite poet is thus crying out for that solitude which makes possible the intimacy and dialogue of love between the two lovers: *By mountain and by hill; to the lofty caves of the rocks...*

> *Then we shall climb up high*
> *to the lofty caves of the rocks,*
> *well hidden from view;*
> *and there we shall enter,*
> *and revel in the first wine of the pomegranates.*[95]

The deepest intimacy of the mystery of love is something that only the two lovers can fully embrace: *He who has an ear, let him*

---

[94]In the original:

> *Gocémonos, Amado,*
> *y vámonos a ver en tu hermosura*
> *al monte y al collado*
> *do mana el agua pura;*
> *entremos más adentro en la espesura.*

[95]In the original:

> *Y luego a las subidas*
> *cavernas de la piedra nos iremos,*
> *que están bien escondidas,*
> *y allí nos entraremos*
> *y el mosto de granadas gustaremos.*

hear what the Spirit says to the churches. To him who conquers I will give some of the hidden manna, and I will give him a white stone, with a new name written on the stone which no one knows except him who receives it.[96] However, in the mystery of divine–human love, the search for solitude does not mean excluding other people or despising other created things. Quite the contrary. Seeking solitude refers simply to the desire of both lovers to have each other totally, and their conviction that that is the only way they can attain perfect love:

> *Lost to myself I stayed,*
> *my face reclining on the Beloved;*
> *everything ceased and I abandoned myself,*
> *throwing my cares*
> *among the lilies to be forgotten.*[97]

Living through the Beloved or living in the Beloved means thinking like Him, feeling like Him and acting like Him. But, as we can well suppose, it is not only that but also *being with Him*, in the strict sense of the phrase. Now at last we can say that love, after many ups and downs, and so much searching and waiting, has attained its supreme goal, the union of the lovers, which is in fact the only thing they wanted. It is no longer a question of running after the

---

[96] Rev 2:17.

[97] St John of the Cross, *Noche Oscura*:

> *Quedéme y olvidéme,*
> *el rostro recliné sobre el Amado,*
> *cesó todo y dejéme,*
> *dejando mi cuidado*
> *entre las azucenas olvidado.*

Beloved, darting here and there, running risks in a long quest. No longer does one have to resign oneself to hearing from him through messengers who can never manage to pass on accurately what the lovers mean and desire to hear:

> *Draw me after you, let us make haste.*
> *the king has brought me into his chambers...*[98]
>
> ....
>
> *I adjure you, O daughters of Jerusalem,*
> *if you find my beloved,*
> *that you tell him I am sick with love.*[99]

St John of the Cross says this, again very beautifully, in his *Spiritual Canticle*:

> *O, who will be able to heal me!*
> *Come, give yourself completely to me now*
> *From now on send me*
> *no more messengers,*
> *for they cannot tell me what I wish!*[100]

---

[98] Sg 1:4.
[99] Sg 5:8.
[100] In the original:

> *¡Ay!, ¿quién podrá sanarme?*
> *¡Acaba de entregarte ya de vero;*
> *no quieras enviarme*
> *de hoy más ya mensajero*
> *que no saben decirme lo que quiero!*

The bride is no longer satisfied with the news about the Bridegroom with which his messengers might provide her. There is only one thing that is able to fully satiate her heart: the words heard directly from the Bridegroom's mouth:

> *Tell me then, sweetheart,*
> *where will you lead your flock to graze,*
> *where will you rest it at noon?*
> *That I may no more wander like a vagabond...*[101]

And St John of the Cross:

> *The creatures all around me*
> *speak of your thousand gifts,*
> *yet they wound me even more.*
> *Something that they stammer*
> *leaves me dying.*[102]

And, as happens with all roads, this was just one more stage to cover, prior to the goal. Love does not understand separations; its only aim is to unite the lovers forever. Therefore, our Lord's words should be interpreted in an ontological sense; they are not meant to

---

[101] Sg 1:7.

[102] In the original:

> *Y todos cuantos vagan*
> *de ti me van mil gracias refiriendo*
> *y todos más me llagan*
> *y déjame muriendo*
> *un no se qué que quedan balbuciendo.*

be merely exhortative or sentimental: *As the Father has loved me, so have I loved you; abide in my love. If you keep my commandments, you will abide in my love, just as I have kept my Father's commandments and abide in his love.*[103] Here it is not a matter of holding on to certain feelings but of staying in a Love which, because it is something absolutely real, equally embraces the two lovers as if they were just one thing. No longer are there two people with the same feelings, but two *in the same love*. But because that love is a real entity, and even a Person, it mysteriously ensures that the two lovers, while keeping their personal individuality inviolable, join to become one,[104] as it were, as a result of the *total* self–surrender each makes to the other: *the Spirit of truth, whom the world cannot receive, because it neither sees Him nor knows Him; you know Him, for He dwells with you, and will be with you.*[105] In fact, all the *as ifs* that are continuously resorted to, to try to explain the mystery, are simply due to the limitation of a language which is incapable of expressing realities which are outside the range of man's imagination. How could man conceive with his intellect or express in language everything the mystery of Love involves? It is worthwhile stressing again: what we have here is not just a merging or convergence of feelings, but a permanent and stable state which in some way turns the two lovers into one. Not simply two in one flesh, as the Book of Genesis said; what we now have is two in one love, becoming as it were one thing in the bosom of the divine life itself: *even as thou, Father, art in me, and I in thee, that they also may be in us, so*

---

[103] Jn 15: 9–10.

[104] It should not be forgotten that we are speaking here about divine–human love, which, as far as man is concerned, is also a participated love. In subsistent Love, the Lovers and their Love form one single nature.

[105] Jn 14:17.

that the world may believe that thou has sent me.[106] United now for evermore in the banquet of the Kingdom which will never end:

> *He brought me to the banqueting house,*
> *and his banner over me was love...*
> *O that his left hand were under my head,*
> *and that his right hand embraced me.*[107]

And so St John of the Cross says:

> *The bride has now entered the pleasant garden*
> *as she has long desired,*
> *and she rests in delight,*
> *her neck reclining*
> *on the gentle arms of her Beloved.*[108]

As anyone will readily notice, the theme given for this chapter has not even been broached. In fact it would have been difficult, not to say impossible, to try to lead up to it in any other way. The best way to approach matters that have to do with love —perhaps the only way— is to try to open up paths in the hope that they lead somewhere. Everyone knows that love —at least for now—

---

[106] Jn 17:21.
[107] Sg 2: 4–6.
[108] In the original:

> *Entrado se ha la esposa*
> *en el ameno huerto deseado*
> *y a su sabor reposa*
> *el cuello reclinado*
> *sobre los dulces brazos del Amado.*

is something much more easy to understand than it is to explain. *Si intelligis, non est Deus.* And, yet, true lovers are always ready to swear that they know very well what they want. How could it be otherwise? If they were in any doubt, they could not be in love. They must know something (or perhaps quite a bit) about the Bridegroom since they feel so much in love with Him: *I have made known to them thy name, and I will make it known, that the love with which thou have loved me may be in them, and I in them.*[109] It is true that the devil and sin managed to bring ugliness and pain into the world, but not to the extent that beauty and joy were uprooted, never to grow again (Sg 8:7). Therefore, from now onwards it is still possible for men to be happy —at least ever since the beatitudes were promulgated in the Sermon on the Mount, and the paths of love were opened once more, never again to be closed.

---

[109] Jn 17:26.

Third Part

Delicate is the fragrance of your perfumes.
Your name is oil poured out:
Therefore the maidens love you.

(Sg 1:3)

CHAPTER I

THE FRAGRANCE OF THE BRIDEGROOM

In fragrantiam unguentorum tuorum optimorum. It is always pleasant to catch the aroma of a perfume, especially if it is the perfume of the loved one. When the perfume comes off things he uses, bringing him vividly to mind even though one does not actually see him, his presence is in some sense created: *See, the smell of my son is as the smell of a field which Yahweh has blessed.*[1] The fragrance of the perfume ceases to matter; it has given way to the evocation of the loved one. It is a fragrance that is more pleasing to the senses than ever because it is his own perfume —that of the loved one— and carries his unmistakable seal.

***

---

[1] Gen 27:27.

However, before we enter our theme proper, let us make some important preliminary points. The commentary on these verses of the *Song* can be described in advance as difficult work, but then that is true about commentary on any part of the Bible. Anyone bold enough to try it will soon see his spiritual wretchedness and be brought face to face with the truth about himself: *The word of God is living and active, sharper than any two-edged sword, piercing to the division of soul and spirit, of joints and marrow, and discerning the thoughts and intentions of the heart.*[2] If a person who writes something down commits himself to the truth more than one who simply speaks —since *scripta manent*—, then a person who comments on the Word of God commits himself even more seriously. Even a large dose of good will is not enough to put him at ease. The first obstacle the commentator encounters is his own limitations: they block his way; he can see nothing else. The stark contrast between human wretchedness and the riches of the Word of God is not slow to appear; convinced though he is that the Word was spoken and written for man's benefit, and even for his joy and consolation,[3] that does not help, because the commentator realizes the great distance there is between the Word and the reality of his own life. So, there is a serious risk of discouragement. It is a proven fact that, the deeper one goes into the content of what God has revealed, the more inaccessible the ideal proposed there for the daily life of man seems to be. And if the commentator's aim is to bear witness —as is normally the case— a point can come when his task seems impossible.

---

[2] Heb 4:12.
[3] Cf. Rom 15:4.

The fragrance of the Bridegroom

Anyone who makes bold to embark on this venture is likely soon to feel unable to go ahead, no matter how much goodwill he has: *And I said, Ah, Lord, Yahweh! Behold, I do not know how to speak, for I am only a youth.*[4] Thus, the words St Peter addresses to our Lord when he is just on the point of being called to the apostolate, seem both sensible and opportune: *Depart from me, for I am a sinful man, O Lord.*[5]

It is true that the Christian, and particularly the apostle, can always take refuge in the thought that his role is rather like that of a bridge —*Omnis namque pontifex...*[6]—, that he is simply an instrument to be used to get from one side to the other, in this case from God to the people, and from the people to God. And, no one pays any attention to an instrument that is just a bridge: the only thing that he is really concerned about is to cross over in order to be on one side or the other.

But the apostle knows well that things do not go that way and that people do end up focussing on him. There is no way to avoid this, because what he is doing is bearing witness —and by its very nature that is something eminently personal and most important. *You are the light of the world. A city set on a hill cannot be hid. Nor do men light a lamp and put it under a bushel, but on a stand, and it gives light to all in the house. Let your light so shine before men, that they may see your good works and give glory to your Father who is in heaven.*[7] It is impossible to separate testimony from the person who gives it. That is in fact what lies at the basis of the glory and the tragedy of the apostle and even of every Christian, a tragedy that

---

[4] Jer 1:6.
[5] Lk 5:8.
[6] Heb 5:1.
[7] Mt 5: 14–16.

prompts the Apostle to utter a moving cry: *If I do preach the gospel, that gives me no ground for boasting. For necessity is laid upon me. Woe to me if I do not preach the gospel! For if I do this of my own will, I have a reward; but if not of my own will, I am entrusted with a commission.*[8] From this we can deduce that, for St Paul, the only thing which justifies the incongruity between word and preacher is the mandate he has been given: *Woe to me if I do not preach the gospel...!* The genuine apostle, who quite rightly feels that he is a poor man like everyone else, is paradoxically sent to make many rich.[9] And he is made aware, through a warning which surpasses all purely human logic, that the impoverished state —real poverty— in which he finds himself is an indispensable condition for his work to bear fruit. *Take no gold, nor silver, nor copper in your belts, no bag for your journey, nor two tunics, nor sandals, nor a staff; for the labourer deserves his food.*[10] Hence the obligation and the pressing need for testimony expose the apostle's wretchedness, not just to himself but also to others. *Where is the wise man? Where is the scribe? Where is the debater of this age? Has not God made foolish the wisdom of the world? For since, in the wisdom of God, the world did not know God through wisdom, it pleased God through the folly of what we preach to save those who believe... For consider your call, brethren; not many of you were wise according to worldly standards, not many were powerful, not many were of noble birth; but God chose what is foolish in the world to shame the wise, God chose what is weak in the world to shame the strong.*[11] Therefore the preaching of the Gospel message has to be proposed both as a

---

[8] 1 Cor 9: 16–17.

[9] Cf. 2 Cor 6:10.

[10] Mt 10: 9–10. Cf. Mk 6:8; Lk 9:3; 10:4; Acts 3:6. The definitive text on this subject may be 2 Cor 6: 3–10.

[11] 1 Cor 1: 20–21.26–27.

goal and as a hope, for those to whom the testimony is offered and for him who offers it.

From this we can deduce that the only ones equipped to bear witness to Christ are those who are convinced that they are incapable of doing so. Christian witness does not acquire legitimacy from the personal superabundance of the witness,[12] but from his obedience to a mandate given him. Since the apostle is aware that he is no teacher or leader, he also knows that there is nothing he is equipped to teach, no orders he is qualified to give (Mt 23: 8–10). Nor can he give anything, because he owns nothing, ever since the moment he became a good disciple of the Lord (Lk 14:33), which one must suppose he is.

However, his strength lies in this very fact. Because he has been sent in this way and even with the express instruction to carry *no gold, nor silver, nor copper in your belts, no bag for your journey, nor two tunics, nor sandals, nor a staff,*[13] he does not run the risk of giving people something which, because it belongs to him, might betray the Message that has been entrusted to him. That is how Christian Poverty, once it has been lovingly accepted by the apostle, enables him to speak about God, removing any impediments and at the same time giving him what he needs for his testimony to make its impact: *And he said to them: When I sent you out with no purse or bag or sandals, did you lack anything? They said, Nothing.*[14] Certainly the apostle feels confronted by an obligation to obey the commandment and carry out the mission entrusted to him: *Go therefore and make disciples of all nations, baptizing them in the name of the Father and of the Son and of the Holy Spirit, teaching*

---

[12] Only Jesus Christ is truly the *faithful witness* (Rev 1:5; cf. 1 Tim 6:13).
[13] Mt 10: 9–10.
[14] Lk 22:35.

them to observe all that I have commanded you.[15] Jesus chose *those whom he desired*[16] and gave them the key role of continuing his mission: *You did not choose me, but I chose you and appointed you that you should go and bear fruit and that your fruit should abide.*[17]

However, there are many people nowadays who, due to the influence of Protestant theology and the effects of the crisis of faith caused by neo–modernism, try to undermine the mission of the apostle. Throwing out, as obsolete and harmful, what they call *medieval notions of pastoral practice*,[18] they have developed a series of theological speculations to do with odd doctrines such as the so–called *maturity of the laity*, to give just one example; this explains why faculties of Catholic theology so often concentrate nowadays on amazingly "way–out" subjects of scandalizing naivety.

One of these themes, which will do by way of a sample, is that which is usually pompously described as *From clerical pastoral domination to lay maturity*, no less. It is certainly a subject to which one cannot help having two immediate and different reactions. On the one hand, a feeling of shock and surprise at the very subject. On the other, a painful feeling of absence, lack, or nostalgia at the sad

---

[15] Mt 28: 19–20.

[16] Mk 3:13.

[17] Jn 15:16. Cf. Jn 15:19; Lk 6:13.

[18] One of the many descriptions people use to run down (without proving any justification for doing so) institutions of the past which have always been held in high regard and been blessed by the Church. These neo–Modernist trends are in fact the result of setting aside valuable *medieval ideas.* The ditching of venerable medieval institutions such as the theology and philosophy of St Thomas, with the Thomist metaphysic of being, came about with the appearance of such phenomena as idealism (with all the evil it brings in its trail including Marxism, existentialism, and philosophical and theological relativism, to mention a few), whose most obvious results are the crisis of faith the Church is undergoing today, and contemporary neo–Modernism itself.

fact that the *Enchiridion Symbolorum* has nothing to say by way of condemning such naivety.

What would someone capable of studying the matter dispassionately and serenely make of the *clerical pastoral domination* referred to? If it means that there have always been clerics who made improper use of their power, that is something which must be accepted as absolutely true. It is a natural consequence of the weakness of human nature and it is a permanent feature of all institutions and social classes. It applies not just to clerics but also to governors, politicians, academics, teachers, writers, military men, doctors and lots more. Given that there have always been good and bad people around, in all situations, it is clearly unfair to generalize and make a blanket condemnation of some particular group or social class. Up to this point no new discovery has been made. But if what it really means is that the clergy in their pastoral work have acted with authority towards lay people, then this criticism is serious since it is nothing but an outrageous mischief. For it was Jesus Christ Himself Who, when He instituted the Hierarchy in the Church, gave authority to some members of his flock to teach and govern the others. If by *domination* is meant an inequality among members whereby some have functions and powers which others do not have, powers whose foundation is of divine institution, then one has to admit that there is such a thing as clerical pastoral domination. But in that case one needs to underline that it is a domination established and specified by the Church's very Founder. Clearly, in that case, one needs to tread very carefully, so as not to run any risk of harming the basic organic structure of the Church.

Moreover, what logical meaning can be given to the notion of *lay maturity*? We must hasten to say that this so–called problem is of fairly recent vintage, because prior to this no one thought that lay people were in a situation of *immaturity*. Over the course of the twenty centuries during which they were regarded as responsible adults, both in the faith and in ordinary life, no one thought that lay people had any need to free themselves from the apron-strings of overpowering nursemaids or spiritual ayahs. The clergy and the laity each performed their own functions, although occasionally, here and there over the course of history, it is true that each interfered in the other's territory. Everyone knows that clericalism and clerical privilege have always existed, both in the form of political Popes and bishops, and in the form of kings and other secular powers intruding on the sacristy. The interesting thing about this phenomenon, though, is the fact that the clergy, the true discoverer of the disease, were quite unaware until now of the *immaturity* under which lay people laboured for so long.[19] There are even those who have come round to the view that the evil was not denounced because it did not in fact exist —although there are others, more sensitive types, who say that it is all due to the fact that the clergy had not previously appreciated the need to proclaim the *maturity* of the laity. For clergy of the old school, lay same as night following day, and vice versa. But modern progressivist clergy think that the maturity of lay people must be given due credit and therefore they need to be upgraded, given a new status.

However, it is quite probable that the new situation has not come from a desire to put things in proper order, as some might think, but from an itch caused by the same inferiority complex as inspires the weak to kowtow to those they regard as strong. In

---

[19]Perhaps it is something like one of those diseases such as cancer and AIDS, which have only recently been discovered —with the difference that cancer or AIDS are fairly recent diseases, but the immaturity of lay people, although it is only now being diagnosed and treated, seems to have existed all along. Or at least that is what some pastoral *experts* think.

the last analysis, it is not so much recognition of the maturity of a class different from one's own: it all stems from a personal identity crisis. C. S. Lewis, on this matter of inferiority complex, refers to "the feeling that prompts a man to say *I'm as good as you*. The first and most obvious advantage is that you thus induce him to enthrone at the centre of his life a good solid, resounding lie. I don't mean merely that his statement is false in fact, that he is no more equal to everyone he meets in kindness, honesty, and good sense than in height or waist measurement. I mean that he does not believe it himself. No man who says *I'm as good as you* believes it. He would not say it if he did. The St Bernard never says it to the toy dog, nor the scholar to the dunce, nor the employable to the bum, not the pretty woman to the plain. The claim to equality, outside the strictly political field, is made only by those who feel themselves to be in some way inferior. What it expresses is precisely the itching, smarting, writhing awareness of an inferiority which the patient refuses to accept. And therefore resents. Yes, and therefore resents every kind of superiority in others; denigrates it; wishes its annihilation. Presently he suspects every mere difference of being a claim to superiority. No one must be different from himself in voice, clothes, manners, recreations, choice of food: 'Here is someone who speaks English rather more clearly and euphoniously than I —it must be a vile, upstage, la–di–da affectation. Here's a fellow who says he doesn't like hot dogs —thinks himself too good for them, no doubt. Here's a man who hasn't turned on the juke–box —he's one of those goddam highbrows and is doing it to show off. If they were honest–to–God all–right Joes they'd be like me. They've no business to be different. It's undemocratic.'"[20] However, it must be pointed out that the inferiority complex Lewis is talking about is not

---

[20]C. S. Lewis, *Screwtape Proposes a Toast and Other Pieces*.

exactly the same as the disability the clergy is suffering from. The cases are not identical, because here it is not a matter of refusing to recognize the superiority of others; it is something much more refined and subtle. What pushes the modern clerics to extol the laity does not come from the demands of some hypothetical justice, but from a pernicious desire to see themselves on a lower level. The problem, therefore, is essentially not so much an attempt to upgrade the laity; it has to do with the sad contempt in which the clergy hold themselves. However, one certainly cannot exclude, as a purely logical consequence, a certain sense of envy of the laity.

If by *lay maturity* is meant raising lay people to a higher plane than they have been on prior to this, in order to equiparate their functions to those of clerics, nothing could be more absurd. All one has to do to see such absurdity is to remember the traditional teaching of the Church. Even though all the faithful form part of the flock of the *great Shepherd of the sheep*,[21] the members of the Church of Christ are by divine institution grouped into two different estates, that of Pastors and that of ordinary sheep. In a real sheep flock, every sheep develops, stage by stage, until it reaches adulthood: they are born, they grow up until they can fend for themselves within the flock, they come to produce more milk and more wool..., but even so they continue to be sheep; adult sheep, but sheep nonetheless, and therefore destined to be led by a shepherd as long as they live, because no matter how mature they are they do not change genus

---

[21] Heb 13:20. Texts such as this, or John 10:16, do not cast doubt on the doctrine of the organic structuring of the Church into Pastors and ordinary faithful —a doctrine which, besides, is clearly revealed and has been repeatedly defined. Against the notion of non–existence of Pastors in the Church, men endowed with real power to govern and teach, cf., among others, Acts 20:28, Jn 21: 15–17, 1 Pet 5:4, Heb 5: 1–5, 1 Cor 4, and Eph 4: 11–12, as well as the Letters to Timothy and Titus, etc.

or species. All the faithful of Jesus Christ's flock, both Pastors and ordinary faithful or sheep, are destined to reach maturity: *until we all attain to the unity of the faith and of the knowledge of the Son of God, to mature manhood, to the measure of the stature of the fullness of Christ.*[22] But that process takes place *through each part working properly,*[23] which means that it takes place within the estate proper to each person.[24] The maturity of lay people is as desirable as the maturity of any Christian (maturity is a goal all should seek), but it can never make them anything other than lay people. There is no reason why it should. Things are lovable or desirable to the extent that they are what God made them. So, clearly lay people are happy within their own state–in–life; they have quite enough responsibilities and problems to keep them occupied and they are in no way diminished by them. Besides, their particular vocation and their specific way of holiness are well delineated and perfectly clear: they sanctify themselves in the midst of the world by doing their secular tasks and duties. These are things which only they can do since it is their vocation to do them. The immense majority of lay people never thought of *rising up* through the ecclesial —or, better, ecclesiastical— ranks, and very few felt they had a vocation

---

[22]Eph 4:13.

[23]Eph 4:16.

[24]Otherwise it would lead to so–called *substantial change*, the point of the following old chestnut:

On a certain occasion two men met in the street, and one of them hastened to greet the other profusely:

—Hello, Charlie, how you've changed...!

—Sorry, friend, —the man replied—, but I think you're mistaken. I'm not Charlie.

To which the first man replied, even more emphatically:

—Well, that just proves my point...!

to be sacristans.[25] But now a whole new field has been opened up between the clerical and lay fields and through it troop a host of people, hybrids as it were. Why are lay people carrying out almost all the ministries proper to the priest? Is this a crisis solution to the serious problem of shortage of priests? Avant garde theologians would reject this latter explanation out of hand. It is not, they say, a question of first aid but of *advancement of a laity which has reached maturity*. In modern theology's view the new situation should not be in any sense seen as a mere recourse or remedy but as a welcome achievement which should have come about much earlier.

This would have made everyone happy... were it not for the presence of annoying objections which keep raising their heads all over the place. Unfortunately the whole matter is so abominably tangled as to be almost unintelligible. After years of criticism of Pius XI's well–known definition of Catholic Action,[26] and the Second Vatican Council's emphasis on the *status* of lay people —stressing to the point of boredom that lay people enjoy their own sphere of action, a specific one, quite well defined—, what is now happening is that,

---

[25] Old–style sacristans were very different from the new breed of modern *sacristans*. The office of sacristan, which for centuries was a profession proper to laymen, was always filled by worthy men who, in countless churches in towns and cities, co–operated in and made a valuable contribution to the tasks involved in divine worship. Their secularity was never in doubt: theirs was an office like any other, a very honourable one, if not the finest of all. At the present time the old sacristans have been replaced by a swarm of men and women who perform a complex mosaic of so–called *ministries*. However, their appearance has created a problem which is no less real simply because no one talks about it —the danger of blurring the figure and role of the priest due to the fact that the area of competence of priest and sacristan are not clearly distinguished from one another, and the further risk of lay people being taken away from doing the tasks which constitute their specific vocation.

[26] Pius XI defined the now practically dead Catholic Action as *participation of lay people in the hierarchical apostolate of the Church*.

through one of those strange, mysterious twists of history, lay people are being elevated to performing the duties proper to the priestly office. And this is being done on the grounds that they have attained the maturity necessary to develop themselves and be freed from their previous subordination to the clergy. This creates the strange paradox that lay people need to stop being lay people in order to be truly lay people. As if that were not enough, to complicate things even further, the clerics who insist that lay people should rise up through the ecclesial and ecclesiastical ranks are the very ones who are bent on living like and looking like lay people —to the extent of giving the impression that they are ashamed of their own clerical status.[27] The whole thing is an enormous, complicated mess: if it can be sorted out, it will take a lot of work.

At this point a number of interesting questions might be asked. What is the source of all this interest in proclaiming the maturity of lay people? What leads people to believe, with such unwonted conviction, that lay people have been in a state of spiritual inferiority for the past twenty centuries? It certainly cannot be said to be a matter of claiming rights: it is not lay people but clerics who have been making all these demands. Nor is it a matter of justified recognition of a situation of oppression of laity by clergy, because it comes across as an attempt more to blur and lower the

---

[27]The students of a certain Church Faculty of Theology, candidates for the priesthood, told the author about a particular clerical professor in the Faculty who used to repeat quite often the phrase, *really, in the last analysis, we are all lay people*. Apart from the fact that the words are untrue —a cleric is not a layman, neither in the last analysis nor even superficially, if words mean anything and if the Law signifies anything— they do express aspirations, more or less conscious, held by clerics who see the laity as the apex of the ecclesial structure. What is the origin of this absurdity? A sense of nostalgia and envy for the lay state in life? Perhaps a lack of appreciation of their own clerical state? All the indications are that both these feelings underlie this sort of attitude.

clerical state than to exalt the laity, as we saw earlier. It is quite likely that the *rabies theologica* we are witnessing against an institution as venerable as the Catholic priesthood has its roots pretty deep down in fairly muddy waters. Certainly some of the blame must be laid at the door of the crisis of faith and the movements of ideas which have been going on ever since the eighteenth–century Enlightenment and even earlier, which are what caused the crisis of faith. Henri de Lubac already spoke[28] of the *suspicion towards the father*, spread worldwide by minds as twisted as that of Freud. And it should be remembered that the priest, precisely because he is a Good Shepherd, is also a Father who looks after the sheep entrusted to Him. However, the attempt made to destroy the ideas of dependence, filiation, submission and being sheep in Christ's flock leads to the suppression of the corresponding ideas of fatherhood and shepherding. The sheep have grown up now and no longer need the Pastor's voice or his crook; besides, the Pastors have also left their duties and prerogatives aside and begun to mix in with and become indistinguishable from the sheep.[29]

There is absolutely no justification for the accusation of overweening power made against Pastors. Given that the role of the priest is to continue the work of Jesus Christ, his mission is simply that of the Good Shepherd: *As the Father has sent me, even so I*

---

[28] In his book *The Drama of Atheist Humanism*, The World Publishing Co., Ohio, 1963.

[29] It is worth noting the strange vehemence with which the clergy in recent times have striven to take on the lifestyle and manners of lay people, even to the point of hiding and disguising their clerical conditions (and generally failing to do so, as one might expect, for, just as it tends to be said that the habit does not make the monk, similarly it is equally true that a jacket and trousers does not make a layman).

*send you.*³⁰ The devil has done quite a lot to spread the idea that the exercise of authority by Pastors is a type of tyranny. The truth is quite the opposite: *The Son of man came not to be served but to serve.*³¹ Jesus had quite different ideas about the world's reactions to the disciples he would send; he spelt out those ideas, to make sure his disciples should be under no illusion: *Beloved, I send you out as lambs in the midst of wolves.*³² His teaching about the exercise of apostolic authority is one of the clearest in the Gospel: *When he had washed their feet, and taken his garments, and resumed his place, he said to them, "Do you know what I have done to you? You call me Teacher and Lord; and you are right, for so I am. If I then, your Lord and Teacher, have washed your feet, you also ought to wash one another's feet. For I have given you an example, that you also should do as I have done to you. Truly, truly, I say to you, a servant is not greater than his master; nor is he greater than he who sent him."*³³ Here two things can be seen very clearly: the existence of authority, about which there is no question, and the serving of others in love as the only possible way to exercise that authority. Something similar can be said of the other texts in which the Master repeats the same teaching: *Whoever would be great among you must be your servant, and whoever would be first among you must be your slave; even as the Son of man came not to be served but to serve, and to give his life as a ransom for many.*³⁴ The texts leave no door open, not even

---

[30] Jn 20:21. Cf. 17:18.
[31] Mt 20:28. Cf. Phil 2:7.
[32] Lk 10:3. Cf. Mt 10:16; 2 Cor 6: 3–10.
[33] Jn 13: 12–16.
[34] Mt 20: 26–28. Cf. Mk 10: 42–45.

a chink, whereby the least little bit of tyranny might enter.[35] If one reads chapter ten of St John's Gospel, which contains the allegory of the Good Shepherd, this teaching is profiled even more clearly: *Truly, I say to you, he who does not enter the sheepfold by the door but climbs in by another way, that man is a thief and a robber; but he who enters by the door is the shepherd of the sheep. To him the gatekeeper opens; the sheep hear his voice, and he calls his own sheep by name and leads them out. When he has brought out all his own, he goes before them, and the sheep follow him, for they know his voice... I am the good shepherd. The good shepherd lays down his life for the sheep. He who is a hireling and not a shepherd, whose own the sheep are not, sees the wolf coming and leaves the sheep and flees; and the wolf snatches them and scatters them... I am the good shepherd; I know my own and my own know me.*[36] Here, plain for all to see, is the shepherd's affection and respect for his sheep, and the close intimacy he has with them: he knows each of them, he calls them by name, he goes on ahead, leading them to good pastures, and when danger threatens he is ready to defend them with his life. He knows his sheep as well as they know him: *I know my own and my own know me...* If anyone here has, by his office, the responsibility to be concerned and to sacrifice himself, it is the shepherd, not the sheep. As regards the knowledge of the sheep, which we are told here the Master has, this is in no sense superficial acquaintance, as can be seen from verses 14 and 15, which are all of a piece: *I am the good shepherd. I know my own and my own know me, as the Father*

---

[35] Some may think that the argument is not centred on doctrinal points, which are evident and clear, but on the fact that Pastors have abused their authority over lay people. However, that is not the point being made. We are not discussing here a question of fact *but of law*, because the aim is to raise lay people to a status which, the argument goes, is one to which they have a right.

[36] Jn 10:1 ff.

knows me and I know the Father; and I lay down my life for the sheep. So, there is a parallel between the intimate knowledge and self–surrender that exists between Father and Son and the touching knowledge and self–surrender of the Son towards his sheep.[37]

Overweening power and pastoral domination by the clergy are as far removed from this as could be possible. They exist only in the minds of people who cannot appreciate the greatness of Christian priesthood. On the other hand, it is clear that those who conceive of their priesthood in terms of loving service and self–surrender, to the point of forgetting themselves and being committed to giving their life for others, would never, even for a moment, think in terms of *pastoral domination by the clergy.*

Once the Second Vatican Council ended, suspicion towards authority in the Church led to a high–flying campaign which produced considerable results, results which are surprising and odd from the historical point of view. Everyone knows that the Council was held under the aura of being the Council of Bishops, the Council which would considerably increase and reinforce episcopal authority.[38] The results were not slow in coming and they were quite spectacular. However, contrary to what some people might naively have expected, the authority of the Bishops was not reinforced; it was weakened: this must have been due to circumstances which may well have been unexpected and yet which respond to a certain

---

[37] Here again one needs to bear in mind the analogy but that does not in the least diminish the force of the argument.

[38] Although it is a subject for the historical researcher of the future, it is clear that the dialectic of papal authority/episcopal authority was only too much in the air in those years. The more or less admitted and declared aim was nothing less than to accentuate and strengthen the authority of Bishops, especially vis–...–vis the Pope. Earlier there had been a lot of talk about the need to open wide the windows of the Vatican, so the climate was being well prepared.

logic. The main result to come out, thanks to the good intentions of the Council Fathers, was that of Episcopal Conferences, organisms whose creation was supported by a series of arguments which, though on the one hand sound enough, on the other failed to take account of all aspects of the matter. One of these aspects was the danger that these bright new mechanisms of ecclesiastical government might become subject to manipulation.

Clearly it is easier for ideological pressure groups to manipulate a structure —Bishops' Conference, Commission or groups of Committees— than to manipulate each Bishop separately. Experience bears this out even more. Once certain ideological pressure groups manage to get control of Bishops' Conferences, as has often happened, it is no longer difficult for them to influence the Bishops themselves. However much the autonomy of Bishops in their own dioceses is recognized in theory, what Bishop is going to oppose agreements made within an entity of which he himself is a member? If the Bishops' Conference of a particular country, for example, has worked out agreements (public or secret) with the Government in power —whose ideology may leave quite a lot to be desired—, it is very difficult for a Bishop, in his own diocese, to make decisions which in any way go against those agreements, no matter how much he thinks he is in the right, no matter how pastorally necessary they may be.

And yet, given the organic structure which Jesus Christ gave his Church, the function of government which each Bishop is supposed to exercise in his own diocese is an essential one. The one Body of the Catholic Church is made up of all the various churches, each governed by its own Bishop, with the Pope, the visible head of the Body, being the uniting link. The dogmatic truth that the Pope is in fact the Supreme Pastor, and not a *Primus inter pares*, cannot be relegated to the lumber–room. But once this submission to the Pope and union, through him, with the entire Apostolic College is in place, there is no doubt but that each Bishop has authority and jurisdiction at the head of his diocese. In the Book of Revelation the Spirit spells out very precise and specific instructions for *each of the seven angels* in charge of the seven churches of Asia.[39] Besides, the appropriateness of requiring that the ecclesial norms laid down for each country[40] should be democratically approved by the Bishops of the area is very debatable: the organic structure that its very Founder gave the Church cannot and should not be ignored.

The Church of the last third of the twentieth century often seems not to take things very seriously. Over–influenced by pagan humanism, suffering from a lack of confidence in supernatural values and resources, paralysed by a boorish amazement at the apparent achievements of the physical, social and political sciences, and frightened moreover by the advances and sheer power of a System which she thinks is unstoppable and irreversible, she has adopted an attitude of listening to the world and has rendered it obeisance.

If the Church wants to survive —and survive she undoubtedly will— she will have to turn again to true Theology and to Holy Scripture read and preached as Holy Scripture. She will have to preach the dogma in its entirety. She will have to put before people once more the demands and sublimity of genuine Christian morality —and do so unambiguously, with no omissions. The Mass will have to be made once again the centre of Christian worship and even of Christian life, in such a way that it no longer looks like a mere show of purely human values and content, but is seen instead as the

---

[39] Cf. Rev 2–3.

[40] Or perhaps for each region. Another questionable development, liable to cause serious contention in places where there are strong independence movements.

renewed Sacrifice of the Cross and the Banquet at which the Body and Blood of Christ is eaten and drunk. The Church will realize her urgent need to exercise the functions of the Magisterium, to speak clearly and firmly and to point to the things which really do concern salvation. She will concern herself with re–evaluating and promoting sound spiritualities, so as to make it possible for people to return to the true virtues of the Christian life; at long last she will utterly abandon compromises and arrangements whose only purpose is to please the world.

A certain sector of Catholicism nowadays tends to make caricatures of Christian virtues. For example, to foster devotion to the Pope, there are those who have recourse to pious untruths which are, at least, inappropriate. In the ecclesiastical sphere and that of clerical and allied *mass media* it is quite common to use *slogans* which are trotted out time and time again. One of these has to do with the Pope who happens to be in office, irrespective of who he is; and takes it as read that *the reigning Pope is a genius.* But of course one does not need to be very clever to know that history has known Popes who were not geniuses. That does not justify the lack of loyalty towards them that so many Catholics have paraded over the course of the centuries. Then, as everyone knows, when a Pope dies, his reputation is left at the mercy of history, and his quality of genius passes automatically to his successor. Fortunately a son does not need his father to be a genius for him to love and revere him: it suffices simply that he is his father. So, any attempt to encourage feelings and convictions on grounds which have no basis is, at the very least, a grave imprudence which can lead to the collapse of the edifice one is trying to build. Nowadays one frequently hears on the lips of members of a certain distinguished modern religious Family the daring assertion that *if the Pope goes wrong, we are perfectly ready to go wrong with the Pope.* But once one admits, in theory, that the Pope is wrong, and also admits that one is ready to go along with that error, it is clear that that person in turn is guilty of a further error, and no longer just in theory —for the simple reason that *going along with an error amounts to committing an error.*[41] From all of which one can deduce the need for loyalty to the Pope to be based on a better, sounder foundation and not to be slow to bar the way to demagogic motives and manoeuvres, whose only object seems to be to make a lot of noise in order to attract some people and please others. It is clear that solid devotions and ideas need to be built on no less solid foundations, but trying to ensure that truth is the first of those foundations.

Something similar, though more serious, happens with the virtue of poverty, which comes in for so much praise these days... and which is proclaimed so much. One reason for this is the fact that poverty is one of the most amphibological concepts to be found. Its *wealth* of meaning is one of the many ironies of language, but in this particular case it has given rise to countless mistakes and endless arguments.[42] Always regarded as one of the worst misfortunes to plague mankind, it was, however, raised by Jesus Christ to the status of a beatitude. The Master did not mind being born or living in the most absolute poverty, going so far as to wed poverty on the cross, to quote the language of St Francis of Assisi. And it was from that moment onwards that many men and women stopped running away from poverty and even began to love it and eagerly try to build it into their lives.

---

[41] In reply to any objection that this is only a matter of words, or mere hypotheses which have no basis in fact, one must say that these ways of speaking and mere hypotheses are equally erroneous.

[42] The author's thinking on this subject is given at length in *El Amigo Inoportuno*, Shoreless Lake Press, New Jersey, 1995, pp. 109 ff.

But that did not mean that things stayed that clear for ever. Contrary to what one might expect, they became much more complicated. As proof of this, there is the fact that exegetes continue to argue about who is the more accurate interpreter of the beatitudes of poverty —St Matthew or St Luke. The main problem has to do with the distinction between real poverty and poverty of spirit, which seem to be two different kinds of poverty.[43] The debate on this subject has gone on for centuries and will undoubtedly be labelled (indulgently) as petty and trivial. For it is clear that any Christian poverty must be as *real* (if it wants to be poverty) as *spiritual* (if it wants to be virtue). There is no such thing as two distinct modes or two different versions of poverty: there is just Christian poverty, one and unique. The whole affair seems to be due to an unfortunate confusion of language, and perhaps to a desire to complicate things which in themselves are quite simple and straightforward. Be that as it may, and given that the last word on the subject was said by St Thomas Aquinas and others,[44] we have no need to go into the question in any detail: we shall simply refer in passing to some of its more contemporary manifestations.

In order to make clear what we shall go on to say, and to avoid explanations which are out of place, perhaps it would be a good idea to simplify the question for the moment. Thus we could say that poverty can be divided into three different categories: official poverty, material poverty and real poverty. Having made the point that this is a purely provisional, over–simplified classification, we should hasten to add that although the three can aspire to constitute

---

[43] Cf. Mt 5:3; Lk 6:20.

[44] There would be no point in prolonging a discussion which, besides, might give the false impression that no answer was possible. Cf. note 42 of this chapter, citing the work which provides the necessary references.

the prototype of true poverty, the content of each is quite different from that of the others, as we shall see.

One of the most outstanding characteristics of *official* poverty is the fact that it can easily be recognized and everyone is all in favor of it. This is quite logical and not at all surprising, once one remembers that it is, in the last analysis, a matter of *official* poverty. To make it easier to grasp the structure and functioning of this type of poverty, it will help to use a simple example. In modern Catholicism *nuns who are poor* and *priests who are poor* get a good press, whereas *poor nuns* and *poor priests* are far from enjoying the same prerogatives. Far from being a joke or a mere play on words, if you study the matter you will soon see that the distinction has great practical importance, with very different results in each case. As everyone knows, there are Institutions and Families within Catholicism which, thanks to the stamp of approval their official poverty wins them, enjoy such influence and such abundance of resources that they could quite properly be called multi-nationals. And there are also lots of individual apostles who avail themselves of the current climate of confusion to make skilful use of the flag of official poverty to obtain rich pickings in terms of finance and influence and power. In fact both sets of people take advantage of the fact that modern Catholics have forgotten the incontestable fact that, as far as true poverty is concerned, no one bothers about it. It never happens that those who are truly poor come in for applause and consideration. But official poverty attracts lots of attention; it is everywhere lauded and applauded, and it has considerable influence and power.

True poverty is quite a different affair. Those who properly understand this virtue know that one needs to be a truly *poor man* before becoming a *man who is poor*. Luckily there are quite a number of men and women in the world whom no one pays attention to, people practically unknown because they don't count, people who have absolutely no influence at all. Men and women who, despite the fact that they know suffering very well through personal experience, distress and deprivation, receive no one's applause and are never taken for heroes. Naturally it is among them one needs to go to find the true poor.

Although *material poverty*, or simply deprivation, is closer to true poverty, it would be risky to say that it overlaps completely with the evangelical concept of poverty. The similarity which many people see between material poverty and Franciscan poverty,[45] even though there is some basis for it, is inexact and confining. What we are calling here material poverty, as well as involving practical difficulties as an ideal for life, is far from being the same thing as the evangelical concept of poverty. In fact poverty needs to be animated by charity if it is to be considered a true virtue; that holds good for all the other virtues too, but for some unknown reason people tend to forget it when poverty is being discussed. The complex history of the Franciscan movement shows that the *Moderators* of the Order, in the time of St Francis —Popes, Cardinal protectors, and various quite competent members of the Franciscan Family— had to make quite an effort to *bring* St Francis *down* to the real world.[46] Quite early on, St Bonaventure had to bring his genius and his enormous personality to bear to impose order: rules of conduct, regulations

---

[45] By Franciscan poverty we mean the poverty practiced by St Francis of Assisi and his true disciples, whether or not contemporaries of the saint.

[46] Once again, the eternal struggle, so often verified in the history of the Church, between charism and *reality*. One might ask here whether the reality referred to is the reality of things or the reality of men's mediocrity. And, although probably only God knows the right answer, who knows if perhaps both of these things are not involved.

about books and libraries, about studies, and some degree of much needed organization, everything seasoned with suitable amounts of common sense and all applied to very concrete and practical details. For example: none of this lending books to friends, because that only leaves one —the saint said— without books and without friends.[47] As everyone knows, St Francis did not want his order to have anything that smacked of big buildings, studies, books or anything else that could awaken the ownership instinct. Nor was he keen to elaborate Rules which might endanger the simplicity and clarity of the Gospel message.

But true Franciscan poverty, at least in its spirit and objectives, is fully in line with evangelical poverty. For, although it is true that it coincides with material poverty as far as external practice is concerned —which is precisely the non-viable element in it—, it really goes much further than that simplistic concept of poverty.

It is this last-mentioned aspect that differentiates it from poverty as understood in many Catholic orders today, affected as they still are by Marxism and unable to appreciate the true Gospel meaning of this virtue. Poverty as a social phenomenon is, as far as these circles are concerned, the *wretched and deplorable* situation in which poor or marginal countries find themselves. As a personal phenomenon this is an attitude or form of witness which is marked by *edginess and anger*; an attitude freely adopted by some who claim to be in solidarity with those countries. The practical result of all this is that, one way or another, poverty as a virtue has disappeared from the horizon of Christian life. For those who still believe in the beatitudes, poverty is the virtue closest to charity. It consists in voluntary detachment from everything —not just material things—,

---

[47]Étienne Gilson, *La Philosophie de Saint Bonaventure*, Vrin, Paris, 1943.

in the reciprocity of pure love. It is what the bride in the *Song* would do in order to make her self–surrender to the Bridegroom a reality.

Another grave situation is that which has arisen in Catholicism through the ousting of the concept of charity in favor of that of *welfare*. Despite the fact that charity or *agape*[48] is far from being the same as mere welfare, much Catholic pastoral policy in recent times is centred exclusively on helping the underprivileged. Nowadays the activity of many religious Families within the Church is totally focussed on this objective. To this must be added the impact of a vast number of documents, emanating from Congresses, Meetings and Conferences, in which Bishops and theological *periti* provide guidelines more sociopolitical than religious in character, and in which the supernatural horizon —not to mention Love, with or without the capital letter— has been lost sight of completely.

Love for God should be projected onto and made co–extensive with love of neighbour, according to a sound doctrine deeply rooted in the New Testament and in the most explicit teaching of Jesus Christ Himself.[49] It is not surprising therefore that works of charity should be a centuries–old and constant feature of Church life. The problem arises when people forget that *charitable works* are not charity, but simply a possible form that charity can take.[50] St Paul speaks of there being heroic acts of service which have nothing to do with charity (1 Cor 13:3). And as far as the other Apostles are

---

[48]Whether they be different things, or whether agape consists rather in love for one's neighbour, which is the horizontal dimension of charity.

[49]There is no need to insist on this. Cf., for example, as relevant classical texts, 1 Jn 4: 20–21 and Jas 2: 14–16.

[50]However much charity *calls for* works of charity (as it does), although that itself shows that they cannot be regarded as identical with charity. Therefore good works on their own have an ambiguous meaning; insofar as they can be the result of charity or of other quite different motivations.

concerned, they were careful to make the point that they were not ready to devote themselves to the service of tables at the expense of the service of the Word (Acts 6:2), which would suggest that they did not see works of this kind as constituting the essential core of Christian life. If to all this one adds that the supposed love for the poor and the marginalized often becomes politicized anger, one can be sure that, where that does happen, charity is no longer — in its double direction, vertical and horizontal— the supreme law governing the Mystical Body of Jesus Christ.

***

That is why there is need to speak about true Love once again. More need than ever. To speak about Christ and about the sweet aroma of Christ, for that and nothing else is the perfume that wafts from the Bridegroom. And we need to speak seriously and sincerely, with none of the honeyed words of media demagogues, none of the vacuous language of discourses prefabricated in pastoral program think-tanks. But first there is need to get the *pastoral experts* to keep quiet —those who devise doctrines that have no content, political and rabble-rousing Pastors who manipulate the word of God to suit themselves (2 Cor 2:17) and, in general, everyone who has compromised with the world in one way or another. It will be much better to let others speak in their place —those who eagerly seek God through their life of sacrifice and through prayer, those who truly love Jesus Christ, the genuine poor and forgotten of the world...

> *Delicate is the fragrance of your perfumes.*
> *Your name is oil poured out:*
> *therefore the maidens love you.*

Reading this text of the *Song* can be a good occasion to recall an interesting text from St Paul: *Thanks be to God, who in Christ constantly*[51] *leads us in triumph, and through us spreads the fragrance of the knowledge of him everywhere. For we are the aroma of Christ to God among those who are being saved and among those who are perishing, to one a fragrance from death to death, to the other a fragrance from life to life. Who is sufficient for these things?*[52] *For we are not, like so many, pedlars of God's word; but as men of sincerity, as commissioned by God, in the sight of God we speak in Christ.*[53]

So, according to St Paul, God relies on his true disciples to spread abroad the fragrance of the knowledge of Christ: *through us he spreads the fragrance of the knowledge of him everywhere.* This means that, according to God's design, Christ must be manifested through his disciples. If one were to borrow the language of the *Song* one would have to say that the Bridegroom must come to be known through the bride. Our Lord has said this very clearly: *You shall receive power when the Holy Spirit has come upon you; and you shall be my witnesses in Jerusalem and in all Judea and Samaria and to the end of the earth.*[54]

It is quite clear that the perfume the Apostle is speaking about is that of the Bridegroom: *the aroma of Christ.* St John of the

---

[51] Another possible reading: *always.*

[52] Another possible reading: *Who is equipped for this task?* or *Who is up to this task?*

[53] 2 Cor 2: 14–17.

[54] Acts 1:8.

Cross is in no doubt but that it is the fragrance given out by the Bridegroom's perfume that attracts the maidens who:

> *Following your footprints,*
> *the maidens run along the way*
> *touched by the spark*
> *and by the taste of your spiced wine,*
> *flows forth the Divine balsam.*[55]

The *Song* tries its best lavishly to describe the intoxicating fragrance that wafts from the Bridegroom:

> *What is that coming up from the wilderness,*
> *like a column of smoke,*
> *perfumed with myrrh and frankincense,*
> *with all the fragrant powders?*[56]

Elsewhere it is the Bridegroom Himself Who claims to be the owner and origin of the spices and essences that give off these aromas, although he knows that these perfumes burst into the bride's garden and therefore also enwrap her:

---

[55] In the original:

> *A zaga de tu huella*
> *las jóvenes discurren al camino*
> *al toque de centella*
> *al adobado vino;*
> *emisiones de bálsamo divino.*

[56] Sg 3:6. These words, which some put on the lips of the chorus and others on those of the author of the poem, do not seem to have been said by either of the lovers. Be that as it may, and leaving aside exegetical questions which do not concern us here, it is clear that the description can be fittingly applied to the Bridegroom.

> *I come to my garden,*
> *my sister, my bride,*
> *I gather my myrrh with my spice*
> *I eat my honeycomb with my honey...*[57]
>
> ....
>
> *A garden locked is my sister, my bride,*
> *a garden locked, a fountain sealed.*
> *Your shoots are an orchard*
> *of pomegranates with all choicest fruits,*
> *henna with nard, and saffron, calamus and cinnamon,*
> *with all trees of frankincense,*
> *myrrh and aloes,*
> *with all chief spices.*[58]

If the bride is to be always and *everywhere* the sweet aroma of Christ, that is, the Bridegroom, then obviously she needs to be completely imbued with the perfume that emanates from Him, because there is nothing more ephemeral, fleeting and delicate than a delightful perfume. That is why the Apostle does not confine himself to saying that the disciples should pass on the aroma of Christ, but he daringly says that they *are the aroma of Christ*, which is something quite different and, quite clearly, the first rule —practically the only rule— that needs to be borne in mind in Christian pastoral activity. St Francis of Assisi, who was very familiar with it, sometimes preached by the simple device of letting himself be seen by people without his saying one word, thereby putting into practice a method with roots deep in the Gospel: *Let your light so shine before men, that they may see your good works and give glory to*

---

[57] Sg 5:1.
[58] Sg 4: 12–14.

your Father who is in heaven...[59] *It is to the glory of my Father that you should bear much fruit, and be my disciples.*[60]

But if the bride is imbued with the Bridegroom's perfume, to the point of actually becoming the aroma of the Bridegroom, it is because there is such intimacy between them that it leads to an interchange of lives. The spice, the perfume and the aromas belong to the Bridegroom and come from Him, even though now they also belong to the bride:

> *My beloved is to me a bag of myrrh,*
> *that lies between my breasts.*
> *My beloved is to me a cluster of henna blossoms*
> *in the vineyards of Engedi.*[61]

What belongs to the Bridegroom is now the bride's, and what belongs to her is also His. This community of property is the result of total, mutual self–surrender, which gives rise to such a superabundance that others can be called to share in it.

> *I come to my garden,*
> *my sister, my bride,*
> *I gather my myrrh with my spice,*
> *I eat my honeycomb with my honey,*
> *I drink my wine with my milk.*
> *Eat, O friends, and drink:*
> *drink deeply, O lovers!*[62]

---

[59] Mt 5:16.
[60] Jn 15:8.
[61] Sg 1: 13–14.
[62] Sg 5:1.

Here again we found the golden rule of pastoral activity, the only one that can successfully call all and sundry to eat and drink their fill at the divine–human banquet. What we have here is a superabundance of love (responded to, of course) which reaches its peak in an interchange of lives. Hence the last exclamation of the stanza: *Eat, O friends, and drink: drink deeply, O Lovers.* This is rather like an anticipated echo of the invitations and calls made in the Gospel: *Tell those who are invited, Behold I have made ready my dinner, my oxen and fat calves are killed, and everything is ready; come to the marriage feast... Go to the thoroughfares and invite to the marriage feast as many as you can find...*[63] *Go out to the highways and hedges, and compel people to come in, that my house may be filled.*[64]

For it is Christ Who attracts, and he does so irresistibly: that is the meaning of the intoxication caused by the perfume, the fragrance, the aroma of Christ. However, the disciple who is in love is so identified with Him, thanks to love, that he can substitute Him and take his place: *It is no longer I who live, but Christ who lives in me.*[65] One can say, taking a further step, that the divine plan is not just for the disciple to stand in for the Master, *but to do so effectively*, for testimony is the only way to bring men to know of Jesus Christ. Therefore it is not surprising that the friends who accompany the bride should ask her to describe the Bridegroom to them and speak to them about Him:

> *What is your beloved more than another beloved,*
> *O fairest among women?*[66]

---

[63] Mt 22: 4.9.

[64] Lk 14:23.

[65] Gal 2:20.

[66] Sg 5:9.

Nor is it surprising that they should repeatedly ask her to show them the way, so that they can all go with her to search for and find the Bridegroom:

> Whither has your beloved gone,
> O fairest among women?
> Whither has your beloved turned,
> that we may seek him with you?[67]

Both questions —about describing the Bridegroom, and what route to take to find Him— are so linked in logic that the second depends on the first. But let us look at the subject more closely.

We have already seen that her companions eagerly press the bride to describe the Bridegroom to them:

> What is your beloved more than another beloved,
> O fairest among women?

Responding to this question by providing a description of the Beloved, just as the bride does (Sg 5: 10–16), is the function of Pastoral practice, of Christology and of Theology generally.[68]

However, it is not difficult to see that these descriptions are inarticulate and insufficient. It is not surprising that all the bride in the *Song* can do is string together a series of poetic metaphors. Therefore, although it is true that *fides ex auditu*,[69] there is also a need for visual testimony to be given by the life of the witness: *Let*

---

[67] Sg 6:1.

[68] Christ is the only way and the only means to know the Father and to reach Him (Jn 14: 5–11). All genuine Theology (with the exception of Theodicy) must start out from Christology and be based noetically on it (Jn 1:18).

[69] Rom 10:17. Cf. Rom 10: 14–18.

your light so shine before men that they may see your good works and give glory to your Father who is in heaven.[70] One can say that the testimony provided by the life of the disciple is found, with respect to preaching, in a relationship which is in some way analogous to that between seeing and believing: *If I speak in the tongue of men and angels, but have not love, I am a noisy gong or a clanging cymbal.*[71] Hence the need for the life of Jesus to be made manifest in that of his disciple,[72] which is what causes the beauty of the Bridegroom to be reflected in the bride, as her own companions acknowledge:

O fairest among women![73]

This leads us to conclude that the aroma of Christ is nothing other than Christ's own life reflected in the disciple; although, if one thinks about it carefully, the word to use here should be *being* rather than *being reflected.* Testimony refers to someone else but it involves making him present in some way in the very life of the person who bears testimony. All that remains is to stress that in discussing this subject one must preserve intact the unicity and individuality of the persons concerned; otherwise love cannot exist: *It is no longer I who*

---

[70] Mt 5:16.

[71] 1 Cor 13:1. God's plan is for both things to be seen as forming one, as the Apostle himself says earlier in the same text: *We are not, like so many, pedlars of God's word; but as men of sincerity, as commissioned by God, in the sight of God we speak in Christ.*

[72] A very poor way of putting it and one which falls far short of the reality. The true relationship between Jesus and disciple is that of an interchange of lives which ends up making them one thing (Jn 6: 56–57).

[73] The theme of the bride's beauty is as ever-present in the *Song* as that of the Bridegroom's beauty. Cf. Sg 1:5; 1:8; 1:15; 2:2; 4: 1–15; etc. —which is only logical when one remembers that love tends to equalize and to make the two lovers one single thing.

live, but Christ who lives in me.[74] St John of the Cross also touches on this subject in his *Canticle*:

> *When you were gazing at me,*
> *your eyes left on me the imprint of their grace:*
> *because of this you loved me greatly,*
> *whereby my eyes deserved*
> *to adore that which they saw in you.*
>
> *Do not scorn me,*
> *for if you first found me to be dark,*
> *now you can indeed look at me,*
> *after you have gazed upon me,*
> *for you have clothed me in grace and beauty.*[75]

However, just as the bride speaks of the Bridegroom, so the testimony the disciples give refers to the Master. They speak about Him, point Him out, follow in his footsteps. The bride is not confused with the Bridegroom, nor the disciple with Jesus Christ. One thing that all come to realize —both the companions of the bride

---

[74]Gal 2:20.

[75]In the original:

> *Cuando tú me mirabas,*
> *su gracia en mí tus ojos imprimían;*
> *por eso me adamabas*
> *y en eso merecían*
> *los míos adorar lo que en ti vían.*
> *No quieras despreciarme,*
> *pues si color moreno en mí hallaste,*
> *ya bien puedes mirarme*
> *después que me miraste,*
> *que gracia y hermosura en mí dejaste.*

and those who receive the witness the disciple bears of Jesus— is that they have to set out on a journey if they are to reach the Lord:

> *Whither has your beloved gone,*
> *O fairest of women?*
> *Whither has your beloved turned,*
> *that we may seek him with you?*[76]

And, as St John of the Cross says in his *Canticle*:

> *Following your footprints,*
> *the maidens run along the way*
> *touched by the spark*
> *and by the taste of your spiced wine,*
> *flows forth the Divine balsam.*[77]

But no one would have felt any eagerness to follow the Bridegroom or to find Christ if the bride had not sung the Bridegroom's praises or if the disciple had not borne true, convincing witness. Given that God's plan is for the aroma of the Bridegroom, the sweet fragrance of Christ, to be first perceived through the bride or the disciples, then the need for testimony is clear: *Through us spreads*

---

[76] Sg 6:1.

[77] In the original:

> *A zaga de tu huella*
> *las jóvenes discurren al camino*
> *al toque de centella*
> *al adobado vino;*
> *emisiones de bálsamo divino.*

the fragrance of the knowledge of him everywhere. For we are the aroma of Christ to God among those who are being saved and among those who are perishing. This is a testimony which, because it is a testimony through one's life and a testimony to Him Who is Life itself, cannot be anything other than a living testimony: *It is no longer I who live, but Christ who lives in me.*[78]

It is not surprising that, given the scale of the enterprise, even St Paul asks in amazement: *Who is sufficient for all these things?*[79] The reply he gives is so surprising that one does not know really whether it is strange or excessively profound: *We are not, like so many, pedlars of God's word; but as men of sincerity,*[80] *as commissioned by God, in the sight of God we speak in Christ.* Whatever meaning St Paul may attribute to the fact of being the aroma of Christ —or whatever way testimony to Jesus must be borne— clearly it must be the very opposite of what those do who adulterate or manipulate the word of God. It is undeniable, therefore, that true Christian witness —of which preaching is a part— must be located somewhere the opposite side of the world from where manipulation or adulteration of the Word of God are to be found.[81]

Having drawn attention to the negative content of the question, we shall have to discuss the most difficult part. What we must now

---

[78] Gal 2:20.

[79] Or also: *Who is equipped for this task?*

[80] Or *integrity*, which is the meaning both of the word *sinceritas* used in the *New Vulgate* and of the word used in the Greek text.

[81] As everyone is well aware, the ways of adulterating the word of God are legion. Nowadays it most commonly takes the form of spiriting away or omitting the content of New Testament revelation, by concentrating on subjects which either have nothing to do with the Gospel message or else are completely incidental to it (ecological problems, the struggle for democracy, consumerism, minority rights...), while at the same time leaving to one side matters which have supernatural content and relevance.

do is to analyse St Paul's teaching on how Christian witness is to be borne —how to be the aroma of Christ—, specifically with reference to preaching: *...as men of sincerity, as commissioned by God, in the sight of God we speak in Christ.* Naturally the exegesis ought to be quite long, although here all we can do is analyse briefly those three phrases of the Apostle.

The first thing St Paul calls for is sincerity, integrity, which can also be safely translated here as holiness of life. And, because it is the first thing the Apostle counterposes to those who adulterate the word of God, it is reasonable to suppose that sincere and genuine preaching of the Word requires a certain holiness or purity of life. For it seems impossible for anyone to preach the *entire* Gospel message sincerely unless there first exists, on the part of the one bearing witness, a sincere effort to put that message into practice. And it is not just a matter of the possibility of someone being able to preach correctly without being convinced, because everyday experience shows that that just does not work. When integrity is lacking, something happens which is a universal phenomenon in contemporary Catholicism: the tendency to deflect the content of preaching towards themes which have nothing to do with the Gospel message or which are trivial or unimportant, at best.[82]

The second part of Pauline thinking on this point really contains two statements and has to do with the fact that those who bear

---

[82]What St Paul expounds in Philippians 1: 12–20 is not at odds with what is being said here. The Apostle states that, not only does he not mind Christ being preached insincerely or even hypocritically, but he rejoices at it provided that Christ is proclaimed. But his joy does not stem in any way from the outcome of a preaching which, though in itself vitiated, ends up bearing fruit. If he rejoices it is simply because such things which, as he himself says, *afflict him in his imprisonment... turn out for his deliverance.* And he also makes the point that by them *Christ will be honoured in his body, whether by (his) life or by (his) death.*

witness to Christ, or those who truly are the aroma of Christ, always speak *as commissioned by God... and in the sight of God.*

Clearly, a person who bears witness must behave *as an envoy of God*, fully aware of what he is doing and faithfully performing the office given him. This is particularly important when the witness is a person consecrated to God, or an apostle on whom a specific ministry has been conferred. As the Apostle says, making a point which one can quickly sense to be of fundamental importance: *This is how one should regard us, as servants of Christ and stewards of the mysteries of God. Moreover it is required of stewards that they be found trustworthy.*[83] Accordingly, the witness —especially if he is a consecrated apostle— must be seen by men as a servant of Christ and a steward of God's mysteries who is fully loyal to the mission given him. This is how one *should* regard us, the Apostle says. He must not therefore be caught up in matters which have nothing to do with his mission, nor should he offer solutions —no matter how good they seem, perhaps from a purely human point of view— which are not strictly in line with the instructions given him.[84] Because he is a steward of the *mysteries of God*, his province must always be within the sphere of the supernatural: *Every high priest is taken from among human beings and is appointed to act on their behalf in relationship with God, to offer gifts and sacrifices for sins...*[85] He should not, for example, put before young people as a focus for their ideals the content of this or that Constitution or

---

[83] 1 Cor 4: 1–2.

[84] The perfection of the Aristotelian ethic, for instance —leaving aside now its possible lights and shades—, does not justify in the least its being utilized by the apostle as the foundations of his message, disregarding even the revelation of the New Testament, on the pretext that now the message will be better accepted by men.

[85] Heb 5:1.

Charter of Rights, no matter how perfect it seems. It is difficult not to see here demagogic intentions which the true apostle must, by the same token, avoid at all costs.[86]

The witness also needs to be aware that the testimony he bears before men should be given *in the sight of God*. What this probably means is that the Christian should always have his eyes and thoughts on his God and Lord. Everything he does he should do through Him and for Him. When bearing his witness he should never seek himself (2 Cor 4:5), or try to please men: *Am I now seeking the favor of men, or of God? Or am I trying to please men? If I were still pleasing men, I should not be a servant of Christ.*[87] The Church and the world are in need of Pastors —Bishops and priests— who are ready to bear their witness before men and aware that they are doing so *in the sight of God*. Nothing else should concern them, for they have their eyes on Christ alone. Pastors whose heart is like that of the bride in the *Song*, who lived in eager expectation of the presence of the Bridegroom, yearning to hear his beloved voice:

---

[86] As happened in the World Youth Meeting, held in Denver (Colorado, USA) on 14 and 15 August 1993. No Charter of Rights devised by men is perfect; no such charter can even embrace all human ideals. One does not need to compare such charters and declarations with the content of New Testament revelation to realize immediately how much they fall short and how many limitations they have —even from the point of view of a purely natural ethic, not to mention higher values. One of the grave dangers these attitudes involve is that of teaching people to think that this is all the apostle has to say to them, because he lacks supernatural points of reference to guide them. The minister of the mysteries of God has become a mere *manager* or mere mouthpiece of a huge multinational concerned with social welfare or social justice.

[87] Gal 1:10. Something which seems to be forgotten by the many Pastors of the People of God who so often preach to the gallery.

> *I slept, but my heart was awake.*
> *Hark! my beloved is knocking.*[88]

The Church alone has the solution to the problems of the world today —but it does not lie in her Social Teaching, as many mistakenly think. And, in turn, the solution to the problems of the Church will only be found through saintly Pastors. Unfortunately no one nowadays seems to think along these lines; indeed, many people jeer at solutions of this kind. Yet it is a fundamental truth. The Church is in need not so much of politician–Pastors and sociologist–Pastors as of Pastors who are in love with Jesus Christ, even though that is a phrase one hears only rarely nowadays. She needs Pastors —and also ordinary faithful, though the need for holy Pastors is more gravely felt— who have in their hearts the same sort of eagerness as St John of the Cross speaks about in his *Canticle*:

> *Reveal your presence,*
> *and may the vision of your beauty be my death,*
> *for the sickness of love*
> *is not cured*
> *except by your presence and image!*[89]

And, finally, the witness will never bear valid testimony in the sight of God unless he does so also in *Christ*, as St Paul says: ...*as*

---

[88] Sg 5:2.

[89] In the original:

> *¡Descubre tu presencia,*
> *y máteme tu vista y hermosura;*
> *mira que la dolencia,*
> *de amor, que no se cura*
> *sino con la presencia y la figura!*

commissioned by God, in the sight of God, we speak in Christ. Anyone who understands the content of the New Testament will readily see the reason for this: because it is impossible to love God without loving Jesus Christ. Or to put it even more correctly: without falling in love with Jesus Christ and without living his very life, in accordance with the bartering and reciprocity of self-surrender that love requires. It is just as the bride says in the *Song*:

> *I am my beloved's and my beloved is mine;*
> *he pastures his flock among the lilies.*[90]

That is the only way the witness can be the good aroma of Christ; and only in that way are the perfume and the aroma able to bear effective witness and win people over. Only then can the witness also say, as the bride in the *Song* does:

> *Awake, O north wind, and come, O south wind!*
> *Blow upon my garden,*
> *let its fragrance be wafted abroad.*[91]

It is true that there are those who think that all this is only poetry and old-fashioned. Yet others like to live on nostalgia; they think that Catholicism has changed, not just in accidental, marginal things, but in many things to do with faith and morals: as they see it, Catholicism is no longer the same as was preached and practiced fifty years ago. And there are even those who go a step further and say that the Church, which at one point in Antiquity found, to her

---

[90]Sg 6:3.
[91]Sg 4:16.

surprise, that she had suddenly become Arian, may one day suffer a new and terrible shock to find that she has become atheist. Could there be any truth in all this...?

It is undeniable that the world is confronted by a number of serious questions which may simply have to be left to the judgment of God, that judgment which will take place when history has become metahistory, having reached its final end. In the meantime the Christian believes in Jesus Christ's promises about the Church lasting forever, while also he lives in hope and full confidence that the *Unam, Sanctam, Catholicam et Apostolicam* will only disappear if Love disappears. But nothing should cause us concern. For, as we already know, and as the ancient text tells us,

> *Many waters cannot quench love,*
> *neither can floods drown it.*[92]

---

[92] Sg 8:7.

CHAPTER II

ON CONTEMPLATION AND ON THE HUMANITY OF OUR LORD

The story is told of how a blind man was going along a road, walking very cautiously, one cold evening in autumn. The unfortunate man had a stick to help him, which he used to check the ground in front, to avoid obstacles, and his journey was made more difficult by a strong wind that was blowing. Suddenly a gust enveloped him in dust and dry leaves. One leaf hit him in the face and he hardly had time to catch it with his hand. The blind man stopped for a moment, sighed deeply and eagerly breathed in the pleasant, faint perfume that the leaf still gave off.

—Oh...! —he said— are you a rose...?

—No, I'm not, —the leaf replied. But I was a leaf of a rosebush, and I have spent so long beside the rose that even now I still carry a trace of its perfume.

Despite the time that had elapsed, the flower's perfume was still there. And thanks to it, it was still possible for a mere dry leaf, tossed around by the wind and taken for a rose on a miserable autumn night, to bring momentary joy to the steps of the blind wayfarer.

Something similar happens in the Christian life, whose ideal, for every Christian, can be none other than to make our Lord's life his own, to such an extent that he might even be mistaken for him as people said in the case of the *Poverello* of Assisi, or like St Paul, who could say of himself: *It is no longer I who live, but Christ who lives in me.*[1] The parable of the blind wayfarer could be glossed along these lines:

—Are you Jesus Christ...?

—No, I'm not Jesus Christ... But I have lived with him so long that I have some of his aroma...

> *Delicate is the fragrance of your perfumes,*
> *your name is oil poured out;*
> *therefore the maidens love you.*[2]

The inspired author avails himself of poetry to express his feelings, or at least to try to express them. For it is undeniable that the Bridegroom is to his mind greater than the most beautiful and sublime thing imaginable, and that is why he says that his fragrance is so delightful. This is simply a poetic way of saying what he feels. The exquisiteness of the fragrance derives, in turn, from the fact that the aroma comes from Him, betraying his presence. It is *his aroma*, and this means that He has come at last. *The Master is here* is an evangelical phrase which sounds even better when it is

---

[1] Gal 2:20.
[2] Sg 1:2.

said in secret, *in a whisper*.³ But at other times, as in the parable of the virgins, the arrival and presence of the Bridegroom is the time for breaking out into joyful acclamations: *Behold the Bridegroom! Come out to meet him...!*⁴

> *The voice of my beloved! Behold, he comes,*
> *leaping over the mountains,*
> *bounding over the hills.*⁵
>
> ....
>
> *I slept, but my heart was awake.*
> *Hark! my beloved is knocking.*⁶

To the author of the *Song*, the name of the Bridegroom is *oil poured out*. This is a poetic way of expressing his enthusiastic conviction that the Bridegroom is truly wonderful —indescribably wonderful; as though he were saying: so wonderful that no one has ever been able or will ever be able to properly describe him. After this there is nothing surprising in the fact that he adds in the next line, *therefore the maidens love you.*

Here the poetic metaphor takes account of a familiar biblical device (quite often used) whereby an allusion to a *name* is the same as a reference to a particular person (Acts 4:12). When it is applied to animals, the name correctly conveys *what* each specifically *is* (Gen 2:20), while when it refers to people, it designates *who* each particular person *is*. So, whereas in the first case it always points to

---

[3] Jn 11:28.
[4] Mt 25:6.
[5] Sg 2:8.
[6] Sg 5:2.

genera and species and really has a collective meaning, in the second use it is exclusively individual, singular and personal. In rational beings therefore the name designates the person[7] and his uniqueness: it identifies him as unique, even as he continues to develop as the person he is..., as we shall see further on.

Of all the beings in the universe, the person is the one most closed in on himself, most autonomous and independent,[8] able to act freely, and the one who by nature has the ability to open himself to other rational beings. His world of autonomy, individuality and unicity, which defines his being a person, is what also makes it possible, by a strange paradox, for Him to establish a relationship with other

---

[7]Hence, for those who have no way of knowing the essentiality or the characteristic properties of a particular person, that person's name is ineffable (Judg 13:18).

[8]The individual substance of a rational nature, which Boethius spoke of. For St Thomas, the person is a complete substance, subsistent in himself, and independent of every other subject (*S. Th.*, III^a, q. 16, a. 12 ad 2); according to the Saint, a thing subsists when it has its existence in itself, with complete independence of any other subject and with absolute incommunicability (*De Pot.*, q. 9, a. 2 ad 6). St Thomas makes very good use, once again, of analogy to explain the concept of person, whether applying it to God or to creatures. He distinguishes between a common concept of person, which is analogous to God and to creatures, and a proper concept in each of the analogues. The common concept of person has two essential notes, *substantiality* and *incommunicability*. These two notes or characteristics, however, are found in very distinct ways in the divine Persons and in created persons. This makes the objective concept of person, which is common to God and to creatures, not univocal or equivocal but analogous. One must remember that in creatures the two notes derive from the substance or from the essential principles, which makes the concept of person in their case something absolute and substantial. But this in no way occurs in God, for in Him the distinction and incommunicability of the persons come from the relations, which are really identical with the divine essence; this means that they are also substantial and possess the two essential notes that constitute the person. Therefore, the persons in God mean the relations; although here the relations must not be considered in themselves only (for that would mean that they only refer to their correlative and would not be subsistent) but rather as identical with the divine essence. From this it follows that the persons in God are subsistent or substantial relations.

personal beings. God, Who is Love, created man in His image and likeness and endowed him with the ability to love, as his own special last end. If, in spite of this, man does not love, he closes in on himself and in some way loses his essentiality —the orientation to which his nature is fundamentally destined—: he is reduced to a condition which becomes definitive when his impossibility of loving is irreversible, as is the case of the damned or of devils in hell.[9] These latter are no longer persons in the strict sense nor do they possess an individual and unique name: theirs is, rather, a collective or crowd name, proper to and characteristic of a *massa damnata* which has cut itself off, freely and forever, from any possibility of loving: *My name is Legion, for we are many*, the unclean spirit replies to Jesus when he asks him his name.[10]

So, a person's name, insofar as it designates him in a manner that allows for no confusion, merges with him and acquires his own qualities (Phil 2: 9–11). By evoking this name one can actualize the presence of the person to whom it belongs: one has only to say it and one gets the same feelings the person's presence would cause:

---

[9] This is not to say that the damned in hell have lost their personal condition. But the destiny of the person consists in opening himself to others in a donation of love, which is not possible for one who is damned, because he is closed in on himself in a loneliness that is irreversible. As a result of this, the personality of a damned person is not so much annihilated as broken and divided, immersed in a kind of unimaginable schizophrenia which tears him apart, seeing (as he does) the failure he has made of his life.

[10] Mk 5:9. It is interesting to note, a propos of the exegesis of this episode in the Gospel, that the author of the account speaks of the demon in the singular, except in verse 13 and perhaps verse 15; whereas Jesus always speaks of him in the singular when he upbraids the devil, there is no exception. The parallel text in St Luke (8: 27–33) is more vacillating, and the narrator speaks sometimes in the singular and sometimes in the plural, except in the case of Jesus, Who is never in doubt. The slight vacillations in the text may be explicable by the exceptional nature of the event, which astonished the chroniclers. Mk 1: 21–28 and its parallel Lk 4: 31–37 are even clearer relevant texts.

love or hate, joy or sorrow, and even tears of tenderness or sadness. The bride in the *Song* describes the tender feelings she experiences when she hears the Bridegroom's name:

> *Your name is oil poured out.*[11]

The mere mention of the Bridegroom's name fills her with enthusiasm. Her feelings are so overcome, due to all that the Person of the Bridegroom means to her, that it is quite beyond her to express her admiration, her eagerness and her love. The Bridegroom is beauty, goodness and truth —all overflowing and all perceived and grasped as an astounding epiphany of being. That is why she cannot describe her feelings: she cannot do so to herself or to the Bridegroom, much less to strangers.

> *Behold, you are beautiful, my beloved, truly lovely!*[12]
> ....
> *As an apple tree among the trees of the wood,*
> *So is my beloved among young men.*[13]

Her proclamation that the Bridegroom is unique is simply another way she tries to say something about her feelings for Him:

> *My beloved is all radiant and ruddy,*
> *distinguished among ten thousand.*[14]

---

[11] Sg 1:3.
[12] Sg 1:16.
[13] Sg 2:3.
[14] Sg 5:10.

This last exclamation is very like another one in which the Bridegroom expresses feelings parallel to those of the bride. And it only makes sense that the same love should provoke similar states of soul, and even similar situations in both lovers:

> *My dove, my perfect one,*
> *is only one, the darling of her mother,*
> *flawless to her that bore her.*
> *The maidens saw her and called her happy;*
> *the queens and concubines also, and they*
> *praised her.*[15]

This is how love turns into the sweetest feeling and most powerful force that exists in the universe —to the point that it seems to be the only source of energy, the power that moves all things:

> *l'Amor che move el sole e l'altre stelle.*[16]

Since Love is in the last analysis God Himself (1 Jn 4:8), it is therefore identical with fullness of Being. Therefore Love is ineffable to the same extent as Being is ineffable. And human love, in turn, is nothing but a real participation in the divine life (2 Pet 1:4), which is the same as saying in the mystery of Love, to which man is called from the moment that he is raised, by the gift of grace, to the supernatural order.

This makes it clear that Love is the last end of man. From what has been said, this must be taken as meaning infinite Love or Love

---

[15] Sg 6:9.

[16] Dante, *Divine Comedy*, at the end.

with a capital letter: that is the Love to which human nature is orientated once it is gratuitously elevated to the supernatural order. However, the world around him, which every man must constantly face, seems to contradict this orientation.[17] The undeniable fact that man often does not love, or loves badly, allows certain questions to be asked which are not easy to answer and which put a question–mark over the happy outcome of human nature's destiny. For example: how is it possible that human nature could be essentially orientated in this direction and yet so often end in failure? How can one explain the fact that the fragrance of the Bridegroom's perfumes, exquisite though it is, is not always noticed by people? Why is it that many people, including not a few Christians, never manage to get to experience true love for Jesus?

The mystery of the indifferent reply, or even negative reply, to the call of love[18] is closely connected with the mystery of sin. Scheeben said that sin is a mystery *sui generis*, even a real *mysterium iniquitatis*.[19]

---

[17]What should have been easy and natural became difficult due to sin. Ever since then man's life on earth has been an armed struggle, even a very difficult one.

[18]Inevitably we must constantly face the difficulties posed by human language. It would probably have been more correct to write "love" with a capital letter here, as elsewhere. But apart from the fact that it would be out of place here to try to achieve linguistic accuracy by using technically the exact words, it is worth remembering that what we are mainly trying to do is to outline some ideas on the subject of love, and to do this we need to speak about God as the infinite and the primary source of love.

[19]M. J. Scheeben, *The Mysteries of Christianity*, IV, § 38. Scheeben rightly applies this expression to sin, echoing St Paul's words in 2 Thess 2:7. To explain the mystery of lack of love would involve explaining the mystery of defectible human freedom, which is also afflicted and weakened by a certain inclination to evil, as a consequence of sin.

The possibility of the aromas of the bridegroom being counterfeited is also connected with the mystery of sin. The theme of the devil disguised as an angel of light is a familiar one in Christian spiritual literature. As regards contemplation, one must admit that, due to the climate of evil and horizontalism which the Church has to deal with at the present time, fake contemplation is quite prevalent. This is made all the easier by the fact that contemplation is a very subtle thing; it is something ineffable, difficult to attain and almost impossible to explain.

The first question one might ask here is why contemplation is faked. But, because this is not the appropriate place to discuss that subject, we shall confine ourselves to making a few observations in passing. Very few people would be rash enough to deny that it is quite likely that the devil is fairly happy about the way things have gone during these closing years of the twentieth century. Despite efforts made to disguise and hide it, it is easy enough to see that Christianity is undergoing a serious crisis, both within Catholicism and in the other Christian Churches. The very depth of this crisis is what has led many people, many of those who are still believers, to search actively for something *genuine* to cling to, a plank to keep them afloat. The lack of a firm, decisive Magisterium, rather than excessive tolerance based on a strange kind of respect for any and every idea,[20] has made for ambiguity in dogma and moral teaching, not to mention liturgical anarchy. The result has been a climate of permissiveness and confusion which has blurred the doctrinal frontiers between Catholicism and Protestantism and even those which separate Christianity from purely worldly systems of thought. It is

---

[20]Modern Catholic pastoral policy has confused respect for persons with respect for error. Cf. Étienne Gilson, *Dogmatism and Tolerance*, International Journal, 8 (1952), pp. 7–16.

not surprising, therefore, that people of good faith should look for certainties and security, or should fight despair and try to escape from a situation where all they find is vacillation, doubt, insecurity, and rejection (in practice) of everything that might have any kind of supernatural character. All this has given rise to the existence of a field where traders in lies can sell their products without hindrance... and, incredible as it may seem, those products include even contemplative prayer. However, in spite of what has just been said about people's good faith, one needs to remember that deception always counts on a degree of complicity on the part of those who fall into its nets; God never lets those who seek the truth in sincerity and good faith to fall victim to lies —or at least not for long. However painful it is to say it, we must admit that acceptance of certain aberrations always implies that there is already some dark corner in the heart of the one who accepts them.

It is important to note that contemplative prayer is something which should be spoken about *cum timore et tremore*.[21] It is not something that can be offered for sale in the markets of the world, for the simple reasons that love cannot be bought or sold (Sg 8:7), and contemplative prayer has to do with the intimacy of loving self–surrender, which always takes place in the exclusive and unique sphere of an *I* and a *thou* (Rev 2:17), marking the culmination and apex of what is a personal relationship. So, given the fact that contemplative prayer is the proper place for the perfect relationship of divine–human love to reach its consummation in this life, we can be absolutely sure that it can in no sense be manipulated by man.

Contemplative prayer is something so subtle and sublime, and also so inaccessible to human efforts alone, that one could not even think of its being something offered to people who put their names

---

[21] Cf. 1 Cor 2: 3–5.

down for a course. To give an example whose vulgarity is matched only by its current popularity: the very latest *courses* on the theory and practice of contemplation which one hears so much about are, at best, pretentious frauds. They claim to be the "flavour of the month," but everyone knows that divine love —or even human love— cannot be acquired by paying the fee for a course. The audacity and shamelessness of those who promote such frauds are (in this case) comparable only with the naivety of the poor unfortunates who let themselves be taken in.

Love, particularly divine–human love, is much more serious than all that. And people should distrust those who put themselves forward as masters of the contemplative life, claiming that they have sufficient experience to allow them to teach others how to *practice it*.[22] The very least one could say about a timetable (to give just one example) which lays down that contemplative prayer is to happen between such a time and such another time is that it is a jest bordering on sacrilege. What kind of contemplative prayer are they talking about? For, true contemplation, which is always accompanied, naturally, by a life of purification and great affinity with Jesus Christ, only happens *where God chooses, when He chooses and how He chooses.* And, of course, it is a complete waste of time to try to confine God to a timetable. If love, of any type, is essentially freedom, what can one say when the loving person is pure Love, or infinite Love. *The spirit blows where it wills, and you hear the sound of it; but you do not know whence it comes or whither it goes...*[23] *Where the Spirit of the Lord is, there is freedom.*[24] Those who

---

[22] If contemplative prayer is not taken very seriously, it indicates a supine ignorance of the subject (at best). In the huge bibliography on this subject, cf., for example, Jean Baruzi, *Jean de la Croix et le Problème de l'Expérience Mystique*, Presses Universitaires de France, Paris.

[23] Jn 3:8.

[24] 2 Cor 3:17.

trade in contemplation, pedlars of the supernatural and of things most sublime, are totally unaware, in this area —how could they not be?— that a certain *unpredictability* is part-and-parcel of the Bridegroom's style, as one can see from Holy Scripture in general (in both Testaments) and in the *Song of Songs* in particular. This *unpredictability* is really something which can be appreciated by the very few people who are au fait with the ins and outs of true love: *The unspiritual man does not receive the gifts of the Spirit of God, for these are folly to him, and he is not able to understand them.*[25] And it is also one of the most profound and strangest mysteries of love:

> *Tell me, you whom my soul loves,*
> *where you pasture your flock,*
> *where you make it lie down at noon;*
> *for why should I be like the one who wanders*
> *beside the flocks of your companions?*[26]
>
> ....
>
> *My beloved is like a gazelle, or a young stag...*
> *Behold, he comes,*
> *leaping upon the mountains, bounding over the hills.*[27]
>
> ....
>
> *Upon my bed by night*
> *I sought him whom my soul loves;*
> *I sought him, but found him not.*[28]
>
> ....

---

[25] 1 Cor 2:14.
[26] Sg 1:7.
[27] Sg 2: 8–9.
[28] Sg 3:1.

> *I opened to my beloved,*
> *but my beloved had turned and gone.*
> *I sought him, but found him not;*
> *I called him, but he gave no answer.*[29]

The New Testament, for its part (and it is rather exceptional), approaches the subject in a way that would merit detailed study. There are all kinds of passages: *As the Bridegroom was delayed, they all slumbered and slept. But at midnight there was a cry...*[30] *Take heed, watch and pray; for you do not know when the time will come. It is like a man going on a journey, when he leaves home and puts his servants in charge, each with his work, and commands the doorkeeper to be on the watch. Watch therefore —for you do not know when the master of the house will come, in the evening, or at midnight, or at cockcrow, or in the morning...*[31] *You yourselves know well that the day of the Lord will come like a thief in the night.*[32] As one can see, the Bridegroom is slow in coming, and one even gets the impression that his delay is fairly intentional. One never knows when exactly he will come, but one can be sure that it will be when least expected —like a thief, when those at home are least watchful.

All this indicates that it is up to the bride to await and seek the Bridegroom, and that He comes only as and when He wishes:

> *Before the day–breeze rises,*
> *before the shadows flee,*
> *return! Be, my love...*[33]

....

---

[29] Sg 5:6.
[30] Mt 25: 5–6.
[31] Mk 13: 33–35.
[32] 1 Thess 5:2. Cf. also Lk 17: 26–35, etc.
[33] Sg 2:17.

> *Upon my bed at night,*
> *I sought him whom my soul loves*
> *I sought him, but found him not;*
> *I will rise now and go about the city,*
> *in the streets and in the squares;*
> *I will seek him whom my soul loves...*
> *Have you seen him whom my soul loves?*[34]

> ....

> *I hear my love. See how he comes*
> *leaping on the mountains,*
> *bounding over the hills...*[35]

At least that is what is implied by texts which, in turn, seem to echo another, very primitive, text: *To the woman he said... Your desire shall be for your husband, and he shall rule over you.*[36] This subject is all the more interesting insofar as it seems to confirm the correctness of attributing to God the character of Father, rather than Mother, and the vanity of the dreams of certain *antimachistas* who would claim the priesthood for women.[37]

Be that as it may, everything seems to indicate that the apparent *versatility* of the Bridegroom is one of the most profound laws of love. A careful —but not easy— study of this subject might well show that the alleged initiative and undoubtedly active role played by God in

---

[34] Sg 3: 1–3.

[35] Sg 2:8.

[36] Gen 3:16.

[37] Although this is a subject which merits detailed study when viewed from this angle (a study which would undoubtedly produce some strange and interesting conclusions), this is not the place to go into it. It suffices to say in passing that the Word made his own a human nature in the masculine sex, and that the priest always acts *in persona Christi*. Worth consulting on this is Aidan Nichols, *Holy Order*, Veritas Publications, Dublin, 1990, pp. 144 ff.

contemplation, about which there has been so much talk, have much to do with the problem.[38] Clearly, it is impossible for the creature to *provoke* contemplative prayer at will, as if he could call God to make appearances when and where it suited him (the creature). Any such attempt can derive only from malice or from a high degree of ignorance, and has nothing to do with true contemplative prayer. What the bride certainly can do is wait for the Bridegroom and seek Him as best she can:

> *Tell me, you whom my soul loves,*
> *where you pasture your flock,*
> *where you make it lie down at noon...*
>
> ....
>
> *If you do not know,*
> *O fairest among women,*
> *follow in the tracks of the flock,*
> *and pasture your kids beside the shepherds' tents.*[39]

---

[38] As is logical, here we are not discussing merely the undeniable need for grace, and even for special supernatural graces, for contemplation to take place —an ingredient which those who trade in the *minutiae* of contemplative life seem to have forgotten. Here we are dealing rather with the role of the Bridegroom as *bridegroom*, in which a certain and apparent pre–eminence vis–...–vis the bride seems to be the result of a general law of love and therefore is valid also for divine–human love. While it is for the bride to search and wait, not knowing when the moment will come, it seems to be the bridegroom's role to come, to appear and to act as he chooses. It is also clear, though, that, if the initiative and the decisions are more the competence of the Bridegroom, the role of the bride is by no means limited to pure passivity: at the very least she has to undertake a search for the Bridegroom, a search which the Book of Genesis does not hesitate to call *ardent*. This is not unimportant when it comes to studying the mystery of contemplation. Nor is it necessary to add that all this in no way diminishes the dignity of either of the sexes. The theme of the undeniable essential equality of both sexes should not be confused with the mystery of the mechanics of love.

[39] Sg 1: 7–8.

> *I will rise now and go about the city,*
> *in the streets and in the squares;*
> *I will seek him whom my soul loves.*[40]

The strange thing is that the texts seem to indicate that the Bridegroom comes only *when He chooses*, very much on purpose, after he has made the bride wait and search for Him:

> *The voice of my beloved! Behold, he comes,*
> *leaping upon the mountains, bounding over the hills.*
> *My beloved is like a gazelle, or a young stag...*[41]

That exactly describes the Bridegroom —light, agile, fleet of foot, alert, elusive, unpredictable in his movements so that one never knows when to expect Him; like the gazelle or the young stag. But this is not at odds with the deep mystery of reciprocity and equality that the mutual self–surrender of love involves. And so the Bridegroom for his part comes to implore the bride, knocking at her door, to have her open it as and when she pleases: that is the extreme to which the essence and inexplicable freedom of love goes. This freedom and reciprocity are completely imbued with the intimacy of a *thou* and an *I* who surrender themselves entirely to one another:

> *Open to me, my sister,*
> *my love, my dove, my perfect one;*
> *for my head is wet with dew,*
> *my locks with the drops of the night.*[42]

---

[40] Sg 3:2.
[41] Sg 2: 8–9.
[42] Sg 5:2.

Any claim to *manipulate* the Bridegroom by trying to practice contemplation at the whim of the creature is, in addition to implying total ignorance of the way love works, the result of the crisis of horizontalism (the product, in turn, of neglect of supernatural values) which is the scourge of the Church at the present time. It is the logical consequence of a marked withdrawal from authentic supernatural life and of ignorance of the structure and genesis of love.

What has been said so far also applies to the use of special devices and techniques for *practising* contemplative prayer, such as the Zen cushion or the Carmelite stool, etc., not to mention, even in passing, the importation of oriental techniques into Christian prayer, which have featured so much in recent decades.[43] One always comes up against the same problem: the employment of certain techniques (such as, for example, that of using breathing, to develop deep concentration) may prove very useful psychologically, but it has little to do with Christian prayer, still less with contemplation, which is an eminently supernatural activity; moreover, there is the danger that techniques of this sort tend further to blur supernatural values in direct proportion to the degree to which they put the stress on the purely natural.

That is why it is likely to prove more fruitful to continue our, albeit modest, outline of the way love works as far as can be seen from the verse of the *Song* this third part of our book deals with:

> *Delicate is the fragrance of your perfumes,*
> *your name is oil poured out;*
> *therefore the maidens love you.*

---

[43] Within Catholicism it is the Jesuits perhaps who have done most to propagate those methods. It would be interesting to study the connexion —if there is one— that these techniques have with the Ignatian method of prayer, as also the reason why they have found such a degree of acceptance precisely among the Jesuits.

We can see that love is always found surrounded by an exuberant festival of the senses. In this particular context the reference is to smell and touch: *Delicate is the fragrance of your perfumes... Your name is oil poured out...* If the fragrance given off by the Bridegroom's perfumes is quite exquisite, exceptionally delightful to the smell, the oil with which he is anointed evokes the gentle sensation of a sweet and finely excited sense of touch, such as the psalmist already described: *It is like the precious oil upon the head, running down the beard, upon the beard of Aaron, running down the collar of his robes.*[44] But the *Song*, in fact, is an overflowing, kaleidoscopic canvas that takes in all the senses, so that one can say, in all justice, that it is a genuine pictorial sketch of love from the angle of each of the senses. Sight, for example:

> *Beloved, you are beautiful, my love,*
> *behold, you are beautiful!*
> *Your eyes are doves behind your veil.*[45]
>
> ....
>
> *You have ravished my heart, my sister, my bride,*
> *you have ravished my heart with the glance of*
>   *your eyes,*
> *with one jewel of your necklace.*[46]

And also hearing:

> *The voice of my beloved! Behold, he comes,*
> *leaping upon the mountains,*
> *bounding over the hills.*[47]
>
> ....

---

[44] Ps 133:2.
[45] Sg 4:1.
[46] Sg 4:9. Cf. 1:5; 1:10; 1:15; 2:14; 6:5.
[47] Sg 2:8.

> *O my dove,*
> *in the clefts of the rock,*
> *in the covert of the cliff,*
> *let me see your face, let me hear your voice,*
> *for your voice is sweet, and your face is comely.*[48]

And the sense of smell:

> *How sweet is your love, my sister, my bride...!*
> *how much better is your love than wine,*
> *and the fragrance of your oils than any spice.*[49]

And, of course, touch:

> *O that his left hand were under my head,*
> *and that his right hand embraced me!*[50]

What does all this mean...? It must certainly mean something, because, according to the teaching of St Paul himself, *whatever was written in former days was written for our instruction.*[51] However, everything, of course, depends on the value one attributes to the *Song of Songs* —on whether it is simply a wedding song; or a collection of metaphors or poetic sayings dedicated to carnal love, or to an idealized or perhaps purely spiritual love (the familiar nuptials of Christ with his Church); or perhaps some other meaning entirely.

This brings up a series of questions: is what is called "carnal love" genuine love or simply the satisfaction of a selfish appetite?

---

[48] Sg 2:14. Cf. 5:2; 8:13.
[49] Sg 4:10. Cf. 1: 3.12–14; 2:13; 3:6; 4: 11.13–14.16; 5:1; 7:9.
[50] Sg 2:6. Cf. 1:2; 4:10; 8: 1.3.
[51] Rom 15:4.

Or, in the case of purely spiritual love, what does this mean for a being composed of matter and spirit, as man is?[52]

The significance and meaning which undoubtedly must attach to the multi–coloured and very rich love–picture of the *Song* should be absolutely intelligible to man. It is, after all, a divinely inspired book, with all that that involves; what purpose could a revealed book have if not to convey meaning? And all the indications are that what the book seeks to describe is *human* love albeit divinized; and so one can also say that it deals with divine–human love mutually reciprocated —but with no trace either of Manichaean scruples about matter (unknown to the Old Testament or to Old Testament literature) or of Platonic disdain for the body.

It is widely known that Platonism and neo–Platonism have influenced Christianity over the course of its history and still do so. St

---

[52] As far as the loves between Christ and his Church are concerned, it should be remembered that the Mystical Body that the Church is is made up of individual members who are persons (1 Cor 12: 12–31). As regards Platonic love (of which the prototype is taken to be Dante's love for Beatrice) one needs to recognize that it is not all that clear a concept: Are we not confusing clean, pure love with *purely spiritual* love? Was Dante, for example, merely in love with Beatrice's soul or was he in love with Beatrice, however disinterested his love was as regards carnal relations? This is a question worth exploring further, bringing it on to the purely theological level, and involving such questions as: Was St Joseph in love with the Virgin Mary, or did he love her with a purely spiritual love? Or, to put it another way: Did St Joseph love the soul of the Virgin Mary or did he love the Virgin Mary, even though his love involved no carnal relationship of any kind whatsoever (not just like Dante's love for Beatrice, but sanctified in Joseph's case by a true virtue of perfect chastity)? Certainly at least two fairly clear conclusions can be drawn: the first refers to the fact that an absolutely pure and clean love (even if supernaturalized) has, as always, the loved person and not merely that person's soul as its object and end. The second has to do with the problems that arise, and become virtually insolvable, when one fails to see man as a genuine composite of matter and spirit in substantial unity.

Augustine himself, who was not exactly exempt from such influence, said that *Deum et animam scire cupio... Nihil amplius*;[53] to which he added that *man, as he sees himself, is a rational soul that uses a mortal and earthly body.*[54] However much one tries to tone down the importance of these and other statements by the brilliant Bishop, they are there nonetheless, totally in line with a tradition which goes back more than twenty centuries. The root of the problem is well–known: matter, and therefore the corporality of the human being, is viewed with suspicion once one argues that perfection is found only in the world of pure ideas. For the Docetists, for example, the Incarnation is mere appearances; Spinoza went further: he regarded the whole notion as contradictory and absurd in itself. And certainly, for Platonists and neo–Platonists, whatever else one might say, the Incarnation cannot but involve a *fall*, more or less recognized or disguised. Hence the doctrine that one needs to be detached from the body, a doctrine that has a long tradition. From Pseudo–Dionysius down to our own time,[55] passing through Eckhart and the other German mystics (with their theory of the soul alone and of the apex of the soul for finding God), to cite just a few, a large body of doctrine seems not to have found (as far as the search for God is concerned) exactly where to put the human body. The natural result of this is to depreciate the mystery of the Incarnation,

---

[53] *Soliloquies*, 1, 2, 7.

[54] *De Moribus Ecclesiæ*, 1, 27, 52.

[55] This does not mean failing to recognize the valuable contribution that neo–Platonism, with Pseudo–Dionysius at its head, has made to the correct understanding and formulation of the doctrine on this point. It is simply a matter of light and shade. Apropos of this, Delacroix says that the doctor of mysticism par excellence, Pseudo–Dionysius, summed up mystical experience definitively in three words: Passivity, Obscurity and Disappropriation (quoted in Baruzi, *op. cit.*, IV, II, note 46).

not to mention the consequent danger of man's not finding the right road to take in his ascent to God.

However, the *Song of Songs*, as far as human love is concerned, seems to come down firmly in favor of the complete man, including therefore his corporality. This implies a teaching much more in tune with all that one can glean from the content of both Testaments. For St Paul, for example, who, better than anyone, sang of the destiny and excellence of the resurrected body (1 Cor 15), neither the human body nor indeed any part of creation is destined to annihilation; all will be glorified, but it must undergo purification and redemption: *For the creation waits with eager longing for the revealing of the sons of God; for the creation was subjected to futility, not of its own will but by the will of him who subjected it in hope; because the creation itself will be set free from its bondage to decay and obtain the glorious liberty of the children of God. We know that the whole creation has been groaning in travail together until now; and not only the creation, but we ourselves, who have the first fruits of the Spirit, groan inwardly as we wait for adoption as sons, the redemption of our bodies.*[56]

Von Balthasar,[57] among others, has pointed to the contradiction or at least dissonance that exists on this point between the two foremost mystics of the Renaissance, St John of the Cross and St Teresa of Avila. All St Teresa's mystical life was marked by locutions and visions of the Humanity of Christ; St John of the Cross, on the other hand, devoted his entire life as a teacher to uprooting from the contemplative life anything that smacked of things deriving from the imagination or the senses, or from the various faculties of the soul (including extraordinary phenomena which might be supernatural

---

[56] Rom 8: 19–23.

[57] Hans Urs von Balthasar, *The Glory of the Lord*, Ignatius Press, San Francisco.

in origin),[58] according to his famous doctrine: *Por la nada, al todo* (through nothingness to totality). The problem is in itself a fairly complex one, and if one adds to it the fact that both mystics are Doctors of the Church, it leads easily to two clear conclusions: on the one hand, the question is obviously an open one; on the other —this is said in passing, as something that is a source of consolation and wonder— we can also clearly see the Church's enormous capacity for understanding in its recognition that some things are indeed still *quæstiones disputatæ*.

Be that as it may, it is clear that no genuine Christian spirituality can ignore the body;[59] this holds true for both lovers; hence the need for the Humanity of Christ and the appropriateness of the Incarnation.[60] In human love, whether it be purely human or divine–human, it is the whole man that loves and is loved: his body and soul, his senses and potentialities, his spiritual as well as his psy-

---

[58] In the *Ascent of Mount Carmel*, book I, chap. 5, for example, the Saint says that *it is supreme ignorance for the soul to think that it will be able to pass to this high estate of union with God unless it first empty itself of the desire of all things, natural and supernatural, which may hinder it.*

[59] In the last analysis man was created as a substance made up of body and soul, matter and spirit: *Formavit Dominus Deus hominem pulverem de humo et inspiravit in nares eius spiraculum vitæ, et factus est homo in animam viventem* (Gen 2:7).

[60] Accepting the reality of intermediate eschatology, it is a matter of faith that the blessed contemplate and love God in heaven, despite the fact that, being temporarily separate from their bodies (with which they will be joined again at the the moment of the resurrection), they are not persons (St Thomas, *Summa Theologiæ*, I\u1d43, q. 75, a. 4 ad 2), even though they are subsistent realities. Anyway, given that this is not the place to go into such a subtle theological question, it is enough to say that we are talking about the souls *of the blessed*, which will attain their perfect mode of loving when they, once more, receive the ultimate perfection of being, that is, their personality, on being re–united to their bodies. Cf. *Summa Theologiæ*, Iᵃ, q. 75, a. 2 ad 2.

chological and physical components; everything the human person is made of and involves, that is precisely which loves and is loved. This is a fundamental truth which, however, has been forgotten or at least blurred too frequently throughout the history of Christian spirituality.

It is easy to see the special point the risen Christ makes of showing his disciples that his glorious body is really *his own body*, in some way different from what they perceived and experienced through their senses, and not an ethereal or astral being.[61] This leads one to think that one of the most important objectives of the decree of the Incarnation was to make it possible for man to draw very close to, to *avail himself of*, the Humanity of Christ: *Something which has existed from the beginning, which we have heard, which we have seen with our own eyes, which we have watched and touched with our own hands, the Word of life, this is our theme. That life was made visible; we saw it and are giving our testimony, declaring to you the eternal life, which was present to the Father and has been revealed to us. We are declaring to you what we have seen and heard, so that you too may share our life. Our life is shared with the Father and with his Son Jesus Christ.*[62] Despite this nothing could prevent a

---

[61] He eats food with his disciples a number of times, and he shows them the wounds in his side and feet and hands. Not only is he ready to let the unbelieving Thomas touch the wounds with his own hands: he invites the other apostles to do so as well (Lk 24: 38–40). He allows the holy women to clasp his feet... St Luke expressly points out how mistaken the Apostles were in thinking Jesus to be a ghost (Lk 24:37).

[62] 1 Jn 1: 1–3. Notice how the evidence of the senses is piled one on the other. By emphasizing in this way the fact that the disciples had an opportunity to exercise all their senses to know the Body of the Lord, St John seems to be trying to show the *reality* of Christ's Humanity, which is now *available* to believers.

series of unexpected obstacles[63] undermining such a basic element of Christian faith and spirituality: *They have taken away my Lord, and I do not know where they have laid him,*[64] Mary Magdalene said when she was looking for the body of Jesus. The loss of the real meaning and of the immediate presence of the Humanity of Christ, and therefore of its *availability* to the believer, has meant irreparable damage for Christian spirituality. In this connexion it is worthwhile pointing to some of the more recent examples of this phenomenon. There is no denying the darkening of faith in the real presence of Christ in the Eucharist, however much people try to disguise it and avoid referring to it; almost all Faculties of Catholic Theology put a question mark over the dogma of the real presence, when they do not openly deny it (as yet clear interventions of the Magisterium and of ecclesiastical discipline to prevent this loss of faith are virtually not existing). Another eloquent example is to be found in certain versions of the new canons of the Mass: for example, in canon II of the eucharistic sacrifice, in the words immediately prior to the consecration that refer to the gifts being offered for consecration, what is one to think of the reference to these offerings becoming *for us* the Body and Blood of the Lord? Are they proclaiming the usefulness

---

[63]The progressive *volatilization* of Christ's Humanity, which has been taking place ever since the foundation of the Church, would be a subject for a useful monograph to complete the history of Christian spirituality. There is no doubt but that devotion to the *Person* of Christ as Incarnate Word has become more blurred over the course of the history of Christianity (the way a torrent spreads out into rivulets that grow smaller and smaller) —taking the form of all kinds of *devotions* which have tended to divert attention from the essentials; yet what is essential in love is the *loved person* as such, just that —not things associated with her or parts of her entourage. Devotions such as that of the Five Wounds or of the Sacred Heart (to mention just a couple), orthodox and commendable though they be, can carry the risk of diverting attention from the whole to the part.

[64]Jn 20:13.

of something that is recognized as an objective reality, or do they rather insert into the faithful's belief the idea that the whole thing is merely subjective? One has to admit that the expression is, at least, fairly ambiguous.[65]

Human nature is so designed that man needs the physical reality of the *corpus* in order to love —the reality of his own body and of the body of the loved one, of course. For it should not be forgotten that the object of love is certainly a person, but a person always perceived through his tangible humanity. This is the same as saying that the person is apprehended through a soul and a body; or, more correctly, through two souls and two bodies, given that loving involves both the complete nature of the person who knows and loves, and the entire nature of the one known and loved. That is the only way love can operate as far as the human creature is concerned. Nor should one forget that, in keeping with the law of reciprocity that always applies in things to do with love, each of the lovers is in turn lover and loved one.[66]

---

[65] Another sign of the same sort of trend, which while being much less important is nevertheless significant, is closely connected with the previous one and it has to do with the feast of *Corpus Christi*, which has now practically disappeared. It has been transferred to the following Sunday, where it gets lost; gone are the eucharistic processions associated with it; and it is no longer a holiday of obligation on its own day; and gone too is the noisy, cheerful splendour of the feast —yet another instance of the Christian people being deprived of precious, attractive, festive devotions (in this case, one centred on the very core of the faith).

[66] This is not the place (which belongs to treatises and monographs on dogmatic theology) to go into the difficult question of the mode of knowledge (the mode of love could also be included) of separated souls, of which St Thomas said *quod ista quæstio difficultatem habet* (*S. Th.*, I^a, q. 89, a. 1). Cf. in addition to I^a, qq. 89 and 90, *Magister Sententiarum* 3, d. 31, q. 2, a. 4; *De Veritate* q. 19, a. 1; *Contra Gentiles* 2, 81; *Quæstio de Anima* a. 15; *Quodlibetales* 3, q. 9, a. 1.

Among the accounts of the events that occurred from Easter Sunday onwards, there is a very interesting text which points both to the reality of our Lord's body and to the form human love takes: *They (the holy women) departed quietly from the tomb with fear and great joy, and ran to tell his disciples. And behold, Jesus met them and said, "Hail!" And they came up and took hold of his feet and worshipped Him.*[67] The Spartan simplicity of the narrative does, however, let us capture the tenderness and emotion of the situation and it also, in a very few words, conveys something that is very much part of the feminine character: the women took hold of his feet and worshipped Him *with both fear and great joy.* It is true that the *Song of Songs* can be interpreted, if one so wishes, as an inspired poem full of metaphors which refer to purely spiritual realities. However, the real problem arises the moment one tries to specify precisely what those *purely spiritual* realities involve. Questions arise, piling on top of one another, as many as one likes, and they all expect an answer which one can say in advance is not going to be easily or readily provided: in a human being can there be such a thing as a purely spiritual love...? Is not love always something *bipersonal* that always requires a thou and an I if it is to develop...?[68] What in fact is the form of love proper to man...? St Thomas, who admits that this is a difficult question, reminds us in this connexion that the *modus operandi unius cuiusque rei sequitur modum essendi ipsius*,[69] thereby

---

[67] Mt 28: 8–9.

[68] In perfect and infinite Love, as a logical consequence of the relationships found within the Trinity, three Persons exist who are absolutely distinct as Persons but really identical with the divine essence —the two Lovers and the Love with which they love one another. But in order to understand love in created beings, or beings who are called to live the divine realities by way of participation, one always needs to resort to analogy, where dissimilarity is always greater than similarity.

[69] *Summa Theologiæ*, I^a, q. 89, a. 1.

repeating a fairly general doctrine.[70] For, once it is established that everything acts in accordance with its nature —elevated by grace, true, but not destroyed— one must admit that man always has to love as a complete being or, to put it another way, with his soul and with his body. At least one has to admit that that, and none other, is his most proper and perfect way of taking part in the mysterious reality of love. Thanks to the *truth*, or the realism, of the Incarnation (whose objectives were never solely to redeem man from sin) and of the Resurrection, the holy women could affectionately embrace the feet of the Lord, now in his glorified state but with a real body and a real soul: *Why are you troubled, and why do questionings rise in your hearts? See my hands and my feet, that it is myself; handle me and see.*[71] The New Testament has no scruple about admitting that the disciples arrived at the conviction that a real Resurrection took place, and came to the tenderness of perfect love for our Lord by a process of seeing and touching. And, while it is true that those who believe without seeing are declared to be blessed (Jn 20:29), it is no less true that that faith is based, in turn, on the testimony of those who have seen, heard and touched with their own hands (1 Jn 1: 1–3).

---

[70] It is interesting to note, however, that the Angelic Doctor seems to feel forced on this point to recognize that there are two distinct modes of knowledge in the human soul, but both are in conformity with his nature, depending on whether the soul is united to the body or separate from it (cf. the text cited in the previous note, *Respondeo dicendum* and *ad* 3). To explain how the separate soul can know angels he even goes so far as to posit special images infused by God (*op. cit.*, I^a, q. 89, a. 2 ad 2).

[71] Lk 24:38.

> *O that you would kiss me with the kisses of your mouth!*
> *For your love is better than wine.*[72]
>
> ....
>
> *O that his left hand were under my head,*
> *and that his right hand embraced me!*[73]
>
> ....
>
> *How fair and pleasant you are, O loved one,*
> *delectable maiden.*[74]
>
> ....
>
> *Come, my beloved, let us go forth into the fields,*
> *and lodge in the villages.*[75]

Given the reality of the Incarnation, the Redemption and the Eucharistic Presence, it follows logically that the expressions found in the *Song* are something more than metaphors that point to purely spiritual realities. If this sacred book has any meaning at all, it can be taken as certain that man has a capacity to feel for his God, made flesh in Jesus Christ, something that, as well as having very little to do with a disincarnated or purely spiritual love, is nothing less than ardent tenderness and blood inflamed by a heart overflowing with love. As certain as the fact that man can love in no other way, is the fact that in this case the Loved One, or the object of man's ardent love, is absolutely perceptible to the senses: *A spirit has not*

---

[72] Sg 1:2.
[73] Sg 2:6; 8:3.
[74] Sg 7:7.
[75] Sg 7:12.

flesh and bones as you see that I have.[76] That does not gainsay the equally certain fact that the Christian is living at present under a regime of faith.[77] For the New Testament, the irruption of the Kingdom of Heaven, albeit in the form of an earnest or first fruits, is *already* a reality for believers: from now on they are enlightened, they already taste the heavenly gift and partake of the Holy Spirit and savor the word of God and the marvels of the world to come (Heb 6: 4–5).[78]

There is another text of St John which might seem to go against the exegesis given on the text of Matthew 28:9 above. It has to do with the account of the appearance to Mary Magdalene: *Jesus said to her, "Mary." She turned and said to Him in Hebrew, "Rabboni!" (which means Teacher). Jesus said to her, "Do not hold me, for I have not yet ascended to the Father..."*[79] However, as we know, these texts do not contradict one another; they are complementary; and that of St Matthew is sufficiently clear on this. The key may lie in the fact that St John seeks to transmit a much more profound teaching than might at first appear: Jesus Christ has not yet ascended to

---

[76] Lk 24:39.

[77] Cf. 1 Cor 13: 10.12. But the exigencies of faith only bring in a special regime; they in no way cancel the laws of love.

[78] Cf. Lk 10:9; 17:21. Some texts of St Paul are very relevant in this connexion; for example Col 2:12: *You were buried with Him in baptism, in which you were also raised with Him through faith in the working of God, who raised Him from the dead.* The Apostle establishes a perfect parallel between the creature's participation in Christ's death, on the one hand, and his participation in his Resurrection, on the other. And he implies that both facts have *already taken place*. Moreover, it is logical that, if participation in the sufferings and death of our Lord are already a reality for believers (as is obvious to all), then their participation in his Resurrection and his glory should also be a reality already. At least this is what the text clearly indicates.

[79] Jn 20: 16–17.

the Father... and therefore the Holy Spirit has not yet been sent.[80] But physical contact and intimacy with our Lord necessarily require a love purified in the white–hot crucible of the Holy Spirit; for, only the overpowering fire of the Spirit can equip the believer to explore the profound and wonderful mysteries of the Heart of Jesus Christ. And, of course, physical intimacy clearly has no place in love unless there first exist a communion of ideas, of affections, of feelings, and of life, between the two lovers.[81]

The entire problem we are discussing is centred, ultimately, on the role and reality which is attributed to the Humanity of Jesus Christ; or to his human nature, if one prefers, made up as it is of body and soul and made his own by the Person of the Word. The problem, which to put it at its simplest has to do with the role that is really played by the Humanity of Christ in the economy of salvation, once more refers directly to the objectives and the reality of the Incarnation: what are the objectives of the Incarnation, and what order do they come in? Or to put it another way, in the classical formula: *Cur Deus homo?* For, once one admits that the Incarnation has other objectives in addition to the plan of Redemption of mankind, is it licit to say that a time must come for man, as he makes his way upwards to God, when he can (or even must) do without the Humanity of Christ?

---

[80] Jesus always links his going up to the Father with the sending of the Holy Spirit: *I tell you the truth: it is to your advantage that I go away, for if I do not go away, the Counsellor will not come to you; but if I go I will send him to you* (Jn 16:7. Cf. Jn 14:26; 15:26; 16:14).

[81] The carnal union of human love is but a distant analogate of the absolute self–surrender, total and reciprocal, which the lovers achieve in genuine love (hence mere carnal union is really an aberrant caricature of genuine love). In divine–human love, given the status of the divine Lover, the creature's affection for God cannot but be an absolutely divinized love.

As far as mystical theology is concerned, there is a centuries-long tradition of thought, fed by profound Platonic and neo–Platonic roots,[82] which tends to ignore or at least underestimate the reality and role of the Humanity of Christ. Basically it involves a more or less conscious refusal to admit the consequences which flow from the realism, or the reality, of the Incarnation. A refusal which in turn is based on Manichaean suspicion of matter and on Platonic over–valuation of pure ideas. In the last analysis, transferring the problem to the sphere of theology, it involves a strange resistance to recognizing both the essence of human nature as created by God and the fact that God really did become man. This explains how some have come to quite absurd conclusions, such as that of making a distinction between the Incarnate Word and a strange and mysterious apophatic God absolutely distinct from, unconnected with and far beyond anything else which might smack of matter or something created, including of course the Humanity of Christ. This distinction is used to justify the suspicion that the objectives of the Incarnation are being cut back and that man is thereby being deprived of the only accessible route to God that has been given him. This approach tends to forget that the God, who is Absolutely One and Transcendent, who is above all concepts, numbers, genera and species, is the same God as took a human nature in Jesus Christ, and that since then there is no other way by which man can obtain access to the Father: *No one comes to the Father, but by me.*[83] Baruzi himself, in his impressive work on St John of the Cross, goes as far as to say that *in the theophatic state to which we will be led we are not going to discover a God scarcely detached from human experience. St John of the Cross will not submerge himself in the*

---

[82]Particularly from Pseudo–Dionysius onwards, and up to the present time.
[83]Jn 14:6.

God Man, but rather (to the degree that his metaphysical culture permits) in the incomprehensible, unlimited God. Whatever they may say, those mystics who, like St Teresa, encountered a Lord who was the master of their actions and the shaper of their thoughts, are on quite a different plane —a human plane. And in a footnote he adds: *G. Belot is right in observing that it would be better to try to distinguish whether the states that mystics experience have to do with God or with Christ. As far as St John of the Cross is concerned, and with the nuances we try to identify in paragraph VI of this chapter, the answer is not difficult to find.*[84]

Once again the question might be asked: *Cur Deus homo...?* Why did the Word become flesh...? In order to take up a tangible flesh —flesh and blood, a heart that beats like that of any human being, hands that bless and embrace and that have truly been dug by nails, real eyes which gaze lovingly— which the believer then has to ignore in order to reach the unnameable God...? In order to save man from the wretchedness of sin and reconcile him with God, of course. But even though that may already be more than sufficient, it is valid to insist: And for nothing else...? On the other hand, it is not surprising that thinkers of the stature of Baruzi, and eminent theologians like von Balthasar —among others—, should have felt puzzled by the figure of St John of the Cross in particular and by the problem of Christian mysticism in general. As regards the latter, one must recognize that it is only to true mystics that the road lies open which can lead to a deeper understanding of the mystery (we refer only to a way, a route, and not to a solution as yet), but that does not mean that ordinary scholars are banned from following other paths or by–ways; water can always be looked for in the brook if one cannot find the deep river. As regards St John of the Cross,

---

[84] Jean Baruzi, *op. cit.*, IV, II.

it must be said that his person involves not only the inexplicable mystery of a hazardous life and of very esoteric doctrine but also the enigma which is typical of any saint's life: in this particular case, the saint of the nights and the nothings, of the denial of everything to do with the senses, of total detachment and poverty —is this not also the saint who sings of nature and of created things, in poetry that borders on divine, and who speaks of the Bridegroom, glossing the *Song of Songs*, in the same almost aphrodisiac language as the sacred book uses?

This problem, a difficult and thorny one, will always be a subject for experts to study in depth, provided they are not too susceptible to the vertigo caused by sight of the abyss. But we should stress here the need for a Humanity of Christ, *perceived* by the believer, as the only way to reach the Person of the Word and, thereby, the Father. True, that perception has to take place through faith as long as one is making one's earthly pilgrimage; but that does not entail traps or obstacles so grave as to prevent one from somehow reaching the Person of the Lord, and doing so in fact through his glorified Humanity, which one grasps as something that is truly real. Grace perfects and elevates nature, but it does not destroy it; and human nature, in order to be able to love, needs the *real presence* of the loved one, perceiving that person and *grasping* him in the manner appropriate to man: through the spirit, the mind, and the senses. Love is unimaginable without the presence of and contact between the lovers,[85] whose only desire is to be with one another: *Father, I desire that they also, whom thou has given me, may be with me where I am, to behold my glory which thou hast given me*

---

[85] Among the names which Trinitarian theology assigns to the Holy Spirit are *Nexus duorum* and *Osculum suavissimum*.

in thy love for me before the foundation of the world...[86] *I will not leave you desolate; I will come to you. Yet a little while, and the world will see me no more, but you will see me; because I live, you will live also. In that day you will know that I am in my Father, and you in me, and I in you.*[87] Moreover, the risen and glorious Christ has in no way set aside his corporality: *See my hands and my feet, that it is I myself; handle me, and see.*[88] That being so, why would the disciple not want to avail himself of the Humanity of Christ in order to reach the Godhead...? —when, moreover, it is impossible to devise a way of attaining that goal without using the only way that leads thereto: *I am the way, and the truth, and the life; no one comes to the Father, but by me.*[89]

It would be madness to think that St John of the Cross or the neo–Platonist mystics know nothing of the beauties of creation:

> *O woods and thickets,*
> *planted by the hand of the Beloved!*
> *O field of green,*
> *enamelled with blossoms,*
> *tell me if he has passed your way!*[90]

---

[86] Jn 17:24.
[87] Jn 14: 18–20.
[88] Lk 24:39.
[89] Jn 14:6.
[90] In the original:

> *¡Oh bosques y espesuras*
> *plantadas por la mano del Amado!*
> *¡Oh prado de verduras*
> *de flores esmaltado*
> *decid si por vosotros ha pasado!*

> *Scattering a thousand gifts,*
> *he passed through these woods in haste,*
> *glancing around as he went,*
> *clothing them with the beauty*
> *that reflected from his face.*[91]

But, does this refer to the beauty that leads right to the Beloved, or is, rather, something which is there to be ignored, and even denied and annihilated, to the degree that it involves perception? Could this beauty be compared to a series of steps, which one uses to ascend all the way to uncreated Beauty, or, perhaps better, should it be compared to a ballast which one must leave in order to attain the Absolutely Transcendent? The last stanza of the *Dark Night*, a passage of sublime and unbelievable poetic beauty, seems to say that all the undeniable beauty of created things has no purpose other than to be forgotten or left behind;[92] perhaps to be done without, by the most radical of negations, because that is the only way to reach the Beloved:

---

[91] *Spiritual Canticle*; the last line of this stanza (vestidos los dejó de hermosura) has the *h* aspirated in hermosura; or perhaps the transcription should be *fermosura*, in line with Old Spanish.

> *Mil gracias derramando*
> *pasó por estos sotos con presura*
> *y yéndolos mirando*
> *con sola su figura*
> *vestidos los dejó de hermosura.*

[92] In connection with this, the fact that creation has not been destined to be destroyed becomes very significant: *It was not for its own purposes that creation had frustration imposed on it, but for the purpose of him who imposed it —with the intention that the whole creation itself might be freed from its slavery to corruption and brought into the same glorious freedom as the children of God* (Rom 8: 20–21).

> *Lost to myself I stayed,*
> *my face reclining on the Beloved;*
> *everything ceased, and I abandoned myself,*
> *throwing my cares*
> *among the lilies to be forgotten.*[93]

There would be no sense in raising these hypotheses did we not have the saint's prose commentaries, in which he expounds at such length and so radically his doctrine of total despoliation. And again in the *Canticle*, after describing in almost divine verses the work of the Beloved and the scenario prior to the moment of the happy encounter with Him:

> *My Beloved the mountains,*
> *the lonely wooded valleys,*
> *the strange islands,*
> *the sonorous streams,*
> *the whisper of the amorous breezes.*[94]

---

[93]In the original:

> *Quedéme y olvidéme,*
> *el rostro recliné sobre el Amado,*
> *cesó todo, y dejéme,*
> *dejando mi cuidado*
> *entre las azucenas olvidado.*

[94]In the original:

> *Mi amado, las montañas*
> *los valles solitarios nemorosos*
> *las ínsulas extrañas*
> *los ríos sonorosos*
> *el silbo de los aires amorosos.*

> *Before the dawn appears*
> *here is the night, resting quiet;*
> *the music hushed,*
> *the sounding solitude,*
> *the supper that revives us and brings love.*[95]

he adds another stanza in which he speaks of the need to withdraw from things, in order to submerge oneself in the silence of total solitude and be able to find the Beloved and hear his voice:

> *Catch the little foxes for us,*
> *for our vineyard is in flower,*
> *while we make a bunch of roses,*
> *and let no one appear upon the hill.*[96]

And let no one appear upon the hill. Total solitude and complete despoliation —quite essential if the Bridegroom is to show Himself.

---

[95] In the original:

> *La noche sosegada*
> *en par de los levantes de la aurora*
> *la música callada*
> *la soledad sonora*
> *la cena que recrea y enamora.*

[96] In the original:

> *Cazadnos las raposas,*
> *que está ya florecida nuestra viña,*
> *en tanto que de rosas*
> *hacemos una piña,*
> *y no parezca nadie en la montiña.*

The last stanza, as always, is a paraphrase of the well–known passage in the *Song*:

> *Catch us the foxes,*
> *the little foxes,*
> *that spoil the vineyards,*
> *for our vineyards are in blossom.*[97]

As the Saint himself explains, in detail and at great length, it has to do with the famous *appetites*, which can do so much harm to the soul, preventing it from reaching God. The Bridegroom Himself, according to the paraphrase and exegesis the poet makes of the *Song*, is also keen that the hubbub of the world should not disturb the bride. Tranquility and rest. Let nothing be there, but only the Beloved:

> *You birds that fly with ease,*
> *lions, stags, skipping fallow deer,*
> *hills, valleys, river–banks,*
> *waters, winds, heats,*
> *and watchers that fill the night with fear:*[98]

---

[97] Sg 2:15.

[98] In the original:

> *A las aves ligeras,*
> *leones, ciervos, gamos saltadores,*
> *montes, valles, riberas,*
> *aguas, aires, ardores*
> *y miedos de las noches veladores:*

> *By the sweet lyre*
> *and song of sirens I conjure you*
> *to cease your wrath.*
> *Do not even echo on the wall,*
> *that the bride may sleep more securely.*[99]

This is simply an echo of the no less lovely verses of the *Song of Songs*:

> *I adjure you, O daughter of Jerusalem,*
> *by the gazelles or the hinds of the field,*
> *that you stir not up nor awaken love*
> *until it pleases.*[100]

So, what sort of silence is being referred to? The silence of things that go on in the background, acting as it were as a backdrop to a wedding scene, whose rustling can still be heard, as a sign that they are still there, forgotten perhaps and relegated, but never obliterated completely? Or is it perhaps the silence and repose the wayfarer experiences once he has rid himself of a dead weight, left behind, jettisoned forever as useless? It is certainly true that the moving words of the Bridegroom cannot be heard unless things have been silenced through being renounced and surrendered as a proof and sign of love. But is it a matter of annihilating or perhaps making

---

[99] In the original:

> *Por las amenas liras*
> *y cantos de sirenas os conjuro*
> *que cesen vuestras iras*
> *y no toquéis al muro*
> *porque la esposa duerma más seguro.*

[100] Sg 2:7. Cf. 3:5; 8:4.

an offering of things? —of destroying them or perhaps surrendering them? —of shedding them, as a weight that troubles or disturbs, or of bringing them along with one until one reaches the place where the Beloved awaits, in order to give them to Him...? In the epilogue of the *Song of Songs*, almost at the very end, the inspired poet has the bride say some words, addressed to the Bridegroom, which sound like a song of offering. An offering to the Bridegroom, and also a generous offering to all other creatures, of every kind, who in one way or another have helped to make it easier for the bride to reach the Bridegroom. For it seems clear that things can either be burdensome obstacles...or else be converted into a shining path which leads to the Holy Mountain on which the divine–human nuptials take place:

> *My vineyard, my very own, is for myself;*
> *You, O Solomon, may have the thousand,*
> *and the keepers of the fruit two hundred.*[101]

What would man do if he no longer had the sacred Humanity of our Lord or could nowhere find his holy corporality? Would it really be easier for him to fall in love with a God Who is transcendent Being above every other name, pure Spirit without flesh like his, without a heart like his, and without a soul full of tenderness like his? For now, with Jesus Christ, he has a God Who has taken a human body and a human soul, which man can therefore look upon, hear and embrace, knowing that it is God Himself that he is seeing, hearing, and touching. A God with eyes of flesh that can shed tears, and with a heart of flesh that is able to feel, and to provoke an almost infinite tenderness. What would man do without that Christ Who is for him his very life?[102] Does he not feel compelled to turn to

---

[101] Sg 8:12.
[102] Cf. Col 3:4.

him, time and time again, restless and hungry for tenderness, after experiencing the inadequacy of things, in order to say with St Peter: *Lord, to whom shall we go? You have the words of eternal life?*[103]

---

[103] Jn 6:68.

CHAPTER III

THE BRIDEGROOM'S FRAGRANCE AND CHRISTIAN PASTORAL ACTION

According to the *Song*, the Bridegroom's perfume is exquisitely fragrant. And because this fragrance is the most pleasant, most attractive thing one could ever find, and the only thing which can win man over completely, Christian pastoral action need talk about nothing else if it truly desires to bear genuine and effective witness to Jesus Christ. That is all it needs to do, all it can do; because if it wants to adhere strictly to our Lord's commandment, its sole aim must be to bear witness to Him and to his teaching: *Go therefore and make disciples of all nations, baptizing them in the name of the Father and of the Son and of the Holy Spirit, teaching them to observe all that I have commanded you...*[1] *You shall receive power when the Holy Spirit has come upon you; and you shall be my witnesses in Jerusalem and in all Judea and Samaria and to the end*

---

[1] Mt 28: 19–20.

*of the earth.*² It can be taken as read that the world, which has no wish to be spoken to about Jesus Christ and still less about Jesus Christ crucified, will be looking for something else. And that is a temptation for a Christian, in particular for an apostle, so grave a temptation that it can be compared only with the urgency of the need to reject it. Hence St Paul, with a healthy, glorious shamelessness, can take pride in proclaiming that although the Jews demand signs and Greeks seek wisdom, we preach Christ crucified —a stumbling block to Jews and folly to Gentiles.³

Any kind of incredulous feeling that pastoral activity might stray from its goals or that Christian witness may be somehow spoiled would evidence great naivety, because that is in fact what is happening all the time. To find the reasons for this one has to look no further than the weakness of human nature, aggravated in recent times by the crisis of faith the Church and the world are undergoing. St Paul himself, even in his own time, felt it necessary to give his disciple Timothy an appropriate warning: *Do not be ashamed of testifying to our Lord, nor of me his prisoner;*⁴ and this despite the fact that the Apostle was well aware of the valiant profession of faith which his spiritual son had already given in the presence of many witnesses (1 Tim 6:12). And it is a fact that embarrassment and fear of the world, possibly causing one to play down strictly supernatural criteria and concentrate on natural criteria, are realities already at work. Given the considerable likelihood of the mountain never coming to Mohammed, there will always be ingenuous people who are inclined to think that the best thing is for Mohammed to go to the mountain. That being so, to give an example, it is not

---

[2] Acts 1:8.
[3] 1 Cor 1: 22–23. Cf. 1 Cor 1:18.
[4] 2 Tim 1:8. Cf. Rom 1:16.

surprising that the Church should sometimes feel obliged to proclaim, to the assemblies of the world, that it believes in the validity of human rights: a very odd declaration, whatever way one looks at it, because it could similarly and for the same reason also proclaim that it believes in the usefulness of multiplication tables. Certainly, the Church can be in no doubt about the value of both things, even though they are on different planes. It would be much more useful to reject the validity of human rights, if what it wants to do is attract attention, because that would ensure that the media would make a lot of noise.

If pastoral activity has as its only objective to spread throughout the world the aroma of the Bridegroom's perfume, or *the good aroma of Christ*,[5] it must be said that that is not always the impression one gets. Even taking for granted the good will that underlines the intentions, it is plain to see that one cannot always say the same about the licitude or at least the appropriateness of the means used. The question as to whether certain means are justified by the good end one is pursuing is as old as mankind,[6] though no one has put it as trenchantly (referring to Christianity) as the Apostle St Paul: *And why not do evil that good may come? —as some people slanderously charge us with saying. Their condemnation is*

---

[5] 2 Cor 2:15.

[6] Machiavelli, in his famous book *The Prince* said, apropos of the need for an ethic, that *if all men were good, this would constitute a precept; but, given that evil men exist who are inclined not to keep a promise, then there is no need why you should see yourself obliged to keep yours. And a prince can always find legitimate ways of dissimulating his bad faith.* The success of this book, which appeared in the heyday of the Renaissance, clearly shows that, despite certain Pharisaical outrage, it reflected a fairly generalized state of opinion. Nowadays the book is no longer an outrageous manual of instruction, dedicated to unscrupulous politicians: it has virtually become an obligatory code of conduct for all who desire to be a success in life.

just.[7] Of course, it is true that, in this case, the problem is even more complicated, because it is no longer a matter —at least so it seems— of doing evil in order to achieve a good end, but of using whatever means one judges most opportune for achieving a good end..., abstraction made as whether or not that means is in fact most in line with New Testament revelation.[8] It may not even be very exact to describe it as an abstraction, because the means are always portrayed, when this matter is discussed, as being the best available means for attaining an end which is undoubtedly honest and praiseworthy. In fact no one even mentions the possibility of the means not being morally good, once the person using them seems convinced that they are good. And yet one has to recognize that certain methods often used in evangelization have a feature which is out of keeping with the spirit of the New Testament and which even very intelligent people can fail to notice. And yet that is really not so surprising, for one must make allowances for fallen, weakened human nature, for one thing, and the sublimity and elevation of New Testament revelation for another. To say, for example, that the poor or those who mourn are blessed, or that one should love even one's enemies, can seem to be going too far, even allowing for the restoration of human nature that grace brings about.

---

[7]Rom 3:8.

[8]Machiavelli's thesis has nothing to do with the principle that *the end justifies the means*, a principle which at least has pretensions (albeit mistaken) to having an ethical basis. The only goal of the Machiavellian doctrine is that the prince get what he wants, without any reference to ethics, and often guided by purely worldly criteria. Once supernatural and even natural ethics is rejected, the eventual result is a corruption of concepts and of language whereby the terms good and evil, and the concepts to which they refer, can mean anything, depending on what the individual chooses to base his own particular system of values.

The acquisition of power and influence by spiritual Families is a revealing example in this connexion. This is a subject, certainly a serious and delicate one, which has always been important down the ages and which continues to be so today. It has to do with the temptation that is so strong and so subtle that one could go so far as to say that it is almost impossible to avoid it or even notice it without special help from heaven. Those who fall into this temptation try to use their power and influence, inside and outside the Church, to do good (pure and simple), never anything else. They work on the assumption (a common and generally accepted one) that the ability to bring influence to bear and the opportunities that wealth offers are things that open the door to an immense array of activities which hugely help the spread of the Gospel, just as they prove useful everywhere else; consider that well-known saying of Quevedo: *Poderoso caballero es Don Dinero* (Mr. Money is a powerful gentleman); or the less well-known adage of Machiavelli, to the effect that *the man who has gold is the one who makes the rules.*

Put like that it may sound a bit harsh. And we know that no one finds it easy to accept painful truths, or even truths that are a nuisance, no matter how true they be. Hence the custom (very widespread nowadays) of toning down language and going in for euphemisms; whereby, for example, what has always been known as a *concubine* is now called a *lady friend*. So it can be said that there are very few, within and without the spiritual Families to be found in the Church, who are prepared to admit, in their own case, instances of misuse of Power —and even less ready to admit that that evil has found its way into their own house. And yet it is clear to see that Power, as a method of spreading good doctrine, not only has nothing to do with the New Testament but is something absolutely at odds with its spirit.[9] Whether one accepts it or not, one cannot deny that the propensity to corrupt people that is to be found in purely worldly things like Money or Power is such that they cannot be handled without impunity.[10]

However paradoxical it may seem, power and influence increase the more one boasts that one doesn't have them. The repeated claim to practice a life of radical poverty has proved to be very profitable, as some spiritual Families very well know. The reason for this is that Christian poverty must surely be the easiest of all the virtues to forge: anyone who preaches poverty to the four winds and proclaims his radical poverty for all to hear will have no difficulty in winning praise and attracting a good following. When practiced noisily by vanguard groups who have the unconditional support of the media, this attracts the attention of simple folk —and not so simple folk. Hence the emergence of spiritual Families whose great influence and tremendous power (through the control of enormous amounts of capital, and other methods) it would be naive to deny.

On this point, as on so many others, human nature demonstrates just how naive it can be. People tend to forget that true poverty, as

---

[9] It would be so easy to produce texts (all of them important) to prove this; but it would extend my text unduly, and would really need a separate study.

[10] We do not mean to dismiss money as something intrinsically evil, or to deny its obvious usefulness as a means of exchange; but it is clear that our Lord, as the texts amply show, was very careful to disabuse his disciples of the idea of using it in pastoral activities. He must surely have had two main reasons for this: the danger money involves in itself, as possibly a serious obstacle to the key virtue of Christian poverty, on the one hand; and, on the other, to get rid of the false belief that a message of such eminently supernatural content like the Gospel can be transmitted by means of purely natural factors: *"When I sent you out with no purse or bag or sandals, did you lack anything?" They said, "Nothing"* (Lk 22:35). Cf. Mt 10: 9–10; 20: 26–27; Mk 9:35; 10: 43–44; Lk 9:58; 10:4; 22: 25–27; Jn 13: 3–15; Acts 3:6; 2 Cor 8:9; etc.

well as being practically unknown, little respected and not at all held in high regard, has very few followers. Far from being surrounded by courtiers and fanfare, it lives in fact in total solitude, left entirely to fend for itself, like the truly poor Christ on the Cross: *My God, my God, why hast thou forsaken me?*[11] It has never attracted much attention; so it is not surprising that St James, a man gifted with a profound knowledge of human nature, had to warn Christians, even in his own time: *My brethren, show no partiality as you hold the faith of our Lord Jesus Christ, the Lord of glory. For if a man with gold rings and in fine clothing comes into your assembly, and a poor man in shabby clothing also comes in, and you pay attention to the one who wears the fine clothing and say, "Have a seat here, please," while you say to the poor man, "Stand there," or "Sit at my feet," have you not made distinctions among yourselves and become judges with evil thoughts?*[12] This is a passage which clearly shows that the human being has a great tendency to incline towards whomever he regards as most worthy and important, despising the poor and unfortunate. However, no longer is the deduction so easily made from this text that greatness (which the human being is so much drawn to) seems to have found in modern times a way of portraying itself also wearing an appearance of wretchedness, always of course with the purpose of greater effectiveness. In modern times, poverty has become an interesting source of income; it only needs to be proclaimed to the four winds, appearing in front of the people as a virtue, and, above all, to be donned with certain nuances of *rebelliousness* —although nobody exactly knows against what or whom that rebelliousness is directed. What this means is that human nature continues to be in awe of the grandiose, but now it wears the rags of radical poverty,

---

[11] Mt 27:46; Mk 15:34.
[12] Jas 2: 1–4.

which is the same as saying that it has the trappings of the great hero extolled on all sides.[13]

In connexion with power and influence, it is worth stressing here something which we also referred to earlier when discussing intentions. It would be highly unjust to attribute to founders of spiritual Families, whether ones which existed at one time in the past or ones which still exist in the Church, intentions which are anything but a desire to do good. The rightness of their intentions is confirmed once and for all by the Church herself when she canonizes or beatifies many of these founders; moreover, they (very justifiably) have a great popular following. And it would be equally wrong not to recognize the immense good work that spiritual Families of this kind have done the world over.

But things are not always simple. And it is not possible to ignore the undeniable fact that human thought is governed by rules of logic which are as precise and as necessary as those of mathematics. For example, once certain bases or starting–off points are established, inevitably certain logical developments occur[14] even though they

---

[13] It would be interesting to make a sociological study of the causes of the inane respect which quite a number of Christians today have for poverty. Given that it in no way has to do with the true Christian virtue of poverty, one would not be surprised to find the roots of this naive attitude in the remnants that still survive of Marxist philosophy, and along with that the underlying feeling of guilt and inferiority which are so often to be found, within the Christian milieux, as a result of that now out–moded ideology.

[14] History of Philosophy proves this fact with all evidence. It seems that ideas have life on their own: they germinate, grow, develop all their virtualities... Modern thought, which very often considers itself to be original, sometimes is but a logical consequence of ideas established many centuries ago. Cf. following note.

were not perceived or foreseen at the outset.[15] And that is precisely what has happened in regard to the Rules and Constitutions of some spiritual Families: they seem to contain *in nuce* certain principles of political philosophy which, even though they were not very much in agreement with the content of the New Testament, were things which the original drafters overlooked. Over the course of time these principles have germinated and have produced results which are quite logical but rather unfortunate.[16]

Given that History is a good teacher, it can sometimes be useful to call in her help to get guidance and draw sound conclusions. And even at the risk of being misinterpreted (or, worse, accused of bearing a grudge over this or that), there are times when one has to draw attention to particular instances. In doing so, one is not arrogating to oneself the right to judge anyone —that is up to History, and ultimately to God alone— but simply giving a concrete example of

---

[15]In the history of thought, Descartes is regarded as the most direct father of modern Idealism. Although his inner intentions will probably never be discovered, there is no denying that it was he, in the main, who made it possible for that ideology to develop. Did the French thinker believe in God or did he not? Did he really try in all good faith, as seems most likely, to provide a definitive proof of the existence of God? Whatever the answer to that question may be, the important thing here is that, by trying to replace the philosophy of realism by the philosophy of the famous *cogito*, he opened the way to the idealist trend in modern philosophy, and all the consequences brought with it. All his disciples and followers did was to work out the logical implications of the premises he established. Cf. for example, É. Gilson, *The Unity of Philosophical Experience*, Charles Scribner's Sons, New York, 1941, pp. 125 ff.; *Le Réalisme Méthodique*, Vrin, Paris, n. d., pp. 1–15.

[16]A different, and perhaps insoluble, problem is whether these results *could* and should have been foreseen. There is no denying that the Church, the teacher and arbitrator of ethics, principles, customs and moral behaviour —although she does not make judgments on matters to do with political philosophy and their possible derivatives— did approve the Constitutions and By–laws, thus rendering them legitimate.

what one means in order to forestall any possible accusation that one is sounding off without justification. Past events can be used as an example (events which still exercise an effect today); but one could equally have chosen other more recent events instead.

No one can question, for example, the noble intentions or the wonderful work of a man as eminent as St Ignatius Loyola. Yet one cannot turn one's back on the factual evidence of the remarkable political activity the Society of Jesus has engaged in, in so many different countries, from its foundation right down to our own time —political activity which no one will deny has had a considerable impact on the course of History. The causes of a complex phenomenon of this kind will probably remain one of the great mysteries of History; but it is difficult to reject the theory that particular principles of political philosophy, devised by the founder with the best of intentions and then spelt out in official documents, may eventually have germinated and produced their logical effects. In the Society's Constitutions one finds it said that *since good is more divine the more universal it is, preference should be given to those persons and places which, having been taken advantage of, are able to bring it about that good be spread to many others who acknowledge their authority or are governed by them; [such persons include] princes, magistrates, administrators of justice, prelates, distinguished men of letters and people in authority...*[17] Following the same line, it is quite normal, therefore, for Father Polanco to say also, referring to the people one has to have dealings with, that *it can be said as universally applicable that one should deal with those one can expect to do greater good in the service of God and the common good in themselves or in others, and not with those who profit little or even hinder (the*

---

[17]St Ignatius' Constitutions, no. 622; quoted by B. Jiménez Duque, *Historia de la Espiritualidad*, II, Flors, Barcelona, 1969, p. 221.

progress of) good. One should deal with important people because, by rendering them help, they in turn help many others; with secular princes, because the good done to their souls can spread to many of their subjects; with persons in authority, because people of that kind can help many others spiritually and temporally, if they themselves are helped.[18] This is why a historian as careful as Lortz says (apropos of the instructions the Society gives the master of the spiritual exercises) that *the invitation given the master not to say anything against prelates or princes had enormous effect in environments used to the merciless criticism handed out by humanists and reformers. But it also put at risk the truthfulness and liberty of the Christian.*[19] It would take too long to discuss the political consequences that principles of this kind could lead to, nor is this the place to do so; besides, much has been written on this subject that can be easily consulted. Here it will suffice to mention, in passing and by way of preference, the things Elliot has to say about the Count–Duke de Olivares and the Portuguese question in the times of Philip IV of Spain;[20] or what such a balanced person and one as well disposed to the Society as Marañón has to say about the Society's political activity in the reign of Philip IV.[21] The only other thing we would say is that more recent historians have, as one might expect, different approaches to the matter: Domínguez Ortiz, for example, tries to study the matter very objectively and, although a supporter of the Society, he does not accept that its expulsion from various countries

---

[18] Tercera Industria del Padre Polanco, quoted by B. Jiménez Duque, *op. cit.*, p. 219.

[19] J. Lortz, *Historia de la Iglesia*, Cristiandad, Madrid, 1982, p. 194, n. 24.

[20] J. H. Elliott, *El Conde–Duque de Olivares*, Crítica, Barcelona, 1990, pp. 393, 426, 590, etc.

[21] Gregorio Marañón, *El Conde–Duque de Olivares*, Espasa Calpe, Madrid, 1980, pp. 182–3, 188, 191, etc.

in the 18th century was caused solely by masonic Voltairian or in general anti–Catholic activity;[22] and there are others, such as Ricardo de la Cierva, who are not slow to criticize the present general of the Jesuits for his apparent passivity towards Freemasonry.[23]

It is easy to appreciate that it is unpleasant and sad to speak of things like this —and dangerous also, because it gets a bad press and no one, or almost no one, wants to accept unpleasant evidence, no matter how true it is. Human nature, because it is more inclined to follow self–interest than a sincere love for the truth, often ends up by substituting spontaneity for logic. We can see this from the following anecdote about a young priest well known to the author.

As well as being young and recently ordained, he was rather naive, which is what usually happens since God so arranged things that the priestly character neither adds nor subtracts anything to the advantages and disadvantages which are a feature of the various stages in the life of man. Due to his parish priest being unexpectedly called away to some duty, the young priest was charged with chairing a meeting of some rather grand ladies in the parish where he was working. So, the poor man felt it incumbent on him to prepare a long and profound discourse full of theology and edifying advice — work he could have saved himself... if he had had the gift of foresight, or at least a better knowledge of female psychology.

---

[22] He may be trying to redress the balance after Menéndez Pelayo's bitter complaint about the expulsion and suppression of the Jesuits in his *Historia de los Heterodoxos Españoles*. A. Domínguez Ortiz, *Carlos III y la España de la Ilustración*, Alianza Editorial, Madrid, 1988, p. 85.

[23] Ricardo de la Cierva, *El Triple Secreto de la Masonería*, Fénix, Toledo, 1994, pp. 14 ff.; although De la Cierva is often accused of being too radical by opponents who are much more radical than he, and who are not slow to bend the truth, his study is certainly a well–documented one. One would be very rash to dismiss him airily.

The meeting had no sooner begun than the young priest got a terrific surprise. There on the table lay a sheet of paper with an *agenda* which, to his amazement, listed a series of speeches with the names of the lady speakers and the subject each would address; at the bottom of the agenda, as an epilogue and finishing touch was an item which read, *concluding prayer and final greeting: by the priest.* But his tribulation was only beginning.

As one might have guessed already, the various speeches were such that if an impartial observer described them as interminable, boring, banal, insubstantial and exasperating, he would be rightly accused of being too kind. The young priest, in anguish and frustration, reflected on the ingenuity of the human imagination's capacity to devise ways of wasting time, when he for his part had to put off doing lots of things, all of them important, just to chair a symposium of people who had nothing to do. One of the speakers, who went on and on about the need to pray more intensely for the persecuted Church behind the Iron Curtain, was followed by another eloquent lecturer who produced from her handbag a letter which she read and commented on at length. It was written by a brother of hers, a Jesuit missionary in Japan, full of generous desires of self-sacrifice and with other not very original accounts of the famous cherry trees. The aforesaid letter went on with paragraphs more or less like this:

—And when, after a life of difficulty and self-surrender, I eventually fall and my bones fertilize the land in which the cherry trees grow...

The good lady was so overcome that she wept, all the time making edifying remarks about the undoubtedly good spirit of the brave missionary...; meanwhile the other ladies waited impatiently for their turn to speak. But it was the young, muzzled priest who was the most impatient of all, thinking of how far away Japan was and the Iron Curtain, whereas here in his own parish there were so many people in need of food and good doctrine; and one didn't have to go beyond the church building itself, to find plenty that needed doing: the main altar, for example, was filthy, not to speak of the corporals, purificators and altar-cloths, which were so full of grime and grease that they had lost their original whiteness.

And so, after a series of other equally passionate speeches, the end eventually came, because nothing in this world ever lasts forever. And the time came for the final prayers, which were the priest's responsibility (the least one might expect). However, presumably due to the desire for revenge which is a typical defect of fallen human nature —from which clerics are not immune— the young priest saw that his chance, *his hour*, had come:

—My dear ladies: —he began, clearing his throat a little and in a slight tone of edginess (not very well disguised)— I have listened with interest to and been moved by what you have said and I can assure you that I have taken note of it. However, I hope you will allow me to make a few observations to bring the meeting to a close: why do you have to go so far afield to find causes —to the Iron Curtain, the cherry trees of Japan and places like that— when here in your own parish, and in your own homes, you get so many opportunities to practice your undoubted Christian zeal? Beginning with your homes, for example: are you sufficiently attentive to your husbands and children, by being very dedicated and heroic in your domestic duties, like the Christian mothers and spouses you are? And even in our parish church we don't have the wherewithal to ensure that the Lord's own house is kept neat and clean: what about helping us (starting today) to wash the vestments and keep the church clean? You can be sure that God would be quite grateful for that, because it is much more practical —and close to home— than bemoaning things which you can do nothing about. Besides...

At this point he was interrupted by an uproar of shouts and protests which drowned his words. The meeting came to an end without any closing prayer, and the young Quixote, who had to make his way out as best he could, was effectively called to order by his parish priest the next day.

And the fact is that, as we have already said, since human feelings are rarely ruled by logic, truth recognized is something very precious and in very short supply. Therefore, whereas few will say they agree with what has been said above, detractors and even angry opponents are two-a-penny. This proves, once again, that the true stuff of New Testament revelation is something so subtle, so elevated, that not only does it often go over the average man's head but it even escapes people who are highly intelligent. And, if it is true that revelation has been given to man in his present situation —in a state of fallen nature and restored by grace—, that in no way takes from the sublimity of revelation, nor does it excuse man from the obligation he is thereby placed under, to accede to revelation through prayer and an attitude full of humility: *I thank thee, Father, Lord of heaven and earth, that thou hast hidden these things from the wise and understanding and revealed them to babes.*[24] As regards the subject under discussion, it is worth pointing out that holiness does not always bring with it the charism of historical insight, nor is there any reason why it should. And yet that is no reason why things should cease to be the way they are, as one can learn by close study, for example, of a parable which is often less understood than it should be: the parable of those invited to the

---

[24] Mt 11:25; Lk 10:21.

wedding. Something has already been said about it earlier in these pages, apropos of the life of ideas.[25]

The first thing one notices, when one reads St Luke's version, is that the host initially applied the same logic as St Ignatius. It is clear to see that those he first invited were not exactly the common people, and that they did have some degree of social standing: one of them had just bought a field, another had bought five yoke of oxen, another had just got married and was getting ready to celebrate his marriage —all things which could not be said, in the ancient world, to be within the scope of simple, humble people.

This comes to prove that purely human logic, human though it be, is still logic, and therefore is not bad in itself. So one can say that it can be quite permissible and even opportune to be logical... even if only to begin with, as in the case of the host in the parable. However, given that purely human logic has been superseded by divine or supernatural logic, anyone who is even averagely sensible can avoid wasting time and can go directly to what is worthwhile; that is certainly one of the lessons of the parable worth learning: *The sons of this world are wiser in their own generation than the sons of light.*[26]

Besides, the facts speak for themselves, for those who were invited so enthusiastically declined to a man: *They all alike began to make excuses* —which is a way of saying, not to put too fine a point

---

[25]Lk 14: 15–24 and Mt 22: 2–10. Our commentary is based on St Luke's version. The text of the various parables is still a very rich vein of the living waters of the Gospel, and one still to be explored. In recent times, except for the short, simple, and already classical commentary by Lucien Cerfaux, (*Le Trésor des Paraboles*, Desclée & Cie., Tournai, 1967), very little profound, useful work has been done on them. Apparently, the whole field of parables, despite its rich potential, is one whose main crop is clichés and superficiality.

[26]Lk 16:8.

on it, that they could not be counted on for anything; this is not surprising if one bears in mind that, *ad mentem Novi Testementi*, and as the facts confirm, it is not usually the rich and powerful who respond to the call of the Gospel, as the Apostle himself pointed out: *Consider your call, brethren; not many of you were wise according to worldly standards, not many were powerful, not many were of noble birth; but God chose what is foolish in the world to shame the wise, God chose what is weak in the world to shame the strong.*[27] This is something our Lord Himself experienced and had very hard things to say about (Mk 10: 17–27).[28]

The host in the parable was annoyed by all these invitees not accepting, so he decided to adopt a different approach and call another type of person: *He said to his servant, "Go out quickly to the streets and the lanes of the city, and bring in the poor and maimed and blind and lame."* So the host did not simply look for other guests, once the first ones failed to accept: he sent out for *entirely the opposite* sort of people from those he originally invited; then, he had gone for important people, now he prefers the poor, the crippled, the blind, the lame, and in general the sort of people found *in the highways and by–ways.*[29] An interesting pastoral tactic which some spiritual Families could heed.

---

[27] 1 Cor 1: 26–27.

[28] Cf. Mt 19: 16–26; Lk 18: 18–27.

[29] What this clearly means is *ordinary people*, simple people. One should be careful not to make the mistake of thinking that what is being proposed has anything to do with the *preferential option for the poor*. That is an acceptable option only if the following conditions are met: (a) that it is cleansed of its Marxist associations; (b) that the concept of the *poor* is taken in the biblical sense and not a merely sociological or Marxist one; (c) that that option is not exploited (as is in fact happening with certain groups within Catholicism) to obtain financial gain or political or social influence. If these conditions are not met, the preferential option for the poor is, at best, simply a joke.

So, here we have an example which clearly shows that the worldly criteria —or at least criteria which have little to do with the content of the New Testament— can worm their way unnoticed into Christian pastoral activity; and as a result it would no longer be a matter of spreading the fragrance of the Bridegroom's perfumes, but something quite different.

And yet it is absolutely basic that these perfumes should keep their fragrance: *Lord, to whom shall we go? You have the words of eternal life.*[30] As the bride in the *Song* tells us, it is a most pleasing, lovely and fragrant perfume, poured out on things, making them beautiful and desirable. It comes from the Bridegroom Himself, causing one to love Him —*therefore the maidens love you*—; it makes things lovable and delightful, revealing them to be the work of love. That is why the creation account says that when God created the heavens and the earth, the Spirit of God moved over the waters,[31] and also that God at the very moment of creating things saw that they were good.[32] It could equally have said that things were full of beauty since, to the same extent they were real things

---

[30] Jn 6:68.

[31] The Book of Genesis begins by saying *In principio creavit Deus cœlum et terram. Terra autem erat inanis et vacua, et tenebræ super faciem abyssi, et spiritus Dei ferebatur super aquas.* Some, such as *La Bible de Jérusalem*, say that this does not refer to the spirit of God or his role in creation, because creation is the work of the Word (as one can see from vv. 3 ff.) But in fact the presence of the Spirit, or of the Love of God, cannot be excluded from the act of creation according to these verses. Apart from the fact that every *ad extra* action of God is an action of the three Divine Persons, as far as attribution is concerned creation is also and above all a design of Divine Love.

[32] It is quite interesting to observe that goodness and beauty, both transcendentals of being, always appear joined together with love. Love as a new transcendental?

and good things, they also were beautiful.[33] Obviously, the study of the transcendentals is not complete yet.

It is important to note that beauty is perceived mainly and above all through the eyes —*pulchrum oculis* is how the Book of Genesis describes the fruit of the tree of Paradise— but not only by the eyes; it is also perceived by hearing, and therefore one can speak of a beautiful voice, a beautiful melody or a beautiful poem. St Thomas says pertinently that the other senses do not perceive beauty, which is why one never describes tastes or odours as being beautiful. Being a participation in uncreated Beauty and therefore having a reference to it, the beauty that man knows and contemplates can never fully satisfy him; this holds good also as regards his apprehension of partial goodness and truth.[34]

So, God is the cause and the source of all beauty, even though beauty may be said to originate in the Word, insofar as He is the

---

[33] According to the Genesis account, the fruit of the tree set in the centre of Paradise —the tree of the knowledge of good and evil— was desirable and attractive; not for nothing was it, too, the work of love: *Vidit igitur mulier quod bonum esset lignum ad vescendum et pulchrum oculis et desiderabile* (Gen 3:6).

[34] Apropos of beauty and of the senses which perceive it, St Thomas says that *pulchrum est idem bono, sola ratione differens. Cum enim bonum sit "quod omnia appetunt," de ratione boni est quod in eo quietetur appetitus: sed ad rationem pulchri pertinet quod in eius aspectu seu cognitione quietetur appetitus. Unde et illi sensus præcipue respiciunt pulchrum, qui maxime cognoscitivi sunt, scilicet visus et auditus rationi deservientes: dicimus enim pulchra visibilia et pulchros sonos. In sensibilibus autem aliorum sensuum, non utimur nomine pulchritudinis: non enim dicimus pulchros sapores aut odores. Et sic patet quod pulchrum addit supra bonum, quendam ordinem ad vim cognoscitivam: ita quod bonum dicatur id quod simpliciter complacet appetitui; pulchrum autem dicatur id cuius ipsa apprehensio placet.* In *Summa Theologiæ*, I^a–II^æ, q. 27, a. 1, ad 3.

Image of God, or of the Father (2 Cor 4:4; Heb 1:3).³⁵ Also, the Word, made man in Jesus Christ (Jn 1:14), *recapitulates* all things in Himself (Eph 1:10), and is even the efficient and final cause of all things, because they were made through Him and for Him (Col 1:16) and now hold together in Him (Col 1:17). He upholds the universe by his word of power (Heb 1:3), He is the first–born of all creation (Col 1: 15–18) and in Him all the fullness of God dwells (Col 1:19). In one of his most daring and profound passages, the Apostle goes so far as to say that *in Him the whole fullness of deity dwells bodily*.³⁶ We can say, therefore, that in the Word made man, in Whose face shines the very glory of God,³⁷ is the first and last source of all the beauty that things have.³⁸ But it must be remembered that this does not just mean that He is the most beautiful of all the sons of man, as Old Testament revelation already observed prophetically (Ps 45:3); it goes further, making it clear that he is also the cause and reason for *all* beauty that is found in creation. The perfume of the Bridegroom has imbued all things with its fragrance and made

---

³⁵Once again we find the Image and the Word (referring to sight and hearing) as places of perception of beauty. For a being whose nature is also corporeal, as is the case with man, beauty must necessarily be something *perceivable by the senses*. As regards where man can go to quench his thirst for uncreated Beauty, there can only be one such place: the Word made flesh, Whose human nature contains the fullness of the Godhead (Col 2:9) and is, therefore, for the human being, the inexhaustible source of all beauty.

³⁶*Quia in ipso inhabitat omnis plenitudo divinitatis corporaliter* (Col 2:9); σωματικῶς means *vere, realiter* (cf. Col 2:17), or *incarnate*, which is the same as saying *corpore assumpto* (cf. Zerwick, *Analysis Philologica Novi Testamenti Græci*).

³⁷*For it was God who said, "Let light shine out of darkness," who has shone in our hearts to give the light of the knowledge of the glory of God in the face of Christ* (2 Cor 4:6).

³⁸St Thomas has very beautiful and interesting things to say in this connexion in his *In Isaiam*, 63, and *In Psalmos*, 44, no. 2.

them beautiful and desirable. As St John of the Cross says in his *Canticle*:

> *Scattering a thousand gifts,*
> *he passed through these woods in haste,*
> *glancing around as he went,*
> *clothing them with the beauty*
> *that reflected from his face.*[39]

Since, according to the Father's plan it is in Him alone that man can quench his desire for truth and goodness —He is the Way, and the Truth and the Life— then clearly He alone is where man can quench his insatiable thirst for beauty:

> *Do not scorn me,*
> *for if you first found me to be dark,*
> *now you can indeed look at me,*
> *after you have gazed upon me,*
> *for you have clothed me in grace and beauty.*[40]

---

[39] In the original:

> *Mil gracias derramando*
> *pasó por estos sotos con presura*
> *y yéndolos mirando*
> *con sola su figura*
> *vestidos los dejó de hermosura.*

[40] In the original:

> *No quieras despreciarme,*
> *que si color moreno en mí hallaste,*
> *ya bien puedes mirarme*
> *después que me miraste,*
> *que gracia y hermosura en mí dejaste.*

Obviously neither the bride in the *Song* nor St John of the Cross are interested in the Bridegroom as the source or cause of beauty: theological or metaphysical speculation is not what these writings are about. In fact, whereas the *Song* never mentions this subject, St John does refer to it incidentally; in the stanza we have just quoted, for example, although the bride in her love notes that the Bridegroom has bestowed upon her loveliness and beauty, what really interests her is the fact that He looks upon her and does not despise her:

> *Do not scorn me,*
> *for if you first found me to be dark,*
> *now you can indeed look at me...*[41]

It is not so much that the Bridegroom is the cause of all beauty as that He *is really beautiful.* For no one is impelled towards love by theological or metaphysical considerations, but by personal reasons which are always reciprocal in character: a *thou* who captivates and to whom an *I* gives itself entirely, out of love; and this in turn is reciprocated.[42] No one falls in love with the beauty another has: one falls in love with the person who possesses that beauty. What really interests the person in love is not the graces or charms of the other person, but the person who has those graces or charms. These, in the last analysis and none too easily, can perhaps be described;

---

[41] In the original:

> *No quieras despreciarme,*
> *que si color moreno en mí hallaste,*
> *ya bien puedes mirarme...*

[42] When love is strong, the gift it makes of its possessions to the loved one is a large one; when love is total, the gift it makes is a total one: *the Father loves the Son, and has given all things into his hand* (Jn 3:35).

but one cannot ever manage to describe that ineffable, mysterious something which they bestow upon the loved one:

> *The creatures all around me*
> *speak of your thousand gifts,*
> *yet they wound me even more.*
> *Something that they stammer*
> *leaves me dying.*[43]

When the bride in the *Song* refers at one point to the sweetness of the Bridegroom's love, she is not thinking so much of the love itself as of the fact that it derives from Him. Her joy really has its source not in the fact that she is loved but in the fact that *it is the Bridegroom Who loves her*:

> *Your love is better than wine.*

Also, given that the bride would never fall in love with the Bridegroom were it not that she sees his graces and his beauty, she really does need to have that perception. For beauty is something which by its essence has to be perceived, since it is nothing other than the splendour, the glory and the luminosity of being.[44] Moreover, the

---

[43] St John of the Cross, *Cántico Espiritual*:

> *Y todos cuantos vagan*
> *de ti me van mil gracias refiriendo*
> *y todos más me llagan*
> *y déjame muriendo*
> *un no se qué que quedan balbuciendo.*

[44] Of all the sacred authors, St John is the one who best knows how to link love, perception (sight) and knowledge; if any of these three is absent, then so are the others: *no one who sins has either seen Him or known Him* (1 Jn 3:6).

Bridegroom well knows the rules and requirements of the game of love, and so He knows very well that He must manifest Himself to the bride:[45] *He who has my commandments and keeps them, he it is who loves me; and he who loves me will be loved by my Father, and I will love him and manifest myself to him.*[46] And this self-revelation, in turn, tends more and more towards total intimacy and union: *If a man loves me, he will keep my word, and my Father will love him, and we will come to him and make our home with him.*[47] If the Lord is known as a great *seducer* (Mt 27:63), this must be because he has shown Himself to be so and been seen to be so.[48] To perceive Him as such the disciple needs only one of the two senses that can grasp beauty —sight or hearing—, although it can sometimes happen that one of these is expressly excluded, as can be seen from St Luke's account of the disciples of Emmaus: according to the evangelist, while the disciples were talking and debating with one another, Jesus drew near and walked with them, but *their eyes*

---

[45] This idea of *need* must be understood here in a broad and in a strong sense, and it is not difficult to see that it is determined not only by the knowledge that comes from the requirements of the laws of love, but also from the impulse which moves the Bridegroom and leads Him to manifest Himself to the bride. In fact the feeling is a mutual one, part of the basic fabric of the great mystery of love.

[46] Jn 14:21.

[47] Jn 14:23.

[48] It is important to note that St John, from the very beginning of the Letter, puts the stress on the perceptions of sight and hearing as the two most important factors which determine whether the disciples can bear witness to the Word made man: *That which was from the beginning, which we have heard, which we have seen with our eyes, which we have looked upon and touched with our hands, concerning the word of life —the life was made manifest, and we saw it, and testify to it, and proclaim to you the eternal life which was with the Father and was made manifest to us— that which we have seen and heard...* (1 Jn 1: 1–3).

*were kept from recognizing Him;*⁴⁹ and then later on, as he spoke to them and explained the Scriptures to them, they came to realize that their hearts were burning with an intense feeling of emotion: *Did not our hearts burn within us while he talked to us on the road, while he opened to us the Scriptures?*⁵⁰

Since the evangelist provides no explanation, we might ask here why it was that the disciples' eyes were prevented from recognizing Jesus. No doubt all kinds of explanations might be suggested..., though none of them particularly convincing. But there is something which, strange as it may seem, does come across fairly clearly from the narrative —the fact that hearing sometimes seems more useful than sight to grasp the things of love: *The wind blows where it wills, and you hear the sound of it, but you do not know whence it comes or whither it goes.*⁵¹ After the Master's resurrection Mary Magdalene fails to recognize Him, despite the fact that He is in front of her; she mistakes Him for the gardener; only when He calls her directly by her name does she realize, eventually, Who He is.⁵² In the Apocalypse it is said: *Beloved, I stand at the door and knock; if any one hears my voice and opens the door, I will come in to him and eat with him, and he with me.*⁵³ In the allegory of the good shepherd we also find this stress on hearing as the decisive factor: the sheep recognize the voice of the Shepherd and follow it: *He who enters by the door is the shepherd of the sheep. To him the gatekeeper opens; the sheep hear his voice, and he calls his own sheep by name and*

---

⁴⁹Lk 24:16.
⁵⁰Lk 24:32.
⁵¹Jn 3:8.
⁵²Jn 20: 11–16.
⁵³Rev 3:20.

leads them out. When he has brought out all his own, he goes before them, and the sheep follow him, for they know his voice. A stranger they will not follow, but they will flee from him, for they do not know the voice of strangers.[54]

This must surely be due to the fact that, in this present age, the Christian is still living in an economy of faith: *for we walk by faith, not by sight.*[55] Moreover, *faith comes from what is heard.*[56] St Paul reminds the faithful of Corinth that *now we see in a mirror dimly, but then face to face.*[57] St Thomas comments, following Dionysius, apropos of this mysterious or dim knowledge, that this hazy, distant light does not lead to knowledge of what God is but to knowledge of what he is not, or at most to the idea of his existence; so it follows, the saint says, that the best way open to man to know God in this life is by way of negation (what creatures or creaturely concepts are not).[58] However, dim or enigmatic vision of the type referred to must be interpreted in the light of what the Apostle immediately goes on to say in the same passage: *Now I know in part, then I shall*

---

[54] Jn 10: 2–5.

[55] 2 Cor 5:7.

[56] *Fides ex auditu* (Rom 10:17).

[57] *Videmus enim nunc per speculum inænigmate, tunc autem facie ad faciem* (1 Cor 13:12).

[58] *Cognitio qua Deus per creaturas videtur, non est ipsius essentia, sed ænigmatica et specularis, et a remotis. Job XXXVI, 25: "omnes homines vident eum," aliquo dictorum modorum, "sed unusquisque intuetur procul," quia per omnes illas cognitiones non scitur de Deo quid est, sed quid non est, vel an est. Unde dicit Dionysius libro Mysticæ Theologiæ quod perfectus modus quo Deus in vita præsenti cognoscitur, est per privationem omnium creaturarum, et intellectorum a nobis* (St Thomas, *Super Evangelium Iohannis Lectura*, c. 1, lec. 11).

know fully, even as I have been fully understood.[59] For, although it is true that *no one has ever seen God*, it is no less true that *the only Son, who is in the bosom of the Father, he has made him known*.[60] Therefore, the partial sight St Paul speaks of must refer to the full sight one will eventually have, which will come about in the end in Heaven; but that does not mean that the Christian cannot now acquire, through the action of the Spirit, a knowledge of the Lord which can lead to total love (not yet consummated, of course). When St Peter speaks in praise of the faithful who love Jesus Christ even though they have not seen Him,[61] he has in mind a merely natural sight that the senses provide, or even a knowledge in the flesh (2 Cor 5:16), but not the supernatural knowledge that is acquired through faith.

The dim, mirror–like knowledge of God is so unclear and partial that it is valid to say that the Christian, in this present life, walks in the Dark Night of his pilgrim way —a *Dark Night* that is also called faith, as the Letter to the Hebrews (Heb 11) so beautifully described it, and yet one which is filled with security and nostalgia. Therefore, St John of the Cross is quite right to lament the fact that the Beloved has hidden Himself:

---

[59] *Nunc cognosco ex parte, tunc autem cognoscam sicut et cognitus sum* (1 Cor 13:12).

[60] Jn 1:18.

[61] Cf. 1 Pet 1:8.

> *Whither have you hidden yourself,*
> *O Beloved, leaving me to lament?*
> *Like the stag you have fled*
> *having wounded me;*
> *I went after you, calling, and you were gone.*[62]

This lament is, as always, simply an echo of the pain and anguish of the bride in the *Song*:

> *Upon my bed by night*
> *I sought him whom my soul loves;*
> *I sought him, but found him not;*
> *I called him, but he gave no answer.*
> *"I will rise now and go about the city,*
> *in the streets and in the squares;*
> *I will seek him whom my soul loves."*
> *I sought him, but found him not.*
> *The watchmen found me,*
> *as they went about in the city.*
> *"Have you seen him whom my soul loves?"*[63]

But, contrary to what we might expect, this Night is in no way Night of sorrow. That could happen only in the sense that the new day has not yet dawned: *but there is no reason to be sorry*

---

[62]In the original:

> *¿A dónde te escondiste,*
> *Amado, y me dejaste con gemido?*
> *Como el ciervo huiste,*
> *habiéndome herido;*
> *salí tras ti clamando, y eras ido.*

[63]Sg 3: 1–3.

for the portion of the night already elapsed. One must not forget that the light that faith provides is much more reliable than that which comes through the senses; it is more than sufficient to allow the bride to see the graces and charms of the Bridegroom. So, it is really a Night *more lovely than the dawn,* as St John of the Cross says in verses which are almost divine and in which the spouses even achieve complete loving union:

> *O night that guided me!*
> *O night more lovely than the dawn!*
> *O night that has joined*
> *the Beloved with his lover,*
> *lover transformed into the Beloved!*[64]

It is not surprising therefore that the bride in the *Song* ends up finding the lover of her soul, and does so just at the point where she moves away from the watchmen, whom she has been questioning in anguish during the night.

> *Scarcely had I passed them,*
> *when I found him whom my soul loves.*
> *I held him, and would not let him go*
> *until I had brought him into my mother's house and*
> *into the chamber of her that conceived me.*[65]

---

[64]In the original:

> *¡Oh Noche que guiaste!*
> *¡Oh Noche amable más que el alborada!*
> *¡Oh Noche que juntaste*
> *Amado con amada,*
> *amada en el Amado transformada!*

[65]Sg 3:4.

And it cannot be otherwise if one accepts that the Christian is capable of falling madly in love with Jesus Christ. No one falls in love with someone without first knowing him: where could the enthusiasm that provokes love come from other than through perception of the charms and graces of the loved one?

> *My love is fresh and ruddy,*
> *to be known among ten thousand...*[66]

Apophatic theology, which is quite correct about how difficult it is for man to develop a concept of God, seems to leave the fact of the Incarnation on a kind of second level. But while it is undeniable that no one has ever seen God, it should not be forgotten that He has revealed Himself to men in Jesus Christ: *Philip said to Him, "Lord, show us the Father, and we shall be satisfied." Jesus said to him, "Have I been with you so long, and yet you do not know me, Philip? He who has seen me has seen the Father; how can you say, 'Show us the Father'? Do you not believe that I am in the Father and the Father in me?"*[67] Since it is true that human reason is quite incapable of working out a precise concept of God, except for the very limited one it develops by the use of analogy, it must be accepted that apophatic theology is right to propose the method of negation and subtraction.

That is easy to see. But at the same time one should not forget that, from the point of the Incarnation onwards, any attempt made to develop a purely metaphysical or theological concept of God that does not take Jesus Christ into account is quite inadequate. That is not to say that speculation is wrong or useless, but it does warn us that it is of little practical use to rest satisfied with a knowledge of God which, due to its being merely philosophical, fails to go further and draw on the wealth of information which the fullness of

---

[66] Sg 5:10.
[67] Jn 14: 8–10.

revelation provides.⁶⁸ If man has been created to love God, even in this life, then one needs to accept that he has been created to know God even in this life too. And, since knowledge must clearly be proportional to the intensity of a love that should be total —*He said to him, "You shall love the Lord your God with all your heart, and with all your soul, and with all your mind"*⁶⁹— it would be rather difficult, not to say impossible, to rest content with an idea of the loved one based on a method of negation, abstraction and subtraction.⁷⁰ Our Lord's clearly rather brusque reply to the apostle Philip's insistence that He show them the Father (Jn 14: 8–10) makes it plain that that sort of approach is invalid now that He Himself —the Word made flesh— is present among men.⁷¹ St Paul, for his part, when reminding the faithful of Corinth that no one knows the thoughts of God except the Spirit of God —just as in

---

⁶⁸Philosophy, of course, is an autonomous and independent science. Far behind are the times when it was seen as merely an *ancilla theologiæ*. Philosophy has its own proper sphere —like any other science and like human reason itself— in which its activity is more than adequately justified. However, given that the last end of man is God, and given that loving God is his true destiny, any human activity other than loving God must always be seen as subordinate. In the last analysis, as our Lord Himself said, only one thing is necessary.

⁶⁹Cf. Mt 22:37.

⁷⁰It would be difficult, to say the least, to make a colour–blind person grasp what a particular colour is (if he could not see that colour) by the method of telling him that *it is not* any of the colours which he does recognize. The author of this book once knew a high school religion teacher —who suffered no doubt from the strange sort of inferiority complex which often seems to attack clerics— who spent his time in classes telling his pupils *what religion was not*. No one would have any difficulty in working out what would happen to a teacher of exact sciences if he spent the school year telling his students what mathematics *was not*.

⁷¹The passage has been traditionally quoted to prove that the Father and the Son have one and the same nature. But maybe not enough use has been made of the episode to stress that from this point onwards it is no longer appropriate or useful to try to reach the Father without availing oneself of the Son made man in Jesus Christ: cf. Jn 14:6, *in fine*.

man no one knows the heart of a man except the spirit of the man himself—, goes on to say: *Now we have received not the spirit of the world, but the Spirit which is from God...*,[72] and he rounds off his thought, a little further on, with a truly surprising statement: *Who has known the mind of the Lord so as to instruct Him? But we have the mind of Christ.*[73]

These passages from St Paul, as well as being fairly expressive, clearly show the way to approach this matter. It is the Holy Spirit Who is charged with the task of engraving on the Christian's soul the image and knowledge of Jesus Christ,[74] and it is for theologians to do what they can to explain the (also mysterious) mode and manner in which this comes about through the ins and outs of the faith. But clearly there must be a degree of knowledge adequate to the love that God expects from his creature. Since that is a "mad" love, it has to come from an absolutely adequate degree of knowledge — and abstractions and negations are just not good enough to provide that. The image of the loved one that the lover possesses is a very concrete one: there is nothing abstract about it; it is the parallel of something as definite and particular as the ideas of an *I* and a *thou*. That is why any attempt on the lover's part to describe the loved one is always based on absolutely tangible or *listable* features:

> *My beloved is all radiant and ruddy,*
> *distinguished among ten thousand.*
> *His head is the finest gold;*
> *his locks are wavy,*
> *black as a raven.*

---

[72] 1 Cor 2: 11–12.
[73] 1 Cor 2:16.
[74] Cf. 2 Cor 3:18; 4:6.

> *His eyes are like doves*
> *beside springs of water,*
> *bathed in milk,*
> *fitly set.*
> *His cheeks are like beds of spices...*[75]

Such are the feelings of the bride of the *Song*. But, as one might expect, the Bridegroom expresses Himself no differently:

> *Behold, you are beautiful, my love,*
> *behold, you are beautiful!*
> *Your eyes are doves behind your veil.*
> *Your hair is like a flock of goats,*
> *moving down the slopes of Gilead.*
> *Your teeth are like a flock of shorn ewes*
> *that have come up from the washing...*[76]

Metaphors and metaphors, of course. But they all derive from a desperate attempt by the lover to avail himself of things, entirely concrete and familiar —sonorous, luminous, tangible, very real, very sharp— to tell himself and to tell the loved one who this *thou* he is addressing is and what she is like. And there is nothing in the universe —in this world or in the next— more absolutely tangible and concrete, better defined and more *personal*, than that *I* and that *thou*, the very ones who later constitute the substantial (and sufficient) elements of the love–relationship.

The *glory* of Christ, which is the epiphany of his graces, of his charm and of his beauty, needs to shine in the heart of the Christian

---

[75] Sg 5: 10–13.
[76] Sg 4: 1–2.

—not just so that the disciple burn with a fire of uncontainable love, but in order that his transformation in Christ may take place (2 Cor 3:18). It should not be forgotten that love also has the effect of transforming persons, as St John of the Cross expresses it in his *Dark Night*:

> *O night that guided me!*
> *O night more lovely than the dawn!*
> *O night that has joined*
> *the Beloved with his lover,*
> *lover transformed into the Beloved!*[77]

A pastoral approach involving functional church buildings or churches without sacred images; biblical and liturgical translations *designed for the people*; a liturgy of *bearing witness* and therefore an insipid, banal liturgy, with Mass celebrated or concelebrated in playful alternation; charity reduced to *solidarity*; chastity ridiculed; preaching politicized; itinerant Pastors who are never to be found where their flock needs them; prayer yielding its place to bearing witness; and a mania for being present in a world which quite justifiably answers with contempt; the cross forgotten when it is not vilified... and so on and so on —all this has brought ugliness into the Church and has served to cover over the image of the glory and beauty of Jesus Christ. The only sure way to uncover that image once more —which is something the Church and the world urgently need to do— is the way of pure faith, with no need of additives (they

---

[77]In the original:

> *¡Oh noche que guiaste!*
> *¡Oh noche amable más que el alborada!*
> *¡Oh noche que juntaste*
> *Amado con amada,*
> *amada en el Amado transformada!*

are always better done without, as St John of the Cross so rightly and so often stresses). Faith is the only sphere in which the Holy Spirit operates; he is the true Teacher of men and the only one able to lead them to know and love Jesus Christ: *When the Spirit of truth comes, he will guide you into all the truth; for he will not speak on his own authority, but whatever he hears he will speak, and he will declare to you the things that are to come.*[78] But it is worthwhile making two important points about the action of the Spirit in the Church and in the hearts of the faithful.

In the first place the Spirit we are speaking of here is not a Spirit of legend or a Spirit that can be manipulated, which is something that contemporary charismatic movements should bear in mind. Not only does He breathe where He wills, paying no attention to men's forecasts (Jn 3:8), but He acts in a way that has nothing to do with statistics or with the fuss and fanfare of publicity. Moreover, the effectiveness of his activity is always in inverse proportion to human standards of measurement, which does not mean that it cannot be easily recognized. The truth is quite otherwise, although the activity of the Spirit is often not perceived as such if human criteria are used. The fullness of his gifts and the superabundance of his fruits are to be found rather by ways which, as well as not being much favored by the world, are not very compatible with publicity: true joy and love, peace of soul, humility, obedience, goodness unconfined, gentleness, spirit of poverty and clarity of soul, love for the cross, relishing the truth and thirst for justice, magnanimity of a mind and generosity of a heart which have been sealed with love: these are some of the things which, since they have little to do with worldly tastes and appetites, despite coming from the Spirit, usually pass unnoticed by

---

[78] Jn 16:13. As regards *all the truth*, it should not be forgotten that Jesus Christ said of Himself that He is the truth (Jn 14:6).

men. The Spirit of the Lord is discreet and humble; He is gentle, a whisper, and He likes to enter man's heart quietly and tenderly, making no noise, like a morning dew which settles quietly on the plants of the field: *A great and strong wind rent the mountains, and broke in pieces the rocks before him, but Yahweh was not in the wind; and after the wind an earthquake, but Yahweh was not in the earthquake; and after the earthquake a fire, but Yahweh was not in the fire; and after the fire a still small voice. And when Elijah heard it, he wrapped his face in his mantle and went out and stood at the entrance of the cave. And behold there came a voice to him...*[79]

Secondly, although it is true that the Spirit always acts within the sphere of faith, his teaching cannot be regarded as vague or nebulous. Since the way of faith is the only sure way, it cannot lead through by-ways of fog or darkness. Our lack of vision in this life (2 Cor 5:7) or the fact that we can understand only partially (1 Cor 13: 9.12) does not mean that we do not have certainty. Besides, if it is the Spirit Who leads us to know and love Christ, his action needs to be so clear, so positive, as to cause us to fall madly in love. And it is well known that love is never the result of foresight or likelihood, nor does it fit in well with confused or nebulous images (no one ever falls in love with a phantasm). Love only comes about through the contemplation of beauty, which is the same as saying that it is called into being by clarity and light, by order and harmony, by grace and charm, goodness and truth, generosity and self-surrender..., and all of that *concretized* in a unique individual being, who is able to go out of himself towards the *other*, who exists in the real universe: the person.

Modern Catholic pastoral policy actually has forgotten that its one and only task is to speak about the person, and especially about

---

[79] 1 Kings 19: 11–13.

the Person of Jesus Christ, without down–playing anything which might rub the world up the wrong way: *We preach Christ crucified, a stumbling block to Jews and folly to Gentiles, but to those who are called, both Jews and Greeks, Christ the power of God and the wisdom of God.*[80] It seems to be suffering from a strange sort of inferiority complex, a sort of fear; it spends itself on the vain task of healing structures, directly, and nothing else. It does not realize that human beings, who only feel attracted and seduced by beauty —it is the only thing that can content their hearts— have never been able to find beauty in structures.[81] That is the reason why they are not following a Church which, in its pursuit of its "structure–oriented" pastoral program, talks itself hoarse telling people that it too is in solidarity with the world and its problems.[82] Whereas, in reality, a pastoral program of that sort can never be the program of Christian charity —for the simple reason that persons (never structures) are alone capable of loving and being loved. The world today, to its amazement and indifference, is presented with the spectacle of a pastoral program which, instead of preaching, as it has been told to do, the everlasting charity which never passes away (1 Cor 13:8), speaks almost all the time about *solidarity*. This is a cold and lifeless concept, devoid of tenderness, virtually empty, once it is made out to be anything but a sub–product of love. However, if one thinks about the matter, what purpose can a hackneyed, tired *solidarity* have for people who do not love one another other than playing on logomachy. Language manipulation and deterioration certainly

---

[80] 1 Cor 1: 23–24.

[81] Beauty is always attractive, but only the beauty found in persons is able to cause the human being to *fall in love*

[82] The Church is bent on appearing as *modern*, yet it is about to enter in its 21st century of existence. The words the Lord uttered do not need any additives in order to be always alive, timeless, and effective (Jn 6:64).

are one of the saddest and most disastrous phenomenon of modern times.[83]

Undoubtedly the Catholic Church of the 21st century will hold a new Council. It will be forced to do so just to survive, and its survival does not even depend on itself, because it has its Founder's promise that it will last till the end of time. One can almost be sure, even now, that that council will be more like Trent than Vatican II, because it will have to declare itself from the word go as a dogmatic and defining council —as all councils in fact are, even though, as in the case of the Second Vatican Council, people tried to disguise the fact and even imply the opposite. Certain disingenuous people who have forgotten this —although it is true that they have been echoing words of authority— have drawn conclusions which should be described, at best, as not very bright: they are of the view, for example, that the Church's misfortunes will only cease when the Mass comes to be celebrated again in Latin. This has given rise to the strange paradox that those who failed to take very seriously that first declaration of the Second Vatican Council are the only ones who accepted it openly and wholeheartedly; whereas those others who,

---

[83] If the matter is examined carefully, it would seem that all that is happening is that people are trying to get away from using words or concepts, such as that of charity, on the grounds that they are tired and unpopular. However, linguistics and sociology are not the strength of pastoral policy either, mainly because if it is true that the idea of charity has lost a lot of prestige, then the blame must be placed at the feet of Christian pastoral policy, not elsewhere. But it is also a fact that through an amazing narrow-sightedness, that pastoral policy fails to appreciate that the word *solidarity* does not mean the same thing as *charity*: it is simply one of the many derivatives of charity, or one of its subderivatives (and an abnormal one at that). Besides no one can gaily change one of the basic concepts of evangelical catechesis, as this new and only commandment is, which the Master gave to his disciples. It all comes down to the same thing —fear of the world and a cap-in-hand attitude towards it.

on the contrary took it literally, have ended up jeering at the Council and the Church.

Lying behind all this is the fact that a Council can never begin —much less end— by making declarations which can be interpreted either as somewhat amusing or as at least strange. Nor should a council even give the impression that it is affected by fear or timidity or complexes of any kind —such as fear of the world or of technological advance, for example. And perhaps it is here that one can find some sort of explanation which lessens the blame to be placed at the door of traditionalists, integrists and fundamentalists (supposing, of course, that such races exist in the pure state); for if it is true that no justification can ever be found for evil, it is also true that quite often attenuating circumstances can be found for those who commit it. The truth is that councils are always called either to redefine things which have become somewhat blurred or forgotten, or to set wrongs at right and put a stop to controversy and mischief, or both things at once. This is not very compatible with timidity or fear: definitions and delimitations call for sureness and a firm hand in those who carry them out, if the aim truly is to dispel confusion and fog; and as far as handling a certain rabble is concerned, everyone who lives in this world, with his feet firmly planted, knows very well that one cannot bring it to an end if one starts out by asking for forgiveness.

Be that as it may, the truth is that the world and the Church at the close of the 20th century have lost sight of the horizon of God to such a degree that all they can do is feel compelled to repeat, over and over again, the vehement calls that bring the Book of Revelation to a close: *The Spirit and the Bride say, "Come." And let him who hears say, "Come." And let him who is thirsty come, let him who desires take the water of life without price.*[84] The *kenosis* of the Spirit is also without any doubt that of Jesus Christ:

---

[84]Rev 22:17.

> *Whither have you hidden yourself,*
> *O Beloved, leaving me to lament?*
> *Like the stag you have fled,*
> *having wounded me;*
> *I went after you, calling, and you were gone.*[85]

But both will appear again. In fact Jesus Christ has never deserted his Church: *I am with you always, to the close of the age.*[86] It does not matter that at some point, one can even understand the uneasiness of the disciples when they saw Him asleep in the stern of the boat, impervious to the howling wind (Mk 4:38). And if He is there, hidden or plain to see, then the Spirit is there also, there where he is more needed than ever: in the midst of the chaos and the confusion, living and acting in a Church which seems to be empty and cold and naked, in order to fill her once more with life when the moment comes, that long–awaited point for which the many men and women of good will still on this Earth call out and weep: *The earth was without form and void, and darkness was upon the face of the deep; and the Spirit of God was moving over the face of the waters.*[87]

---

[85]St John of the Cross, *Cántico Espiritual*:

> *¿A dónde te escondiste,*
> *Amado, y me dejaste con gemido?*
> *Como el ciervo huiste*
> *habiéndome herido;*
> *salí tras ti clamando, y eras ido.*

[86]Mt 28:20.
[87]Gen 1:1.

Index of Quotations of the New Testament

Matthew

3: 11, **160**
13–17, **297**
5: 3, **186, 348**
4, **188**
14–16, **329**
16, **357, 360**
6: 21, **70**
22, **307**
7: 13, **248**
13–14, **236, 238**
22–23, **172**
8: 17, **77**
9: 13, **95**
10: 9–10, **330**
16, **341**
24–25, **302**
39, **15, 68, 121, 288, 313**
40, **171**
11: 12, **15**
25, **427**
27, **108**
12: 31–32, **59**
16: 25, **15, 68, 121, 288, 313**
17: 20, **128**
18: 12–14, **254, 271**
19: 4–5, **31**
6, **73**
16–26, **429**
23–24, **60**
20: 15, **307**
25–28, **124**
26–27, **206, 418**
26–28, **341**
28, **341**
22: 2–10, **428**
4, **358**
9, **358**
37, **214, 443**
23: 8–10, **331**
24: 12, **123**
25–26, **251**
25: 1–13, **52**
5, **129**
5–6, **383**
6, **140, 373**
12, **172**
14–30, **143, 296**
20, **121**
34–35, **95**
26: 29, **157, 174, 175, 196**
27: 46, **419**
63, **436**
28: 8–9, **397**
9, **400**
19–20, **332, 413**
20, **174, 452**

Mark

1: 21–28, **375**
2: 17, **95**
3: 13, **332**
4: 38, **452**
5: 9, **375**
6: 8, **330**
8: 35, **15, 68, 121, 288, 313**
9: 35, **418**
10: 17–27, **429**
    21, **97, 157**
    23, **60**
    28, **187**
    42–45, **341**
    43–44, **418**
    43–45, **206**
12: 30, **214**
13: 33–35, **383**
15: 34, **419**

Luke

2: 10, **183**
   35, **146**
4: 31–37, **375**
5: 8, **329**
   32, **95**
6: 13, **332**
   20, **186, 348**
   21, **188**
   38, **157**
7: 36, **58**
8: 27–33, **375**
9: 3, **330**
   24, **15, 68, 121, 288, 313**
   58, **418**
10: 3, **341**
    4, **330, 418**
    9, **400**
    16, **171**
    21, **427**
11: 5–13, **23**
12: 35–40, **52**
    37, **124**
    49–51, **160**
13: 24, **239**
14: 15–24, **428**
    21, **95**
    22, **96**
    23, **358**
    26, **15**
    27, **248**
    33, **186, 331**
15: 4, **81, 95**
    4–6, **254, 271**
    5–6, **86, 271**
    6, **86, 88**

20, **86**
32, **86**
16: 8, **428**
13, **60**
17: 21, **400**
26–35, **383**
18: 18–27, **429**
22, **186**
19: 12–27, **296**
21: 1–4, **157**
3–4, **142**
4, **186**
22: 25–27, **418**
27, **124**
35, **331**, **418**
48, **59**
24: 16, **437**
32, **437**
37, **394**
38, **398**
38–40, **394**
39, 30, **400**, **405**
39–40, **28**
41–43, **29**

John

1: 14, **14**, **275**, **432**
18, **14**, **359**, **439**
39, **187**
45–46, **228**
2: 23, **33**
3: 8, **103**, **251**, **381**, **437**, **447**
29, **31**, **188**
34, **103**, **156**, **210**
35, **434**
4: 7, **95**
8, **17**
13–14, **196**
14, **209**
5: 26, **291**
32, **273**
33, **193**
6: 26–59, **123**
53–55, **287**
55, **123**
56, **307**
56–57, **72**, **121**, **142**, **280**, **288**, **294**, **360**
57, **93**, **122**, **248**
57–58, **15**
58, **304**
60, **123**
64, **449**
66, **123**
68, **412**, **430**
7: 37, **95**, **160**
9: 35–38, **30**

10: 1, **342**
    1–17, **271**
    2, **89**
    2–5, **438**
    3, **89, 92, 182**
    4, **53, 89**
    5, **182**
    10, **233**
    11, **138, 182, 288**
    14, **53, 92, 182**
    14–15, **93**
    15, **138, 288**
    16, **336**
    17–18, **138**
    27, **53**
11: 28, **373**
    45, **33**
12: 25, **15, 313**
13: 1, **156, 210**
    1–8, **69**
    2–15, **124**
    3–15, **418**
    12–14, **112**
    12–16, **341**
    34, **90**
    36, **255**
    36–38, **138**
14: 3, **72, 122**
    4, **252**
    5–11, **359**
    6, **14, 108, 193, 252, 273, 275, 402, 405, 443, 447**
    6–7, **266**
    8–10, **442, 443**
    9, **14, 21, 22, 29, 266**
    12, **127**
    16–17, **52**
    17, **103, 320**
    18, **72**
    18–20, **405**
    19, **306**
    20, **72, 122**
    21, **436**
    23, **307, 436**
    26, **50, 52, 103, 401**
15: 4, **301**
    4–5, **303**
    5, **301**
    8, **357**
    9–10, **320**
    9–11, **173**
    11, **183, 191, 259**
    12, **90**
    13, **136, 142, 209, 295**
    14–15, **69**
    15, **27, 52, 89, 107, 125, 204, 301**
    16, **332**
    18, **301**

19, **332**
20, **302**
26, **103, 401**
16: 6–7, **226**
7, **30, 204, 401**
13, **52, 103, 171, 447**
13–14, **76**
14, **401**
14–15, **171**
15, **61, 143**
16, **226**
19–22, **87**
22, **86, 183, 192, 226, 233**
23, **192**
24, **233**
17: 3, **271, 287**
7, **62**
8, **89**
10, **62, 302**
13, **260**
14, **89**
17, **273**
18, **341**
21, **302, 321**
22, **122**
23, **272**
23–24, **272**
24, **72, 272, 302, 405**

26, **27, 90, 93, 118, 204, 272, 287, 322**
18: 37, **193, 275**
19: 28, **95**
30, **136**
20: 11–16, **437**
13, **395**
16–17, **400**
17, **29**
21, **304, 341**
27, **29, 30**
29, **33, 398**
21: 15–17, **336**

ACTS OF THE APOSTLES

1: 7–8, **306**
8, **171, 354, 414**
2: 2–4, **103**
12–16, **155**
3: 6, **330, 418**
4: 12, **373**
32, **144**
6: 2, **353**
20: 28, **336**
35, **60, 61, 109, 112, 134, 267, 296**

Romans

1: 16, **414**
3: 8, **416**
5: 5, **18, 27, 101, 118, 204, 231, 288, 308**
   8, **295**
6: 3, **255**
   3–4, **140**
   3–5, **304**
   3–11, **296**
   4, **255**
7: 24, **251**
8: 3, **125**
   19–23, **392**
   20–21, **406**
   23, **231**
   26, **103**
   39, **266**
9: 3, **190**
10: 14–18, **359**
   17, **33, 359, 438**
12: 5, **292**
14: 7, **15**
   7–8, **159, 313**
   17, **183, 233**
15: 4, **328, 389**

1 Corinthians

1: 18, **414**
   20–21, **330**
   21–23, **84**
   22–23, **414**
   23–24, **449**
   25, **84, 129**
   26–27, **330, 429**
2: 3–5, **380**
   9, **217**
   10, **169**
   11–12, **204, 444**
   14, **382**
   16, **204, 305, 444**
3: 16, **288**
   21–22, **112**
   23, **72, 112**
4: **336**
   1–2, **365**
   16, **305**
6: 15, **307**
   15–20, **288**
   19, **307**
   20, **305**
9: 16–17, **330**
   24–27, **252**
   26–27, **248**
11: 1, **305**
   23–29, **235**
12: 12, **292**

12–31, **390**
14, **292**
18, **292**
19, **182**
22, **182**
27, **182, 292**
28–14:36, **169**
13: 1, **360**
1–3, **171**
3, **352**
4, **100**
5, **58**
8, **27, 129, 157, 226, 449**
9, **448**
9–10, **100**
10, **35, 130, 400**
12, **52, 92, 100, 233, 234, 256, 262, 400, 438, 439, 448**
13, **27, 100, 199, 234, 236, 247**
14: 1, **100**
15: 19, **10**
54–55, **139**

2 Corinthians

1: 22, **36, 101, 231**
2: 14–17, **354**
15, **15, 415**
17, **353**
3: 17, **138, 251, 381**
18, **444, 446**
4: 4, **432**
5, **366**
6, **432, 444**
10–11, **305, 308**
5: 5, **231**
7, **438, 448**
15, **72, 311**
16, **439**
21, **125, 297**
6: 3–10, **330, 341**
6, **169**
10, **330**
7: 5, **253**
8: 9, **125, 197, 418**
13: 4, **77**

Galatians

1: 10, **366**
2: 19, **241, 294**
20, **15, 72, 143, 280, 294, 307, 313, 358, 361, 363, 372**
3: 13, **125**
27, **306**
27–29, **296**

5: 22, **169, 173, 191**
   22–23, **233, 238**
   24, **238**
   25, **238**
6: 17, **307**

EPHESIANS

1: 10, **432**
   14, **36, 101**
4: 11–12, **336**
   13, **337**
   16, **337**

PHILIPPIANS

1: 12–20, **364**
   20, **305**
   21, **138**
   22–23, **72**
   23, **140**
2: 5, **305**
   7, **341**
   7–8, **125**
   9–11, **375**
3: 12, **66, 72, 276**

COLOSSIANS

1: 15–18, **432**
   16, **432**
   16–17, **52**
   17, **432**
   19, **432**
2: 9, **432**
   12, **400**
   17, **432**
3: 3, **314**
   3–4, **142, 303, 310**
   4, **288, 411**
4: 6, **240**

1 TESSALONIANS

5: 2, **383**

2 TESSALONIANS

2: 7, **378**

1 TIMOTHY

2: 5, **198**
4: 12, **169**
6: 12, **414**
   13, **331**

2 Timothy

1: 8, **414**
   10, **139**
3: 12, **252**
4: 7–8, **140**

Titus

2: 11, **30**
3: 4, **30**

Hebrews

1: 3, **432**
2: 6–8, **113**
   7, **107**
   14–15, **139**
4: 12, **328**
   15, **77**
5: 1, **206, 329, 365**
   1–5, **336**
   2, **77**
   2-3, **206**
   4, **206**
6: 4–5, **400**
11: **439**
   1, **32**
12: 2, **190, 191**
13: 14, **90**
   20, **336**

James

2: 1–4, **419**
   14–16, **352**

1 Peter

1: 8, **33, 439**
5: 4, **336**

2 Peter

1: 3–4, **296**
   4, **377**

1 John

1: 1, **32**
   1–2, 14, **30**
   1–3, **394, 398, 436**
   1–4, **306**
   2, **30**
   3, **171**
   4, **173**
2: 6, **304, 305**
   14, **17**

3: 2, **92**, 100, **233, 262**
   5, **125**
   6, **435**
  24, **288**
4: 8, **19, 26, 36, 45, 56,
    63, 64, 95, 264, 377**
   9, **288, 303**
  9–10, **104**
  13, **104, 288**
  16, **45, 52, 64, 303**
  18, **139**
  19, **48, 60, 104, 145**
  20, **45**
  20–21, **60, 352**

13, **15**
16, **226**
17, **95, 451**

REVELATION

1: 5, **275, 331**
   8, **15**
2: 4, **160**
  17, **187, 202, 293, 317,
    380**
2-3:   **345**
3: 14, **15**
  15–16, **160**
  20, **89, 122, 301, 437**
21: 6, **15, 95**
  22–23, **249**
  25, **249**
22: 5, **249**

Books of the Bible

Acts, Acts of the Apostles	**Jn**, John	**1 Pet**, 1 Peter
Amos, Amos	**1 Jn**, 1 John	**2 Pet**, 2 Peter
Bar, Baruch	**2 Jn**, 2 John	**Phil**, Philippians
1 Chron, 1 Chronicles	**3 Jn**, 3 John	**Philem**, Philemon
2 Chron, 2 Chronicles	**Job**, Job	**Prov**, Proverbs
Col, Colossians	**Joel**, Joel	**Ps**, Psalms
1 Cor, 1 Corinthians	**Jon**, Jonah	**Rev**, Revelation
2 Cor, 2 Corinthians	**Josh**, Joshua	**Rom**, Romans
Dan, Daniel	**Jud**, Judith	**Ruth**, Ruth
Deut, Deuteronomy	**Jude**, Jude	**1 Sam**, 1 Samuel
Eccles, Ecclesiastes	**Judg**, Judges	**2 Sam**, 2 Samuel
Eph, Ephesians	**1 Kings**, 1 Kings	**Sg**, Song of Songs
Esther, Esther	**2 Kings**, 2 Kings	**Sir**, Sirach
Ex, Exodus	**Lam**, Lamentations	**1 Thess**, 1 Thessalonians
Ezek, Ezekiel	**Lev**, Leviticus	**2 Thess**, 2 Thessalonians
Ezra, Ezra	**Lk**, Luke	**1 Tim**, 1 Timothy
Gal, Galatians	**1 Mac**, 1 Maccabees	**2 Tim**, 2 Timothy
Gen, Genesis	**2 Mac**, 2 Maccabees	**Tit**, Titus
Hab, Habakkuk	**Mal**, Malachi	**Tob**, Tobit
Hag, Haggai	**Mic**, Micah	**Wis**, Wisdom
Heb, Hebrews	**Mk**, Mark	**Zech**, Zechariah
Hos, Hosea	**Mt**, Matthew	**Zep**, Zephaniah
Is, Isaiah	**Nahum**, Nahum	
Jas, James	**Neh**, Nehemiah	
Jer, Jeremiah	**Num**, Numbers	
	Obad, Obadiah	

Contents

Introduction 9

FIRST PART

"Let him kiss me with the kisses of his mouth"

I. The desire to be loved 43

II. The notice of love 47

III. The loving kiss or "osculum suavissimum" .... ??

IV. Loving or being in love 63

V. The desire to be desired 79

VI. The desire to be contemplated 97

VII. The self-surrender of the Bridegroom to the bride 111

VIII. The self-surrender of the bride to the Bridegroom 133

SECOND PART

"Your love is better than wine"

I. The intoxication of love 155

II. Christian joy 179

III. Contemplation and poetry 195

IV. Contemplation and Faith 231

V. Contemplation and Happiness 259

VI. Living the life of the other 287

THIRD PART

*"Delicate is the fragrance of your perfumes.
Your name is oil poured out:
Therefore the maidens love you"*

I. The fragrance of the Bridegroom 327

II. On contemplation and on the Humanity of our Lord 371

III. Bridegroom's fragrance and Christian Pastoral Action 413

www.ingramcontent.com/pod-product-compliance
Lightning Source LLC
Chambersburg PA
CBHW080500240426
43673CB00006B/251